The Journal of Military History

☆

Volume 69, No. 1   January 2005

Editor: Bruce Vandervort

Managing Editor: Larry I. Bland
Assistant Editor: Blair P. Turner
Assistant Editor: Spencer C. Tucker
Assistant Editor: Anne S. Wells
Assistant Editor: Rose Mary Sheldon

Office Manager: Wendy Vandervort

Published quarterly by
The George C. Marshall Foundation
and The Virginia Military Institute
for the

SOCIETY FOR MILITARY HISTORY

Cover illustration: Portrait of Korean Admiral Yi Sunsin (1545–98) in Chesŭngdang (Victory Hall) on Hansan Island, by Kim Ŭnho. Adapted from the frontispiece in *Imjin Changch'o: Admiral Yi Sun-sin's Memorial to Court* (Seoul, South Korea: Yonsei University Press, 1981).

For article reprints, please go to the website of the Copyright Clearance Center at www.copyright.com or contact a customer representative at 978-750-8400. All reprinted articles must be bear a credit line acknowledging the source of the article.

Correspondence concerning essays submitted for publication, editorial content, reprint permissions, back issues, advertising, institutional subscriptions, and mailing should be sent to Bruce Vandervort, Editor, at this office.

Books for review, book reviews, and correspondence concerning reviews should be sent to Bruce Vandervort, Editor, at the editorial office. Unsolicited book reviews are not accepted.

Annual memberships in the Society for Military History (including subscriptions to the newsletter and *The Journal of Military History*):

Regular Membership:	$50.00
Student (with professor's signature): (limited to 3 years—renewable annually)	$25.00
Institutional subscriptions:	$75.00

Additional overseas postage: Members and subscribers outside the United States-Canada-Mexico add $10.00 for postage (all prices in U.S. funds only). Time for issues to reach members varies, particularly for non-U.S. addresses.

Individual articles are available online at some libraries through ProQuest, MUSE, or JSTOR (for which there is a three-year lapse before online access). If you cannot access these databases, contact the Journal office at 540-464-7468 or e-mail: jmhsmh@vmi.edu. The article will be sent to you at a charge of $10.00 postage paid.

Back Issues of *Military Affairs* and *JMH*

When available, back issues may be purchased from the editorial office for $12.00 per copy ($14.00 outside the United States–Canada–Mexico). Missing issues will be replaced free within six months of the date of publication.

Back issues are now available online, to SMH members only, through JSTOR's individual access program. Full-text searches can be made of all issues from 1937, excluding the most recent three years, for $15.00 annually. Please contact the *Journal* office for details.

Contents

Contents

Contents

Manuscript Submission Guidelines

Manuscripts should be sent to:

Editor
The Journal of Military History
George C. Marshall Library
Lexington, VA 24450–1600.

Authors should submit four paper copies of the manuscript. Do not include your name on any of the copies and, at this initial stage, please do not send a diskette or CD.

It is also understood that your manuscript has not been published elsewhere, nor is it under consideration with another publisher. Text, indented quotations, and footnotes should be double-spaced with wide margins. Footnotes must be numbered consecutively from the beginning and appear in a separate section at the end of the article.

The editors prefer to work with manuscripts that are about thirty double-spaced pages in length (not counting notes, tables, and charts) in pica-size (12 pt.) type. Authors should not include their names on the printed copies, as these are sent anonymously to our referees.

Style will conform to *The Chicago Manual of Style* (15th ed.). The editors may suggest changes in the interest of clarity and economy of expression; such changes will not be made without consultation with the author. The editors are the final arbiters of usage, grammar, and length.

Authors are encouraged to supply relevant artwork (maps, charts, line drawings, and photographs) with their essays. The author is responsible for obtaining permission to publish any copyrighted material.

The submission of an article, book review, or other communication with the intention that it is to be published in this journal shall be taken as *prima facie* evidence that the author willingly transfers the copyright to the journal and its parent society, which will, however, freely grant the author the right to reprint his or her piece, if published, in the author's own works. In the case of articles, upon acceptance the author will be sent a contract and an assignment of copyright. For more information, see the Society's internet site at www.smh-hq.org.

The Society for Military History, the Virginia Military Institute, and the George C. Marshall Foundation disclaim responsibility for statements, either of fact or opinion, made by contributors.

MEMBER ONLINE ACCESS

The *Journal of Military History* (JMH) has been part of JSTOR s
scholarly online archive since 1997. We are happy
to announce that past issues of the *Journal* are now available
electronically to Society members. Users will be able to
browse and conduct full-text searches of all issues of the JMH
from its inception in 1937, excluding the most recent three years.
Of particular interest will be the issues that are currently
out-of-print and no longer available.

If you are interested in joining the JSTOR individual
access program, and are currently a member of the Society, please
go to the member online access link at www.smh-hq.org
and submit your application, or download the form and send to
the *Journal of Military History*, George C. Marshall Library,
Virginia Military Institute, Lexington, VA 24450. If you have any
questions about the program, please contact the *Journal* office
by e-mail at jmhsmh@vmi.edu.

JSTOR is an independent not-for-profit organization
with a mission to create a trusted archive of scholarly journals
and to increase access to those journals as widely as possible.
Information regarding JSTOR is available at
http://www.jstor.org

The Journal of Strategic Studies

A Refereed Journal

FOUNDING EDITOR:
John Gooch, *University of Leeds, UK*

6 issues in 2005

EDITORS:
Thomas G. Mahnken, *The Johns Hopkins University, USA*
Joseph A. Maiolo, *King's College London, UK*

Over the last twenty years, the reshaping of the world politics and the development of innovative military technologies has placed a huge question mark beside the efficacy of force in contemporary statecraft. Consequently, the field of strategic studies has never been of greater significance than it is today. Since the appearance of the first issue in 1978, *The Journal of Strategic Studies* has taken a lead in promoting fresh thinking in the field among practitioners and academics alike. The defining feature of *The Journal of Strategic Studies* is its commitment to multi-disciplinary approach. The editors welcome articles that challenge our historical understanding of man's efforts to achieve political ends through the application of military and diplomatic means; articles on contemporary security and theoretical controversies of enduring value; and of course articles that explicitly combine the historical and theoretical approaches to the study of modern warfare, defence policy and modern strategy. In addition to a well-established review section, The *Journal of Strategic Studies* offers its diverse readership a wide range of 'special issues' and 'special sections'. Recent editions have focused on land, sea and air warfare, Israeli security policy, women and war, geopolitics, NATO and the proliferation of weapons of mass destruction.

This journal is also available online.
Please connect to **www.tandf.co.uk/online.html** for further information.
To request an online samply copy please visit: **www.tandf.co.uk/journals/ onlinesamples.asp**

SUBSCRIPTION RATES
2005 – Volume 28 (6 issues)
Print ISSN 0140-2390 Online ISSN 1743-937X
Institutional rate: US$591; £375
Personal rate: US$108; £74

Frank Cass
Taylor & Francis Group

ORDER FORM

fjss

PLEASE COMPLETE IN BLOCK CAPITALS AND RETURN TO THE ADDRESS BELOW

Please invoice me at the ☐ **institutional rate** ☐ **personal rate**

Name _____

Address _____

_____

_____

Email _____

Please contact Customer Services at either:

Taylor & Francis Ltd, Rankine Road, Basingstoke, Hants RG24 8PR, UK
Tel: +44 (0)1256 813002 **Fax:** +44 (0)1256 330245 **Email:** enquiry@tandf.co.uk **Website:** www.tandf.co.uk

Taylor & Francis Inc, 325 Chestnut Street, 8th Floor, Philadelphia, PA 19106, USA
Tel: +1 215 6258900 **Fax:** +1 215 6258914 **Email:** info@taylorandfrancis.com **Website:** www.taylorandfrancis.com

Crouching Tigers, Secret Weapons: Military Technology Employed During the Sino-Japanese-Korean War, 1592–1598

☆

Kenneth M. Swope

Abstract

The Japanese invasion of Korea (1592–98) has recently been called Asia's first "regional world war." It marked the first time in Asian history that massive armies equipped with modern weaponry faced one another on the field of battle. The Japanese armies commanded by the warlord Toyotomi Hideyoshi were arguably the most skilled in the world at the time, yet in the end the Japanese were defeated by a Sino-Korean alliance in tandem with Korean guerrillas. Looking at the primary documents of the war, it seems apparent that military technology was the single most important, but not the only, factor that shaped the direction and determined the outcome of the war. This article presents an overview of some of the major military technologies utilized by the belligerents and challenges conventional interpretations of the conflict, passed down through the centuries, that claim Japan's defeat was due to superior allied numbers and Hideyoshi's death.

THE Japanese invasion of Korea (1592–98), masterminded by the upstart overlord of Japan, Toyotomi Hideyoshi (1536–98),[1] was one

---

1. Hideyoshi was the second of the so-called Three Unifiers of sixteenth-century Japan, succeeding Oda Nobunaga (1534–82) and preceding Tokugawa Ieyasu (1542–1616). He rose to high position under Oda and succeeded him in 1582 after

---

Kenneth Swope earned his Ph.D. in History at the University of Michigan for his dissertation, "The Three Great Campaigns of the Wanli Emperor, 1592–1600: Court, Military, and Society in Late Sixteenth-Century China," and he conducted research for that work at the Academia Sinica in Taibei, Taiwan. He is currently Assistant Professor of History at Ball State University, where he is working on a book on the Ming Chinese response to the Japanese invasion of Korea.

The Journal of Military History 69 (January 2005): 11–42 © Society for Military History ★ **11**

of the most significant events in the long history of East Asia. Planned as the first stage in Japan's conquest of China, and eventually India as well, the invasion has recently been called Asia's first regional "world war." It marked the first time in Asian history that massive armies equipped with modern weaponry clashed on the field of battle.[2] Moreover, unlike the Korean War of the 1950s, often called "The Forgotten War" by Americans scarred by the experience of Vietnam, Hideyoshi's Korean War is still very much in the popular consciousness of both Korea and Japan, and to a much lesser degree, China as well. Shrines and memorials to heroes of this saga dot both the Korean and Japanese countrysides. Tourists are encouraged to visit the splendid museum inside Hideyoshi's former castle at Osaka, restored in the militaristic 1930s to serve as a memorial to Japan's glorious military past. Likewise, visitors can view spectacular paintings, statues, and reconstructed turtleboats (kŏbuksŏn) all over Korea. Admiral Yi Sunsin (1545–98), Korea's leading naval commander during the invasions, is regarded as perhaps the single greatest hero in Korean history. It is no accident that Yi's diary and memorials from the war are among the few primary sources of Korean history from the Yi dynasty translated into English.[3] Additionally, some Japanese

---

Nobunaga was surrounded and forced to commit ritual suicide by another vassal named Akechi Mitsuhide (1526–82). Mitsuhide lived barely two weeks after his coup as Hideyoshi soon mustered sufficient forces to crush his rival at the Battle of Yamazaki. After this engagement, Hideyoshi went about the business of defeating or co-opting his other military rivals and establishing a new government order in Japan, one which was federalist in its makeup, but legitimized by the authority of the imperial family, who bestowed high titles upon Hideyoshi, including the title of kampaku (imperial regent) in 1585, and taiko (retired imperial regent) in 1591. Because of his humble birth he could not attain the title of shogun, but by 1590 Hideyoshi had brought all of Japan under his rule and was poised to take the next step on his path to glory. The standard English-language biography of Hideyoshi is Mary Elizabeth Berry, Hideyoshi (Cambridge, Mass.: Harvard University Press, 1982). For a recent biography of Oda Nobunaga, see Jerouen Lamers, Japonius Tyrannus: The Japanese Warlord Oda Nobunaga Reconsidered (Leiden: Hotei Publishing, 2000); for Tokugawa Ieyasu, see Conrad Totman, Tokugawa Ieyasu: Shogun (San Francisco: Heian, 1983).

2. See Jahyun Kim Haboush, "Dead Bodies in the Postwar Discourse of Identity in Seventeenth Century Korea: Subversion and Literary Production in the Private Sector," Journal of Asian Studies 62, no. 2 (May 2003): 416.

3. See Ha Tae-hung, trans., Nanjung Ilgi: War Diary of Admiral Yi Sunsin (Seoul: Yonsei University Press, 1981); and Lee Chong-young, ed., Imjin Changch'o (Admiral Yi Sunsin's Memorials to Court), trans. Ha Tae-hung (Seoul: Yonsei University Press, 1981). Recently, another extremely important document, the account of Korea's prime minister during the war, Yu Sŏngnyong, known in Korean as the Chingbirok, has also been translated into English as The Book of Corrections: Reflections on the National Crisis During the Japanese Invasion of Korea, 1592–1598, trans. Choi Byonghyon (Berkeley: University of California Press, 2002). For a more complete discussion of the historiography of the conflict, see Kenneth M. Swope,

commanders, most notably Katō Kiyomasa (1562–1611), were venerated to the point of deification in the years after the invasion. Even though Japan's designs were eventually thwarted by a Sino-Korean alliance, Hideyoshi's dream of conquering the Asian mainland was revived in the late nineteenth century by Meiji expansionists. In fact, the very route the Japanese invaders followed through China in the 1930s was modeled after Hideyoshi's initial plans. The events of the war also inspired anti-Japanese revolutionaries in Korea in the twentieth century, and the Japanese colonial regime went to great lengths to destroy reminders of the conflict that might provoke anti-Japanese resistance.

The war also has larger international implications. In terms of sheer numbers, the conflict involved armies that easily dwarfed those of their European contemporaries, as more than two hundred thousand regular troops fought for both the Chinese and Japanese sides, in addition to hundreds of thousands of Korean regulars, volunteer militiamen, and monk soldiers. The fluid political environment of maritime Asia in the late sixteenth century also meant that there was a significant European impact on the war as well, manifesting itself both in the form of European observers and chroniclers from afar, and more importantly, in the use of various European military technologies, most notably muskets and cannon, throughout the conflict. It is well known that the Japanese had used European-derived firearms in domestic conflicts since the middle of the sixteenth century, but only recently have other examples of military technological diffusion become apparent with regards to this war.[4] Expanding upon and challenging Michael Roberts's and Geoffrey Parker's thesis of a European military revolution, Sun Laichen has persuasively argued that Ming China was in fact the world's first gunpowder empire and that the Ming were the primary exporters of military technology throughout Asia until at least the late sixteenth century.[5] Japanese scholars have suggested that further technology transfers took place after the war, including a dissemination of firearms technology from Japan to China via captured Japanese prisoners, and the transmittal of Dutch knowledge of cannon making to the Koreans via shipwrecked

---

"The Three Great Campaigns of the Wanli Emperor, 1592–1600: Court, Military, and Society in Late Sixteenth-Century China" (Ph.D. diss., University of Michigan, 2001).

4. The standard English-language treatment of Japan's initial adoption of firearms is still probably Noel Perrin, *Giving Up the Gun: Japan's Reversion to the Sword, 1543–1879* (Boston: David R. Godine, 1979). For a comparative look at Japan's adoption of European firearms technologies, see Geoffrey Parker, *The Military Revolution: Military Innovation and the Rise of the West, 1500–1800,* 2nd ed. (Cambridge: Cambridge University Press, 1996), 140–45.

5. Sun Laichen, "Ming-Southeast Asian Overland Interactions, ca. 1368–1644" (Ph.D. diss., University of Michigan, 2000). Sun is currently expanding his field of inquiry to include Korea, and his preliminary research suggests the same conclusions.

sailors in the seventeenth century.[6] Findings such as these suggest that the war really needs to be evaluated within the larger context of military innovation and international trade, and not just as an isolated phenomenon in Asian history. Thus, it would be useful to ask how this conflict fits into the larger parameters of the so-called military revolution and if this war could not be seen as a test study for the wider application of the theories of Geoffrey Parker and others along those lines, although that is beyond the scope of the present article.[7]

But despite its obvious importance for both East Asian and world history, the War of the Korean Peninsula remains little known and poorly understood in the West. Most textbooks give it scant attention or at best devote a few lines to it, blaming the war for the weakening of the Ming (1368–1644) state, the destruction of Korea, and the victory of the forces of Tokugawa Ieyasu (1542–1616) in the Battle of Sekigahara in Japan in 1600. This situation in itself is baffling, for the war is wonderfully documented in Korea, China, and Japan. Literally thousands of documents on the war remain extant, and a tremendous number of them have been published in various forms in China, Japan, and Korea. Most of these documents are written in classical Chinese, which is fortuitous for someone such as myself who does not read Korean. The sheer volume of material is certainly partly to blame for the lack of scholarly attention to this conflict in the West. This situation has been exacerbated by the general reluctance of Asianists in the West to devote much attention to military affairs, a reluctance perhaps born of the biases inherent in the writings of civil officials trained in Confucian learning.[8]

6. On the transfer of firearms technology from Japan to China, see Kuba Takashi, "Juroku seikimatsu Nihon shiki teppō no Min-Chō he no dempa: Banreki Chōsen no eki kara Banshu Yo Oryo no ran he," *Toyo Gakuho* 84, no. 1 (June 2002): 33–54. On the Dutch connection with Korea, see Shin Dongkyu, "Oranda jin hyōryu min to Chōsen no seiyo shiki heiki no kaihatsu," *Shi'en* 61, no. 1 (November 2000): 54–71. I would add that some of the assertions made in this second piece seem questionable, given that some of the weapons attributed to the Dutch were in fact copied by the Chinese from the Europeans a century earlier and probably transmitted that way.

7. Of course, Parker is not without his critics. For an overview of the discussion concerning technology and the military revolution, see Bert S. Hall, *Weapons and Warfare in Renaissance Europe* (Baltimore, Md.: Johns Hopkins University Press, 1997), 201–35. Also see Clifford J. Rogers, *The Military Revolution Debate* (Boulder, Colo.: Westview Press, 1995).

8. The virtues of civilian control over the military had been extolled in China since the time of Confucius (551–479 BC). Traditional Chinese histories were written by civil officials, who tended to denigrate the influence and achievements of their military counterparts. Periods of military ascendancy were cast as aberrations of the natural order of things. This bias has tended to influence, consciously or not, subsequent scholarship on the Chinese past.

As a result of these and other problems, to date not a single full-length scholarly treatment of the conflict exists in English, although there seems to be a recent resurgence in interest in the war as evidenced by the number of articles published lately in Asia and elsewhere and interest expressed at scholarly conferences.[9] Stephen Turnbull published the first popular account, which, although it provides a solid general narrative of the war, has a number of shortcomings. First of all, Turnbull relies entirely on Japanese- and English-language secondary materials, augmented by a few translations of primary sources. He uses virtually nothing written from the Chinese perspective, not even widely available English-language reference works or monographs. He also leaves out much important Japanese scholarship, most notably the works of Kitajima Manji, who has published extensively on the subject. As a result the work is one-sided and presents a rather flawed interpretation of the war. Turnbull repeats the conventional view that Hideyoshi's death in 1598 was the primary factor in Japan's defeat in Korea. He also seems to adopt a pro-Japanese slant throughout, such as glossing over Japanese atrocities by blaming them on "lesser soldiers not in the first rank of samurai heroes."[10] Nevertheless, Turnbull does deserve credit for making a larger audience aware of this war and its historical importance. His work is also lavishly illustrated and therefore useful for those who would like to see images of some of the personalities, technologies, and sites of the war.

As indicated above, study of this conflict can shed invaluable light on a number of important issues in early modern Asian, or even world history, including the nature of foreign relations and diplomacy between states including the so-called Chinese world order and its attendant tributary system, the importance of ritual and "face" in interstate relations in Asia, the importance of imperial pretensions and motives, military logistics and planning, and the adoption and use of new military technologies in battle, to name just a few. It also helps to put the current tensions on the Korean peninsula in their proper historical perspective as North Korea's current desire for national security is certainly grounded in past experiences. Policy makers and negotiators would benefit by gaining a greater understanding of the historical tensions between China, Korea, and Japan as we move into a new century promising increased involvement on the international stage by all these states.

In this article I concentrate on one very important dimension of the war, military technology. Again, it is somewhat surprising that this aspect of the war has not received more attention outside East Asia. As

---

9. There are also a number of works in progress on various aspects of the war, in addition to my own.

10. Stephen Turnbull, *Samurai Invasion: Japan's Korean War, 1592–1598* (London: Cassell and Co., 2002). The quotation appears on page 86.

will be seen below, traditional accounts generally attribute the complete and utter collapse of Korean regulars in the early stages of the war to their deficiencies in technology. Japanese accounts from the time of the war down to the present highlight this fact. It was only when the Koreans managed to invent their ingenious turtleboats (vessels reinforced with iron plates and ringed with spikes that made them resemble turtles) and the Ming Chinese intervened with overwhelming numbers that the tide was turned against the invaders.[11] Japan's technological and tactical advantages were such that had Hideyoshi not died in 1598, then his dream of creating an empire in mainland Asia may have been realized,[12] or so standard treatments, most of which were written from the Japanese perspective, would have us believe.[13]

While more recent scholarship, most notably the fine work of Kitajima Manji, has tended to adopt a more balanced appraisal of the conflict, for centuries the Japanese perpetuated a myth of victory in Korea, a myth so powerful that it fired the dreams of conquerors in the late nineteenth century until Hideyoshi's dreams were finally realized with the annexation of Korea in 1910. This myth stemmed in part from the various chronicles compiled on behalf of Hideyoshi's retainers serving in Korea, all of whom were eager to attain recognition for their efforts.[14] Thus, official house historians were wont to exaggerate the prowess of their respective employers, and the numbers of enemy troops, for example, were often inflated so that the Japanese were always outnumbered in any conflict. Later historians, who wrote comprehensive accounts of the conflict for Japanese audiences by utilizing these earlier records as their sources, in turn transmitted such tales. The most prominent and

11. See *Chŏson Wangjo sillok (Sŏnjo sillok)* as compiled in Li Guangtao, ed., *Chaoxian "Renchen Wohuo" shiliao,* 5 vols. (Taibei: Zhongyang yanjiuyuan lishi yuyan yanjiusuo, 1970), 15 and 18. This is a collection of Korean historical materials, most of which are derived from the official dynastic histories of the Yi dynasty.

12. For example, see Kitajima Manji, *Hideyoshi no Chōsen shinryaku* (Tokyo: Yamakawa kōbunkan, 2002), 92–98. In fact Hideyoshi's presumed motives for the invasion itself are still very much a matter of debate and range from a desire to monopolize foreign trade to a desire to weaken would-be rivals in Japan to the quest for eternal glory, to name a few. For more on this, see Swope, "Three Great Campaigns," 187–90; and Samuel Dukhae Kim, "The Korean Monk-Soldiers in the Imjin Wars: An Analysis of Buddhist Resistance to the Hideyoshi Invasion, 1592–1598" (Ph.D. diss., Columbia University, 1978), 8–11.

13. For a summary of Japanese interpretations of the war going all the way back to the Tokugawa (1603–1868) period, see Kitajima Manji, *Toyotomi seiken no taigai ninshiki to Chōsen shinryaku* (Tokyo: Azekura shōbo, 1990), 24–82. Also see Ishihara Michihiro, *Bunroku keichō no eki* (Tokyo: Hanawa shōbo, 1963).

14. A number of these family chronicles are still extant in Japan and some have been published. For a representative example, see Yamamoto Masayoshi, comp., *Shimazu kokushi: History of the Feudal Domain of the Shimazu clan,* 10 vols. (Tokyo: Seikyō kappan insatsujo, 1905).

influential of these works, if not the most accurate, were Kawaguchi Choju's *Seikan iryaku,* translated as *A Heroic Account of the Conquest of Korea*; and Rai Sanyo's *Nihon gaishi,* rendered as *A History of Japan's Foreign Relations.*[15] Furthermore, this myth is alive and well today as evidenced by the content of various shrines and memorials to Hideyoshi and the war scattered throughout Japan and by the conversations I myself have had with ordinary Japanese.

What is perhaps more surprising is that modern Chinese histories of the conflict often have the same interpretation. Again, many of these flawed interpretations of the war stem from reliance upon biased or inaccurate source materials. For example, one of the most often cited summaries of the conflict, excerpted from the *Ming shi,* translated as *The Official History of the Ming Dynasty,* relates that "When the *kampaku* [Hideyoshi] invaded the eastern country [Korea] the war lasted seven years from start to finish and resulted in the loss of hundreds of thousands of lives, the destruction of millions of pounds of grain and yet the Middle Kingdom and Korea had still not devised a stratagem for victory. It was only with the death of Hideyoshi that hostilities were brought to a close."[16] Yet throughout this same source, accounts that directly contradict this assessment can be found. Moreover, it must be kept in mind that Chinese historiographical practice virtually required the assignation of praise and blame, and as the history of the Ming was compiled during the succeeding Qing (1644–1911) period, it was necessary for the compilers to look for evidence of Ming military weakness. Since the compilers of this same history blamed the Wanli Emperor (r. 1573–1620) for initiating the period of Ming decline, it was only natural for them to extend their argument to all aspects of his administration. Later Chinese historians have followed this lead, with the notable exception of the late Li Guangtao, who made extensive use of primary sources from all three sides, most notably the Korean.[17]

When I first approached this topic as a graduate student, I was heavily influenced by the standard portrayals, but even a cursory reading of

---

15. Kawaguchi Choju, *Seikan Iryaku* (1831), in Wu Fengpei et al., comps., *Renchen Wohuo zhi yi shiliao huiji,* vol. 2 (Beijing: Quanguo tushuguan suowei fuzhi zhongxin chubanshe, 1990), 471–74. Rai Sanyo, *Nihon gaishi,* 2 vols. (1827; reprint, Taibei: Guangwen shuju, 1982).

16. See Zhang Tingyu et al., eds., *Ming shi* (1739), 12 vols. (Taibei: Dingwen shuju, 1994), 8358.

17. For an example of the lingering influence of traditional historiography in contemporary treatments of the war and the Wanli Emperor, see He Baoshan, Han Qihua, and He Dichen, *Ming Shenzong yu Ming Dingling* (Beijing: Beijing yanshan chubanshe, 1998), especially 98–121. A more balanced appraisal can be found in Fan Shuzhi's biography of Wanli. See Fan Shuzhi, *Wanli zhuan* (Beijing: Renmin chubanshe, 1993), 227–55.

some of the primary sources suggested to me that such stock interpretations were grossly oversimplified and there was far more going on in the war that demanded further study. Additionally, far from conveying images of fearful Chinese and Koreans loath to meet the fabled Japanese war machine head on, I found that the reverse was often the case. In fact, it was the Japanese who often avoided large set piece battles with the Chinese, not because they feared their numbers, but because they had a healthy respect for Ming military technology. This assessment comes from Chinese, Japanese, and Korean sources. Therefore, based on my extensive readings of a number of key primary sources, it is my contention that despite all the rhetoric used by the participants throughout the conflict, in the end it was technological and logistical considerations that probably shaped the direction of the war more than anything else, and everyone knew it. Lest I open myself up to charges of technological determinism, I would add that I do not believe that technology was the only factor that impelled the Japanese retreat, but it was the single greatest variable. Early in the war, before the Chinese got involved and before the Koreans unveiled their turtleboats, the Japanese ran roughshod over the defenders. Technology leveled and then eventually tipped the battlefields in favor of the Sino-Korean allies, along with logistical considerations, of course. Finally, I would add that the present piece is but a tiny sliver of a much larger work in progress and I hope to present a much more thorough treatment of the war and all its myriad complexities in the finished work.

In primary accounts of the war, what is most striking at first is the diversity of technologies employed. All three combatants consistently sought to develop and implement new technologies and strategies throughout the conflict, and all devised countermeasures to combat the perceived advantages of their opponents. This should come as no surprise to most students of military history, but these developments, with the notable exception of Korea's famous turtleboats, have been largely ignored by historians outside Asia. Thus, this war provides an excellent forum in which to pursue comparative military issues. For example, much has been made of the so-called "Military Revolution" in Europe from 1500 to 1800, but hardly any attention has been devoted to Asian developments in this same period, despite the availability of primary source materials.[18] It is taken for granted by many that military and technological innovation was a driving force of Western expansion and dominance and a manifestation of the West's dynamism.[19] But, if one

18. See Parker, *Military Revolution*.

19. A number of scholars have taken up these issues recently in the field of Chinese history, and an impressive body of work is starting to come out. For an overview of these trends, see Hans van de Ven, ed., *Warfare in Chinese History* (Leiden: Brill, 2000), in particular the introduction by van de Ven, 1–32, and the conclusion by Jeremy Black, 428–442.

were to focus on even just this war, much of the same dynamism can be seen, albeit on a more limited scale. Therefore, the Korean War of 1592–98 is of seminal importance in understanding the nature and impetus for innovations in military technology in early modern East Asia and offers a unique setting in which to study both military theory and practice. We also see how fast military technologies can be developed and implemented during a war, a situation that is often discussed with respect to later conflicts, but also seems to apply here.

Before going further, it should be acknowledged that some of the technologies used in this war were in fact developed outside Asia, most notably the arquebus muskets used by the Japanese, while others were fascinating adaptations of designs and technologies developed in a variety of places and times. For example, according to tradition the Japanese first received firearms technology from Portuguese who landed off the island of Tanegashima in 1543. Thus, guns were sometimes called Tanegashima, in addition to the more general term *teppō*.[20] These were small-bore weapons and were actually modeled on designs the Europeans quickly replaced, though they were retained by the Japanese with slight variations almost through the Tokugawa (1603–1868) period. While on the one hand this is certainly evidence of the superior firearms technology of the Europeans as of the sixteenth century, it is also a testament to the willingness of Asian states to adopt and adapt useful foreign technologies. States within Asia and rival groups within states, such as the Japanese *daimyo* (warlords), were very cognizant of the advantages superior military technology could offer them, and they were always on the lookout for something that could give them an edge. Thus, they eagerly adapted any new technology that might be in their means to implement. The ability to manufacture or acquire the technology is therefore key. In some instances it was impossible for states or leaders to use these technologies on a large scale for a variety of reasons, so obviously superior weapons were either not used at all or used only on a limited scale.

20. See Yoshioka Shinichi, "Bunroku Keichō no eki ni okeru kaki ni tsuite no kenkyu," *Chōsen gakuhō* 108 (July 1983): 71. In his excellent study of Korean weaponry, J. L. Boots asserts that the Japanese shogun Ashikaga Yoshimitsu (1358–1408) received a matchlock from the Portuguese as early as 1368. See J. L. Boots, "Korean Weapons and Armor," *Transactions of the Korea Branch of the Royal Asiatic Society* 33, no. 2 (December 1934): 25. Moreover, although the Portuguese are generally given credit for introducing firearms into Japan, Japanese sources written by famous gunsmiths from the early seventeenth century state they learned the art of gunnery from China, not Portugal. See Joseph Needham et al., *Science and Civilisation in China*, vol. 5, part 7, *Chemistry and Chemical Technology: Military Technology; The Gunpowder Epic* (Cambridge: Cambridge University Press, 1986), 390–91. Some argue the Japanese largely discarded earlier technologies when Portuguese weapons were introduced.

Before the coming of the Europeans in larger numbers in the six-teenth century, the Chinese were the major disseminators of military technology in Asia. The Ming Chinese had actually been using weapons similar to the Portuguese arquebus for some two hundred years.[21] As indicated above, one scholar has even called early Ming China the first "gunpowder empire" in the early modern world and asserts that it was the Ming, not the Europeans, who started the military revolution, not only in Asian history, but also in world history.[22] Therefore, when Euro-peans brought their arms to Asia, they did not introduce the technology, but rather they supplemented and expanded the options already avail-able to war-makers. Victory or defeat often came to rest upon the ability to properly use the technologies at one's disposal. Because of this fact, troops which were otherwise overmatched or outclassed could prevail by virtue of the superiority of their weaponry, most often greater range or penetrating power on the part of their ranged weapons. As a result, con-flicts often became testing grounds for new technologies.

When Hideyoshi first set his sights on conquering Ming China, and later, the rest of Asia, he had good reason to be confident. After all, with the use of Western military technology, namely the aforementioned arquebus musket, Hideyoshi had managed to conquer all of Japan and bring it under the rule of one man for the first time in over a century. He knew the Koreans, through whom he would have to go first, were woe-fully ill-equipped to deal with his disciplined, well-armed troops. Indeed, on paper the war looked like a serious mismatch from the start, though the early twentieth century scholar J. L. Boots, writing during the period of Japanese colonial rule over Korea, exaggerated a bit when he said, "The story of Korean arms is a tragedy. . . . It is a story of a people dri-ven in desperation to a task for which they had no heart, forced to learn an art for which they had no aptitude. It is the story of a people who repeatedly had to lay down their honored pen and brush to defend their lands and homes against those who loved the sword."[23]

In fact, Hideyoshi did attempt to learn something of Korea's defenses and armed forces before the invasion via a number of spies and coastal raids. On the whole he was unimpressed. According to a Japanese source, Hideyoshi sent twenty-six ships to ply the waters off the south coast of Korea in 1587 in order to test the strengths and weaknesses of Korea's troops. The Korean troops on land and at sea were timid in these encounters and fled before the Japanese. The only commander who did

---

21. Needham, *Science and Civilisation in China*, vol. 5, part 7, 71.
22. See Sun, "Ming-Southeast Asian Overland Interactions," 31, 75.
23. Boots, "Korean Weapons and Armor," 1.

come forth to fight was killed when his boat was sunk.[24] Therefore, Hideyoshi felt he had nothing to fear whatsoever from the Koreans. Furthermore, he dismissed Ming China as "the country of the long sleeves" and figured that the scholar-bureaucrats who ran the empire would offer little resistance to his forces, saying the armies of the Ming "resemble helpless women in their spirit and fighting ability."[25]

What Hideyoshi did not know was that the Ming had also been developing cannon and other firearms based on Portuguese models since early in the reign of the Jiajing emperor (r. 1522–66). Upon seeing the efficacy of these weapons, the emperor ordered that a bureau be established immediately for their manufacture and that soldiers be trained in their use. After Jiajing's directive, the floodgates were opened for the importation of foreign military technology. In Wanli's reign (1573–1620), other foreign ships arrived bearing what the Chinese called "Red Barbarian Cannon" (*hong yi pao*), a mighty weapon some twenty feet in length and weighing over thirty-three hundred pounds, capable of reducing city walls and making the ground shake for ten *li* (approximately 3.5 miles).[26] The manufacture of these weapons was but an extension of the duties of the Ming firearms division, which was first established by Emperor Yongle in 1407, allegedly with the help of Vietnamese experts captured during the Ming occupation.[27] Equally fascinating is the fact that the Koreans also established their own firearms divisions and eagerly sought help from Ming China in this area.[28] They also apparently made relatively frequent use of these weapons against both pirates and Jurchen raiders from the north, although it seems that they had fallen into disuse by the time of the Japanese invasions.

24. Kawaguchi, *Seikan Iryaku*, 478–79. It should be added that the Koreans did embark upon a haphazard and generally ineffective program of military reforms after these engagements in anticipation of a possible Japanese invasion. See Swope, "Three Great Campaigns," 194–97. Also see Yu Sŏngnyong, *Chingbirok* (ca. 1630; published 1695), 257–470, in Wu Fengpei et al., *Renchen Wohuo zhi yi shiliao huiji*, 281–87.

25. This appraisal comes from a letter Hideyoshi wrote to two of his generals in Korea and is translated in Yoshi S. Kuno, *Japanese Expansion on the Asiatic Continent*, 2 vols. (Berkeley: University of California Press, 1937–40), 1: 323. Kuno's work contains many important translations, but it should be used with caution because it is heavily influenced by the nationalistic Japanese fervor of the 1930s. This work and other sources on the Korean campaign are discussed at length in Swope, "Three Great Campaigns," chapters 4–6; and in Kenneth M. Swope, "Rhetoric, Disguise, and Dependence: China, Japan, and the Future of the Tributary System, 1592–1596," *International History Review* 24, no. 4 (December 2002): 757–82.

26. Zhang et al., eds. *Ming shi*, 2264–65.

27. Ibid., 2264.

28. *Chosŏn Wangjo sillok* as cited in Sun Laichen, "Ming China and Korea, c. 1368–1600: With Special Reference to Gunpowder Technology," unpublished conference paper, 9–10.

Finally, Hideyoshi did not foresee how important control of the seas would be during the campaign. Over the seven-year span of the war, the Japanese found themselves bested time and again by the allies at sea, their supply lines cut. They were never able to close the technological gap between themselves and the Chinese and Koreans in this area. Hideyoshi tried throwing more men at the problem, but the combination of Admiral Yi Sunsin's turtleboats and the naval artillery of the Chinese proved too much for the invaders to handle. In the end the superior experience, skill, and discipline of the Japanese were no match for the technological superiority of the Chinese and the Koreans. It should be added that numbers were not as much of a factor as some Japanese sources would have us believe. As far as I can determine, the Chinese did not have numerical superiority over the Japanese until the very last stages of the war, although the Koreans tipped numbers in favor of the allies. But the popular assertion that the Japanese were grossly outnumbered throughout the conflict is simply not true.

The invasion began on 23 May 1592 as a force of over 150,000 Japanese in several hundred ships landed at Pusan and other ports along Korea's southeastern coast.[29] When Sō Yoshitoshi (1568–1615) and Konishi Yukinaga (1558–1600) arrived at the head of the invading forces, the Koreans were intimidated by their banners "which blotted out the sky" and their cannon which "roared like thunder."[30] The garrison at Pusan was manned by 20,000 troops under the command of General Chŏng Pal, fierce in his black armor. Chong came forth to engage the enemy but he found his forces about to be cut off so he retreated to the city, pursued by the Japanese. The invaders took up positions on the mountain behind the city and fired down upon the Koreans within. Their ranks did not hold, and the Koreans scattered.[31] As they tried to flee, the Japanese cut them to ribbons, killing 8,500 Koreans and capturing alive 200 more. Chŏng Pal himself died in the fighting but was buried with honor by the Japanese.[32] In this engagement, as would be the case throughout the early stages of the war, Japanese muskets gave them a huge advantage over the defenders. Both Japanese and Korean accounts consistently refer to the Japanese use of firearms in land battles as being integral to early Japanese successes, the guns apparently having both greater range and penetrating power than Korean bows and arrows.

29. Li, ed., *Chaoxian "Renchen Wohuo" shiliao*, 1.

30. See Kawaguchi, *Seikan Iryaku*, 507.

31. Sin Kyŏng, *Zai zao fan bang zhi* (ca. 1693), 2 vols. (Taibei: Guiting chubanshe, 1980), 71.

32. See Turnbull, *Samurai Invasion*, 51; Kawaguchi, *Seikan Iryaku*, 509; and Kuwata Tadachika and Yamaoka Shohachi, eds., *Chōsen no eki*, vol. 5 of *Nihon no senshi* (Tokyo: Tokuma shoten, 1965), 255.

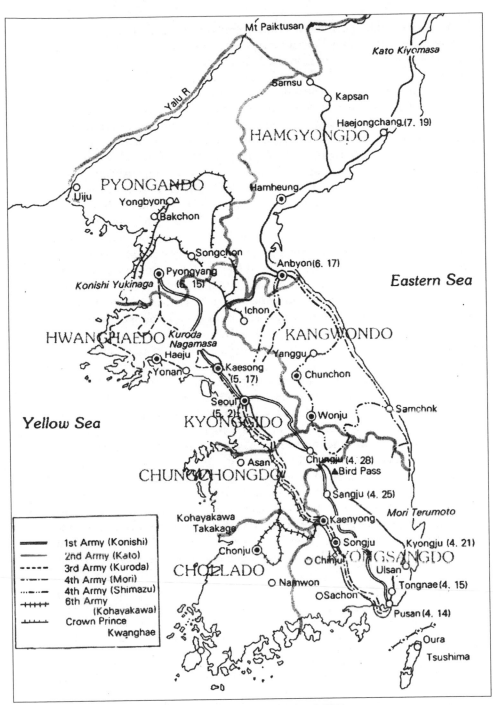

Japanese invasion of 1592

We also see Japanese tactics and organization at work. Throughout the war when attacking Korean cities and mountain fortresses (*san-sŏng*), the Japanese tried to gain the high ground and fire down upon the defenders with volleys of bullets and arrows.[33] Japanese forces were organized into infantry and cavalry divisions with the infantry consisting of units of archers, spearmen, and gunners, while mounted troops tended to carry spears.[34] It is significant to note that they did not generally rely upon the fabled Japanese long swords (*katana*) as their favored weapon in mass combat, although they did carry them. Japanese swords did prove vital in a least a couple of major battles during the war, being longer and sharper than the swords of the Chinese and Koreans. The general tactic adopted by the invaders was to fire musket volleys first, then advance, and fire more volleys before engaging in hand-to-hand combat. Spear units operated in tandem with archery and gun units to provide defense. As noted above, firearms and other light artillery came to be the most important weapons used by the Japanese. Some of them fired shot as heavy as thirty *momme,* or about three pounds.[35] The matchlocks were called *hinawaju* or *hinawajutusu* in Japanese, in addition to the more generic terms mentioned above. Yi Sunsin remarked about how feared Japanese firearms were among the Koreans and how the Japanese often attacked with guns from caves, hideouts, and other fortified positions.

A typical Japanese musket was just over three feet in length and fired shot weighing about six *momme.* The caliber was about 15.8 mm. While the muskets had a range in excess of perhaps six hundred yards, they were actually more effective at longer distances because of the difficulties of loading, aiming, and firing at close range. The Koreans realized this fact early on and tried to exploit it, albeit with limited success. The Japanese also had smaller guns designed specifically for use from horseback; there was a fair variation in the length, weight, and caliber of their muskets, with some versions exceeding five feet in length and weighing approximately twenty pounds while having about the same caliber as the aforementioned models.[36] Heavier hand-held arms weighed over sixty-five pounds and had much larger bores, firing heavier shot in

33. Korean fortresses are discussed at length in Wilbur Bacon, "Fortresses of Kyŏnggido," *Transactions of the Korea Branch of the Royal Asiatic Society* 37 (1961): 1–63. Japanese-built fortresses in Korea, known as *wajŏ,* are treated in Turnbull, *Samurai Invasion,* and in Ōta Hideharu, "Gumbu ni yoru Bunroku-Keichō no eki no jokaku kenkyu," *Gunji shigaku* 38 (September 2002): 35–48.

34. Kuwata and Yamaoka, eds., *Chōsen no eki,* 68.

35. Ibid.; and Yoshioka, "Bunroku Keichō no eki ni okeru kaki ni tsuite no kenkyu," 71.

36. See the chart in Yoshioka, "Bunroku Keichō no eki ni okeru kaki ni tsuite no kenkyu," 78.

Left: "Black" mark cannon fired by fuse. Lead balls or bundles of large arrows were discharged. Right: "Yellow" mark cannon shot lead balls and wing arrows.

a wider arc. Types of shot varied as well, ranging from small single pellets weighing just under half an ounce to balls with tiny hooks suspended from them to scattershot.[37]

Larger guns were used specifically for sieges or sometimes mounted on platforms on ships, especially during the second invasion of 1597–98. But it appears that Japanese cannon never quite reached the massive sizes of their mainland counterparts, perhaps because of their different geopolitical environments, and quite likely in the Korean case, because it may have been too difficult for the Japanese to transport massive cannon through hostile and rugged terrain. Representative examples included in a recent military dictionary depict field pieces that weighed in at a mere ninety pounds or so.[38] They tended to favor a short, heavy musket with a wide bore. Numerous illustrations of Japanese soldiers using these "hand cannons" in combat have survived.[39] The Shimazu clan, in particular, were said to have used these weapons to great effect in the siege of Sachŏn in 1598.[40] In fact, the Japanese came to rely more and more upon firearms as the war dragged on. Letters home frequently beseeched Hideyoshi and other commanders to send more firearms to counteract those of the Chinese. This included requests for heavier cannon.[41]

In discussing firearms used during the war it is interesting to note that while the Japanese specialized in hand-held weapons and light artillery, the Chinese and the Koreans countered with larger cannon and naval weapons.[42] The most plausible explanation for this is the different

37. See Sasama Yoshihiko, *Jidai kosho Nihon kassen zuten* (Tokyo: Yuzankaku shuppansha, 1997), 249.
38. Ibid., 245.
39. An example can be found in Turnbull, *Samurai Invasion*, 211.
40. Yoshioka, "Bunroku Keichō no eki ni okeru kaki ni tsuite no kenkyu," 74.
41. Ibid., 75.
42. Ibid., 71.

types of strategic environments in which the three belligerents operated prior to the war. Korea had long been at peace and faced few external threats other than pirates. It makes sense that their few firearms were concentrated on boats or on the walls of important cities and fortresses. In their rather limited conflicts in other arenas, Korean bows, which were among the best in Asia and will be discussed below, were generally sufficient to carry the day. And as for cavalry, the Koreans preferred either spears or long battle flails, a weapon which has few parallels elsewhere. The Japanese, on the other hand, had been in a state of almost total war for over a century. The adoption of muskets and their deployment in the hands of relatively untrained peasants allowed a few *daimyo* to finally carry the day and defeat their rivals. Meanwhile the Chinese used different weapons in different areas depending upon the type of foe they faced. But they, too, increasingly relied upon firearms in the late Ming period, especially in conflicts with recalcitrant tribespeople along the frontiers who resisted the steady encroachment of the expanding Ming state. Larger cannon were, of course, best for attacking or defending the walled cities common in Ming China.

The Koreans had four primary types of cannon: heaven, earth, black, and yellow, their names derived from the first four characters of an ancient Chinese-language primer and typically inscribed upon the cannon themselves.[43] They also used a variety of small cannon known as "victory mark cannon." These bronze weapons ranged from just under a foot to perhaps twice that in length and had bores of 23 to 29 mm.[44] The Koreans also used mortars and primitive hand grenades, and quickly started manufacturing muskets after being given one as a present by a Japanese ambassador just prior to the war.[45] They had four major sources of guns, namely, old guns they made themselves, the Ming Chinese, the Portuguese, and copied Japanese models. Therefore, most Korean models seem to be derivative though scattered references in Korea's dynastic histories suggest they may have invented some of their cannon or, at the very least, made extensive modifications to Chinese imports. Like the Chinese, the Koreans employed a number of hybrid weapons in their arsenal, most commonly arrows with small explosive

---

43. Turnbull, *Samurai Invasion*, 89–90; and Yoshioka, "Bunroku Keichō no eki ni okeru kaki ni tsuite no kenkyu," 71–72. All of these models were fairly small and portable. Heaven-mark cannon were fired by fuse and discharged both lead balls and arrows. Earth cannon were slightly smaller than Heaven-mark models, and though they also used fuses, they only fired bundles of arrows. Black-mark cannon were also fired by fuse and discharged both lead balls and bundles of arrows, being slightly larger than Heaven-mark cannon. Finally, Yellow-mark cannon were the largest of all and fired lead balls and giant arrows.

44. Yoshioka, "Bunroku Keichō no eki ni okeru kaki ni tsuite no kenkyu," 80.

45. Boots, "Korean Weapons and Armor," 21–24.

charges or incendiary devices attached. They also sometimes used devices that fired a large number of arrows at once using the force of a single explosive charge. The ranges of these models varied, but, as an illustrative example, the Grand General Fire Arrow had a range of nine hundred paces.[46] Modern Japanese texts contain diagrams of similar weapons, but I have seen no definitive evidence of their use in the fighting in Korea.[47]

The most important artillery pieces in the Ming arsenal were the Portuguese-derived *folangji,* sometimes translated as culverin, which were often mounted on ships, and native models such as the Grand General Cannon (*da jiangjun pao*), the Great Distance Cannon (*wei yuan pao*), and the Crouching Tiger Cannon (*hu cun pao*).[48] The latter in particular were used to great effect at the Battle of Pyŏngyang in 1593. They were approximately two feet in length and thirty-three pounds in weight, firing in excess of one hundred (.43 ounce) pellets in one discharge.[49] The Ming also had muskets, mortars, bombards (*fa gong*), fire arrows (another favorite of the Koreans), and a variety of smoke bombs and hand grenades. In addition to the examples mentioned above, both the Chinese and the Koreans also employed a fascinating array of hybrid weapons featuring elements of both more traditional catapults and gunpowder weapons. The most ingenious of these devices included the Korean *hwacha,* or firecart, used at the siege of Haengju in 1593. This was the equivalent of a modern rocket launcher as it consisted of a honeycomb-like framework mounted upon a wooden cart pushed by two to four men. One hundred to two hundred arrows or steel-tipped rockets could be fired simultaneously from the cart.[50] The Ming also reportedly used battering rams loaded with gunpowder, though descriptions of these weapons are confusing. This list is by no means complete, and some of the more interesting weapons will be discussed later.

As the Japanese continued to advance during the last week of May and pushed rapidly towards the Korean capital at Seoul, the Koreans resolved to make a stand at narrow Chŏryŏng Pass, an eminently defensible position along the route to Seoul. Despite their shocking series of defeats up to this point, some Korean commanders, most notably Sin Ip (1546–92), who earned his reputation battling fierce Jurchen tribesmen in the north, still believed the Koreans could prevail.[51] As a result,

46. Technical details on all these firearms can be found in Yoshioka, "Bunroku Keichō no eki ni okeru kaki ni tsuite no kenkyu."
47. Sasama, *Jidai kosho Nihon kassen zuten,* 247–48.
48. Yoshioka, "Bunroku Keichō no eki ni okeru kaki ni tsuite no kenkyu," 72.
49. See L. Carrington Goodrich and Chaoying Fang, eds., *Dictionary of Ming Biography,* 2 vols. (New York: Columbia University Press, 1976), 173–74.
50. See Turnbull, *Samurai Invasion,* 149.
51. See, for example, Sin, *Zai zao fan bang zhi,* 79.

instead of meeting the enemy at the pass itself, Sin resolved to fight a decisive battle in the flatlands beyond the pass, before the hill fort of Ch'ungju, saying, "The enemy are foot soldiers and we are cavalry. If we go forth and meet them on the open plain and use our iron clad cavalry, how can we not be victorious?"[52] Furthermore, Sin thought the Japanese were too short to be capable soldiers and because they relied upon muskets, which were useless at close range, the Korean forces should be able to close and defeat them with their array of polearms and flails.[53]

Korean cavalry were typically equipped with battle flails, glaives, and long spears, in addition to bows, which will be described below. The flail was a round hard wood stick, painted red and 4.5 feet long, with an additional heavier piece fourteen inches long, attached by three links of iron chain and covered with heavy iron nails or knobs.[54] Mounted archers often carried it for use after they had spent all their arrows. Long spears came in all manner of shapes and sizes, including tridents and spears similar to European awls or pikes. They also used glaives, sometimes referred to as "reclining moon knives"; battle rakes modeled on those used by the Chinese; and cross-bladed spears, which were effective in unhorsing enemy cavalry. The Japanese used cross-bladed spears as well; the Japanese commander Kato Kiyomasa's personal weapon of this type has been preserved in Japan and immortalized in statues and artwork.[55]

The Battle of Ch'ungju turned out to be a complete and utter rout for the Koreans. Ignoring the advice of his subordinates, Sin Ip stubbornly insisted upon arraying his forces on the soft ground of the valley, with their backs to a river. The Japanese split up their forces and entered the valley from all sides, rushing in "like the wind and the rain."[56] The combined force of their arquebuses and cannon shook the earth, and several outlying towers quickly fell to the attackers. According to a Japanese source, in the middle of the night the Japanese commander employed a "flaming ox attack" (burning reeds were attached to the tails of cattle which were sent forth) and the Korean lines broke, Sin and many of his men drowning in the Han River.[57] Ch'ungju was taken on 7 June. Altogether, more than three thousand Koreans were killed and one hundred were captured.

At this point a few words should be said about missile weapons other than firearms since they proved nearly as important in the respective

52. Ibid., 93.
53. Yu, *Chingbirok*, 285–87.
54. Boots, "Korean Weapons and Armor," 15.
55. See the illustrations in Boots, "Korean Weapons and Armor," and Turnbull, *Samurai Invasion*.
56. Kawaguchi, *Seikan Iryaku*, 520.
57. Li, ed., *Chaoxian "Renchen Wohuo" shiliao*, 2.

arsenals of the belligerents. According to J. L. Boots, the bow and arrow was the one weapon in which the Koreans excelled, both in use and production. In his usual florid way Boots states, "It was the one military practice in which Korean boys longed to become proficient, the one token of martial skill which ever held its own among a people who for thousands of years have preferred silks, pictures, poems, and music, the stately crane in the paddy fields and the knarled [*sic*] pine on the mountainside."[58] Indeed, the diaries of the famed naval commander Yi Sunsin are replete with references to almost daily archery practice. The Korean bow was a composite reflex bow, usually about four feet in length and made of mulberry wood, bamboo, water buffalo horn, and cow sinew spliced together. The bows could be used in different ways and could fire different arrows. They were sometimes even used crossbow fashion to lay down a barrage of covering fire and could also be used from horseback.[59] The Koreans sometimes employed poisoned, fire, or exploding arrows, much like the Chinese. Most significantly, Korean bows had tremendous range, being able to cover up to 500 yards, compared to about 350 yards for Japanese long bows.

The Chinese also used a variety of bows. They preferred the crossbow, which had been invented in China, and which had both great range and penetration power, its primary limitation being the amount of time it took to load, draw, and fire. The Chinese also used short bows for mounted combat and longer composite bows for their infantry. They especially liked to use fire arrows, particularly in siege and naval warfare. While some of these weapons were simply ordinary arrows wrapped with pitch or other inflammable materials, others contained explosive devices or gunpowder in small amounts. Japanese bows were massive, over seven feet in length, and constructed of bamboo and mulberry, wrapped with reed or lacquered. They fired arrows some three feet in length, tipped with a variety of different heads for specialized purposes, including for killing enemy officers and for signaling by means of attaching a wooden whistling box to the head.[60]

Rocked by the defeat at Ch'ungju, the Korean court abandoned the capital and fled to the north, finally stopping at the town of Ŭiju, located along the Yalu River, the border with China, as the Japanese captured city after city, eventually getting as far as Pyŏngyang. The Koreans requested aid from their nominal tributary overlords, the Ming, who were at the time preoccupied with the suppression of a troop mutiny in

58. Boots, "Korean Weapons and Armor," 4.
59. Ibid., 4–8.
60. Ibid., 9–10. Much more information on Japanese archery can be found in G. Cameron Hurst, *Armed Martial Arts of Japan: Swordsmanship and Archery* (New Haven, Conn.: Yale University Press, 1998), 103–43.

Ningxia in northwest China.[61] Therefore, the Ming dispatched only Zu Chengxun, the Vice Commander of the northeastern city of Liaoyang, and a subordinate named Shi Ru at the head of three thousand troops. Their mission was to investigate the situation in Korea and perhaps send a military message to the Japanese. The Ming crossed the Yalu on 22 August and headed for Pyŏngyang. They encountered difficulties immediately as the Ming were not familiar with the terrain and their cavalry were hampered by heavy rains. The Japanese got word of the Ming approach and opened the gates of Pyŏngyang. The Ming, believing the city to be deserted, entered, only to be lured into an ambush on 23 August, the Japanese emerging from cover "like ghosts in the night," firing upon the Ming forces with their muskets, which the Ming apparently were not aware the Japanese possessed in large numbers, despite Korean warnings.[62] The Ming horses could not maneuver on the muddy ground, and the calvary were almost completely annihilated. Shi Ru was killed, and Zu Chengxun barely escaped with his life.[63] It was said that only a few dozen men survived the Japanese ambush.[64] This would not be the only time during the Korean campaign that Chinese cavalry were undone by poor conditions. Nevertheless, even with their victory, the Japanese commanders were ill at ease. They knew the Chinese would be coming in greater numbers, and despite Hideyoshi's bombast, Japan's generals had a healthy respect for the military prowess of Ming China from the start. Throughout the next several years the Japanese would consistently avoid engaging the Chinese in set piece battles if at all possible and would try to rely on ambushes and terrain advantages to offset their technological shortcomings, which would become apparent in the Battle of Pyŏngyang in early 1593.

At any rate, the Ming was rocked by news of the debacle at Pyŏngyang. Immediate orders were issued for the bolstering of defenses and recruitment of troops in all coastal provinces in anticipation of a possible Japanese invasion. Song Yingchang (1536–1606), a veteran official known for his interest in military defense, training, and preparations, was appointed Military Commissioner (*jinglue*) of Korea, and Shen

---

61. The Ningxia mutiny is discussed at length in Swope, "Three Great Campaigns," chapter 3; and in Kenneth M. Swope, "All Men Are Not Brothers: Ethnic Identity and Dynastic Loyalty in the Ningxia Troop Mutiny of 1592," *Late Imperial China* 24, no. 1 (June 2003): 79–130.

62. Zhuge Yuansheng, *Liang chao ping rang lu* (1606) (Taibei: Taiwan xuesheng shuju, 1969), 239–40.

63. See Mao Ruizheng, *Wanli san da zheng kao* (1621), vol. 58 in Shen Yunlong, comp., *Ming-Qing shiliao huibian*, 83 vols. (Taibei: Wenhai chubanshe, 1971), 33. Also see Gu Yingtai, *Ming shi jishi benmo* (1658), reprinted in *Lidai jishi benmo*, 2 vols. (Beijing: Zhonghua shuju, 1997), 2375.

64. Kawaguchi, *Seikan Iryaku*, 557.

A reconstruction of a turtle ship based on the written description of designs preserved in the Exhibition Hall at the Yi Sunsin Shrine in Asan, Korea.

Weijing (ca. 1540–97), an obscure trader who had connections to the Chinese Minister of War, was made an ambassador to deal with the Japanese and buy the Ming some time as Song gathered men, mounts, and supplies for a large-scale expedition to Korea.

Things would have been even worse for the Koreans at this point had it not been for the heroism of Korea's most revered historical figure, Admiral Yi Sunsin. Yi was the Naval Commander of the Left of Chŏlla Province and soon joined the fight against the Japanese in the waters off the southern coast of Korea. He is famous for his invention of the turtleboats, but in actuality the idea had been around in Korea since at least 1415. Chinese sources from the same period contain pictures of craft that bear a striking resemblance to the turtleboat, in particular a ship known as the "falcon boat" (*ying chuan*), though I have found no evidence that suggests the Chinese used these boats in the war against Japan.[65] The turtleboats were propelled by rows of oars on both sides, meaning they were not vulnerable to the vagaries of wind like the boats of the Japanese. A head was mounted on front, fires were apparently lit

---

65. See Mao Yuanyi, *Wubei zhi* (1601), 22 vols. (Taibei: Huashi chubanshe, 1987), 4762–4821. A picture of the falcon boat can be found on 4797. Also see Turnbull, *Samurai Invasion*, 94.

below decks, and the smoke funneled out the mouth for added effect. The plates and spikes thwarted the favored Japanese tactics of grappling and boarding but more significantly, the ships were equipped with cannon on all sides. This was in marked contrast to the Japanese, who had plenty of muskets on land but virtually no cannon on their ships.[66] Thus, the Koreans were able to create havoc amongst the Japanese fleet by firing away with their cannon, out of range of Japanese bows and catapults. Moreover, the Japanese were scattered and disoriented by the smoke spewing from the mouth of the turtle at the front of the ships.[67] In the Battle of Hansan Island in July 1592, only fourteen of seventy Japanese ships are said to have survived an encounter with Yi and his turtleboats. Korean sources have tended to give Yi and his ships almost all the credit for defeating the Japanese. Though this is an exaggeration in my opinion, the Korean navy did play a vital role in severing Japanese lines of transportation and communication and gave the Koreans a much-needed psychological boost.

It should be added that it was not just the turtleboats that outperformed Japanese naval vessels. In fact, the entire Korean fleet probably did not have more than half a dozen turtleboats in action at any one time. The square sails used by the Japanese were not nearly as effective as Chinese and Korean fore and aft sail designs. Therefore, Chinese and Korean ships were far more maneuverable than their Japanese counterparts, which were essentially appropriated merchant vessels. In fact, Hideyoshi had tried to obtain warships from the Portuguese through Jesuit intermediaries but was rebuffed. A first-class man-of-war (*panok-sŏn*) of the Yi dynasty was "probably not less than seventy feet overall in length and probably went up to one hundred feet with a beam of about one third the length. . . . Along the sides were heavy bulwarks of thick planking loopholed for archery and fitted with ports for small cannon. On some vessels shields were hung along these bulwarks as was the custom in ancient times in the Mediterranean and with the Vikings."[68] Korean sailors wore sea-blue uniforms with black felt hats and used a wide variety of weapons including swords, spears, tridents, battle axes, maces, scythes, grappling hooks and irons, and great bows with large arrows, fire arrows, and darts, some with a range of four hundred yards. They also used crossbows and even pistols for ranged warfare.[69]

66. Horace H. Underwood, "Korean Boats and Ships," *Transactions of the Korea Branch of the Royal Asiatic* Society 23, no. 1 (1934): 59.

67. Kawaguchi, *Seikan Iryaku,* 554.

68. Underwood, "Korean Boats and Ships," 55.

69. Ibid., 58–59. I should add that as far as armor is concerned, Korean armor tended to be leather or even just padding with metal plates sewn in it. Japanese armor varied widely according to station and rank but was generally better, while Ming

Japan's second invasion of Korea, 1597–98

The Chinese navy must also be taken into account when discussing the Korean campaign, although it should be noted that none of the participants in this conflict truly possessed a jurisdictionally separate navy, so readers should not think that these units were all that different from their land counterparts. On the one hand this might seem strange given the lengthy seacoasts of all three states, but this situation also reflects the political realities of the era when the most pressing military concerns (up to this point) were land based. Thus, the Japanese used co-opted pirates and merchants to facilitate their crossing to Korea and had few

---

armor could be anything from simple paper/padding to chain mail, though it was most commonly some variation of studded leather.

commanders with real experience in naval warfare. The Chinese and Koreans had a few officers and soldiers with extensive experience on the sea, but even these soldiers typically rotated inland when needed. Thus, they were typically just called "water soldiers," or *shui bing* in Chinese.

This notwithstanding, from the beginning of the war the Chinese recognized the importance of the navy, realizing they would need both warships and supply vessels. The warships of Fujian were deemed the best, followed by medium-sized vessels (*cang chuan*), flat-bottomed ships (*sha chuan*), and galleys (*hu chuan*). These boats were sturdily constructed of reinforced pine and ironwood and were equipped with cannon and smaller arms, making them very effective in combat. There was nothing that could match them on the seas, and the Japanese did not dare take them on.[70] As soon as the Chinese decided that war with the Japanese was imminent, the Ministry of Works, one of the six branches of Ming government, was ordered to build twenty Fujianese war galleys, eighty to one hundred medium-sized ships, and fifty to sixty flat-bottomed vessels.[71] These vessels were all typically equipped with a variety of firearms, ranging from bombards to falconets to mortars to culverins. Many of the Chinese vessels possessed oars in addition to sails. Bronze bombards sometimes weighed in excess of six hundred pounds and fired solid lead balls weighing about six pounds apiece. Ming mortars fired upwards of one hundred pellets in one discharge, each pellet weighing just under half an ounce.[72]

As preliminary discussions with the Japanese were taking place through the fall of 1592, the Ming were assembling an army for a much larger counterattack. Li Rusong (1549–98), who had been the commander responsible for the Ming victory in Ningxia and was from a prominent military family, was made Military Superintendent, a position which imbued him with sweeping authority for the Eastern Expedition that exceeded that of virtually any Korean official save the king. He led his forces directly from Ningxia to the Korean border where he linked up with other units recruited from all over the empire.[73] According to some sources the Ming assembled as many as seventy thousand troops, but the

70. Mao, *Wubei zhi*, 4775.

71. See Li Guangtao, *Chaoxian Renchen Wohuo yanjiu* (Taibei: Zhongyang yan-jiuyuan lishi yuyan yanjiusuo, 1972), 34–35. Fujian is the southeastern coastal province that faces Taiwan. The larger Fujianese boats typically carried over one hundred men and were equipped with catapults, cannon, and great bows, though they sometimes had trouble dealing with small, fast ships. See Mao, *Wubei zhi*, 4778.

72. Goodrich and Fang, eds., *Dictionary of Ming Biography*, 173–74.

73. Li Rusong's biography can be found ibid., 830–35. The biographies of the entire Li family can be found in Zhang et al., eds., *Ming shi*, 6183–98. Also see Kenneth M. Swope, "A Few Good Men: The Li Family and China's Northern Frontier in the Late Ming," forthcoming in *Ming Studies* 49 (2004).

actual number was probably somewhere in the vicinity of forty thousand, half of whom could be considered seasoned veterans. The Koreans were desperate for Ming assistance, but still reeling from their earlier defeats at the hands of the Japanese, they warned the Ming about the fighting prowess of their foes. Song Yingchang addressed the Korean envoy, saying, "Our army is like the wind and the rain. In the morning they will come together at the Yalu River and by evening we certainly will have smashed the enemy."[74]

The Ming finally crossed the Yalu in January 1593 and were again warned about the Japanese use of muskets in battle. Li Rusong scoffed at this, boasting, "The Japanese may rely on muskets, but we use great cannon which have a range of 5–6 li. What can the enemy do against them?"[75] After a series of skirmishes the main body of the Ming army arrived outside the walls of Pyŏngyang on 6 February, bolstered by Korean forces. That night a Japanese assault on the camp of Li Rubo, Rusong's younger brother, was repulsed by the Ming with fire arrows.[76] The allied commanders deployed their forces around the walls of the city even as some of the Japanese commanders beat a fighting retreat to its innermost defenses. Li had the Korean generals Yi Il and Kim Ŭngsŏ attack the east as he arrayed a variety of large and small cannon and artillery pieces around the other walls, directing his men to fire smoke bombs and flaming arrows into the city.[77]

At dawn on 8 February, the drums within the city sounded and the Japanese attacked, their boulders, bullets, and arrows falling down like rain on the besiegers. The ground shook and smoke filled the sky as the armies joined battle. Losses were heavy on both sides. Japanese armed with great spears and vats of boiling water repulsed the initial assault by Kim Ŭngsŏ and Yi Il on the east wall. Li then had his forces feign a major assault on the southeast corner of the city as he and his brother led their troops against the west walls. As the front ranks began to break, Li personally killed a fleeing soldier to restore order and announced that the first man to breach the walls would receive five thousand ounces of silver.[78] Fires broke out all over the city and noxious vapors filled the air. Li Rusong galloped forth and directed the battle himself from the thick of the fighting. At one point his horse was even shot out from under him.[79] He gathered a group of stouthearted men and hit the wall with "cloud ladders." Li Rusong then directed Commander Yang Yuan to pro-

74. Zhuge, *Liang chao ping rang lu*, 245.
75. Kawaguchi, *Seikan Iryaku*, 575–76.
76. Mao, *Wanli san da zheng kao*, 34.
77. Zhuge, *Liang chao ping rang lu*, 248.
78. See Wang Chongwu, "Li Rusong zheng dong kao," *Lishi yuyan yanjiusuo jikan* 16 (1947): 343–74, 345.
79. Gu, *Ming shi jishi benmo*, 2375.

ceed through the small west gate of the city while his brother, Li Rubo, followed through the great west gate, setting fires so that the smoke and flames blinded and disoriented the enemy. Subsequently Yang Yuan and Li Rubo found themselves in the midst of a bloody street fight with the defenders.

Song Yingchang was present at the battle as well, leading reinforcements at the north, south, and west sides of the city. Konishi Yukinaga boldly led his men forth to break out of the encirclement, but a hail of arrows and cannon fire turned him back. The Japanese then turned to cut their way through the troops stationed to the southwest, whom they believed to be Koreans. To their dismay, however, the troops shed their disguises and revealed themselves to be Ming troops, a revelation which is said to have thrown the Japanese into a panic.[80] Meanwhile, the Ming commander Wu Weizhong was battling the Japanese at the Peony Terrace outside the city, where he continued to lead his men despite taking a bullet in the chest.[81] Japanese resistance remained stubborn, and even though they were badly defeated, Konishi Yukinaga was able to retreat to Pongwŏllu Pavilion outside the city.[82] The Japanese made a fair stand there and cut down a number of their pursuers, which allowed Konishi Yukinaga to cross the frozen Taedong River in the middle of the night, as he retreated south towards Yŏngsan.[83]

The Japanese were sorely shaken after this defeat, and in a sense, after this battle, they never recovered the momentum they had enjoyed up to this point. Therefore, even though the war would drag on for over five more years, this battle was the turning point of the war, not unlike the Battle of Midway in the Second World War. It showed that the Japanese were not invincible and gave the Koreans their first chance to claim a definitive victory. Moreover, the Battle of Pyŏngyang changed the way the Japanese fought the rest of the war. Until the Ming got involved the Japanese largely relied on their superior training, morale, and firearms to carry the day. The Battle of Pyŏngyang convinced the Japanese they could not go head to head with the Ming when the latter could bring their big guns to bear. For the rest of the war the Japanese preferred to use ambushes and hit-and-run tactics against the Ming. They had apparently

80. Kawaguchi, *Seikan Iryaku*, 579.
81. Mao, *Wanli san da zheng kao*, 35.
82. Other sources say he retreated to Yonkwang Pavilion. See Li, "Li Rusong zheng dong kao," 346.
83. Some sources maintain that Li Rusong sent Konishi a letter saying he would allow the Japanese a chance to retreat because of excessive bloodshed on both sides. According to this version of the story, Korean forces stationed along the Taedong mistook a cannon blast in the city for the signal to attack so they cut down the Japanese as they retreated. See Li Guangtao, *Renchen Wohuo yanjiu*, 77, and Wang, "Li Rusong zheng dong kao," 346.

never encountered firepower of this magnitude in their own country. It is said that the great cannon of the Ming shook the earth for tens of li, and even the mountains around the city trembled during the battle. The smoke from the artillery blotted out the sky, and the whole city was ablaze from Ming fire arrows. The surrounding forest also caught fire.[84]

The Japanese commanders retreated in disarray and hastily convened a council of war to determine their next course of action. There were arguments and countercharges hurled about on all sides, but they eventually decided to retreat as far as Seoul, with the Chinese and Koreans in hot pursuit. The allies quickly recaptured the city of Kaesong and recovered the four northern provinces of Korea. The Korean king even returned to Pyŏngyang. The Koreans were duly impressed with Chinese firepower and military prowess as King Sŏnjo (r. 1567–1608) exclaimed, "Their army is said to number 30,000. This is not a lot but they know how to use them. That is military ability!"[85] When the king asked his ministers about Chinese and Japanese firearms, they replied, "When the Japanese fire their muskets, you can still hear, even if they fire from all sides. But when the Chinese fire their cannon, the sky and the earth vibrate and the mountains and plains tremble and you can't even speak." The king replied, "With weapons such as these, how can we not fight and win?"[86] The Koreans also stated, "Military affairs are simple. Big cannons defeat small cannons and many cannon defeat few cannon."[87]

Giddy with his success and possessing faulty intelligence which suggested that Japanese had already abandoned Seoul, Li Rusong sped forth at the head of no more than three thousand cavalry, leaving his train of firearms far behind. In late February Li and his men were ambushed by a large force of Japanese at the postal station of Pyŏkchegwan, some ninety *li* north of Seoul. The Japanese attacked with their muskets from the high ground and then closed in on the Ming cavalry, inflicting heavy casualties with their *katana,* which were longer and sharper than the swords carried by the northern Ming cavalry units that served as Li's vanguard. The battle raged from late morning until early afternoon. Li Rusong himself may well have been killed or captured had it not been for the heroism of his subordinate Li Yousheng, who used his own body as a human shield to save the general.[88] The Ming commander was finally saved when his brothers Li Rubo and Li Rumei arrived and caught the Japanese in a pincer attack. In the end both sides suffered about equal

84. Kawaguchi, *Seikan Iryaku,* 579.
85. Cited in Zheng, *Ming dai Zhong-Ri guanxi,* 597. On Korean observations of the utility of firearms, see Li, ed., *Chaoxian "Renchen Wohuo" shiliao,* 256–57.
86. See Zheng, *Ming dai Zhong-Ri guanxi,* 597.
87. See Li, ed., *Chaoxian "Renchen Wohuo" shiliao,* preface, 15.
88. Mao, *Wanli san da zheng kao,* 36.

losses and both retreated, the allies to Kaesong, the Japanese to Seoul. Soon thereafter the Japanese were forced to abandon Seoul, as a Chinese general led a detachment in burning the Japanese grain stores nearby.

Some sources erroneously refer to the Battle of Pyŏkchegwan as the largest or most important conflict of the entire Korean campaign.[89] While the battle was important, as it temporarily slowed the allied advance and disheartened Li Rusong, in the end the Japanese were still forced to abandon Seoul and retreat all the way to the southeast coast of Korea. The main significance of the battle was probably that it rendered the Ming less aggressive for the remainder of the conflict. The battle also impressed upon both sides the importance of firearms and superior military technology. The Japanese were able to prevail because they possessed more guns and longer, better swords. As the Chinese were soon to find out, northern cavalry-based units were at a serious disadvantage in mountainous Korea. There was not enough grassland to pasture horses, and their mobility was severely curtailed in Korea's rugged terrain. The weapons northern soldiers typically carried, namely bows and short swords, were ineffective against Japanese muskets fired from cover and *katana* used in hand-to-hand combat. Some Ming commanders complained that the Japanese muskets fired too fast for the Ming to counter, while others said once the Japanese fired, it took them a long time to reload. Others said the muskets had range but lacked accuracy and were of little use at close quarters, so the Ming should just close on them.[90] If the troops did this, however, they would have to contend with the longer swords of the Japanese. Therefore, as the war dragged on, the Chinese brought in more southern troops who were infantry based and trained in the tactics first devised by the great Ming commander Qi Jiguang (1528–88) in the 1560s to combat Japanese pirates who plagued the southeast coast of China.

The Japanese withdrew from Seoul on 9 May. They eventually hunkered down in a string of fortified camps along the southeast coast of Korea as peace talks dragged on for over four years. The commanders on all sides disagreed about exactly how to pursue peace negotiations and what the terms would be. Even worse, the envoys consistently misrepresented the demands of the other side to their respective governments.[91] Most of the Ming forces returned to China, though a small number were left to keep an eye on the Japanese and help train the Koreans to defend themselves, using Chinese weapons, strategy, and tactics. There were occasional skirmishes between the two sides, and a

89. See, for example, Turnbull, *Samurai Invasion,* 143–48.
90. The debate is summarized in Wang, "Li Rusong zheng dong kao," 363.
91. For a complete discussion of the failed peace talks, see Swope, "Rhetoric, Disguise, and Dependence."

Japanese massacre of civilians at Chinju in the summer of 1593 put a serious strain on the peace talks. Few at the Ming court trusted the Japanese, and the Koreans continued to press the Ming to help them expel the Japanese from the peninsula altogether. In the end, after a bizarre series of events that included the flight of the chief Ming envoy, the Ming granted Hideyoshi the title "King of Japan." This infuriated the Japanese ruler, who was of a mind to kill the Ming envoys on the spot but eventually just decided to invade Korea in force again.

Just over 140,000 men were mobilized for the second invasion of Korea, which began in early 1597. This time the Japanese were even more brutal, impressing Koreans into service and killing those of no value to them. As many as 50,000 to 60,000 Koreans may have been forcibly taken back to Japan. The Koreans again asked the Ming for help and dispatched Kwŏn Yul and Yi Wŏn'ik, Korea's foremost generals, to the south to rally forces against the enemy. This time the Japanese took pains to build up their navy and tried to supply more of their troops with firearms. They were aided by factional strife in Korea, which had resulted in Yi Sunsin being deprived of his post and replaced by an incompetent drunk, Wŏn Kyun. Thus, early in the second campaign, the Japanese were able to transport troops and supplies to the southern tip of Korea and attack from that direction in addition to the southwest. The Chinese forces still present moved to check the Japanese advance, but they were sorely outnumbered and could do little until reinforcements arrived. For their part, the Ming decided to send another large expeditionary force with the aim of striking the Japanese as quickly as possible.

In terms of military technology, the second campaign was much like the first, though overall the fighting was more bitter and there were more sieges. The Japanese enjoyed initial success in approaching Seoul from the south, but were finally checked in early autumn of 1597 at Chiksan, in the mountains south of the capital.[92] Again, it was firearms that helped the allies carry the day. There are also reports of the Ming developing a type of reinforced, bulletproof armor which made them better able to withstand Japanese musket barrages.[93] At the same time Chinese naval forces were arriving to threaten Japanese supply lines in the south, and an allied land offensive was pushing the Japanese back towards their fortified bases in the southeast.

Though an attempted siege of Ulsan in southeast Korea was foiled by a Japanese relief force at the end of 1597, the invaders never seriously went on the offensive again. They consistently found themselves holed up in strongly fortified castles, often along narrow mountain passes,

92. Mao, *Wanli san da zheng kao*, 53.
93. See Li Guangtao, "Ming ren yuan Han yu Jishan da jie," *Lishi yuyan yanjiusuo jikan* 43 (1971): 1–14.

which precluded the Chinese and Koreans from using their superior cannon. Even when the Japanese managed to save themselves from almost certain defeat, as was the case in Sachŏn when a freak explosion forced the allies to retreat as they breached the wall, they had to pull back for lack of supplies or reinforcements.

Morale amongst the Japanese steadily declined, and many of their commanders began pressing for a withdrawal to the home islands. Even Hideyoshi himself came to have doubts, allegedly saying, "How could I have sent 100,000 soldiers overseas to become ghosts?"[94] When he questioned his generals about the situation in Korea, they said, "Korea is a big country. If we move east, then we have to defend the west; if we attack to our left, then we are assailed on the right. Even if we had another ten years, the matter still might not be resolved."[95] Thereupon Hideyoshi complained of his advanced age and the fact that there appeared to be no way out of quagmire and asked them, "If we were to stop the troops and sue for peace, then what?" At this all the generals answered, "That would be best."[96] Sources such as these indicate that Hideyoshi himself decided to withdraw from Korea before his death from illness on 18 September 1598. This is in marked contrast to the account transmitted in most secondary sources, which maintains that the decision to withdraw from Korea was made by Hideyoshi's inner circle of councilors and commissioners *after* his death. The most senior of these men also served as regents for Hideyoshi's infant son. It is generally held that these men sought to get out of the Korean quagmire so they could devote their full attention to contesting for power in Japan. While all of the information concerning their motives may well be true, it appears from these accounts that the disenchanted conqueror had already made his decision to throw down the sword. In fact, the withdrawal from Korea was well underway by the time of Hideyoshi's death, and less than half of his top commanders remained in Korea as of August 1598. Throughout the summer of 1598 the Japanese troops had become increasingly restless, and their commanders feared they were on the verge of mutiny. Matters were exacerbated when Yi Sunsin was restored to his post and given joint command of the naval forces with the Chinese commander Chen Lin (d. 1607), a noted firearms expert.[97]

94. This quote is taken from chapter 16 in *Nihon gaishi* and is cited in Li Guangtao, *Ming-Qing dang'an lunwen ji* (Taibei: Lianjing chuban shiye gongsi, 1986), 828. Examples of Hideyoshi's regret and disappointment over failing can also be found in Li, ed., *Chaoxian "Renchen Wohuo" shiliao*, preface, 16–19.

95. See Li , *Dang'an lunwen*, 831.

96. Ibid. Also see Park Yune-hee, *Admiral Yi Sun-shin and His Turtleboat Armada* (Seoul: Hanshin Publishing Co., 1978), 227–28, on the Japanese generals' desire to withdraw and their recommendation to Hideyoshi.

97. For more information on Chen Lin, see Goodrich and Fang, eds., *Dictionary of Ming Biography*, 167–74, and Zhang et al., eds., *Ming shi*, pp. 6404–8.

The final three months of the war were nothing short of a disaster for the Japanese, whose retreat was far from orderly. The allies were eager to settle scores for damage inflicted upon them over the previous seven years. After heavy fighting most of the Japanese commanders managed to escape, though the allies inflicted a serious defeat on the Japanese in the Battle of Noryang Straits in mid-December of 1598. Although Yi Sunsin was killed in this engagement, the allies sunk over three hundred Japanese ships and killed as many as ten thousand Japanese. As the hapless Japanese swam to shore and tried to hide in caves in the tiny islets of the straits, allied forces bombarded them with cannon and mortar fire.[98] This marked an ignominious end to Hideyoshi's dream of an Asiatic empire.

While there were many factors responsible for the final defeat of the Japanese in the Korean campaign, I would suggest that military technology was the single most important variable. The Japanese enjoyed great success early in the war when they held a monopoly on superior technology on land. Conversely, the Koreans and Chinese dominated the sea-lanes for most of the war and effectively prevented the Japanese from ever securing stable supply lines. Once they entered the war, the Chinese supplied the Koreans with superior weapons and helped train their troops. Tactically the Chinese and Koreans were often overmatched by their battle-hardened Japanese foes, yet the Japanese were reluctant to engage the allies in set-piece battles because they knew they could not win. Many Japanese accounts suggest that the allies prevailed simply by force of numbers. This was not the case. The Japanese mobilized close to half a million troops over the course of the war, perhaps five times as many as the Chinese. The Koreans were certainly more numerous, but their most notable victories were guerrilla attacks, and the major fighting was carried out by Chinese troops under Chinese commanders. In the end the Japanese commanders pressed their hegemon to pull out and return home where, ironically enough, they would largely isolate themselves from the outside world and its technologies for two and one-half centuries before once again emerging as a military threat to the Asian mainland at the end of the nineteenth century.

98. Zhang et al., eds., *Ming shi*, p. 6405.

WAR & SOCIETY

A journal of the history of warfare and its impact on society
published in two issues in May and October each year.

The journal has a wide international
readership and publishes a broad
range of articles. A complimentary
copy is available on request.

Articles published recently include:

Paul Collier,
'The Capture of Tripoli in 1941: Open
Sesame or Tactical Folly?'
Robert Cribb,
'Military Strategy in the Indonesian
Revolution: Nasution's Concept of
"Total People's War" in Theory and
Practice'
Edgar Jones & Simon Wessely
'The Origins of British Military
Psychiatry Before the First World War'
Jenny Macleod,
'The Fall and Rise of Anzac Day:
1965 and 1990 Compared'
Gervase Phillips,
'"Of Nimble Service": Technology,
Equestrianism and the Cavalry Arm of
Early Modern Western European
Armies'
David J. Ulbrich,
'Clarifying the Origins and Strategic
Mission of the US Marine Corps
Defense Battalion, 1898–1941'
J.Y. Wong,
'The Limits of Naval Power:
British Gunboat Diplomacy in China
from the *Nemesis* to the *Amethyst*,
1839—1949'

New contributors welcome.
Subscription rates
2 issues: AU$30, US$22, stg£12
4 issues: AU$54, US$40, stg£20

All articles are externally refereed and
published within 12 months of acceptance.
They should not normally exceed 7000
words exclusive of footnotes.

All enquiries to:
The Editors, *War & Society*,
School of History,
Australian Defence Force Academy,
CANBERRA, ACT 2600, Australia
Fax: +61 2 6268 8879
E-mail: warsoc@adfa.edu.au
Web pages:
http://www.adfa.edu.au/ajax/article.html

Martial Illusions: War and Disillusionment in Twentieth-Century and Renaissance Military Memoirs

☆

Yuval Noah Harari

Abstract

The twentieth century has witnessed a revolution in the image of war and of soldiers. The age-old romantic image of war has been discredited; war has increasingly been interpreted as a disillusioning experience; and the soldier has been at least partly transformed from hero to victim. This article examines the roots of this revolution, by comparing twentieth-century and Renaissance military memoirs. It argues that this revolution did not result from twentieth-century military or technological changes in the nature of war, but rather from cultural and mental changes in soldiers' self-perception and in their expectations of life, that occurred between 1600 and 1900.

SCHOLARS studying twentieth-century war memoirs have reached the almost unanimous conclusion that in the twentieth century, at least in the West, soldiers have become disillusioned with war, and their own image has partly changed from that of heroes to that of victims. Following Paul Fussell's dictum that "Every war is ironic because every war is worse than expected,"[1] scholars such as Tobey C. Herzog agree that the main themes of twentieth-century war memoirs are "[t]he tension between the soldier's romantic expectations of war and the harsh realities

---

1. Paul Fussell, *The Great War and Modern Memory* (New York: Oxford University Press, 1975), 7.

Yuval Noah Harari received his Ph.D. from the University of Oxford. He is the author of *Renaissance Military Memoirs: War, History, and Identity, 1450–1600,* as well as of several articles on medieval military history. He is a lecturer at the Department of History in the Hebrew University of Jerusalem.

of the battlefield,"[2] and "the soldiers' loss of their youthful naïveté as they acquire a battlefield education."[3]

It is no coincidence that many of the scholars who studied these war memoirs are themselves veterans, including Fussell and Herzog, for the other main conclusion from studying twentieth-century war memoirs is that many soldiers, having become disillusioned with the romantic image of war, have set themselves the task of actively destroying this image, and preventing future generations from falling victim to it. Twentieth-century veterans have produced a growing avalanche of war books, war poems, war paintings, war films, and academic war studies, all geared to tear away the romantic mask of war, and unmask war's "true face."

Already in 1930 a French historian and veteran of World War I (1914–18), Jean Norton Cru, wrote a study of World War I war books, which sets up the following structure: prewar illusions lead men to war, the war shatters these illusions, and the embittered survivors have the duty and the ability to disillusion the public. Norton Cru explains that

> On the score of courage, patriotism, sacrifice and death, we had been deceived and with the first bullets we recognized at once the falsity of anecdote, history, literature, art, the gossip of veterans, and public speeches. What we saw, what we felt had nothing in common with what we expected in view of all we had read and all we had been told.[4]

The true face of war, writes Norton Cru, is

> terrible exhaustion, extraordinary fatigue. War is water up to your belly, and mud, and ordure, and unspeakable filth. War is dead moldy faces and rotting tatters falling away from rotting flesh and corpses which no longer resemble corpses, half afloat on the muddy, voracious earth. War is the never-ending monotony of pure misery, broken by intense and bitter dramas. That's what war is, and not a bayonet sparkling like silver in the sun.[5]

Norton Cru hopes that since

---

2. Tobey C. Herzog, *Vietnam War Stories: Innocence Lost* (London: Routledge, 1992), 13.

3. Herzog, *Vietnam,* 33. See also Ibid., 4, 6, 37, 60; Paul Fussell, *Wartime: Understanding and Behavior in the Second World War* (New York: Oxford University Press, 1989), 268; Samuel Lynn Hynes, *The Soldiers' Tale: Bearing Witness to Modern War* (London: Pimlico, 1998), 16–17, 30, 56, 101–5; Samuel Lynn Hynes, *A War Imagined: The First World War and English Culture* (London: Bodley Head, 1990), xii; Eric J. Leed, *No Man's Land: Combat and Identity in World War I* (Cambridge: Cambridge University Press, 1979), 75.

4. Jean Norton Cru, *War Books: A Study in Historical Criticism,* trans. S. J. Pincetl and E. Marchand (San Diego, Calif.: San Diego State University Press, 1976), 8.

5. Ibid., 19.

man comes to the point of making war only by a miracle of persuasion and deception practiced on the future combatants, in peace time, by false literature, false history, and false war psychology . . . if people knew what the soldier learns at his baptism of fire, nobody would consent to a solution by force of arms.[6]

Veterans have been remarkably successful in undermining the romantic image of war. Though this image is still powerful, today it is strongly contested by a contradictory public image that sees war as hell and soldiers as victims. As Fussell and Samuel Lynn Hynes (another scholar-veteran) emphasize, modern language itself underwent important changes. The old heroic rhetoric of war has come to sound increasingly pompous and ridiculous to Western ears, and has consequently been replaced by a new and much more somber war rhetoric.[7]

The disillusionment with the romantic image of war has been so strong, that narratives that support it are often suspected of being inauthentic or subtly ironic—or are just considered bad literature.[8] Hynes concludes that whereas "[c]ourage and heroism were possible in Vietnam narratives; the ideal of courage, the Heroic Man of the war tradition, wasn't. Or rather, he was, but only as a ridiculous celluloid figure."[9]

This "thesis of disillusionment" has been criticized from several angles, mainly regarding its applicability to World War I. Cultural and literary historians such as Ann P. Linder, Eric J. Leed, Klaus Theweleit, Michael Paris, Joanna Bourke, and Jay Winter have argued that at least Fussell's *Great War and Modern Memory* rests far too heavily on a small elitist canon of English and French writers. Linder, Leed, and Theweleit, who studied German World War I war books, have argued that most German war memoirists were not disillusioned with their prewar ideals.[10] Paris has shown that even British popular culture in the 1920s and 1930s was far from being "disillusionist."[11]

6. Ibid., 18.

7. Hynes, *War Imagined,* 113–14, 182–83; Fussell, *Great War,* 174.

8. Fussell, *Great War,* 170–72; Herzog, *Vietnam,* 88–89; Evelyn Cobley, *Representing War: Form and Ideology in First World War Narratives* (Toronto: University of Toronto Press, 1993), 5; Chris Hopkins, "Beyond Fiction? The Example of Winged Warfare (1918)," in Patrick J. Quinn and Steven Trout, eds., *The Literature of the Great War Reconsidered: Beyond Modern Memory* (New York: Palgrave, 2001), 9–23.

9. Hynes, *Soldiers' Tale,* 214.

10. Ann P. Linder, *Princes of the Trenches: Narrating the German Experience of the First World War* (Columbia, S.C.: Camden House, 1996), 22, 43–48, 53–55. See also George L. Mosse, *Fallen Soldiers: Reshaping the Memory of the World Wars* (New York: Oxford University Press, 1990), 6–7.

11. Michael Paris, *Warrior Nation: Images of War in British Popular Culture, 1850–2000* (London: Reaktion Books, 2000), 112–19, 145, 148–57, 184–85. This view is adopted even by Hynes. In *Soldiers' Tale* he softens the conclusions he reached in *War Imagined,* saying that not all soldiers were disillusioned by war (Hynes, *Soldiers' Tale,* 105).

Joanna Bourke, while accepting much of the disillusionment the-sis,[12] has drawn attention in her *Intimate History of Killing* to the fact that the depiction of soldiers as victims is problematic. Relying on an extensive pool of American, British, and Commonwealth sources, Bourke convincingly demonstrates that soldiers from World War I to the Vietnam War (1961–75) continued to see themselves as killers rather than victims.

Jay Winter has also argued that it is wrong to see World War I as rep-resenting a clean break with the past and as ushering in a new disillu-sioned era. Though "Romantic notions about war did indeed take a battering during the 1914–18 war," and though consequently "the days of [war's] glorification were over,"[13] Winter stresses the continuing appeal of traditional attitudes towards war even after 1918, and argues that 1945 was "the real caesura in European cultural life."[14]

Military historians such as Robin Prior, Trevor Wilson, Brian Bond, Hew Strachan, and Gary Sheffield have also attacked Fussell's thesis as anachronistic when applied to World War I. They, too, have argued that it is based on a very limited canon of elite writers, and that it also ignores many important aspects of the war and all the various fronts except the Western.[15]

They have convincingly demonstrated that during the war itself, few people interpreted it using the paradigm of disillusionment, and even in the 1920s and 1930s the disillusioned view of war was still a minority elitist view, though it began to gain more widespread appeal.[16] It was only in the 1960s, due to the influence of the Vietnam War, of the fear of nuclear war, and of the antiauthority youth culture, that the disillu-sioned interpretation of war in general and World War I in particular became the standard popular view.[17]

12. See, for example, Joanna Bourke, *An Intimate History of Killing: Face-to-Face Killing in Twentieth-Century Warfare* (London: Granta Books, 1999), 16–26, 64–67.

13. Jay Winter, *Sites of Memory, Sites of Mourning: The Great War in European Cultural History* (Cambridge: Cambridge University Press, 1995), 8.

14. Winter, *Sites of Memory,* 228. See also Ibid., 3, 121, 132–33.

15. Robin Prior and Trevor Wilson, "Paul Fussell at War," *War in History* 1, no. 1 (1994): 66–70; Brian Bond, *The Unquiet Western Front: Britain's Role in Literature and History* (Cambridge: Cambridge University Press, 2002), 27–28, 81, 92–100; Gary Sheffield, *Forgotten Victory: The First World War: Myths and Realities* (London: Review, 2002). See also Martin Stephen, *The Price of Pity: Poetry, History and Myth in the Great War* (London: Leo Cooper, 1996), 98–99, 230–31.

16. Bond, *Unquiet Western Front,* 24–25, 28–35; Hew Strachan, "The Soldier's Experience in Two World Wars: Some Historiographical Comparisons," in Paul Addi-son and Angus Calder, eds., *Time to Kill: The Soldier's Experience of War in the West, 1939–1945* (London: Pimlico, 1997), 370.

17. Bond, *Unquiet Western Front,* 51–54, 65; Strachan, "Soldier's Experience," 370.

I believe that these arguments are accurate, yet they do not undermine the disillusionment thesis. They merely move the date when the romantic image of war was publicly discredited from 1916 to the 1960s, and transform Fussell from a distant reporter on the death of this romantic image, into one of its main executioners. Whether or not martial disillusionment was an important experience in World War I, it certainly became the main martial experience in post-1960s Western culture.

As Bond and Michael Paris argue, since the 1960s film, television, popular military history, fiction books, the theater, and other media forms have all tended to transform disillusionment into the most common public paradigm for interpreting martial experience.[18] Pupils in British schools today are consequently more likely to learn about World War I from Wilfred Owen's poems and episodes of the television program *Blackadder* than from military histories, patriotic memoirs, or Rupert Brooke's poems.[19]

Similarly, even if the view of the soldier as victim was initially propagated by a small elitist circle, after Vietnam it gained far wider currency both amongst soldiers and even more so amongst the general public. At least since Vietnam the ethical discussion of soldiering has been replaced by a psychological one, in which the main issue is the psychological damage (grouped under the umbrella of Post-Traumatic Stress Disorder [PTSD]) war may cause soldiers, rather than the crimes soldiers may commit in war.[20] The idea of the soldier-as-victim has become clichéd, adopted by the veteran who argues that "I had been, as we all were, victimized by a romantic, truly uninformed view of war";[21] by governments and veteran associations whose statistical surveys have found that between 25 and fully 100 percent of Vietnam veterans—most of whom never saw combat—suffer from PTSD;[22] and even by hard-core military historians such as Bond, who occasionally refer to the "survivors" of a battle rather than to its "veterans."[23]

It is therefore not surprising that whereas in the 1920s and 1930s only a minority of elitist writers composed their memoirs as disillusion-

18. Bond, *Unquiet Western Front*, 39, 59–68, 76–77, 82–87; Paris, *Warrior Nation*, 236–37, 249–50, 255–56.

19. Ibid., 86–88.

20. Ben Shepard, *A War of Nerves: Soldiers and Psychiatrists in the Twentieth Century* (Cambridge, Mass.: Harvard University Press, 2001), 355–76; Bourke, *Intimate History of Killing*, 114–16, 220, 254–67; Edna Lomsky-Feder and Eyal Ben-Ari, "Trauma, Therapy and Responsibility: Psychology and War in Contemporary Israel," in Monica Boeck, Aparna Rao, and Michael Bollig, eds., *The Practice of War* (Oxford: Berghahn Books, forthcoming).

21. Stewart O'Nan, ed., *The Vietnam Reader* (New York: Doubleday, 1998), 312.

22. Shepard, *War of Nerves*, 366, 392; Hugh McManners, *The Scars of War* (London: HarperCollins, 1993), 370; Bourke, *Intimate History of Killing*, 246.

23. Bond, *Unquiet Western Front*, 63, 70.

ment narratives, in the last four decades a far greater percentage of military memoirs—whether they concern World War I, World War II (1939–45), Vietnam, or the Intifada (1987–)—tend to be disillusionment narratives. They may not necessarily be pacifist or "antiwar," but they are certainly critical of the romantic image of war.[24]

Whether the romantic image of war was discredited in 1916 or in the 1960s, a very big question remains unanswered. If indeed this romantic image is a groundless but dangerous illusion, why did it survive for so many centuries? The usual explanation is that princes, priests, and poets have conspired throughout history to create a heroic mask for war, which hid some of its ugliest features, and transformed those features which could not be hidden into the seductive marks of heroism. They thereby created a powerful cult of war and of heroism. The secrets of this cult were made known only to those select men who passed its bloody initiation rites and became warriors, and who were consequently given a privileged place in society. Throughout history, some civilians repeatedly tried to unmask the true face of war, but the power of this cult and its warrior initiates was so great, that the civilians always failed. Then, sometime between 1916 and 1969, something momentous happened. The initiation rite backfired. Not only were the (surviving) initiates completely disillusioned about the heroic cult, but they used the very power conferred on them through their initiation in order to destroy this cult and successfully unmask the true face of war.[25]

This explanation highlights one important point: throughout history war's "true face" was always familiar to the victims of war. It was only the warriors themselves who needed twentieth-century wars to open their eyes, but without their heroic authority, it was impossible to destroy the heroic cult. Yet this again begs the question: Why did it take warriors so many centuries to become disillusioned with war? One possibility is to argue that the nature of war changed sometime around 1916, which led to a change in its image. Up to 1916, for the soldiers, war was indeed heroic and glorious. This would mean that people like Wilfred Owen and Erich Maria Remarque (author of *All Quiet on the Western Front*) did not unmask war's eternal face, but simply reacted to technological changes in the nature of war, which for the first time transferred soldiers from the ranks of the heroes to the ranks of the victims, and which thereby transformed hitherto heroic truths into "an old lie."[26]

24. It is important to remember that one can support a war even while rejecting its romantic image. See Bond, *Unquiet Western Front*, 31–32.

25. For war as initiation, see Linder, *Princes*, 50–52; Leed, *No Man's Land*, 12–13, 28–33; Barbara Ehrenreich, *Blood Rites: Origins and History of the Passions of War* (New York: Metropolitan Books, 1997), 10–12, 125–28, 145–46, 156.

26. Erich Maria Remarque, *Im westen nichts neues* (Berlin: Propyläen-verlag, 1929, c1928).

Most memoirists and scholars who uphold the disillusionment thesis have toyed with this possibility, but ultimately rejected it and argued that the disillusioning face of war is a permanent and universal feature, that may be masked or unmasked, but not changed.[27] It is clear why the upholders of the disillusionment thesis tend to adopt such a universalistic view. For if Owen, Remarque, and others only reacted to a changing technological reality and did not unmask war's eternal face, there is no reason why their writings should help stop future wars. If war's true face changes, and if soldiers should do their best not to prepare themselves for yesterday's war, then perhaps young people in the future could expect to play the game of dashing hero again.

Yet if Owen and Remarque did unmask the eternal face of war, and if there has been no fundamental change in the nature of war around 1916, why did it take soldiers so many centuries to open their eyes? This article is an attempt to begin exploring this question. It focuses on military memoirs written by Renaissance and late-medieval veterans. It examines whether these veterans write about experiences of disillusionment, whether they try to demolish the romantic image of war, and if not—what could explain their silence.[28]

My choice to focus on late-medieval and Renaissance memoirs is due to two reasons. First, this is the period in which the romantic "old lie" was formulated. Though glorious façades for war have been constructed at least since Biblical times, the particular façade characteristic of the modern West is largely a product of the Renaissance, born out of the marriage of the old medieval chivalric ideals with the rising ideals of statehood and nationalism. Secondly, the Renaissance witnessed the greatest revolution in military technology prior to World War I, namely

27. Fussell, *Wartime*, 294–96; Herzog, *Vietnam*, 4; Hynes, *Soldiers' Tale*, 17–19; Leed, *No Man's Land*, 13; Prior and Wilson, "Paul Fussell," 68.

28. Most medieval and Renaissance military memoirs were composed by noblemen who served as commanders of various ranks. I tried to focus as much as possible on memoirs of common soldiers and junior commanders, but the article still relies on memoirs of medium and senior commanders to a greater extent than studies of twentieth-century military memoirs. However, this is not too problematic, for two reasons. First, though previous studies have ignored this phenomenon, it seems that at least from the 1960s on, many senior-rank military memoirists have been deeply influenced by the anti-romantic model of junior-rank memoirists, so that they, too, began to present a disillusioned image of war (see, for example, Frank Percy Crozier, *The Man I Killed* (Garden City, N.Y.: Doubleday, Doran and Co., 1938, and Moshe Givati, *Three Births in September* [Tel Aviv: Ma'arachot, 1990 (in Hebrew)]. More importantly, the reason previous studies ignored the memoirs of senior-rank officers is that, in Norton Cru's words, they did not "belong to the fighting troops or . . . live with them under fire" (Norton Cru, *War Books*, 6–7). This may be true in the twentieth century, but in the Renaissance even the highest ranking commanders normally lived side-by-side with the common soldiers and fought in the front ranks, so their experience of war was not radically different from that of the common soldiers.

the introduction of firearms. Hence, if there is an inherent connection between technological change and martial disillusionment, we can expect it to be manifested in the Renaissance as well.

Though quite a lot of research has been done on Renaissance military memoirs,[29] no comparison has been made between them and twentieth-century memoirs, especially regarding the question of disillusionment. Scholars of Renaissance warfare have certainly given much attention to the psychology of war, to questions of soldiers' motivation, and to the tension between ideals and reality in war. During the Renaissance itself this tension was a favorite topic of discussion, immortalized in the pages of *Don Quixote*. In his *Waning of the Middle Ages,* which was written during World War I and appeared in 1919, Johan Huizinga argued that in the fifteenth century chivalric ideals were divorced from the reality of war, and were no more than an escapist dream from the harsh reality of peacetime as well as wartime conditions.[30] It was no more than a grand illusion, maintained by the chivalric cult's initiates through a prodigious expense of energy, time, money, and blood.

In following years the pendulum swung back and forth in the argument about the relationship between romantic ideals and realities of war in the late Middle Ages and the Renaissance. Yet though most scholars have stressed the continuing relevance of chivalric ideals and practices even in the sixteenth century, all seem to agree that late-medieval and Renaissance war was nothing like the war portrayed in chivalric culture, and that romantic ideals were useful mainly as a means of constructing noble identity, advancing the interests of the royal state, and ensuring the loyalty of subjects.[31]

29. Philippe Contamine, "The War Literature of the Late Middle Ages: The Treatises of Robert de Balsac and Béraud Stuart, Lord of Aubigny," in Christopher T. Allmand, ed., *War, Literature, and Politics in the Late Middle Ages* (Liverpool: Liverpool University Press, 1976), 102–21; Robert J. Knecht, "Military Autobiography in Sixteenth-Century France," in J. R. Mulryne and Margaret Shewring, eds., *War, Literature and the Arts in Sixteenth-Century Europe* (New York: St. Martin's Press, 1989), 3–21; Henry J. Cohn, "Götz von Berlichingen and the Art of Military Autobiography," in Mulryne and Shewring, eds., *War, Literature and the Arts,* 22–40; Joël Blanchard, "Écrire la guerre au XVe siècle," *Le moyen français* 24 (1989): 7–21; Margarita Levisi, "Golden Age Autobiography: The Soldiers," in Nicholas Spadaccini and Jenaro Taléns, ed., *Autobiography in Early Modern Spain* (Minneapolis: Prisma Institute, 1988), 97–118; Nadine Kuperty, *Se dire à la Renaissance: les mémories au XVIe siècle* (Paris: Vrin, 1997).

30. Johan Huizinga, *The Waning of the Middle Ages: A Study of the Forms of Life, Thought, and Art in France and the Netherlands in the XIVth and XVth Centuries* (London: E. Arnold and Co., 1924).

31. Malcolm Vale, *War and Chivalry* (London: Duckworth, 1981); Maurice Keen, *Chivalry* (New Haven, Conn.: Yale University Press, 1984); Sidney Anglo, ed., *Chivalry in the Renaissance* (Woodbridge: Boydell, 1990); Arthur B. Ferguson, *The Chivalric Tradition in Renaissance England* (Washington: Folger Shakespeare

The study of Renaissance warfare therefore creates the impression that the romantic image of war was an "old lie" already in the Renaissance. However, though some scholars make explicit comparisons between the realities of Renaissance and twentieth-century warfare,[32] they do not proceed to engage with the disillusionment thesis. They are very interested to know how contemporaries could, in Maurice Keen's words, "reconcile the cult of the fighting man with their awareness of those horrors of war that bore on the noncombatant rather than the warrior, in particular the crimes and misdemeanours of soldiers, their pillaging and their brutality?"[33] Yet they show less interest in the tension between the cult of the fighting man and the horrors that bore on the warriors themselves. And they do not attempt to explain how it happened that though the romantic image of war was a lie already in the fifteenth century, it took soldiers another five hundred years to become disillusioned with it and to challenge it publicly.

> If in some smothering dreams you too could pace
> Behind the wagon that we flung him in,
> And watch the white eyes writhing in his face,
> His hanging face, like a devil's sick of sin;
> If you could hear, at every jolt, the blood
> Come gargling from the froth-corrupted lungs,
> Obscene as cancer, bitter as the cud
> Of vile, incurable sores on innocent tongues,—
> My friend, you would not tell with such high zest
> To children ardent for some desperate glory,
> The old Lie: Dulce et decorum est
> Pro patria mori.[34]

Thus ends Wilfred Owen's poem *Dulce et decorum est,* written in 1918. Four centuries before Owen wrote this poem, another English poet, George Gascoigne, wrote about his own military experience in Flanders

---

Library, 1986); J. R. Hale, *War and Society in Renaissance Europe,* 2d ed. (Guernsey: Sutton, 1998), 37–38; Frank Tallett, *War and Society in Early Modern Europe, 1495–1715* (London: Routledge, 1992), 17–18.

32. John Keegan's *Face of Battle* compares the realities of war at Agincourt (1415) and on the Somme (1916), whereas Geoffrey Parker's Army of Flanders repeatedly compares the mutinies of the Spanish army in the Netherlands to the 1917 mutinies in the French army (Geoffrey Parker, *The Army of Flanders and the Spanish Road: The Logistics of Spanish Victory and Defeat in the Low Countries' Wars* [Cambridge: Cambridge University Press, 1972], 187, 199).

33. Keen, *Chivalry,* 220. See also ibid., 233–34.

34. Wilfred Owen, *War Poems and Others,* ed. Dominic Hibberd (London: Chatto and Windus, 1973), 79.

Fields in a poem titled *Dulce Bellum inexpertis,* whose theme he defines
as follows:

> I may confesse that Bellum every way,
> Is Sweete: but how? (beare well my woordes away)
> Forsooth, to such as never did it trie,
> This is my Theame I cannot chaunge it I.[35]

Gascoigne seems to echo the twentieth-century disillusionment
theme, for he repeatedly criticizes and ridicules those who praise war
without ever experiencing it themselves. He begins by surveying what
poets, painters, astronomers, and common people say about war. He criticizes all of them, saying that they know not what they talk about. In his
view, if painters wished to display what war really is, they should show

> townes destroyde, and fields with bloud berayde,
> Yong children slaine, olde widdowes foule opprest,
> Maydes ravished, both men and wives distrest.[36]

He then explains that the expectations that cause men to go to war
are often disappointed. He begins his explanation on a familiar enough
note, saying that

> I set aside to tell the restlesse toyle,
> The mangled corps, the lamed limbes at last,
> The shortend yeares by fret of fevers foyle,
> The smoothest skinne with skabbes and skarres disgrast,
> The frolicke favour founst and foule defast,
> The broken sleepes, the dreadfull dreames, the woe,
> Which wonne with warre and cannot from him goe.
> I list not write (for it becommes me not)
> The secret wrath which God doth kindle oft,
> To see the sucklings put unto the pot,
> To heare their giltlesse bloose send cries alofte,
> And call for vengeance unto him, but softe
> The Souldiours they commit those heynous actes,
> Yet Kings and Captaynes answere for such factes.[37]

Up to now Gascoigne seems to be arguing along similar lines to twentieth-century disillusioned memoirists. However, he now adopts a different course. After dismissing these miseries of war in an aside of about 10
lines, Gascoigne describes in about 150 lines what he considers a much
worse problem with war, which is that those who go there in search of

---

35. George Gascoigne, "The fruites of Warre, written upon this Theame, Dulce
Bellum inexpertis . . . ," in George Gascoigne, *The Complete Works,* ed. John W. Cun-
liffe, 2 vols. (New York: Cambridge University Press, 1974), 1:179.

36. Ibid., 1:144.

37. Ibid., 1:149.

honor and money are often unjustly cheated of both.[38] He then discloses his hand fully, and devotes almost thirty pages to what really incenses him: The fact that he personally was unjustly cheated of his due honor. He narrates at length how after a distinguished career at arms, he was appointed to command an infantry band at the fort of Valkenburgh during the Netherlands War (1556–1648). However, due to impossible conditions, so he says, he abandoned the fort, and a day later surrendered to the Spaniards without a fight.[39] He and the other captains returned to England under a cloud. They were accused of treacherously selling the fort to the Spaniards, and lost both their property and, what is far worse in his eyes, their honor.[40]

Gascoigne now recapitulates his argument that "war is sweet only to the inexperienced," clarifying what he meant by it. And he means something quite different from what Owen means, for he concludes by explaining that:

> These fruits (I say) in wicked warres I founde,
> Which make me wryte much more than else I would,
> For losse of life, or dread of deadly wounde,
> Shall never make me blame it though I could,
> Since death doth dwell on everie kinde of mould;
> And who in warre hath caught a fatall clappe,
> Might chaunce at home to have no better happe.
> So losse of goodes shall never trouble me,
> Since God which gives can take when pleaseth him,
> But losse of fame or slaundred so to be,
> That makes my wittes to breake above their brimme,
> And frettes my harte, and lames me every limme:
> For Noble minds their honour more esteeme,
> Than worldly wights, or wealth, or life can deeme.
> And yet in warres, such graffes of grudge do growe,
> Such lewdnesse lurkes, such malice makes mischief,
> Such envie boyles, such falshood fire doth blowe,
> That Bountie burnes, and truth is called thief,
> And good desertes are brought into such brief,
> That Saunder snuffe which sweares the matter out,
> Brings oftentimes the noblest names in doubt.[41]

Contrary to what we may have supposed on the basis of his earlier references to the miseries of war, Gascoigne is not disillusioned with war as such. He quickly forgets about the miseries of civilians, and even the

38. Ibid., 1:151–55.
39. Ibid., 1:169–75.
40. Ibid., 1:176–78.
41. Ibid., 1:178–79.

danger of death and injury haunting soldiers is no argument against war in his view, for one may just as easily be killed at home. Whereas Owen's message is that the ideals that sent him to war—all the talk about honor and glory—are dangerous delusions, Gascoigne still cherishes honor more than his life. What he complains about is only that he was dishonored unjustly, and what he warns his readers about is that it may happen to them, too—something which always bothered knights and warriors.

To make this completely clear, Gascoigne adds an epilogue to his poem. In it he apologizes to his fellow soldiers if he spoke too harshly of war, and assures the reader that it is definitely possible to win much honor through war. To prove this, he names several of his comrades who won honor through noble deeds of arms. He then assures the readers that "he honors those Which wade in warres to get a woorthie name" and that

> If drummes once sounde a lustie martch in deede,
> Then farewell bookes, for he will trudge with speede.[42]

Gascoigne's poem is characteristic of Renaissance military memoirs in general: they are clearly aware of the ugly and stupid face of war, yet they are not concerned about it very much (unless their honor is at stake), and it does not prevent them from cherishing martial honor and from seeing war as a worthy vocation.

About 250 years before Gascoigne went to the Netherlands, a young knight from Hainault named Jean le Bel made the opposite journey, traveling from the Netherlands to fight in Northern England against the Scots (1327). In the early 1350s le Bel wrote a chronicle of his times, whose first chapters describe this campaign in a manner which would seem familiar to readers of *Catch-22* and *The Good Soldier Švejk*.[43]

Le Bel's narrates how the English army went looking for the elusive Scots in the wilderness of the Anglo-Scottish borderlands. The English knights, hearing the sound of battle cries ahead of them, repeatedly broke their order and galloped ahead impetuously

> through water, stones and flint-stones and through valleys and mountains, with helmet on the head, shield on the neck, glavie or sword in hand, without waiting for neither father nor brother nor companion. And when they thus galloped for half a league or more and arrived at the place whence the cry aroused, they found themselves deceived, because these were deer or hinds or other wild beasts.[44]

---

42. Ibid., 1:183.

43. Joseph Heller, *Catch-22* (New York: Simon and Schuster, 1961); Jaroslav Hasek, *The Good Soldier: Schweik* (New York: F. Ungar, 1930).

44. Jean le Bel, *Chronique de Jean le Bel,* ed. Jules Viard and Eugène Déprez, 2 vols. (Paris: Librairie Renouard, 1904–5), chapter 11.

The English continued these mad dashes all day, "without stopping except in order to piss," until they got completely lost. Le Bel's narrative now switches from a farcical to a more tragic mode, recounting the miserable conditions in which the lost English army found itself. Chapter XII depicts war in its most wretched form, and dispels any remaining inclination in the reader's heart to valorize war. Le Bel gives vent here to the common soldier's resentment towards the lords and commanders. He draws a picture of a military fiasco, in which the common soldier has to suffer for the mistakes of his superiors, while these manage to feather their nests even under the worst circumstances. While the common soldiers are forced to drink filthy water from the river, the lords have their wine-bottles; while the common soldiers—following orders—brought with them neither food nor equipment, the lords themselves did bring along some pack-horses laden with necessities; while the common soldiers have nothing to give their horses, the lords have oats; while the common soldiers have no light, the lords have torches; and finally, when the army is "rescued" by local peasants who inform it of its location, the common soldiers have to wait hungrily for the arrival of swindler merchants from Newcastle, whereas the lords send their servants ahead to bring them food and other essentials.

The sole "heroic" exploit Le Bel recounts is the tale of the squire who discovered the whereabouts of the Scottish army—and even he was captured by the Scots, and was able to return to the English army and report his findings only because the Scots desired the English to attack them.

It seems that this campaign thoroughly disillusioned le Bel about the reality of war. Not long after it he gave up the military vocation, and became instead a canon at St. Lambert's Church in Liège, in which position he composed the above-mentioned chronicle. We might imagine that this chronicle was not very favorable to the heroic war image, a lone voice crying out against the dominant chivalric fantasies of the day.

We could not be further from the truth. Le Bel's chronicle became one of the foundation stones of the Western romantic view of war. Apart from the description of the 1327 campaign, it usually glamorizes war, portraying the chivalric culture at its best, and glorifying the exploits of daring knights. Moreover, this chronicle became the model and founding text of the most influential school of late-medieval chivalric chroniclers. The famed Jean Froissart was le Bel's immediate successor, and copied entire chapters from him. Froissart was then continued by such authors as Monstrelet, Wavrin, and Chastelain (some of whom, like Wavrin, were themselves war veterans). This school made a vital contribution to the formulation of late-medieval chivalry, and bequeathed its heroic image to posterity.

If Gascoigne's and le Bel's writings are uncharacteristic of late-medieval and Renaissance military memoirs, it is only because they express more disillusionment than other memoirists. Quite a few Renaissance memoirists were positively enthusiastic about war. Jean de Bueil, a fifteenth-century French captain, famously wrote:

> What a gratifying thing war is, for many are the splendid things heard and seen in the course of it, and many are the good lessons to be learnt from it. . . . When one feels that one's cause is just, and one's blood is ready for the fight, tears come to the eye. A warm feeling of loyalty and pity comes into the heart on seeing one's friend expose his body with such courage to carry out and to accomplish the will of our Creator; and one makes up one's mind to go and die or live with him, and, out of love, not to abandon him. No man who has not experienced it knows how to speak of the satisfaction which comes from this sort of action. Do you think that a man who acts in this way will fear death? Not at all; for he is so comforted, so much carried away that he doesn't realize where he is. He simply does not fear anything.[45]

Jörg von Ehingen, too, loved war. He began his career as a page to the wife of Duke Sigismund of Tyrol. However, he was annoyed by the peaceful life there, and left in search of warlike adventures. He traveled through Eastern Europe as far as Rhodes and Egypt in search of war, but to his dismay, "there was good peace in all the kingdoms of Christendom."[46] He then traveled west, searching for wars in France and Iberia, until he finally found one at Ceuta on the Moroccan coast. During one sortie there, a Muslim Goliath challenged the Christians to send forth a champion to fight him. Ehingen begged to be chosen, and had his way. His memoirs climax in a blow-by-blow description of this single combat. Ehingen killed his rival, and was afterwards fêted both in Ceuta and in the courts of Europe.[47]

Most memoirists were not so enamored with war, yet none of them described an experience or a process of disillusionment with war, and none lamented that he was victimized by a delusively romantic view of war.[48] Robert de la Marck, lord of Florange and a sixteenth-century

---

45. Jean de Bueil, *Le Jouvencel par Jean de Bueil suivi du commentaire de Guillaume Tringant*, ed. Léon Lecestre, 2 vols. (Paris: Librairie Renouard, 1887–89), 2:20–21. Translation taken from C. T. Allmand, ed., *Society at War: The Experience of England and France During the Hundred Years War* (Edinburgh: Oliver and Boyd, 1973), 27–28.

46. Jörg von Ehingen, *Reisen nach der Ritterschaft,* ed. Gabriele Ehrmann, 2 vols. (Göppingen: Kümmerle Verlag, 1979), 38.

47. For the love of war, see also Yuval Noah Harari, *Renaissance Military Memoirs: War, History, and Identity, 1450–1600* (Woodbridge: Boydell, 2004), 101–3.

48. Harari, *Renaissance Military Memoirs,* 100, 132, 148–50. The closest that memoirists come to describing experiences of disillusionment is in occasional remarks such as when Philippe de Commynes writes that at his first battle, Montlhéry (1465), he was "less frightened than I have ever been anywhere since, because of my

French mercenary captain, is a typical example. His memoirs recount that he embarked on his military career at the tender age of eight or nine, when, inspired by the influence of "some book about adventurous knights of past time,"[49] he left home to join the court of Louis XII, and at eighteen went on to his first campaign. It seems that sixteen years of almost ceaseless campaigns were not enough to disillusion Florange about his childhood dream of emulating the adventurous knights of chivalric romances. Though he suffered much on these campaigns, when he wrote his memoirs (in Habsburg captivity after the disaster of Pavia [1525]) he referred to himself throughout his narrative by the romantic sounding name of "the Adventurer," and never said a bad word about war.

Götz von Berlichingen, too, dreamed of heroic adventures from his early childhood. In 1504 the twenty-three-year-old Berlichingen was hit by a cannonball and lost his hand. According to his memoirs, he was in despair, because "I was finished as a man of war."[50] His spirits revived once he replaced his lost hand with an iron one and resumed his martial career. Throughout his memoirs he never dwells on the issue again, so if the few pages describing his injury had been lost, readers could never have guessed that all the following exploits were performed by a one-handed knight.

Florange, Berlichingen, and most other memoirists describe their various campaigns in a matter-of-fact way, not hiding their injuries and miseries, but not dwelling on them either, and treating war above all as a natural and quite neutral phenomenon. As a cultural institution they tend to see war as positive, inasmuch as it is the source of their livelihood and honor,[51] whereas they hardly ever reflect on it as a personal experience.[52]

Their attitude to war is also apparent from their didactic stance. None of them wrote his memoirs in order to disillusion his readers and help prevent future generations from going to war. On the contrary, many wrote their memoirs in order to inspire their descendants and other readers to take up arms, and to conduct themselves well and honorably in war. The French Marshal Blaise de Monluc, who lost all his sons to war, and wrote in retirement after an harquebus ball hit him in the

youth and because I had no fear of danger" (Philippe de Commynes, *Mémoires*, ed. Joseph Calmette, 3 vols. [Paris: Les Belles Lettres, 1964–65], 1:28). And even such remarks do not necessarily express disillusionment.

49. Robert de la Marck, lord of Florange, *Mémoires du Maréchal de Florange dit le Jeune Adventureux*, ed. Robert Goubaux and P.-André Lemoisne, 2 vols. (Paris: Librairie Renouard, 1913–24), 1:3.

50. Götz von Berlichingen, *The Autobiography of Götz von Berlichingen*, ed. H. S. M. Stuart (London: Duckworth, 1956), 25–26.

51. Harari, *Renaissance Military Memoirs*, 101–3.

52. Ibid., 56–63, 67–88.

face and disfigured him horribly, goes as far as threatening his little grandson that if he does not emulate his dead father by himself going to war, Monluc will disown him.[53]

Why were medieval and Renaissance military memoirists not disillusioned with war? One possibility is that war in the late Middle Ages and the Renaissance was indeed less horrible than it became in the twentieth century—at least for the soldiers. As long as war was fought with sword and harquebus, soldiers were ready to pay the price it demanded; not until the machine-gun and high explosive shell appeared did they cry stop.[54] Yet there is little to support this view. The war experience of medieval and Renaissance soldiers could be as bad as that of twentieth-century soldiers, and most memoirists were fully aware of the uglier sides of war.

Though the absolute numbers of soldiers who were wounded or killed in Renaissance wars were far smaller than in the twentieth-century world wars, the percentage of wounded and killed soldiers was at least as high, with armies losing from a quarter to half their strength on a single day of battle. For example, at Ravenna (1512) the Spanish lost within a few hours nine thousand men out of sixteen thousand, and the victorious French over four thousand out of twenty-three thousand.[55]

Disease and hunger were even more deadly than battles, so that even without pitched battles, armies could suffer a wastage rate of 20 to 80 percent per campaign (though desertion was also an important component of this wastage rate).[56] Geoffrey Parker is probably correct in remarking that hardships similar to those endured by the troops of early modern Europe "would be tolerated by few armies today."[57]

Quite a few memoirists give graphic descriptions of the poor conditions on campaign. Elis Gruffydd, a Welsh common soldier in the English army that invaded France in 1523, writes that the soldiers, who were not equipped for a winter campaign, suffered much from cold, hunger, and inadequate living quarters. "During this time," writes Gruffydd, "grey bearded winter began to show his face in black cold frost wind and short days and long nights which caused the decrepit shivering soldiers to

53. Blaise de Monluc, *Commentaires de Blaise de Monluc, Maréchal de France,* ed. Paul Courteault, 3 vols. (Paris: A. Picard, 1911–25), 2:585.

54. See Prior and Wilson, "Paul Fussell," 63–64.

55. Florange, *Mémoires,* 1:83–94; Charles W. C. Oman, *A History of the Art of War in the Sixteenth Century* (London: Methuen, 1937), 147–48. For the heavy toll of late-medieval and Renaissance battles, see also Keen, *Chivalry,* 222–23; Hale, *War and Society,* 84, 119–20.

56. Hale, *War and Society,* 119–20; Geoffrey Parker, *The Military Revolution: Military Innovation and the Rise of the West, 1500–1800,* 2d ed. (New York: Cambridge University Press, 1996), 53–57; Parker, *Army of Flanders,* 207–11.

57. Parker, *Army of Flanders,* 207. For the difficult conditions, see also ibid., 183, 198–99, 210–11.

complain and groan to each other. Some said it was too much for them to be there lying on the earth under hedges and bushes dying of cold." Gruffydd recalls how he was woken up one night by a soldier who left the tent "to make water," and shouted, "'Ah sirs, if I had known at the beginning of the night that there would be as much frost and snow as this I would not have taken so much trouble to search my shirt for lice, but I should have hung it out in the wind and let them die of cold, as we shall do if we stay here any longer.'"

The soldiers eventually mutinied and forced the commanders to retreat. The retreat was just as horrible: "Many men on horse and on foot died from sheer cold. Others said that some had lost the use of their limbs from the force of the frost wind. . . . and others said that they had lost the use of their water pipes."[58]

It is interesting to note that like Gascoigne and le Bel, Gruffydd was not disillusioned by all this suffering. He stayed in the army for decades more, and as for the misery of his fellow soldiers in 1523, he blames it on them! He writes that "they had no reason to complain except of their own sluggishness and slovenliness. For there was no lack of food or drink or wood for fire or making huts," but they were too lazy to make use of it. Indeed, he blames the mutineers for wrecking the campaign, saying that they were "cowardly men with base hearts who would rather go home to their mothers and fathers, some to plough and thresh, others to follow the cart and hedge and dig and live niggardly," instead of pursuing the honorable career of soldiers.[59]

---

58. M. Bryn Davies, "Suffolk's Expedition to Montdidier 1523," *Bulletin of the Faculty of Arts, Fouad I University* 7 (1944): 40–42.

59. Davies, "Suffolk's Expedition," 39. For the ravages of hunger, cold, and disease, see also, for instance, François de Rabutin, *Commentaires des Guerres en la Gaule Belgique (1551–1559),* ed. Ch. Gailly de Taurines, 2 vols. (Paris: H. Champion, 1932–44), 1:63–183, 2:72; Sebastian Schertlin von Burtenbach, *Leben und Thaten des weiland wohledlen und gestrengen Herrn Sebastian Schertlin von Burtenbach, durch ihn selbst deutsch beschrieben,* ed. Ottmar F. H. Schönhuth (Münster: [s.n.], 1858), 3–4; Fery de Guyon, *Mémoires de Fery de Guyon,* ed. A.-P.-L. de Robaulx de Soumoy (Bruxelles: Société de l'Histoire de Belgique, 1858), 7–9, 40, 90–91; Jacques de Mailles, *La très joyeuse, plaisante et récréative histoire du gentil Seigneur de Bayart composée par le Loyal Serviteur,* ed. M. J. Roman (Paris: Librairie Renouard, 1878), 250; Bernal Díaz del Castillo, *Historia Verdadera de la Conquista de la Nueva España,* ed. Joaquín Ramírez Cabañas, 10th ed. (Mexico: Editorial Porrúa, 1974), 103, 338, 463, 474; Jean de Haynin, *Mémoires de Jean, Sire de Haynin et de Louvignies, 1465–1477,* ed. D. D. Brouwers, 2 vols. (Liège: Soc. de bibliophiles Liégeois, 1904–5), 1:89; Ludwig von Diesbach, *Die autobiographischen Aufzeichnungen Ludwig von Diesbachs,* ed. Urs Martin Zahnd (Bern: Stämpfli, 1986), 39–41; Berlichingen, *Autobiography,* 87–90; Jean de Mergey, *Mémoires militaires du Sieur de Mergey,* in Joseph François Michaud and Jean Joseph Poujoulat, eds., *Nouvelle collection des mémoires pour servir à l'histoire de France, depuis le XIIIe siècle jusqu'à la fin du XVIIIe,* 3 series, 32 vols. (Paris: [s.n.], 1836–39), series 1, vol. 9 (1836), 564, 571.

Gutierre Díaz de Gamez, a fourteenth-century Castilian squire, summarizes the difficulties soldiers had to endure on campaign and in combat, saying that

> Knights who are at the wars eat their bread in sorrow; their ease is weariness and sweat; they have one good day after many bad; they are vowed to all manner of labor; they are forever swallowing their fear; they expose themselves to every peril; they give up their bodies to the adventure of life in death. Moldy bread or biscuit, meat cooked or uncooked; today enough to eat and tomorrow nothing, little or no wine, water from a pond or a butt, bad quarters, the shelter of a tent or branches, a bad bed, poor sleep with their armor still on their backs, burdened with iron, the enemy an arrow-shot off. . . . With the first drowsiness, an alarm; at dawn, the trumpet. . . . Such is their calling; a life of great fatigues, bereft of all ease. But there is no equal to the ill of those who make war upon the seas; in a whole day should I not end my telling of their miseries and their labors.[60]

However, Díaz de Gamez is not disillusioned with war. He cites this list of difficulties merely as proof of the great honor that kings and people in general should give knights, who expose themselves to such hardships in order to pursue honor and protect society.

Renaissance soldiers had to bear these miseries for long periods at a stretch, far longer than in the twentieth century. Though battles were normally one-day affairs, campaigns and sieges stretched for months. Unlike in twentieth-century conflicts, in which soldiers were rotated between frontline and rear areas and seldom spent more than several weeks in the thick of the fighting (three weeks in World War I and up to eleven weeks in Vietnam),[61] units in the Renaissance were seldom rotated in such a way, and individual soldiers were rarely if ever given leave.[62]

For instance, Bernal Díaz del Castillo left Cuba with Cortés in November 1518, and was involved in almost continuous military opera-

60. Gutierre Díaz de Gámez, *El Victorial o Crónica de Don Pero Niño,* in Juan de Mata Carriazo, ed., *Colección de crónicas españolas,* vol. 1 (Madrid: Espasa-Calpe, 1940), 42–43. For a variety of other difficulties memoirists complained about, see Francisco Balbi de Correggio, *La Verdadera Relación de todo lo que el anno de M.D.LXV. ha succedido en la isla de Malta, de antes que llegasse l'armada sobre ella de Soliman gran Turco . . . Recogida por F. Balbi de Correggio* (Barcelona: P. Reigner, 1568), 120; Monluc, *Commentaires,* 1:118, 2:351; Haynin, *Mémoires,* 1:63; Guyon, *Mémoires,* 63; Díaz del Castillo, *Historia Verdadera,* 10, 28, 317–18; Florange, *Mémoires,* 2:136; Rabutin, *Commentaires,* 1:164; Alonso Enríquez de Guzmán, *Libro de la Vida y Costumbres de Don Alonso Enríquez de Guzmán,* ed. Hayward Keniston (Madrid: Ediciones Atlas, 1960), 148; Martin du Bellay and Guillaume du Bellay, *Mémoires (1513–47),* ed. V.-L. Bourrilly and F. Vindry, 4 vols. (Paris: Soc. de l'histoire de France, 1908–19), 3:299. See also Diesbach, *Die autobiographischen Aufzeichnungen,* 39.

61. Prior and Wilson, "Paul Fussell," 67; Stephen, *The Price of Pity,* 117; Bourke, *Intimate History of Killing,* 360.

62. Parker, *Army of Flanders,* 199.

tions until the fall of Tenochtitlán in August 1521. During all that time, writes Díaz del Castillo, many of his comrades were killed and wounded. They had to undergo many hardships and suffering, for conquest, observes Díaz del Castillo, is not like "going to a wedding."[63] He notes that throughout all that time the conquistadors "slept shod and armed and with all our weapons ready."[64] The siege of Tenochtitlán itself lasted ninety-three days of ceaseless hard fighting. When the battle ended at last, writes Díaz del Castillo,

> all we soldiers became as deaf as if all the bells in a belfry had been ringing and had then suddenly stopped. . . . because during the whole ninety-three days of our siege of the capital, Mexican captains were yelling and shouting night and day. . . . Then there was the unceasing sound of their accursed drums and trumpets, and their melancholy kettledrums in the shrines and on their temple towers. Both day and night the din was so great that we could hardly hear one another speak.[65]

Francisco Balbi de Correggio notes that during the five-month-long siege of Malta (1565), in whose garrison he served, the outnumbered defenders had to endure daily bombardments and raids, and daily witnessed "innumerable and horrible deaths."[66] They never had any respite, because "We were now so close to the enemy at every point, that we could have shaken hands with them."[67]

According to the Spaniard Bernardino de Mendoza, during the ten-month-long siege of Haarlem (1572–73), there were military encounters almost every day.[68] The English mercenary Roger Williams recounts that the Spanish soldiers in the siege trenches suffered so much from the cold, hunger, diseases, and the other strains of war, that when Haarlem fell and their commander, the Duke of Alva, decided to go besiege Alkmaar, the soldiers rebelled, "fearing to bee troubled with a more miserable lodging then they had before Harlem . . . . To say troth . . . they had reason to fear Alkmaar, considering . . . their misery endured before Harlem aboue ten monthes."[69]

63. Díaz del Castillo, *Historia Verdadera*, 115.

64. Ibid., 210.

65. Ibid., 369.

66. Balbi de Correggio, *Verdadera Relación*, 94.

67. Ibid., 103.

68. Bernardino de Mendoza, *Comentarios de lo sucedido en las Guerras de los Paises-Bajos desde el año de 1567 hasta el de 1577*, ed. Cayetano Rosell (Madrid: [s.n.], 1853), 479. For the events of this siege, see ibid., 479–93.

69. Roger Williams, *The Actions of the Lowe Countries written by Sir Roger Williams, knight*, in John X. Evans, ed., *The Works of Sir Roger Williams* (Oxford: Clarendon Press, 1972), 131. See also Mendoza, *Comentarios*, book X, chapter 4; Parker, *Army of Flanders*, 198–99.

Memoirists were also well familiar with the atrocities soldiers commit in war, towards both civilians and captive enemy soldiers.[70] Ludwig von Eyb describes in a rather amused way how during the Burgundian invasion of Lorraine Charles the Bold executed many Lorrainers, hanging them on trees and forbidding their bodies to be taken down. Eyb remembers how his friend Wilvot von Schaumburg pitched his tent under a tree on which hung thirty-seven corpses. Some of these corpses were hung so low, that when one wanted to go in or out of the tent, one had to bend down in order not to bang one's head against the dangling feet. Even when a branch on which seven corpses were hanging broke, the soldiers dared not remove the corpses for fear of Duke Charles's wrath.[71]

Alonso Enríquez de Guzmán narrates how after the battle of Las Salinas (1538) he was captured by five enemy harquebusiers, who tortured him in order to extract money from him. They even staged a mock execution, twice firing a blank harquebus at him.[72] Spanish soldiers in Mexico witnessed their captured comrades being sacrificed and eaten,[73] whereas they themselves treated their Indian captives equally badly, even using the fat taken from Indian corpses to dress their wounds.[74]

The killing and maltreating of civilians was so ubiquitous, that most memoirists take it for granted, and report it without any further comment. For instance, Jörg von Ehingen, on his way back from Ceuta, describes the storming of several Muslim towns in Granada, and remarks that "the rank and file had orders also to kill the women and children, which was done."[75]

Even the horrors of twentieth-century *Materialschlacht*—the mass slaughter of soldiers by an overwhelming technological force, wielded by far-off and invisible enemies—were not completely alien to Renaissance memoirists. The mechanical artillery of the Middle Ages could have a devastating psychological effect on soldiers not used to mechanized death. Jean de Joinville writes with terror about the Muslim mechanical artillery at Mansura (1250), which shot stones and pots full of Greek fire. He writes that the Greek fire made a noise "like that of a thunderbolt

70. For atrocities, see Hale, *War and Society,* 184–88, 195–96; Keen, *Chivalry,* 228; Vale, *War and Chivalry,* 160; Nicholas Wright, *Knights and Peasants: The Hundred Years War in the French Countryside* (Woodbridge: Boydell, 1998).

71. Ludwig von Eyb, *Die Geschichten und Taten Wilwolts von Schaumburg,* ed. A. von Keller (Stuttgart: Litterarischer Verein, 1859), 29.

72. Enríquez de Guzmán, *Libro de la Vida,* 178.

73. Díaz del Castillo, *Historia Verdadera,* 352–53, 372.

74. Ibid., 109–10.

75. Ehingen, *Reisen,* 65–66. See also Antoine du Puget, *Mémoires inédits d'Antoine du Puget, Sieur de Saint-Marc, concernant les troubles de religion dans le Midi de la France, depuis l'année 1561 jusqu'à 1597,* in Michaud and Poujoulat, *Nouvelle collection des mémoires,* series 1, vol. 6 (1836), 713.

falling from the skies; it seemed like a dragon flying through the air. The light this huge, flaming mass shed all around it was so bright that you could see right through the camp as clearly as if it were day." Whenever the Muslims shot Greek fire the Crusaders threw themselves on the ground and prayed to God to save them. Joinville writes that when he and his knights were assigned to guard the Duke of Anjou's siege-tower, which was the main target of the Muslim artillery, "we all felt very sick at heart." However, before their shift began the Muslims managed to burn the tower. The Duke of Anjou was beside himself with grief, but Joinville and his men, good Crusaders though they were, "praised God, because if we were to be on guard that night, we should all have been burnt alive."[76]

The effect of cannon was even more fearsome. Though the destructive power of fifteenth- and sixteenth-century cannon was infinitely smaller than in the twentieth century, their psychological and physical effect could be just as devastating. Precisely because artillery was less effective, soldiers were still placed on the battlefield in packed formations, and cannonballs often mowed down whole ranks, causing much slaughter and appalling disfigurement.[77] Renaissance memoirists not infrequently narrate how cannonballs smashed limbs, heads, and entire bodies.[78] Balbi de Correggio describes the Turkish bombardment at Malta, saying that "When all of these batteries began to fire, and all at the same time, the noise and concussion was such that it seemed as if the end of the world was coming."[79]

The effect of the heavy harquebus balls, which were far more massive than twentieth-century bullets, was hardly less atrocious. For instance, Monluc describes the injury that disfigured him and ended his military career, saying that at the storming of Rabastens (1570),

> as I was returning to the rear to command that they bring forward two ladders, an harquebus ball, shot from the corner of a barricade that was adjacent to the tower, hit me in the face . . . All of a sudden I was all blood. I was pouring blood from the mouth, from the nose and from the eyes. . . . I was hardly able to speak, because of the great amount of blood that I was pouring from the mouth and from the nose.[80]

76. Jean de Joinville, *Vie de Saint Louis,* ed. Jacques Monfrin (Paris: Dunod, 1995), section 210. See also ibid., section 213.

77. Vale, *War and Chivalry,* 136–37; Parker, *Army of Flanders,* 168; Oman, *History,* 138–40, 159, 182.

78. Alonso de Contreras, *Vida del Capitan Alonso de Contreras,* in José M. de Cossio, ed., *Biblioteca de Autores Españoles. Autobiografías de Soldados (siglo XVII)* (Madrid: Ediciones Atlas, 1956), 83; Haynin, *Mémoires,* 1:67–68; Florange, *Mémoires,* 1:122–23; Berlichingen, *Autobiography,* 24–26.

79. Balbi de Correggio, *Verdadera Relación,* 78. See also, ibid., 80.

80. Monluc, *Commentaires,* 3:344–45.

Monluc was lucky to survive such an injury. Given the state of sixteenth-century medicine, even minor bullet wounds were usually a death sentence.[81]

Even if all this still seems to be dwarfed by the effects of twentieth-century firepower, we should not forget that hand-to-hand combat with cold steel had its own peculiar horrors, which could be as bad as those of a heavy bombardment. Having to face the hot fury of a berserk warrior at close quarters is not necessarily better than facing the ignorant destruction rained by shells and bombs. For those who imagine war as a heroic contest between brave warriors, the latter option seems worse, because it denies soldiers both glory and the ability to determine their fates through their martial skills. Yet for the majority of soldiers, who are made of softer material, it is not obvious which is the worst option.

Take, for instance, the battle of Novara (1513), which was decided by a clash to the death between a Swiss and a *landsknecht* pike phalanx, each consisting of more than five thousand men. Florange, who commanded the landsknecht phalanx, notes that from the three to four hundred men in the landsknechts' first rank, only six survived the clash, and of all the captains, only two. The losses in the other ranks were hardly less atrocious, and the losses of the Swiss were equally bad. In a few minutes Florange probably saw more of his comrades killed than most American soldiers in Vietnam saw throughout their entire military service. In those minutes Florange must have witnessed many a gory scene: men with heads split open, men with limbs cut off, disemboweled men, men crushed into pulp, men torn asunder by harquebus- and cannon-balls, maddened men trapped with no way to flee. He himself was lucky to get away with only forty-six wounds. Whereas the twenty thousand British dead and forty thousand British wounded on the first day of the Battle of the Somme (1916) were spread over more than twenty kilometers, the dead at Novara were packed into a few hundred square meters. Bodies of friend and foe alike lay in heaps, and streams of blood were not a literary convention. When Florange says he was found "amongst the dead," he is not speaking metaphorically. He must have been covered with bodies.[82]

Moreover, in twentieth-century warfare fighting and killing is a comparatively abstract affair, often done from a distance of kilometers, very rarely from a distance of less than several dozen meters. At Novara, one could touch one's foes, and killing somebody meant plunging your pike or halberd into his stomach or head and watching him screaming in the pain and agony of death.

Taking all this litany of difficulties and miseries into consideration, it is not surprising that late-medieval and Renaissance armies were

81. Parker, *Army of Flanders,* 168; Hale, *War and Society,* 120–22.
82. Florange, *Mémoires,* 1:126–28; Du Bellay, *Mémoires,* 1:27–28.

plagued by desertion and mutiny on a scale unheard of in the twentieth century.[83] Most memoirists recount incidents of desertion and mutiny, and many of the memoirists themselves deserted or mutinied at one point or another of their careers.[84] Nevertheless, even this did not prompt them to condemn war and expose its "true face." Indeed, like many others of their contemporaries, even when they deserted or mutinied they did not part ways with war, for they soon rejoined another army, or even the very same army they had left earlier.[85]

If the face of Renaissance wars was as terrible as that of twentieth-century wars, and if the memoirists saw that face clearly, how can we explain that they were not disillusioned by it and did not expose war's "true face"? It may be argued that the cultural authority of the romantic view of war was so strong in the Renaissance, that veterans did not dare to challenge it, or did not have the literary models to do so.

However, as noted earlier, in Renaissance literary and Humanistic circles, the accuracy of the romantic image of war was often challenged, and the controversy about it was probably the most heated literary debate of the day. Moreover, most military memoirs do not follow the conventions of chivalric romances. Far from it. They depict war in a very different way than the romances do, implicitly contradicting the romances on many points.[86] The only curious thing is that though the memoirists certainly were not bewitched by the romantic image, only a handful challenge it directly, and in general they show no interest in destroying it.[87]

Neither could it be argued that Renaissance memoirists were intimidated by external or internal censorship from exposing war's true face. Many of their writings were private texts written for family members and friends, which did not pass any external censorship. As for inner censorship, Renaissance memoirists did not have any enduring military entitles such as standing armies and regiments to which they were

---

83. Parker, *Army of Flanders,* 210–18, 290–92; Hale, *War and Society,* 171; Tallett, *War and Society in Early Modern Europe,* 116–17; Jeremy Black, *European Warfare, 1494–1660* (London: Routledge, 2002), 18–19, 28; Jan Glete, *War and the State in Early Modern Europe* (London: Routledge, 2002), 132.

84. See, for example, Haynin, *Mémoires,* 1:257–59; Williams, *Actions of the Lowe Countries,* 131–32, 148–49; Pierre de Bourdeille, abbot of Brantôme, *Oeuvres complètes de Pierre de Bourdeille, seigneur de Brantôme,* ed. Ludovic Lalanne, 10 vols. (Paris: Soc. de l'histoire de France, 1864–82), 7:145–49; Du Bellay, *Mémoires,* 4:245; Monluc, *Commentaires,* 1:30; Florange, *Mémoires,* 1:104–5.

85. Parker, *Army of Flanders,* 212–18.

86. For a full discussion of this point, see Harari, *Renaissance Military Memoirs,* 94–98.

87. Ibid., 98, 103.

beholden by ties of loyalty,[88] and they were remarkably free from nationalist attachments. As noted earlier, many Renaissance memoirists deserted the army in the midst of war, changed sides in the middle of a campaign, and even rebelled and fought against their nominal sovereigns—something Owen and Remarque never did.[89]

Another possibility is that like German World War I memoirists, Renaissance memoirists found that the value of martial comradeship redeemed war's horrors.[90] Bueil's praise of comradeship certainly supports this argument. However, though comradeship was of greater importance in Renaissance than in twentieth-century wars (because in the Renaissance formally organized *cameradas* took care of many essential functions that in the twentieth century were taken care of by the army itself),[91] apart from Bueil hardly any Renaissance memoirist ever mentions either his comrades or the abstract ideal of comradeship.[92]

The answer lies elsewhere. First, the differences between wartime and peacetime were less pronounced, and in particular, living conditions during peacetime were harsher in the Renaissance era than in the twentieth-century West, which caused the harsh conditions of war to seem more natural. Death, cruelty, and privation were quite familiar to civilians at home. Seeing people die, suffering from hunger and cold, witnessing extreme cruelty, or being subjected to it was the common fare of most Renaissance civilians from an early age. Whereas in 1916 a realistic report of life in the trenches would have shocked most British civilians, Gruffydd's reports of the miseries his comrades experienced in France would have sounded quite familiar to many of his countrymen.[93] However, the importance of this factor should not be stressed too much, especially since, as Leed points out, in the twentieth century the disillu-

―――――――――

88. Ibid., 53.

89. Many memoirists served in foreign armies, such as Roger Williams, Pierre de Bourdeille de Brantôme, and Ehingen, whereas Bueil, Berlichingen, Commynes, Enríquez de Guzmán, Pedro García de Paredes, Fery de Guyon, Florange, Jacques Pape de Saint-Auban, and Sebastian Schertlin all fought against their prince at one time or the other, either in the service of some foreign prince or in rebellion. See also Harari, *Renaissance Military Memoirs,* 53–56.

90. For comradeship in World War I memoirs, see in particular Linder, *Princes,* 73–81; Leed, *No Man's Land,* 24; Mosse, *Fallen Soldiers,* 167.

91. Parker, *Army of Flanders,* 177; Harari, *Renaissance Military Memoirs,* 139–40. It was very common in Renaissance armies for small groups of soldiers to organize themselves in *cameradas,* sharing their resources and looking after one another. Soldiers often relied on their *cameradas* for the provision of lodging and food and for care while sick or injured.

92. See Harari, *Renaissance Military Memoirs,* 139–41.

93. See also Hale, *War and Society,* 80–84.

sionment with war was partly caused by its being too similar to the peacetime reality of industrialized society.[94]

Secondly, Renaissance soldiers had choices that their twentieth-century counterparts were usually denied. As Gruffydd says, those who "would rather go home to their mothers and fathers . . . to plough and thresh . . . and live niggardly" instead of pursuing the honorable career of soldiers, were usually able to do so. Though conscription became more common towards the end of the sixteenth century, desertion was relatively easy, and thus people tended to stay in the ranks only if military life appealed to them, or at least did not appall them too much.

Yet this alone cannot explain the difference between Renaissance and twentieth-century attitudes. We should not forget that on the one hand, the professional soldiers of the Renaissance did not exalt the romantic image of war—they simply did not make any effort to unmask it. And on the other hand, as we saw above, in World War I it was precisely the elitist volunteers rather than the conscripted working-class men who first wrote narratives of disillusionment.

The most important reason why Renaissance memoirists were not disillusioned with war is that they had a fundamentally different identity and mental outlook than their twentieth-century descendants. As Linder argues regarding German memoirs, and as Leed, Hynes, and Evelyn Cobley emphasize regarding all twentieth-century memoirs, even when twentieth-century soldiers claim to be completely disillusioned with their prewar ideals, they still believe in the traditional Enlightenment ideals of self and of *Bildung*,[95] and use these ideals to construct their identity and understand the war and their lives.[96]

They grew up on the ideal that life is a process through which the experiences one undergoes build and develop one's "self." They consequently entered war not just with rather shallow fantasies of honor and glory, but also with a much deeper expectation that war would provide them with extreme and extraordinary experiences, which would build and develop their selves to a far greater degree than could be accomplished through "ordinary" peacetime experiences.

Accordingly, the main threat war posed to the soldiers' worldview and identity was not the threat to their superficial commitment to honor and glory, but rather—as Leed rightly points out—the threat to their understanding of life as the continuous process of developing and

94. Leed, *No Man's Land,* 48–49, 68–69, 90–96.
95. The ideal of *Bildung* sees the ideal life as a process of experimental learning, through which a person comes to know the world, and develops his or her various abilities to their full potential.
96. Leed, *No Man's Land,* 17; Linder, *Princes,* 45–55, 91, 98–99, 101, 119–20; Cobley, *Representing War,* 5, 26, 69, 75–76, 96–99, 118–31. See also Herzog, *Vietnam,* 14, 60; Fussell, *Great War,* 114–15.

improving an enduring entity called "self." The problem with war, says Leed, was that it was so discontinuous with the soldiers' lives before and after the war, that it made it hard to view life as a process through which a "self" endures and develops.[97] The main task of twentieth-century memoirists has been precisely to overcome this threat, and weave the story of their lives together again.

Thus Linder argues that for World War I German writers, "the idea of random discontinuous experience was intolerable";[98] Miriam Cooke maintains that "[w]ar is messy but . . . [m]en have generally turned their messy war experiences into coherent stories";[99] and Bourke writes that most veterans "refused to narrate their war-stories in self-destructive ways," and it "was precisely this ability to assert their own individuality and sense of personal responsibility even within the disorder of combat that gave meaning to the warring enterprise and to their lives."[100] Leed interestingly draws attention to the fact that Erik Erikson's theory of ego-identity was formulated during World War II in observation of "combat fatigue" cases. Erikson defined those suffering from "combat fatigue" as people whose "lives no longer hung together and never would again. There was a central disturbance of what I then started to call ego-identity. . . . This sense of identity produces the ability to experience oneself as something that has continuity and sameness."[101]

For soldiers who entered war expecting life to be the continuous development of a self, and who then strove to somehow integrate the war into such a life, the idea of "disillusionment" provided the key. By utilizing this key even the worst horrors of war could be transformed into a *Bildungsroman*: "I entered war as a shallow, naïve and partly-formed youth, and was ignorant about my true self and about the true nature of the world. In war I underwent extreme experiences that revealed to me who I really am and what the world is really like, and I consequently returned from war with new insights, a new depth of character, and a new wisdom."[102] Seen in such terms, war is not the death of the Enlightenment view of self, but its epitome, as attested by a British paratrooper in the Falklands War (1982) who shouted to Robert Fox in the midst of battle: "I've just learnt more about myself in the last ten minutes than I knew in my whole life before."[103]

97. Leed, *No Man's Land*, 2–4. See also Hynes, *Soldiers' Tale*, 8.

98. Linder, *Princes of the Trenches*, 99.

99. Miriam Cooke, *Women and the War Story* (Berkeley: University of California Press, 1996), 16.

100. Bourke, *Intimate History of Killing*, 369.

101. Quoted in Leed, *No Man's Land*, 3–4.

102. See, for example, Cobley, *Representing War*, 26, 75–76, 118–31; Hynes, *Soldiers' Tale*, 5; Linder, *Princes of the Trenches*, 101, 105–7, 119–20.

103. Robert Fox, *Eyewitness Falklands: A Personal Account of the Falklands Campaign* (London: Methuen, 1982), 180–81.

Hence, since the deepest ideal of the Enlightenment is "know and develop thyself," martial disillusionment transpires to be not the foundering of prewar cultural expectations, but their fulfillment. Soldiers expected war to present them with special experiences which would change them and provide them with deep insights about themselves and the world—and war obliged them. The only unexpected thing was that the big insight war gave them was the insight of disillusionment. But even this was not completely unexpected. After all, very often in *Bildungsroman* the insights one gains through *Bildung* expose public opinion and one's own received knowledge as illusions. "Disillusionment" is really a not uncommon type of enlightenment.

The fact that the twentieth-century martial experience of disillusionment is the product of prewar cultural expectations more than of any new military realities is confirmed by several factors. First, in World War I the experience of disillusionment was largely a middle-class experience, and working-class memoirists shared it to a far lesser extent, reflecting the way in which at the time, the ideals of selfhood and *Bildung* were adopted by the middle-class to a far greater extent than by the working-class.

Secondly, and even more importantly, already in the nineteenth century, soldiers and civilians who were tuned up to the right mental and cultural trends were able to produce narratives of martial disillusionment even without exposure to the technological and military realities of the following century. In 1897 Léonce Patry published a "disillusionment" narrative about the Franco-Prussian War (1870–71), titled *Guerre telle qu'elle est.*[104] Gerald F. Linderman shows that many memoirs of disillusionment were written by participants in the American Civil War (1861–65).[105] As I intend to show in a forthcoming research project, disillusionment themes also appear in many memoirs of the Crimean (1853–56) and Napoleonic Wars (1800–1815), particularly memoirs of people influenced by the Romantic movement. On the literary front, Stendhal's *Charterhouse of Parma*, Tolstoy's *Sebastopol in August, 1855* and *War and Peace*, Stephen Crane's *Red Badge of Courage*, and several short stories by Ambrose Bierce, all narrate the familiar story of how a young man full of romantic martial dreams is disillusioned by the cruel realities of war.[106]

---

104. Léonce Patry, *The Reality of War: A Memoir of the Franco-Prussian War and the Paris Commune (1870–1) by a French Officer* (London: Cassell and Co., 2001).

105. Gerald F. Linderman, *Embattled Courage: The Experience of Combat in the American Civil War* (London: Collier Macmillan, 1987), 17–20, 240–61.

106. Stendhal, *La Chartreuse de Parme* (Paris: A. Dupont, 1839); Leo Tolstoy, *The Novels and Other Works of Lyof N. Tolstoi*, 24 vols. (New York: Charles Scribner's Sons, 1917), 11: 269–340; Leo Tolstoy, *War and Peace* (Harmondsworth, Middlesex: Penguin Books, 1968); Stephen Crane, *The Red Badge of Courage: An Episode of the*

Thirdly, it is notable that in recent decades, disillusionment narratives have been written not only about apocalyptic wars such as the two world wars, but also about short, victorious, and relatively bloodless campaigns such as the Six Day War (1967) or the Falklands War, as well as about low-intensity conflicts such as the Intifada, which are fought mainly with weapons less lethal even than those of Renaissance wars.

If "disillusionment" is therefore a product of prewar expectations that life in general and war in particular be a process of *Bildung*, it becomes clear why Renaissance military memoirists were not disillusioned with war: They entered war with very different cultural baggage and a very different set of expectations. Though the ideals of both self and *Bildung* were already current in the Renaissance, at least in embryonic form, and were utilized, for example, by writers of religious autobiographies, Renaissance military memoirists rejected them. Almost all of them came from the ranks of the military aristocracy, and they still adhered to the medieval aristocratic worldview, according to which identity was based not on one's developing personality or inner world, but rather on one's honor, which was based partly on being born to the right family, and partly on performing honorable deeds. In their eyes, one could have had a deep and complex inner world, yet if one was from common stock and performed no honorable deeds, one had no honor and therefore one was a nobody with neither an identity nor even a name.[107]

Hence, whereas for twentieth-century soldier-authors such as Owen or Remarque, "life" was the continuous experiential process of developing an inner self, and honor was merely a superficial attribute that a self may or may not acquire during its development, for the Renaissance memoirists inner developments and changes of personality were inconsequential, and life was the discontinuous accumulation (or dissipation) of honor, consisting of the performance of free-floating honorable (or dishonorable) deeds in the outside world. Renaissance memoirists certainly had inner experiences—including experiences of disillusionment—and they probably underwent various inner changes, but these had no place in their preprogrammed idea of "life," and were therefore left out of most memoirs. Only external deeds were thought to be part of life, and they accordingly constitute the bulk of these narratives. (Just as some Vietnam memoirists certainly performed "honorable deeds of arms," yet they could not conceive of life as a mere accumulation of such deeds.)[108]

American Civil War (New York: D. Appleton, 1895); Ambrose Bierce, Shadows of Blue and Gray: The Civil War Writings of Ambrose Bierce, ed. Brian M. Thomsen (New York: Forge, 2002).

107. Harari, *Renaissance Military Memoirs,* 133–48, 152–55; Vale, *War and Chivalry,* 15–31, 166–67, 174.

108. Harari, *Renaissance Military Memoirs,* 146–48, 152–55.

This meant that Renaissance memoirists could not see war as an interruption of their life and as a threat to their ego-identity. Since their identity was based not on an enduring temporal process but on the accumulation of free-floating deeds, it could not possibly be interrupted or disrupted even by the most horrible war. On the contrary, since war was the main occasion when honorable deeds could be performed, war was essential for building their identity, and their main expectation of war was to provide them with honorable deeds, not with deep experiences of mental change.

Just as war complied with the prewar expectation of twentieth-century memoirists, so it also complied with those of Renaissance memoirists. Just as it provided the former with deep insights and inner changes, so it provided the latter with a stock of honorable deeds. Hence, in both cases postwar narratives merely reflect and confirm prewar cultural expectations.

As Leed indicates, when war really contradicts soldiers' prewar expectations, including their deepest expectations of what life should be like, such soldiers completely break down, for they are no longer able to understand what war is and who they are. Such soldiers do not write books. The soldiers who have written books, both in the Renaissance and in the twentieth century, are those who managed to avoid that fate, and their narratives were at least in part an instrument of self-preservation: These narratives were the means by which the dreadful events of war were recast into an acceptable story of a "normal" life. The huge differences between twentieth-century and Renaissance narratives stem only from the fact that Renaissance and twentieth-century soldiers had different pre-programmed ideas of what "life" should be.

We can therefore conclude that there was indeed a revolution in the image of war and of soldiers sometime between 1916 and 1969, but this was largely the result of an earlier mental and cultural revolution in the image of "life," rather than the result of a purely technological or military revolution in the realities of "war." This implies that the twentieth-century revolution in the image of war uncovered neither the eternal nor the changing face of war. Rather, it uncovered the changing expectations of people in general and soldiers in particular from life.

Hence, Fussell's thesis should be turned on its head. It was not that the horror of World War I caused the widespread cultural disillusionment that characterizes the twentieth-century West. Rather, the culture of disillusionment that was emerging already in the nineteenth century caused World War I and subsequent wars to be interpreted as "disillusioning."

This is pretty bad news. From an ethical and political perspective, I am convinced that Owen and Remarque interpreted war in a far better way than Gascoigne or Florange or most other previous war authors. Yet it would be wishful thinking to see their interpretation as a universal truth, and to expect that anyone who becomes familiar with war and who does not delude himself must eventually embrace that truth. As the case of Renaissance military memoirists clearly indicates, there can be warriors and warrior castes that are intimately familiar with war and all its horrors, yet see it as an acceptable and even a desirable vocation. It all depends on people's worldview—not on war's "true face."

Ben Hebard Fuller and the Genesis of a Modern United States Marine Corps, 1891–1934

☆

Merrill L. Bartlett

Abstract

Historians of the smaller of the United States naval services have tended to dismiss or denigrate the career of the fifteenth Commandant of the Marine Corps, usually describing him as an avuncular and uninspiring sinecure holder. An examination of Fuller's tenure at the helm of the Corps at the time of the retrenchment imposed during the Herbert C. Hoover administration and the stimulus for naval growth that followed under the Franklin D. Roosevelt administration reveals an officer far more adroit than usually depicted.

BY the early 1880s, the smaller of America's naval services appeared destined for extinction or absorption into either the Army or the Navy. Increasingly, budgetary watchdogs in Congress and critics within the Department of the Navy questioned the requirement for a separate naval constabulary that appeared more and more an anachronistic vestige of the Age of Sail. While friends of the U.S. Marine Corps (USMC) on Capitol Hill managed to stifle attempts to emasculate the sometimes spirited and colorful force, post–Civil War retrenchment appeared to demand either Herculean reforms or a suitable funeral. Enlisted ranks

Merrill L. Bartlett served as a Marine Corps officer for more than twenty years. He earned his undergraduate degree from Washington State University, and completed graduate studies at San Diego State University and the University of Maryland, College Park. His published works (editor, co-editor, author, and co-author) include seven books on naval history as well as more than one hundred essays and book reviews. While teaching at the U.S. Naval Academy, Bartlett earned the William P. Clements Award as the outstanding military educator, 1979–80. At his retirement in 1983, the Academy honored him by establishing the "Merrill Bartlett Prize in History."

reflecting a scandalous desertion rate, and an officer corps plagued by infighting and career aggrandizement, exacerbated the problem.[1]

In 1880, nearly one-fourth of enlisted Marines were carried on the rolls as deserters, while the officer corps consisted of too many undistinguished sinecure holders. Pungent editorials in contemporary newspapers or in the semiofficial *Army-Navy Journal* appeared increasingly to criticize the Marine Corps through sarcastic commentary. One journalist opined that "The Marine Corps is the oldest, the smallest, and the best uniformed and equipped and most artistically drilled branch of the fighting wing of the government," and another suggested that "the ladies of the Marine Corps represent the feminine counterpart of the officers of wit, culture, social grace, and generous hospitality." Directing criticism at the officers themselves, a member of the Fourth Estate remarked that "a Marine officer parts his hair in the middle and carries a sword; he carves out his career with his pedigree." Another critic suggested that the junior officers reflected an axiom that "USMC meant 'useless sons made comfortable.'"[2]

The Colonel Commandant of the Marine Corps during these troubling times turned to an improvement in the quality of his junior officers to correct serious shortcomings within the Marine Corps. For decades, successive Commandants and various Secretaries of the Navy had expressed dismay over the quality of the second lieutenants. Most new officers earned their commissions through political patronage, served briefly and without distinction, and then went on to whatever outlets their influential parents might provide. Few remained to serve for a full-service career or performed satisfactorily. At other times, Congress or the Secretary of the Navy declined to authorize the commissioning of any new officers to replace shortages on the lineal list.

But in 1882, Capitol Hill passed legislation to correct the overages in the Navy's burgeoning list by curtailing sharply the number of new officers commissioned from among the graduates of the Naval Academy in Annapolis, Maryland. A caveat to the unpopular bill, however, allowed the Marine Corps to fill its shortages with the surplus. Thus, between 1883, when the excess stood at its worst, and 1896, when the demands

1. Jack Shulimson, *The Marine Corps' Search for a Mission, 1890–1898* (Lawrence: University Press of Kansas, 1998), passim.

2. *Army-Navy Journal,* 29 January 1889 and 25 December 1886; *New York Times,* 19 December 1889. For a compelling argument that the problems of the Marine Corps stemmed from a lackluster performance in the Civil War, see Jeffrey T. Ryan, "On Land and Sea: The United States Marine Corps in the Civil War" (Ph.D. diss., Temple University, 1997).

of a rapidly expanding Navy demanded that every graduate serve in the ships of the fleet, all of the Marine Corps second lieutenants came from Annapolis. Ben Hebard Fuller entered the Marine Corps in this way.[3]

A glance at Fuller's seemingly lackluster career for the next three decades suggested that this son of a Michigan circuit-court judge was destined to become merely another sinecure holder blocking the rungs of the promotion ladder to more aggressive officers. At the time of his appointment as commandant in 1930, no less an icon than John Archer Lejeune sniffed despairingly that "at least he [Fuller] is a lively fellow." While official naval circles expressed surprise at Fuller's appointment, losing aspirants sulked and fumed. The indefatigable and irrepressible Smedley D. Butler—winner of two Medals of Honor—claimed that a cabal of "shore-based" admirals had denied him the post he so richly deserved. Logan Feland, a highly decorated infantry commander of World War I, snarled to a powerful Republican supporter that "he had been cast aside for one of the most worthless men in the Corps."[4]

Like most graduates from the Naval Academy who entered the Marine Corps following matriculation, Fuller stood too low in his class to even consider a commission in the Navy. Graduating in 1889, he accepted an appointment in the Marine Corps two years later. He and the other six Marines from that class entered the School of Application at Marine Barracks, Washington. The course that began that year was the result of long-smoldering plans by the Colonel Commandant of the Marine Corps to improve the sorry performance of his junior officers. After a short year of studying and practical application, Fuller assumed the traditional duties of a junior officer. Assignments for almost the next

3. Merrill L. Bartlett, "Two Admirals for an Ensign," *U.S. Naval Institute Proceedings* 124 (February 1998): 55–59. A compilation of the total service of all Marine Corps officers commissioned between 1798 and 1898 may be found as an appendix to Richard Strader Collum, *History of the United States Marine Corps* (Philadelphia: Hammersly, 1903). This summary reveals just how few young officers chose to remain in uniform for a significant length of time.

4. Charles R. Train to Herbert Hoover, 21 July 1930, Candidates for Commandant file, container 36, Herbert Hoover Presidential Library, West Branch, Iowa; Logan Feland to James G. Harbord, 22 August 1930 and 19 September 1930, correspondence file (F), Harbord MSS, New York Historical Society, New York, N.Y.; Smedley D. Butler, "To Hell With the Admirals: Why I Retired at Fifty," *Liberty* 87 (5 December 1931): 14–16, 18, 22–25; and John A. Lejeune (hereafter JAL) to Harbord, 6 August 1930, correspondence file (L), Harbord MSS. See also, Merrill L. Bartlett, "The Inside Track to Commandant," *U.S. Naval Institute Proceedings* 121 (January 1995): 58–63; and Merrill L. Bartlett, "The Shore-Based Admirals Win: The Surprise Selection of Ben H. Fuller as Commandant of the Marine Corps, 1930," a paper presented at the Annual Meeting of the Society for Military History, Fredericksburg, Virginia, 11 April 1992.

decade alternated between guard duties at various barracks and with Leatherneck detachments in ships of the fleet.

Early 1899 found young Fuller, newly promoted to captain, posted to a battalion of infantry formed hastily from a culling of East Coast barracks. The Secretary of the Navy ordered the ad hoc force to deploy to Cavite, the old Spanish naval arsenal now occupied by the United States astride Subic Bay in the Philippines. The deployment in which Fuller participated heralded new and important duties for the smaller of America's naval services. Increasingly, battalions, regiments, and even brigades were formed either from available manpower at the various barracks or from a pooling of detachments from the fleet. For the next two decades, Fuller served in such traditional assignments satisfactorily if not superbly. He displayed none of the panache or élan characteristic of more well-known Marine Corps officers of his era, such as Littleton W. T. Waller or Smedley D. Butler.

While Fuller and his fellow Marines embraced these new-found expeditionary duties following the Spanish-American War in 1898, criticism within Navy circles grew increasingly shrill with regard to an apparent Marine Corps penchant for traditional duties. Luminaries in Navy Blue visualized a new and novel approach to a mission consistent with the advent of the "American Century." William F. Fullam, the top graduate of the Naval Academy Class of 1877, led the charge. Beginning in the 1880s, Fullam and his supporters—known pejoratively for a generation as "The Fullamites"—bombarded senior officials within the Department of the Navy, Congress, and the news media with a variety of material that intimated that the Marine Corps had outlived its usefulness as a source of shipboard police. At one point, Fullam suggested that the term "USMC had become synonymous for a vacuity of intellect," and outraged senior Marine Corps officers responded in kind with invective of their own.

The thrust of Fullam's quest for reforms escaped most hidebound Marines. Fullam and many other Navy officers desired a drastic reorganization of the Marine Corps's operating forces into ready battalions aboard troop transports, always available to fleet commanders. When the Marine Corps countered by pointing out that limited personnel precluded such a draconian change, the suggestion followed that utilization of Marine detachments afloat—removing them from the warships of the fleet—would provide the manpower necessary. Almost all Marine Corps officers of the era interpreted the changes sought by the Fullamites as a veiled attempt to emasculate the Marine Corps and force it either into extinction, or absorption by the Army or the Navy.[5]

5. Jack Shulimson and Graham A. Cosmas, "Teddy Roosevelt and the Corps' Seagoing Mission," *Marine Corps Gazette* 65 (November 1981): 54–61; and John G. Miller, "William Freeland Fullam's War With the Corps," *U.S. Naval Institute Pro-*

Senior Marine Corps officers and their supporters on Capitol Hill managed to deflect the criticism and even roll back a presidential dictum removing the Leathernecks from the fleet. Proponents of the Marine Corps's traditional duties aboard ship argued increasingly, and with fresh currency, that the shipboard detachments provided the necessary manpower for the government to react promptly and decisively as the United States embraced new-found responsibilities. In the two decades following the Spanish-American War, Marines became the tip of the colonialist spear as the United States flexed newly discovered muscles in East Asia and in the Caribbean. Increasingly, legal scholars convinced politicians that while dispatch of army troops ashore on foreign soil amounted to an act of war, the deployment of naval forces did not. Influential advisors in the form of jurists, cabinet members, and even a sitting Major General Commandant (MGC) of the Marine Corps advised Presidents and Congressmen that the projection of seapower ashore, in this instance Marines, amounted to nothing more than sending in the police or a fire brigade and thus did not constitute a violation of international law.[6]

Between 1898 and the beginning of America's embrace of colonialism, and the post–World War 1 era when Congress and the Oval Office began to lose their enthusiasm for altruism and overseas naval adventures, naval landing parties went ashore on foreign soil routinely in East Asia or the Caribbean. Usually, the dispatch of an armed party of bluejackets and Leathernecks came at the request of the U.S. ambassador and local officials to restore order and otherwise protect American lives and property. Such deployments consisted of nothing more than sailors and Marines from the ships of the fleet, and never evolved into a semi-permanent naval presence. Sometimes, such as in China, Panama, Cuba, Vera Cruz in Mexico, Haiti, and Santo Domingo, the dispatch of a small naval force ashore was followed quickly by additional Marines from barracks in the continental United States. On occasion these forays ashore grew to regimental or even brigade size, and the naval presence became semi-permanent. A generation of Marine Corps officers, typified by the frenetic and ambitious Smedley Butler, became convinced increasingly

---

ceedings 105 (November 1975): 38–45. For enlightening correspondence on the contentious issue of Marines serving on the ships of the fleet, see William F. Fullam to [Edward L.] Beach, 21 November 1908; and William S. Sims to Fullam, 31 October 1908, container 3, Fullam MSS, Manuscripts Division, Library of Congress (hereafter MD-LC), Washington, D.C.

6. Secretary of State Philander C. Knox to President William H. Taft, 29 August 1912, quoted in Richard D. Challener, *Admirals, Generals, and American Foreign Policy* (Princeton, N.J.: Princeton University Press, 1973), 25–26; Secretary of the Navy Curtis D. Wilbur to President Calvin Coolidge, 23 June 1924, reel 24, Coolidge MSS, MD-LC; and Commandant of the Marine Corps John A. Lejeune, U. S. Congress, Senate, Hearings Before the Senate Naval Affairs Committee, 69th Cong., 2nd sess., 10 June 1927.

that the small-wars environment embracing America's era of colonialism had become the *raison d'être* for the smaller of the naval services.

As the career of Ben Hebard Fuller plodded on, he served in such ventures as well as traditional Marine Corps duties. Returning from East Asia in 1901, Fuller served first on recruiting duty in Manhattan and then at the barracks in New York. Two years later, he returned to conventional duties at sea, but this time Fuller commanded the Marine Detachment on the battleship *New York*. Late in 1903, newly promoted to major, he served first at the barracks at Mare Island, California, and then in Honolulu. Recognizing his cerebral talents, the Colonel Commandant of the Marine Corps posted Fuller to Annapolis, where he commanded the School of Application. Following his promotion to lieutenant colonel in 1911, he assumed command of the barracks in Charleston, South Carolina.

Coincident with the mission of the Marine Corps to fulfill an expanding role as a naval constabulary in colonial infantry assignments ashore, the General Board of the Navy defined an additional new mission for the Corps. To operate any distance from the shores of the United States, the fleet required either an extensive supply train or advanced bases established to provide supplies, munitions, and repair facilities for the ships. Proponents pointed to the successful seizure of Guantánamo in support of operations in Cuban waters during the Spanish-American War. In 1901, the General Board ordered the organization of a fixed-defense regiment consisting of a thousand men to be trained at Annapolis and Newport, Rhode Island. For the next decade, ships of the fleet experimented with the landing of naval guns ashore to defend advanced bases, while naval planners formulated lists of equipment deemed necessary. Within Marine Corps circles, however, the dictum by Navy superiors drew a tepid response. Already over-committed, and his personnel stretched to the limit, Major General Commandant George F. Elliott ignored the entreaties emanating from the luminaries within the Department of the Navy.[7]

The intransigence of the Marine Corps, however, did not fail to attract the attention of senior Navy officers still intent on forcing Leatherneck support for a fleet already geared up for the American Century. Fullam, now the Aide for Inspections, Department of the Navy, had the ear of President Woodrow Wilson's Secretary of the Navy, Josephus Daniels. Following an inspection of the Philadelphia Navy Yard in May

7. "History of Advanced Base Training in the Marine Corps," General Board Study 408, 1 May, 15 May, and 29 September 1913; and General Board Study 432, 28 August 1931, General Records of the Department of the Navy, Record Group (hereafter RG) 80, National Archives and Records Administration (hereafter NARA), Washington, D.C.

1913, Fullam growled that "practically nothing [with regard to the advance-base force] has been accomplished during the past thirteen years." The following fall, Fullam intoned that "the present lack of adequate material [for the advance-base force] clearly indicates the condition of unpreparedness for meeting the demands of war."[8]

With continual nagging emanating from Fullam and his coterie, Secretary Daniels took the initiative. Already convinced that too many lethargic bureaucrats occupied padded office chairs within the Department of the Navy, he approved the board's recommendation that the advance-base concept be exercised and tested during the 1914 winter maneuvers in the Caribbean. For a decade, naval leaders had postulated just such a mission for the Marine Corps. Fullam and his following even went so far as to recommend the permanent establishment of such a force aboard troop transports.

By 1913, the size of the advance-base force had grown from a slim battalion of infantry into an entire brigade of Marines. Besides a headquarters, planners foresaw two 1,300-man regiments: one, a fixed-defense regiment employing shore-emplaced naval guns, searchlights, machine guns, and mining equipment; the other, a mobile-defense regiment composed of six companies of infantry, reinforced by field artillery and machine guns. In its initial deployment and test on the small island of Culebra off Puerto Rico, observers declared it successful. Nonetheless, Headquarters Marine Corps had provided the manpower necessary by scouring the barracks of the eastern seaboard; once the maneuver had ended, it ordered the Marines involved to return to their parent naval stations.[9]

Unlike many contemporaries, who scoffed at time spent in the classroom or contemplating missions statements—such as the advance-base concept—Fuller sought assignments that furthered his professional education. Early in 1913, he completed the Army's Field Officers' Course at Fort Leavenworth, Kansas, as a precursor to joining the 1913–14 Army War College course. After he served a short stint in command of the barracks at Norfolk, Virginia, Major General Commandant George Barnett selected Fuller as Fleet Marine Officer, Atlantic Fleet, and he followed the admiral's flag in a succession of battleships for the next two years. Then, in 1916, Fuller reported to the Naval War College as a student. Few

8. William F. Fullam to the Secretary of the Navy, 1 May and 29 September 1913, General Board Study 408, RG 80, NARA.

9. "Marine Corps Advanced Brigade," Army-Navy Journal, 13 December 1913, 472; file 1975-80-20, routine correspondence, Entry 18, Records of the U. S. Marine Corps, RG 127, NARA; and Jack Shulimson and Graham A. Cosmas, "The Culebra Maneuver and the Formation of the U. S. Marine Corps' Advanced Base Force," in Robert W. Love, Jr., ed., Changing Interpretations and New Sources in Naval History (New York: Garland, 1980), 293–308.

of his fellow officers sought professional education; most considered recourse to the classroom as an outlet for less vigorous and effete Marines. Writing from Haiti, the irrepressible Smedley D. Butler took umbrage at the tactics of his brigade commander, Eli K. Cole, who had earned diplomas from both the Naval Academy and the Army War College: "Now this sort of warfare will gain you much credit and high marks in a million-dollar war college, where all the students are gaining military experience . . . over excellent food and good, dry beds," Butler snarled in a letter home, an opinion intended primarily for his father, who chaired the powerful House Naval Affairs Committee.[10]

America's entry into the World War in 1917 provided a curious interlude in the naval mission of the Marine Corps. As the United States drifted toward inevitable participation in the conflagration in Europe, Commandant George Barnett paved the way for participation of his forces with an adroitness and political acumen that beguiled observers. From the parochial perspective of Barnett, failure of the Marine Corps to participate in the war would give a hollow ring to the proud slogan "first to fight" that had adorned recruiting posters since the turn of the century. The MGC argued, increasingly and stridently, that in time of war every asset should be brought to bear in the conflict without regard to branch of service. In congressional testimony just after the United States declared war on Germany, Barnett presented his case and even took the unusual step of arguing with Admiral William S. Benson, the Chief of Naval Operations (CNO). Benson had grown chary of Marine Corps plans to inculcate itself into the American Expeditionary Forces (AEF) earmarked for France (in the event of U.S. entry into the war), fearing a diminution of traditional responsibilities to the fleet. The MGC deflected the CNO's protestations with the promise that the Marine Corps would honor commitments to the fleet through the simple expedient of personnel expansion.[11]

Convinced, Congress passed legislation that increased the size of the smaller of the naval services in quantum leaps. By the time the guns had fallen silent on the Western Front in November 1918, the Marine Corps had grown from 27,749 men to 74,832. Two brigades deployed to France, but only one formed up with an infantry division, while the other was frittered away as replacements or on rear-echelon duties. Combat casualties—half the Marines that served in the Fourth Brigade (Marine), AEF, suffered wounds or were killed—consumed manpower at a furious pace. After June 1918 and the epic battle at Belleau Wood, two replacement

10. Smedley D. Butler to his father, 5 October 1915, Butler MSS, Marine Corps Research Center, Quantico, Virginia.

11. U.S. Congress, House, Committee on Naval Affairs. *Hearings on Estimates Submitted by the Secretary of the Navy, 1917* (Washington: GPO, 1917), 30–31.

battalions of Marines left Quantico, Virginia, for the Western Front every month until the cease fire.[12]

For more than a generation, many Marine Corps officers believed that only those who had proved themselves in France deserved benefits and promotion. But not every Leatherneck had that opportunity. The MGC had kept his promise to Congress and the Department of the Navy to honor traditional commitments in support of the fleet, and at naval stations at home and abroad. With the personnel expansion, Congress authorized an increase in the number of general officers. On 1 July 1918, Fuller became a brigadier general and was deployed to command the brigade in Santo Domingo. But postwar retrenchment cost him his star, and Fuller reverted to colonel in less than a year. Navy Secretary Daniels interjected himself into the demotion process, arguing that he wanted to "reward those who had been at the cannon's mouth." Scrutiny of the canny political hack's involvement in the affair suggests that he wanted simply to ensure that the indefatigable Smedley D. Butler retained his own promotion to brigadier general.[13]

Returning to the United States in October 1920, Fuller used political leverage to regain his lost star after a disillusioned body politic turned out the Democrats in the presidential election that year. His daughter had married the son of Michigan Congressman Joseph W. Fordney, and this fortuitous alignment convinced Secretary of the Navy Edwin H. Denby—another Michigan Republican—to press for the return of Fuller's promotion to flag rank. Fuller assumed duties at Headquarters, and Major General Commandant Lejeune made him his assistant on 2 July 1928. Fuller remained in that post through Major General Commandant Wendell C. Neville's debilitating illness and death, earning a reputation for steady and unflappable performance among the staff and senior officers within the Department of the Navy. From this vantage point he watched the progressing military and naval retrenchment of the 1920s gut the Marine Corps.

Congress and the three Presidents who served in the 1920s took their cue from a populace grown apathetic toward America's involvement in foreign imbroglios. While the current, and perhaps questionable,

---

12. Jack Shulimson, "First to Fight: Marine Corps Expansion, 1914–1919," *Prologue* 8 (Spring 1976): 5–16; and Merrill L. Bartlett, "Leathernecks, Doughboys, and the Press," *Naval History* 7 (September–October 1993): 46–53. For a complete study of Marine Corps participation in the American Expeditionary Forces, see George B. Clark, *Devil Dogs: Fighting Marines of World War I* (Novato, Calif.: Presidio, 1999).

13. Josephus Daniels to Josephus Daniels, Jr., 1 August 1919, container 23, Josephus Daniels MSS, MD-LC; and Merrill L. Bartlett, "Josephus Daniels and the Marine Corps, 1913–1921," in William B. Cogar, ed., *New Interpretations in Naval History: Selected Papers from the Eighth Naval History Symposium* (Annapolis, Md.: Naval Institute Press, 1989), 190–208.

interpretation of international law with regard to the deployment of naval forces ashore remained in vogue, lawmakers increasingly looked askance at such adventures overseas. During hearings on Capitol Hill in 1922, an exasperated Congressman asked Lejeune, "will we ever get out of Santo Domingo?" to which the MGC responded in kind, "that is for you to decide." While the death knell to colonialism would not be sounded until the threat of a war in the Pacific became a reality more than a decade later, senior officers in naval and military circles pored over contingency plans with new vigor. Even before Fuller reported to Headquarters, the MGC had approved the dispatch of the mercurial, brainy, and alcoholic Earl H. "Pete" Ellis to the Western Pacific to view firsthand just what the Japanese had accomplished in the mandated islands.

Earlier, Marines serving on planning staffs had alerted the MGC that major revisions to War Plan Orange for a war with Japan had begun. Hard on the heels of Ellis's prophetic study, "Advanced Base Operations in Micronesia," the Joint Army-Navy Board approved the amphibious assault mission for the Marine Corps. Thus, as Fuller took up his new assignment in 1928, the smaller of the naval services had a *raison d'être* that would preordain it as a key contributor to the war in the Pacific to follow.[14]

When Fuller assumed the commandancy in 1930, President Herbert C. Hoover had already indicated a willingness to fulfill a promise of military and naval retrenchment. Secretary of the Navy Charles Francis Adams proved a willing subordinate in the program to reduce the assets of the Department of the Navy to near impotence. Nonetheless, worldwide commitments for the Marine Corps remained the same, and traditional missions in support of the fleet continued. In the year Fuller assumed the commandancy, the strength of the Marine Corps stood at 19,380 men. Although brigades had deployed to Nicaragua and China in 1927, only a regiment of Marines remained as semi-permanent fixtures in each troubled country. Meanwhile, Marines continued to serve in the warships of the fleet, man the two skeletonized expeditionary brigades at

14. U.S. Congress, House, 66th Cong., 3rd sess., Hearings Before the Naval Appropriations Committee, 21 January 1922. See also, General Board Study 432, 11 February 1922, RG 80, NARA; General Board of the Navy Study 432, 11 February 1922, RG 80, NARA; and Joint Board Serial 280, 21 July 1928, Records of the Joint Army-Navy Board, RG 225, microfilm series 1421, NARA. For a useful, final postscript on the mission of Pete Ellis, see Dirk Anthony Ballendorf, "Earl Hancock Ellis: A Final Assessment," *Marine Corps Gazette* 74 (November 1990): 78–87; and Dirk Anthony Ballendorf and Merrill L. Bartlett, *Pete Ellis: An Amphibious Warfare Prophet, 1880–1923* (Annapolis, Md.: Naval Institute Press, 1997). The assignment of the amphibious assault mission to the Marine Corps may be found in *Joint Action of the Army and Navy* (Washington: GPO, 1927), sections IV and VII.

Quantico and San Diego, California, and provide sentries at Navy stations at home and abroad. Despite these burgeoning commitments, the Marine Corps was only slightly larger than a decade before.

President Hoover came to the Oval Office in 1929 determined to bring efficiency to the government and to reduce expenses. The world-wide depression only fueled his fervor to cut federal outlays. Secretary Adams fulfilled his role as a zealous subordinate by whittling away at the perceived excesses in the naval services. Fuller, like Neville before him, argued that the minuscule figures forced an inordinate number of Marines to serve overseas; his entreaties went unheard. Although in the second year of Fuller's tenure, the Department of State called for a sharp reduction in the size of the Marine force in Nicaragua, the numbers in-country remained fairly constant. In 1931, the personnel strength of the Marine Corps dropped to 18,782 men. The nagging from the administration irritated Fuller, who shared his frustration with Lejeune: "This is some job now with the Secretary [of the Navy] telling me not to spend $700,000 of our appropriations for this year."[15]

The curtailment continued into Hoover's third year in office. Although the legal strength of the Marine Corps was 27,400 enlisted men in 1931, Congress had appropriated funds to pay for only 18,000. In that year, the Secretary of the Navy even recommended cutting the daily enlisted allowance for rations from fifty-two and one-half cents to forty-eight. Fuller reminded Hoover, Adams, and the congressional naval affairs committees of the dismal statistics: there were only 9,014 Marines in the United States; 4,657 men on foreign duty; 2,093 in the ships of the fleet; 1,073 Leathernecks in aviation duties; and 355 men in sick or casual status.

Ruefully, he noted that most of his Marines were either overseas or with the fleet, or coming from or going there. Still, Hoover and Adams pushed for further reductions. Half of the Navy and Marine Corps recruiting stations closed, Navy bands were abolished, and the Marine Corps Recruit Depot, Parris Island, South Carolina, was reduced in status; ominously, the Hoover administration recommended closing Parris Island and establishing a single recruit training facility at Quantico. Appearing more sympathetic, Congress raised Marine Corps personnel levels to 17,500 men, but Adams just as forthrightly cut them back to 16,000. Fuller and his senior officers testified before Congress that any further cuts, reportedly to 13,600 men as hinted by Hoover and Adams, would devastate the Corps. In the last year of Hoover's administration, Fuller exclaimed to the House Naval Affairs Committee that the reductions "have made it impossible to carry out [the Marine Corps's] primary

15. Fuller to JAL, 18 September 1930, reel 4, Lejeune MSS, MD-LC.

mission of supporting the United States Fleet by maintaining a force in readiness to operate with the fleet."[16]

Meanwhile, as manpower cuts threatened to emasculate the Marine Corps, Fuller faced continuing problems with his ambitious and frenetic senior officers. Although Butler claimed at the time of his failure to achieve the commandancy that he would remain in uniform to lead the Marine Corps, he began almost immediately to cast about for a civilian position. Increasingly, the Corps's *enfant terrible* became embarrassing to the administration because of his irresponsible public utterances. Butler had earned the ire of Adams and Hoover by suggesting that the Department of State rigged elections in Latin America. Although appearing subdued after a severe dressing down in the Secretary's office, Butler then insulted the Italian dictator, Benito Mussolini, in a speech to a private club. In the imbroglio that followed, Butler faced a threatened court-martial, accepted a letter of reprimand, and marched noisily into retirement.[17]

Other officer personnel problems plagued Fuller, just as they had Lejeune and Neville. The stagnation of the officers' lineal list that had persisted since the end of World War I continued, and Congress appeared

16. U. S. Congress, House, 71st Cong., 3rd sess., Hearings Before the House Naval Affairs Committee on Appropriations for FY 32, 9 February 1931; [Fuller to Adams?], 20 May 1931, container 36, Hoover MSS; Fuller to the Secretary of the Navy, 17 January 1931, in General Board Study 432, RG 80, NARA; "Will Destroy Marine Corps," *Army-Navy Journal*, 14 January 1932, 1; "Navy Estimates Cut, Sent to White House," *Army-Navy Journal*, 17 October 1931, 145; "Marine Cut to Stay," *Army-Navy Journal*, 12 September 1931, 30; "Oppose Marine Cut," *New York Times*, 16 December 1932, 14; "House Fights Cuts in Marine Corps," *New York Times*, 12 January 1933, 2; "No New Cut in Marines," *New York Times*, 7 August 1931; "Economy Plans Cut Naval Air Program," *New York Times*, 12 June 1931, 42; "Marine Corps Stops Enlisting in Effort to Save $1,000,000; May Cut Force to 16,000," *New York Times*, 11 June 1931, 1; and "Marine Corps Economy," *New York Times*, 15 June 1931, 18. For a scholarly overview of the Department of the Navy during the Hoover Administration, see John Richard Meredith Wilson, "Herbert Hoover and the Armed Forces: A Study of Presidential Attitudes and Policy" (Ph.D. diss., Northwestern University, 1971), chapters 2–3.

17. Merrill L. Bartlett, "Old Gimlet Eye," *U.S. Naval Institute Proceedings* 112 (November 1986): 65–72; Robert B. Asprey, "The Court-Martial of Smedley Butler," *Marine Corps Gazette* 43 (December 1959): 28–33; Hans Schmidt, *General Smedley D. Butler and the Contradictions of American Military History* (Lexington: University Press of Kentucky, 1987), 202–13; "General Butler Ordered Before Court-Martial," *Army-Navy Journal*, 31 January 1931, 513, 531; "Secretary Reprimands Gen. Butler; Trial Off," *Army-Navy Journal*, 14 February 1931, 1; and "Gen. Butler to Quit Soon," *New York Times*, 6 August 1931, 21. For Butler's noisy polemic, see Butler, "To Hell with the Admirals," 14–16, 18, 20, 22, and 23. A former Secretary of the Navy, Curtis Wilbur, suggested the way for the Hoover Administration to extricate itself from the controversy; see Wilbur to Hoover, 7 February 1931, container 36, Hoover MSS.

reluctant to authorize the creation of selection boards in order to removed the aged and redundant. Although in 1931 President Hoover approved a plan to retire officers who had failed selection for promotion, he reneged when advisors informed him that it required an additional $170,000 beyond existing costs to fund the plan. Fuller and his staff testified that graduates of the Naval Academy Class of 1906 then serving in the Marine Corps were still captains, while Navy officers of the Naval Academy Class of 1918 would become lieutenant commanders on 1 July 1931. Their Marine Corps counterparts were not due for promotion to major for another ten years at the present rate of promotion. Although the House Naval Affairs Committee approved HR 5344, Congress failed to pass the promotion bill.[18]

Not satisfied with eroding the personnel strength of the Marine Corps, Hoover and Adams then began steps to disband the Corps and transfer its assets to the Army. By 30 June 1931, Fuller counted only 1,196 officers and 15,365 enlisted men in his ranks. But Hoover and Adams sought to inflict further reductions. The Oval Office worked through a compliant General Douglas MacArthur, Chief of Staff of the Army, who apparently harbored little affection for the Marines as a result of their unwarranted publicity garnered during World War I. A MacArthur protégé, Major General George S. Simonds, prepared a proposal arguing that the Marine Corps duplicated much of the Army's function. He proposed that the Army could easily absorb the Corps's overhead and avoid unnecessary duplication. Simonds's position paper contended that a savings of twenty-five million dollars was attainable: "It represents a clear possibility of saving money without impairing national defense."

Unknown to Fuller, the triumvirate of Adams-MacArthur-Simonds had enlisted the support of an unlikely ally. The Chief of Naval Operations, Admiral William Veazie Pratt, had, by that time, fallen under the MacArthur spell and agreed with the argument that the Marine Corps should be limited simply to traditional duties aboard ship. The CNO, Fuller's Naval Academy classmate, agreed that the combined-arms aspect of Marine Corps organization overlapped and duplicated that of

---

18. U. S. Congress, House, 72nd Cong., 2nd sess., USMC Commissioned Officer Distribution, Promotion, and Retirement Provisions, Hearings, Naval Affairs Committee, 2 February 1932; J. Clawson Roop, Director, Bureau of the Budget, to Hoover, 13 October 1931, container 36, Hoover MSS. See also, JAL to Burton C. French, 19 May 1931; JAL to Rufus H. Lane, 19 May 1931; JAL to Frederick D. Hale, 20 May 1932; and Lane to JAL, 24 May 1932, reel 5, Lejeune MSS, MD-LC; "President Approves USMC Promotion Bill," *Army-Navy Journal,* 10 October 1931; and "Promotion Bill Fails," *Army-Navy Journal,* 5 December 1931, 319.

the Army. But this time, congressional supporters of the Marine Corps rose to the challenge and the proposal died.[19]

The year before, Fuller noted in his annual report that the personnel situation could not become worse; he had Marines serving in thirty-three ships plus aviation detachments on the carriers *Lexington* and *Saratoga*; early in January 1931, a battalion was formed from Marines at Cavite and Olongapo, and then sent hurriedly to reinforce the 4th Marines in China. The proposed reduction in end-strength, from 18,000 men approved by Congress to 15,343 recommended by the administration, made the Corps's position untenable. On 30 June 1932, Fuller counted only a slight increase to 16,561 Marines, and a year later that number dipped to 16,068. "With the present enlisted strength, the Marine Corps is not prepared to perform its allotted task in the event of a national emergency," Fuller warned in his annual report to the Secretary of the Navy. Then, as if to underscore the crisis, he issued a terse statement to the troops: "I wish to record my appreciation of the efforts put forth by all ranks during a trying year."[20]

In 1933, the dismal outlook for the Marine Corps took an upturn. Entreaties by the Department of State and congressional criticism had convinced the Oval Office to begin withdrawing the Marines from Nicaragua and otherwise implement a "Good Neighbor" Policy in Latin America. The election of Franklin D. Roosevelt, an unabashed supporter of the Marine Corps, buoyed hopes at Headquarters Marine Corps for relief of the personnel situation. Fuller took the opportunity to begin major shifts in senior personnel. The departure of the troublesome Butler in 1931 and the disappointed Feland in 1933 cleared the way to realign the ranks of general officers. Brigadier General Robert H. "Hal" Dunlap, a promising and popular officer considered by many observers as a potential MGC, lost his life in an accident. To fill the vacant major general's slot vacated by Feland, Fuller nominated Dion Williams. He sent forth the name of another Naval Academy graduate, Charles H.

---

19. George S. Simonds, "Amalgamation of the Marine Corps with the Army," 8 May 1931, folder M (correspondence, 1929–31), Simonds MSS, MD-LC; and George Van Horn Moseley, "One Soldier's Journey," 159–62, Moseley MSS, MD-LC. William Veazie Pratt's diary is silent on the affair, but his biographer notes that many senior officers considered the Chief of Naval Operations somewhat of an unprotesting agent of the Hoover Administration. See Craig L. Symonds, "William Veazie Pratt as CNO," *Naval War College Review* 30 (March-April 1980): 17–38. Douglas MacArthur's papers are also silent on the proposal; but see Pratt to MacArthur, 18 January 1952, RG 10, MacArthur MSS, MacArthur Memorial, Norfolk, Virginia, in which Pratt compares MacArthur to Winston S. Churchill.

20. *Annual Report of the Secretary of the Navy, 1932* (Washington: GPO, 1932), 1141–63; and "USMC Aviation Units Placed on Carriers," *Army-Navy Journal,* 26 September 1931, 1.

Lyman—a protégé of Major General Joseph H. Pendleton—to become a brigadier general and fill Williams's vacancy.

Fuller's foes had either departed the scene or muted their disappointment in his selection. Lejeune, Superintendent of the Virginia Military Institute in Lexington, Virginia, remained distant and occasionally badgered the MGC for additional commissions for Institute graduates. From retirement, Butler observed the progression in the ranks of general officers with scorn and dismay. Obviously, Fuller had undertaken a shuffling of senior officers to prepare the ascension of an heir to the commandancy. Worse, the officers elevated possessed diplomas from the Naval Academy. Smedley D. Butler lost no time in storming the barricades, this time in a characteristic diatribe to President Roosevelt.

The Marine Corps's stormy petrel observed tartly that upon the retirement of Dion Williams for age in January 1934, Fuller planned to elevate John H. Russell to the vacant major generalcy. Clearly, this move paved the way for the despised Russell to succeed Fuller. Butler argued passionately for Brigadier General Harry Lee to receive a promotion to major general and referred to him as a member of a group "which is fast passing out, discouraged and broken in spirit." Butler added that: "The class to which I refer is composed of those officers who did not have, at least, some Naval Academy education, but who, notwithstanding this handicap, is . . . almost entirely responsible for the proud record of the Marines." Butler and his coterie hoped that Lee—ranking one number senior to Russell in 1931—would retain seniority and succeed Fuller as MGC.[21]

President Roosevelt and Secretary of the Navy Claude A. Swanson ignored Butler's protestations. Russell commanded at Quantico from 1 December 1931 until assuming the position of assistant to the Major General Commandant in February 1933. Fuller finally had his team in place, and then began to focus on a major realignment of the Marines as expeditionary forces in support of the fleet. Beginning in 1931, the General Board of the Navy had intermittently studied the role of the Marine Corps in support of the fleet. In that year, the CNO demurred with the MGC's request to increase the number of aircraft at the expense of personnel assigned to fleet or shore activities. Fuller hoped to increase the assets of aviation squadron VO-7M from six to twelve aircraft, thus giving the Marine Corps a total of seventy-four operational planes plus

---

21. Smedley D. Butler to Franklin D. Roosevelt, 17 July 1933, file 18E, Roosevelt MSS, Franklin D. Roosevelt Presidential Library, Hyde Park, N.Y.; see also, "Major Generals Appointed," *Army-Navy Journal,* 9 September 1933, 21, 39; Fuller to Adams, 7 June 1933, file 18E, Roosevelt MSS; Ernest L. Jahnke to Walter H. Newton, 15 and 20 October 1931, and Jahnke to Herbert Hoover, 5 September 1931, container 36, Hoover MSS.

twenty-one spares. Then, in the summer of 1932, the War Plans Division made a significant recommendation to the General Board concerning the organization and establishment of the Marine Corps.

In its conclusions, the body emphasized that the Marine Corps must only be responsible for the seizure and defense of advanced bases; subsequent operations ashore would then pass to the Army. Planners argued that the Marines should only be employed as an adjunct to the Army if necessary, because in any likely scenario the Marine Corps would be busy supporting the fleet. Prophetically, the Director of the War Plans Division posited that Marine Corps air assets should always remain an integral part of naval aviation and never operate as a separate component; otherwise, it would open the way for criticism from the Army Air Corps, "which has for its purposes the abolition of all Marine Corps air activities, and the diversion of the present appropriations for this component to its purposes."[22]

Knowing of the Board's deliberations, Fuller and his staff invited its attention to an important study, "History of Advanced Base Training in the Marine Corps." As the General Board of the Navy appeared increasingly to dwell on the Marines with the fleet as the primary source of expeditionary forces, Headquarters Marine Corps argued emphatically for the separate organization and maintenance of Marines intended primarily for deployment overseas: "Marines in ships' detachments [should] not be considered available for duty with expeditionary forces," Fuller intoned. In the same study, the General Board made several recommendations and observations that failed to get the attention of Headquarters and attain some measure of agreement. Clearly, the Marine Corps had matured sufficiently to no longer play the handmaiden's role for the admirals.

The use of the Marine Corps as part of a field army, such as in World War I, was considered a special case. In future wars, planners anticipated the requirement for all Marine Corps assets in support of the fleet. Marine aircraft must be considered part of naval aviation, and never be deployed separately from the fleet. Senior Marine Corps and Navy officers scored the inclination toward indoctrination of scenarios drafted by the Army, because potential deployments of Marines appeared most likely to be in naval and not land warfare: "The idea that the Marine Corps is an amphibious organization should not be lost sight of in the composition, organization, training, and equipment."[23]

22. Director, War Plans Division, to the General Board, 10 August 1931, file KA-KV (secret), RG 80, NARA; see also, CNO to CMC, 20 April 1931, in the same file.

23. General Board Study 432, 28 August 1931, RG 80, NARA; and Director, War Plans Division, to the General Board, 10 August 1931, file OP 12F-CD, and CMC to CNO, 3 November 1931, SecNav/CNO Secret files, RG 80, NARA. See also, CMC to

Late in 1932, another study by the General Board arrived at Headquarters. Fuller repeated his objection to counting Marine ships detachments as part of available expeditionary forces. The MGC wondered if such detachments could be available to deployment, then who performed their normal duties aboard ship? But a statement relegating the Marine Corps to an obscure, secondary role to that of the Navy raised Fuller's ire. He took umbrage at the suggestion that naval strength had priority over that of the Marine Corps. In the Navy's view, manning the ships of the fleet should be given priority; if the Marine Corps lost numbers in the process, so be it. Then in an obvious rebuke to the Director, War Plans Division, General Board of the Navy, Fuller informed him that he intended to conform solely to the requirements resulting from Naval War College Advanced Base Problem No. 1. Just a week before, Fuller told the same admiral that he had ordered a study of the organization of the Advance Base Force to support the major strategic plan—obviously, War Plan Orange.[24]

A year later, however, the General Board appeared more supportive of the Marine Corps position. The General Board reported that the strength of the Marine Corps should be 21,000 men to support the fleet adequately; however, the Chief of Naval Operations increased that figure to 27,400 in his endorsement of the study. Fuller and his staff objected to the Navy's position that any artillery larger than 3-inch caliber reduced the mobility of the landing force; experience had shown the requirement for 155mm guns or howitzers. Finally, the Chief of Naval Operations expressed concern over the shortages of Marines assigned to the fleet; specifically, he wanted Marine detachments in the new light cruisers and more Leathernecks assigned to the battleships. Both the Chief of Naval Operations and the Major General Commandant agreed that the time-honored figure of Marine Corps strength being one-fifth that of the Navy no longer appeared valid. Less than a month later, Fuller asked the Secretary of the Navy to approve the assignment of a Marine officer to the General Board because of the increasing number of matters of interest and vital importance to the Marine Corps.[25]

Director, Division of Operations and Training, HQMC, Commandant, Marine Corps Schools, Quantico, and Director, War Plans Division, General Board of the Navy, 29 November 1932, SecNav Confidential files, RG 80, NARA.

24. CMC to CNO, 3 November 1932, KA-KV secret file; and CMC to Division of Operations and Training, and War Plans Section, Marine Corps Schools, Quantico, 24 November 1932, KG-KW confidential file, RG 80, NARA.

25. CNO to SecNav, with CMC's comments, 2 March 1933; CMC to SecNav, 11 April 1933; Admiral J. V. Chase, Chairman, General Board, to SecNav, 10 August 1932; and Admiral William Veazie Pratt to SecNav, 2 March 1933, file 1240-30, Entry 18, General Correspondence, RG 127, NARA.

Fuller's final step, one that altered the operating forces of the Marine Corps substantially, was to recommend the dissolution of the expeditionary forces and replace them with fleet marine forces placed under direct control of fleet commanders. As part of the process, he criticized the lack of suitable doctrine, as evidenced by the gyrations of the General Board of the Navy over the previous two years. Fuller ordered the Commandant, Marine Corps Schools, to "proceed as expeditiously as practicable to prepare for publication a manual for landing operations." Fuller directed Quantico to begin work no later than 15 November 1933, and authorized the suspension of classes to use the staff and students to work on the project.[26]

Fuller's career, dating from an appointment as a midshipmen in 1884 until his retirement in 1934, saw the Marine Corps not only retain traditional duties in support of the Navy at sea and ashore, but also adopt new missions as colonial infantry, an advanced-base force, and finally an amphibious-assault force for the projection of a sizeable element of America's seapower ashore. Fuller's commandancy, especially the prophetic evolution of a doctrine for amphibious assault, suggests that the role of the Marine Corps as a subsidiary of the Navy had ended. For more than a century, captains and admirals had dictated policies and directives with regard to the smaller of the naval services; insipid and compliant Secretaries of the Navy had, for the most part, supported senior Navy officers. That Fuller was able to stand up to the admirals successfully on subjects of mission and doctrine suggests that his commandancy has been both ignored and underrated. He proved a stellar Major General Commandant of the Marine Corps, and he surpassed the meager expectations of his critics. Fuller's commandancy represented a clear change in the sea dynamic of the Marine Corps.

Fuller's career, especially his commandancy and the events of 1933–34, is fraught with irony. When President Hoover's naval aide-de-camp prepared the memorandum on the subject of a successor to Neville, he argued strongly for Fuller's appointment. Commander Charles R. Train noted, *inter alia,* that Fuller's appointment would promote better relations within the Department of the Navy. He reminded the Chief Executive that Fuller's Naval Academy classmate, William Pratt, had just been appointed to the position of Chief of Naval Operations, "and this can only afford good results." But Fuller stood firm every

26. Ben H. Fuller to Commandant, Marine Corps Schools, Quantico, 28 October 1933, file 1520-30-120, Entry 18, RG 127, NARA. John Russell, however, lays claim to initiating this change, even though Fuller himself signed the directive; see Russell, "The Birth of the Fleet Marine Force," *U.S. Naval Institute Proceedings* 72 (October 1946): 49–51.

time the admirals attempted to gain ground at the expense of the Marine Corps, and he never hesitated to take issue with Pratt or his coterie.[27]

The admirals wanted Marines posted to the new light cruisers, and additional Leathernecks assigned to existing detachments in the warships of the fleet. In a complete reversal from the arguments of the Fullamites at the turn of the century, senior Navy officers argued now for the increases in ships' detachments as a source of expeditionary forces readily available to fleet commanders. Beginning in the 1880s, Fullam and his supporters took just the opposite view, positing that Marines should be formed into battalions readily available as expeditionary forces. Senior Marines of that era opposed the notion, and argued vehemently against any change in traditional missions in support of the fleet. More than three decades later, the admirals and generals reversed their positions to provide the ultimate irony of Fuller's commandancy.

27. Train to Hoover, 21 July 1930, Candidates for Commandant file, container 36, Hoover MSS; for examples of Fuller's willingness to thwart the wishes of the admirals, see the SecNav/CNO KA-KV files (secret), RG 80, NARA; and CNO to SecNav, with CMC's comments, 2 March 1933, and CMC to SecNav, 11 April 1933, file 1240-30, Entry 18, General Correspondence, RG 127, NARA.

This organization is dedicated to the study and preservation of military history in the Americas. Its objectives are to promote and advance the research of military history and traditions through publications, exhibits and meetings. Members include anyone interested in military history and others such as historians, collectors, writers, artists, and those involved in living history.

The Company publishes the quarterly journal
MILITARY COLLECTOR & HISTORIAN

and an ongoing series of color plates, the MILITARY UNIFORMS IN AMERICA

For Membership Information Contact:

THE COMPANY OF MILITARY HISTORIANS

David M. Sullivan, Administrator

P.O. BOX 910 · RUTLAND, MA 01543-0910
Phone: 508-845-9229

e-mail: comhhq@flash.net   or   DSulli7875@aol.com

Billy Yank and G.I. Joe: An Exploratory Essay on the Sociopolitical Dimensions of Soldier Motivation

☆

Thomas E. Rodgers*

Abstract

This article provides an explanation of how Union soldiers could fight so effectively in the Civil War with so little training by comparing their prewar socialization experiences with those of infantrymen in World War II. Billy Yank's society inculcated concepts of masculinity, patriotism, and citizenship that were major factors in his ability to function under fire. G.I. Joe's society instilled different concepts of masculinity, patriotism, and citizenship that could not provide him with the same ability as Billy Yank to function on the battlefield. Extensive training and unit cohesion were necessary to compensate for what socialization did not provide G.I. Joe.

AT the beginning of his memoir of his military service in World War II, Leon Standifer recounts witnessing ceremonies honoring Civil War veterans when he was growing up in the 1930s. Indeed, America's entry into the Second World War took place less than seventy-seven years after the end of the War Between the States. In those eight decades, however, America, its political culture, and its military forces changed dramatically. These changes made significant differences in how Billy Yank, the Union infantryman of the Civil War, and G.I. Joe, the

* The author wishes to thank Dr. Jerry K. Sweeney and audience members for instructive comments on an earlier version of this work presented in a session sponsored by the Society for Military History at the Missouri Valley History Conference, Omaha, March 2003, and the anonymous readers who evaluated the article for the *Journal of Military History*.

Thomas E. Rodgers, adjunct professor of history at the University of Southern Indiana, received his Ph.D. in American history from Indiana University. He has published numerous essays on Civil War subjects.

regular army or marine infantryman of World War II, responded to their nation's call to arms and to the experience of military combat.[1]

In comparing soldiers of the Civil War and World War II, this article will focus on frontline combat troops. Among Civil War soldiers it will concentrate on the vast majority who entered service in state regiments, rather than on the small minority who served in the regular army. Among World War II soldiers, it will center on those men who joined combat infantry units in the regular army and the marines. It will not consider other combat arms, career soldiers who joined in the prewar years, or National Guard infantrymen. In short, it will focus on the most common experiences in both wars of private citizens who entered the military during a time of crisis and were assigned to fight as infantry. Since the article examines the relationship between socialization experiences in America in two different time periods, its major focus will be on native-born soldiers.[2]

Men entering the regular army or marines to serve as combat troops in World War II had a very different experience from those entering the

1. Leon C. Standifer, *Not in Vain: A Rifleman Remembers World War II* (Baton Rouge: Louisiana State University Press, 1992), 17–18. I have adopted the term "Billy Yank" from Bell Wiley's seminal work on the Union soldier, even though, as Wiley himself notes, the term was not in common use until after the war. Bell I. Wiley, *The Life of Billy Yank: The Common Soldier of the Union* (Baton Rouge: Louisiana State University Press, 1952), 11–12. "G.I. Joe" was a commonly used nickname for American fighting men during World War II.

2. The scope of the study is limited to the groups described in the text in order to be able to focus on changes over time. Although National Guard units were organized from a local area or region, it should be noted that they do not seem to have had the same level or kind of community base as Civil War volunteer companies or even regiments. Lester Tenney, for instance, knew no one from civilian life in his guard unit. Lester I. Tenney, *My Hitch in Hell: The Bataan Death March* (Washington: Brassey's, 1995), especially 1–41. Immigration was so low in the eleven years preceding World War II that recent immigrants could have constituted only a very small part of the army and marine recruits. Most immigrants in 1941 had been in the country for a long time and presumably had become somewhat assimilated. In contrast, immigration in the fifteen years before the Civil War was very high, especially in proportion to the native population and especially in the North. While English Protestant immigrants assimilated fairly quickly, the major groups, the Irish and the Germans, did not do so. Catholics among these latter two groups faced a very hostile nativist movement. Although many immigrants served in the Union army, they appear to have tended to join in smaller percentages than the native born. Why this is so would require at least a full article to explain, and, thus, must remain beyond the scope of this article. Steven J. Buck, "'A contest in which blood must flow like water': Du Page County and the Civil War," *Illinois Historical Journal* 87 (Spring 1994): 2–20; William L. Burton, *Melting Pot Soldiers: The Union's Ethnic Regiments* (New York: Fordham University Press, 1998); Roger Daniels, *Coming to America: A History of Immigration and Ethnicity in American Life,* 2nd ed. (New York: Perennial, 2002), 121–84, 265–70, 287–302.

Union army. They went through a basic training designed to separate them from civilian society. Their individuality was muted by standardized haircuts and clothing. They were put into units filled with strangers from all over the country. They underwent extensive training in the use of various weapons, in hand-to-hand combat techniques, in physical conditioning, in maneuvers, and much more. They were trained until they could act automatically without thinking. The concept of unit cohesion was drilled into them until they came to see their squad members as virtual brothers. All of this was seen as necessary for success or even for functioning on a battlefield.[3]

Men entering the Union army in the Civil War were not separated from civilian society. Men routinely joined units with brothers, cousins, brothers-in-law, and even their fathers. In many companies two-thirds to four-fifths of the men were from the same county, and many were from just a few communities within that county. There was no standard grooming, uniforms and equipment were routinely supplemented by clothes from mothers and wives, and extra weapons were purchased in the private sector. Most soldiers received no training except marching and drilling. It is rare to find references to things so basic as target practice or field maneuvers. In some instances men did not even receive weapons until a few days before leaving for the front, and in some extreme cases they did not receive weapons until after they were in or near a combat zone.[4] How could men whose indoctrination and training

3. John Ellis, *On the Front Lines: The Experience of War through the Eyes of the Allied Soldiers in World War II* (New York: John Wiley and Sons, 1990), 13–20; Gerald F. Linderman, *The World Within War: America's Combat Experience in World War II* (Cambridge, Mass.: Harvard University Press, 1997), 4, 185–87; Lee Kennett, *G.I.: The American Soldier in World War II* (paperback ed., Norman: University of Oklahoma Press, 1987), 24–90; Peter S. Kindsvatter, *American Soldiers: Ground Combat in the World Wars, Korea, and Vietnam* (Lawrence: University of Kansas Press, 2003), 17–26. For individual and group memoirs that contain significant discussions of basic training, see E. B. Sledge, *With the Old Breed: At Peleliu and Okinawa* (New York: Oxford University Press, 1990); Stephen E. Ambrose, *Band of Brothers: E Company, 506th Regiment, 101st Airborne from Normandy to Hitler's Eagle's Nest* (New York: Touchstone, 1993); Standifer, *Not in Vain*; Robert Kotlowitz, *Before Their Time: A Memoir* (New York: Anchor Book, 1998); Francis B. Catanzaro, *With the 41st Division in the Southwest Pacific: A Foot Soldier's Story* (Bloomington: Indiana University Press, 2002); Robert Leckie, *Helmet for My Pillow* (1957, reprint ed., New York: ibooks, 2001). Leckie is especially good on clothes and haircuts.

4. For background on the training of Union troops, see Wiley, *Billy Yank*, especially 25–28, 49–55; James M. McPherson, *Battle Cry of Freedom: The Civil War Era* (New York: Oxford University Press, 1988), 330–31. For specific examples of things mentioned in the text, see Benjamin F. Scribner, *How Soldiers Were Made . . .* (1887; reprint ed., Huntington, W.Va.: Blue Acorn Press, 1995), 20–33; Dale E. Linvill, ed., *Battles, Skirmishes, Events and Scenes: The Letters and Memorandum of Ambrose Remley* (Crawfordsville, Ind.: R. R. Donnelley & Sons, 1997), 11; Richard S. Skid-

were so rudimentary—so different from that of the fighting men of World War II—have any success on the battlefield? Why, in the vernacular of the Civil War, did they not all skedaddle as soon as they got their first glimpse of the elephant?

The thesis of this article is that the answer to this question lies in the social and political experiences of these Civil War soldiers, and that the extensive training of men preparing to fight in the Second World War was made necessary, in part, because of the changed social and political milieu in which these men came to maturity in the 1930s and early 1940s. An analysis of the courage and of the patriotism of the fighting men of these two different eras can provide historians with insights that cannot be easily obtained by studying the combatants of one era in isolation. Such a cross comparison will illustrate that even though there are certain commonalities to soldiers and combat across the centuries, how

more, ed., *The Civil War Journal of Billy Davis: From Hopewell, Indiana to Port Republic, Virginia* (Hanover, Ind.: The Nugget Publishers, 1989), 26; Robert H. Rhodes, ed., *All for the Union: The Civil War Diary of Elisha Hunt Rhodes* (New York: Vintage Civil War Library, 1992), 11–12; Oscar O. Winther, ed., *With Sherman to the Sea: The Civil War Letters, Diaries, and Reminiscences of Theodore F. Upson* (Baton Rouge: Louisiana State University Press, 1943), 31; Mildred Throne, ed., *The Civil War Diary of Cyrus F. Boyd: Fifteenth Iowa Infantry, 1861–1863* (1953; reprint ed., Baton Rouge: Louisiana State University Press, 1998), 18; James S. Thomas Papers, SC 1448, Indiana Historical Society, Indianapolis, Indiana; Richard S. Skidmore, ed., *The Alford Brothers . . .* (Hanover, Ind.: The Nugget Publishers, 1995), 61. (The manuscript reproduced in the book is in the Indiana Historical Society, Indianapolis.) Urban companies appear to have had more transients than rural ones, and as bounties became a factor, recruits were increasingly attracted from outside the county raising a company. Still, most units appear to have continued to be recruited largely from the inhabitants of the local area. For community studies of Civil War recruitment, see Thomas E. Rodgers, "Republicans and Drifters: Political Affiliation and Union Army Volunteers in West-Central Indiana," *Indiana Magazine of History* 92 (December 1996): 321–45; Russell L. Johnson, "'Volunteer While You May': Manpower Mobilization in Dubuque, Iowa," in *Union Soldiers and the Northern Home Front: Wartime Experiences, Postwar Adjustments,* ed. Paul A. Cimbala and Randall M. Miller (New York: Fordham University Press, 2002), 30–68; Thomas R. Kemp, "Community and War: The Civil War Experience of Two New Hampshire Towns," in *Toward a Social History of the American Civil War: Exploratory Essays,* ed. Maris A. Vinovskis (New York: Cambridge University Press, 1990), 31–77; Emily J. Harris, "Sons and Soldiers: Deerfield, Massachusetts and the Civil War," *Civil War History* 30 (June 1984): 157–71; W. J. Rorabaugh, "Who Fought for the North in the Civil War? Concord, Massachusetts, Enlistments," *Journal of American History* 73 (December 1986): 695–701; J. Matthew Gallman, *Mastering Wartime: A Social History of Philadelphia during the Civil War* (Cambridge: Cambridge University Press, 1990), 11–84.

a man performs on a battlefield may be more deeply influenced by his premilitary service life than is normally supposed.[5]

The exercise of courage is an integral part of military conflict. There are many similarities in the memoirs and diaries of frontline troops of both wars as men express their private apprehensions upon facing battle for the first time. Will they freeze? Will they run? Will they perform with courage? Likewise, acts of courage—risking or sacrificing one's life for one's comrades and the success of the mission—were very similar in both conflicts. Nevertheless, there are subtle, but important, differences in the forms of courage and the sources of courage between many of the men who fought in the Civil War and many of those who fought in World War II. To understand these differences one must look at how most of the men of each era were socialized and how this socialization experience influenced their ability to show courage under fire.

A good starting point for understanding the social organization in which Civil War soldiers were raised, how it promoted courage, and how it differed from that of the frontline troops of World War II is the overview of American social structure proposed by John Higham in the printed version of his presidential address to the Organization of American Historians in 1974. Higham contends that early American social structure can be understood in terms of what he labels primordial and

---

5. Some authors have used or suggested the use of studies of soldiers done during World War II by S. L. A. Marshall, Samuel A. Stouffer, and others as models for studying Civil War soldiers. Such historians appear to assume that there are many commonalities between soldiers in different wars. The position I take in this article is that one should assume soldiers in the two wars to be different until it can be proven otherwise. I am also uneasy with trying to apply the questions used by World War II interviewers in a fairly mechanical way so as to achieve some kind of scientific analysis, such as was done in the study by Pete Maslowski (see below). It seems to me that one cannot simply abstract statements as if they are answers to a questionnaire. If one, for instance, looks at the letters of Jacob Ritner of the 25th Iowa Infantry Regiment, one can find complaints about the government, expressions of longings for home, and suggestions of disgruntlement interspersed among some remarkable outbursts of florid patriotism and strongly stated political and ideological comments. Trying to determine what his ultimate feelings might be requires a nuanced reading of all his expressed opinions within the context of all that he wrote. James M. McPherson's work on the motivation of Civil War soldiers seems to do a good job of allowing World War II studies to enhance the depth and sophistication of his analysis without assuming Civil War soldiers were just like soldiers of the Second World War (in fact, he found substantial differences). Marvin R. Cain, "A 'Face of Battle' Needed: An Assessment of Motives and Men in Civil War Historiography," *Civil War History* 28 (March 1982): 5–27; Peter Maslowski, "A Study of Morale in Civil War Soldiers," *Military Affairs* 34 (December 1970): 122–26; Charles F. Latimer, ed., *Love and Valor: Intimate Civil War Letters between Captain Jacob and Emeline Ritner* (Western Spring, Ill.: Sigourney Press, 2000); James M. McPherson, *For Cause and Comrades: Why Men Fought in the Civil War* (New York: Oxford University Press, 1997).

ideological organization, while American social organization in the twentieth century is best understood in terms of what he calls technical unity. Borrowing from the anthropologist Clifford Geertz, Higham defines the primordial relationship as "a corporate feeling of oneness that infuses a particular, concrete, unquestioned set of inherited relationships." He defines ideology as "those explicit systems of general beliefs that give large bodies of people a common identity and purpose, a common program of action, and a standard for self-criticism." While Higham believes that these two forms of organization can overlap each other, he thinks that by the mid-nineteenth century the geographical mobility of the American people had led to a breakdown of primordial relationships except in a few isolated southern communities and among Indian tribes. With the widespread collapse of the primordial social organization, most of America had, he believes, come to be organized around ideological ties.[6]

The findings in the field of social history in the nearly three decades since Higham proposed his organizational scheme require that a few modifications be made to it. Americans may have been highly mobile, but rural Americans, who were the vast majority in the mid-nineteenth century United States, tended to move in chain migrations and to settle in open-country communities with kith and kin who possessed similar cultural values. The core of these communities was the persisters who remained for many years in the same place and largely gave shape to the community over time. If relationships within rural communities were not as intense as those of an isolated tribe, they still had the same dynamic and were rooted in shared cultural and religious values. I will call this less intense version of primordialism that I believe existed in much of mid-nineteenth century America "organic communities."[7]

Concerning ideology, Higham was correct in seeing this as a way of organizing society on a scale primordial relationships could not, but his view that ideology replaced crumbled cultural communities is, in the light of subsequent research, wrong. Higham attempted to discern a kind of national American ideology shared by most of the people in the country. His national ideology can now be seen as consisting of ideological

6. John Higham, "Hanging Together: Divergent Unities in American History," *Journal of American History* 61 (June 1974): 5–28. The quotations are from 7 and 10.

7. For background on geographical mobility, see Richard S. Alcorn, "Leadership and Stability in Mid-Nineteenth Century America: A Case Study of an Illinois Town," *Journal of American History* 61 (December 1974): 685–702; Don H. Doyle, *The Social Order of a Frontier Community: Jacksonville, Illinois* (Urbana: University of Illinois Press, 1978); John Mack Faragher, *Sugar Creek: Life on the Illinois Prairie* (New Haven, Conn.: Yale University Press, 1986); Hal S. Barron, "Staying Down on the Farm: Social Processes of Settled Rural Life in the Nineteenth-Century North," in *The Countryside in the Age of Capitalist Transformation,* ed. Steven Hahn and Jonathan Prude (Chapel Hill: University of North Carolina Press, 1985), 327–43.

tenets shared by the members of the Whig and later the Republican parties rather than the vast majority of the nation's population. Organic cultural communities aligned themselves with the major political party whose ideology most coincided with their cultural values: the greater the coincidence of values, the stronger the attachment to the party. In essence, organic communities tried to project their cultural beliefs to the county, state, and national levels through the agency of the political party whose ideology most closely resembled their values. The values and structure of organic communities also subtly influenced how the tenets of national party ideology were understood. In essence, local conditions and values mediated one's understanding of the political pronouncements of national leaders and party organs and of how one defined America and its meaning. Nationalism and localism were intertwined, as were the ties of the organic community and ideological commitments.[8]

If there was in reality no one American ideology, Americans still tended to believe in the existence of only one true ideology. Higham gives little attention to the concept of republicanism because he composed his organization theory before research on this subject had become fully developed. Republicanism originated in England, and during the colonial period became a widely held ideology in the American colonies. Among its central tenets were fear of government power as the enemy of liberty, virtue in the sense of putting the good of the community above one's own interests, a sense that liberty could be threatened by internal subversion as well as foreign enemies, and the need for some kind of mechanism for containing the powers that of necessity had to be given to government. Part of the power of republicanism was that it was vague enough to blend with other value systems. For instance, the concept of virtue could be given a religious element in New England, an element of disinterestedness by a gentleman class promoting deference, or an element of aggressive masculinity in the South. In other words, as James Roger Sharp has shown in his study of politics in the 1790s, different groups could come to see their combination of republican ideas and other values as the true republicanism. If Americans defined "republicanism" in different ways, they all agreed on the belief that male citizenship required a willingness to fight at the polls or on the battlefield for true republicanism. America was created in a war to stop Great Britain from destroying American republican liberties, and each male

8. For a more detailed discussion of these points, see Thomas E. Rodgers, "Northern Political Ideologies in the Civil War Era: West-Central Indiana, 1860–1866" (Ph.D. diss., Indiana University, 1991), 597–624.

heir of the Revolution was obligated to fight as the Founding Fathers had whenever those liberties were threatened.[9]

Members of the Democratic and Republican parties saw their cultural and ideological values as the embodiment of true republicanism and, consequently, as the true definition of what the American Republic was and should be. Their versions of republicanism were not the same as any form of the ideology that existed before the Revolution, but each contained enough elements of republicanism for each group to see their composite of ideas and values as republicanism. In other words, no Revolutionary-era form of republicanism determined the content of their ideology, but instead, their ideology determined how they defined "republicanism." If republicanism did not, by the mid-nineteenth century, have the power to determine beliefs, it still had great motivational power. However a man defined "republicanism," he believed that it was his duty as an American to defend the Republic from external and internal threats to what he saw as the true republicanism.[10]

9. The nature of republicanism and how much influence it had on post-Revolutionary America is a highly contested issue among historians of the Early Republic. What is suggested here is that republicanism had influence even if it was not one cohesive ideology. For background on republicanism, see James Roger Sharp, *American Politics in the Early Republic: The New Nation in Crisis* (New Haven, Conn.: Yale University Press, 1993), especially 34; Robert E. Shalhope, "Toward a Republican Synthesis: The Emergence of an Understanding of Republicanism in American Historiography," *William and Mary Quarterly*, 3rd ser., 29 (January 1972): 49–80; Robert E. Shalhope, "Republicanism and Early American Historiography," ibid., 39 (April 1982): 334–56; Lance Banning, *The Jeffersonian Persuasion: Evolution of a Party Ideology* (Ithaca, N.Y.: Cornell University Press, 1978); Lance Banning, "Jeffersonian Ideology Revisited: Liberal and Classical Ideas in the New American Republic," *William and Mary Quarterly*, 3rd ser., 43 (January 1986): 3–19; Bernard Bailyn, *The Ideological Origins of the American Revolution* (Cambridge, Mass.: Harvard University Press, 1967); Forrest McDonald, *Novus Ordo Seclorum: The Intellectual Origins of the Constitution* (Lawrence: University of Kansas Press, 1985), especially 66–96; Jean H. Baker, "From Belief into Culture: Republicanism in the Antebellum North," *American Quarterly* 37 (Fall 1985): 532–50; Rodgers, "Northern Political Ideologies," 680–86.

10. Earl Hess has made some very interesting arguments for the importance of republican ideology to the performance of Union troops. One difference between his position and mine is that he sees republican ideology as something coming down intact from the Revolution and serving as a motivation only for Union forces. I would argue that while republicanism had the power to motivate behavior, what that behavior would be was determined by a variety of political ideologies that claimed the mantle of republicanism. Thus, I would contend that not only northern soldiers, but also northern Democratic dissenters, Confederate soldiers, and Unionist dissenters in the South all saw their ideological beliefs as the true republicanism. In a sense, all major native-born factions, including African American volunteers for the Union army, were fighting for republican liberty, but they did not see how the definition of republican liberty had become contested years earlier. They chose to see the views of other groups as illegitimate and as threats to the "real" republican liberty they espoused.

The family was the basic building block of the organic community. The male head and adult sons were the family's representatives to the community: they were their family's politician, its policeman, and its soldier. Males were the only full-fledged citizens. Each male had a duty and a responsibility as a citizen and as a man to protect his community and to defend its values. This duty was carried out in a number of ways. Political participation allowed a man to help protect his community by supporting the political party whose ideology would project the community's version of true republicanism and help make it dominant in the country as a whole. Such participation involved more than just voting. Hundreds of thousands of voting-age males engaged in township, county, congressional, state, and national conventions. Millions participated in massive daylight or torchlight parades and attended endless rounds of political debates. Voters also sometimes held conventions to pass resolutions expressing the community's views on the urgent issues of the day. During the war, soldiers as well as civilians got together to pass such resolutions. After all of these pre-election activities, male voters turned out to vote in percentages far greater than those seen in twentieth-century America.[11]

A male citizen's responsibilities to the community did not end with politics. In many areas of the Midwest, South, and West men might join together to form regulator groups, vigilante organizations, or lynch mobs to protect their communities from criminal gangs, horse thieves, and other threats. Across the country, men also bore many responsibilities in helping to create local social safety nets. This was especially true in the

James McPherson has also suggested patriotism and ideology as a major stimulus for what he calls initial motivation, sustaining motivation, and combat motivation. He suggests that this may have been true for Civil War soldiers, but not necessarily true for combatants in other wars. I am not using his three-part division of motivation, but I am contending as he does that ideology was a major motivation in everything from enlistment to showing courage in battle. It should also be noted that both McPherson and Hess propose a variety of forces that reinforced courage in addition to ideology. I would not dispute that such factors as the valorous leadership by officers and the security of being in a line that Hess describes, and the form of comradeship (not the same as later unit cohesion) that McPherson describes might enhance courage, but I would contend that what I am describing here is the most important factor by far in the behavior of Civil War soldiers. Earl J. Hess, *The Union Soldier in Battle: Enduring the Ordeal of Combat* (Lawrence: University Press of Kansas, 1997), especially 73–126; McPherson, *For Cause and Comrades,* especially 46–116. Also see Earl J. Hess, *Liberty, Virtue, and Progress: Northerners and Their War for the Union,* 2nd ed. (New York: Fordham University Press, 1997), 13, 86.

11. For background, see Jean H. Baker, *Affairs of Party: The Political Culture of Northern Democrats in the Mid-Nineteenth Century* (Ithaca, N.Y.: Cornell University Press, 1983); Joel H. Silbey, *The American Political Nation, 1838–1893* (Stanford, Calif.: Stanford University Press, 1991); Rodgers, "Northern Political Ideologies," 125–72.

open-country communities across rural America in which neighbors and relatives provided an informal system of aid for the sick, injured, or misfortunate. This kind of aid could even extend beyond the neighborhood, as was evident in the Civil War when male farmers would parade into towns with wagons full of foodstuffs and firewood for the wives and children of town-based soldiers who did not have the support of rural community networks.[12]

In addition to all of these duties, male citizens had a responsibility to fight to defend the nation. Republicanism held as its highest virtue putting the good of the nation above one's own interests. To fight for one's country was not only a duty, it was also part of a man's self-definition. To fight was to show that one was a true republican. Revolutionary leaders had seen military service both as an expression of virtue and also as a way of reinforcing this virtue within the citizen. By 1861, men had come to define "republicanism" in different ways, but however they defined it, it included an imperative to be willing to fight for what one believed just as it had in earlier times. Civil War soldiers were enormously conscious of being the heirs of the Revolutionary forefathers and of needing to do their duty, just as those before them had done in the Revolution and other wars. Because ideology linked the local organic community to the larger society, fighting for the nation was to fight for one's community and one's family. A man's decision to enlist and to fight once on the battlefield was thus intertwined with his sense of manhood, his dedication to family, his loyalty to his community, his duty to country and ideological ideals, and the value he placed on his own personal liberty and rights. To not show courage in battle would be a dereliction of duty to nation and community, a betrayal of everyone one loved, and proof that one was not a man or deserving of the liberty won by one's forefathers. As Private Wilbur Fisk of Vermont put it: "Unless a man has patriotism of the most exalted kind, a high sense of duty and an undoubting faith in the righteousness of our cause to lean back upon in his hour of trial, he has a poor support."[13]

12. Paul A. Gilje, *Rioting in America* (Bloomington: Indiana University Press, 1996), especially 80–84; Rodgers, "Northern Political Ideologies," 87–90; Thomas E. Rodgers, "Hoosier Women and the Civil War Home Front," *Indiana Magazine of History* 97 (June 2001): 114.

13. Emil Rosenblatt and Ruth Rosenblatt, eds., *Hard Marching Every Day: The Civil War Letters of Private Wilbur Fisk, 1861–1865* (Lawrence: University Press of Kansas, 1992), 150. Charles Royster provides a useful discussion of how, ideally at least, the interconnection that republicanism made between the qualities of the individual and his ability to defend the Republic was seen during the American Revolution in his *A Revolutionary People at War: The Continental Army and American Character, 1775–1783* (1979; paperback ed., New York: W. W. Norton & Company, 1981), especially 28–39.

If republican manhood required a man to show courage and fight, the cultural values by which organic communities defined their form of manhood and courage varied. These alternative views of republican manhood can, I believe, be grouped into two basic categories, which are rooted in the cultural values of groups that aligned themselves with either the Republican or Democratic political parties. The ideology of the two parties reflect many of the shared values of their major constituent groups, and can thus instruct historians in how young men aligned with the two parties differed in their conceptions of republican virtue and duty and how these conceptions could become the source of their courage on the battlefield.[14]

A good example of how young men who associated with the Republican party defined their role as citizens of the Republic can be found in the correspondence of the Dooley family of Parke County, Indiana. For this family, as it was for most Republicans, the key ideological concept was character. Character was developed over time through the development of self-control. Self-control was fostered by a systematic adherence to moral absolutes, the suppression of bad emotions called passions, and the development of one's reason to guide one's life and to help control the passions. The Dooleys and many other Republicans saw the Civil

14. Rodgers, "Northern Political Ideologies," 269–487, 597–624; Rodgers, "Hoosier Women," 105–28; Randall C. Jimerson, *The Private Civil War: Popular Thought during the Sectional Conflict* (Baton Rouge: Louisiana State University Press, 1988). Reid Mitchell and Gerald Linderman have written perceptive works on Civil War soldiers, their courage, and their connections to their communities. Linderman has called courage "the cement of armies," while Mitchell has suggested that love of home was "'the cement of the armies.'" Both of these scholars deal with community and courage, and both cite numerous soldier quotations to demonstrate that such connections existed and that at least some soldiers were somewhat aware of them. Neither of them, however, make the kind of systematic connections I am attempting to make in this paper between ideology, community, and sense of manhood. It is also interesting that both scholars, but especially Linderman, suggest that an alienation between soldiers and their communities grew over time. I simply have not found such an alienation in the scores of manuscript and published collections I have studied in my research on the Civil War in Indiana and the Midwest. In Hoosierdom, soldiers were often given banquets on their return, the state had its own sanitary commission whose agents provided all kinds of services to soldiers in the field, soldiers' letters and resolutions were sought out and published in newspapers, and many male kin and neighbors looked out for the wives and children of soldiers. Gerald Linderman, *Embattled Courage: The Experience of Combat in the American Civil War* (New York: Free Press, 1987); Reid Mitchell, *The Vacant Chair: The Northern Soldier Leaves Home* (New York: Oxford University Press, 1993), quotations are from 31; Reid Mitchell, *Civil War Soldiers: Their Expectations and Their Experiences* (New York: Viking, 1988), especially 81–82; Emma Lou Thornbrough, *Indiana in the Civil War Era, 1850–1880* (Indianapolis, Ind.: Indiana Historical Bureau and Indiana Historical Society, 1965), 164–79; Rodgers, "Hoosier Women," 114–19.

War as having been created in large part by the unrestrained passions of southern men and their northern Democratic allies. True individual liberty could be obtained only through character and self-control, and the Republic would be safe from internal decay of virtue only if a large part of the American male population were persuaded to exhibit such character. As happened to so many other young Republicans, when Rufus Dooley went off to war his family barraged him with moralizing homilies. It was not enough for Rufus to show character by fighting bravely in battle; he must also show character by avoiding the vices of camp life. Courage in battle and morality in camp were simply two sides of the same coin of character. Fighting the passions within oneself—whether they be cowardice or lust—was part of the same war. The struggles to preserve self-control within oneself and to preserve the Union from southern demagogues were simply the microcosm and macrocosm of the same struggle. The way in which Rufus Dooley and thousands of others had been socialized provided them with the motivation and the courage to persevere in both aspects of this struggle to save the Union.[15]

15. Rufus Dooley Papers, M 383, Indiana Historical Society. For elaboration on these points, see Thomas E. Rodgers, "Dupes and Demagogues: Caroline Krout's Narrative of Civil War Disloyalty," *Historian* 61 (Spring 1999): 621–38; and Rodgers, "Hoosier Women," 122–25. Rufus did succumb for a time to the vice of alcohol, but exhortations from home brought him back to the straight and narrow as he, an older brother, and other members of his unit formed their own temperance society. It should be noted that not all young soldiers went directly from home to the army. Significant numbers of these footloose young men may have joined for adventure more than for patriotism, but I would contend that even though adventure, money, and other enticements might play a role in motivating enlistment for this type of young man, the things I am proposing in this paper as the motivation for enlistment and courage in battle were more important factors for the actions and behaviors of most soldiers. In addition, I think that these footloose young men were politically malleable, and that once they were in the army, the Republican-based courage and patriotism of those around them and the politicized efforts of Republican officers led many to share the kind of values of a young Republican such as Rufus Dooley. Hence, the overwhelming Republican votes of recruits from even heavily Democratic counties is explained by substantial enlistments by Republicans, lack of enlistments by staunch Democrats, and the political conversion of footloose young men. Rodgers, "Northern Political Ideologies," 102–3, 529–71; Rodgers, "Republicans and Drifters"; Rodgers, "Sacrifices on the Altar of Her Country: A Hoosier Mother [Sarah Dooley] in the Civil War" (presentation at the Indiana Historical Society Annual History Conference, Greenwood, Indiana, November 1995); Arnold Shankman, "Soldier Votes and Clement L. Vallandigham in the 1863 Ohio Gubernatorial Election," *Ohio History* 82 (Winter/Spring 1973): 88–104; Oscar O. Winther, "The Soldier Vote in the Election of 1864," *New York History* 25 (October 1944): 440–58; T. Harry Williams, "Voters in Blue: The Citizen Soldiers of the Civil War," *Mississippi Valley Historical Review* 31 (September 1944): 187–204; Frank L. Klement, *The Copperheads of the Middle West* (Chicago: University of Chicago Press, 1960), 213–20; Joseph T. Glatthaar, *The March to the Sea and Beyond: Sherman's Troops in the Savannah and Carolinas Cam-*

Democratic ideology revolved around the concepts of self-interest and will. White men were all equal to each other because all understood and acted upon their self-interest and no one—regardless of wealth, education, or piety—could do otherwise. White males also possessed the will to defend their liberty. The will to use violence to protect and preserve one's own liberty and the will to fight for the nation as a bastion of liberty were the hallmarks of anyone deserving to be a full-fledged citizen. Democrats did not see women, children, and black males as having the level of will necessary to be legitimate participants. The intense opposition of northern Democrats to African American men serving in the military was rooted not only in racism, but also in the view that it was an assault on Democratic conceptions of masculine citizenship. To show courage in battle was to demonstrate that one had the will and virtue of a true American. To not show courage was to relegate oneself to the ranks of women, children, and blacks. Thus, the socialization of men associated with the Democratic party gave them a remarkably strong impetus to show courage in battle.[16]

Democratic courage was prone to be emotional, while Republican courage was more phlegmatic. However the source and style of courage differed, the individual's imperative to perform courageously on the battlefield was inextricably intertwined with his sense of manhood and duties of citizenship. The fact that most Civil War soldiers served in units with so many family and friends increased the pressure to perform. The company was in many ways an extension of one's organic community. This fact was often symbolized in the flag presentation ceremonies in which local women presented a flag they had made to departing troops who pledged dramatically to defend the flag, the nation, and the honor of the local community. Failure by Billy Yank to perform endangered his sense of self-worth and his place within a community where he would

paigns (1983; paperback ed., Baton Rouge: Louisiana State University Press, 1995). 39–51; and the mobility studies listed in note 7.

16. For a more elaborate discussion of these points, see Thomas E. Rodgers, "Liberty, Will, and Violence: The Political Ideology of the Democrats of West-Central Indiana during the Civil War," *Indiana Magazine of History* 92 (June 1996): 133–59; Rodgers, "Northern Political Ideologies," 378–487. For background on Democrats, see John Ashworth, *'Agrarians' and 'Aristocrats': Party Political Ideology in the United States, 1837–1846* (Cambridge: Cambridge University Press, 1983); Joel Silbey, *A Respectable Minority: The Democratic Party in the Civil War Era, 1860–1868* (New York: W. W. Norton and Company, 1977). The Confederate experience is beyond the scope of this article, but in many ways it may be similar to that of Billy Yank. For instance, Charles Brooks's study of the intertwining of male identity and broader political concepts of liberty in John Bell Hood's Texas Brigade seems to parallel much of what is said here about Union soldiers. Charles E. Brooks, "The Social and Cultural Dynamics of Soldiering in Hood's Texas Brigade," *Journal of Southern History* 67 (August 2001): 535–72.

probably live or with which he would have some type of contact all of his life. It would also be a betrayal of forefathers who had defended liberty in the Revolution and the War of 1812. These forefathers had shown the kind of republican virtue that was needed to sustain the American experiment in liberty. Democrats and Republicans might disagree on how to define that virtue, but they did agree that however they defined it, they must show they possessed it and were willing to fight as valiantly as had their fathers.[17]

The fact that midwestern Democrats did not join the army in large numbers during the Civil War does not mean they were deficient in meeting their civic responsibilities. Their reluctance to join is explained, in large part, by the fact that they saw the war as promoting a Republican version of American republicanism that was quite different from their own. They preferred to fight for ideological control of the government and the nation at the ballot box before they turned their attention to the South. Democrats in Illinois and Indiana, in fact, turned out in such large numbers in 1862 that their party was able to take over the legislatures of both states. In addition, it should be noted that whenever the Republicans appeared to not allow fair contests at the ballot box, Democrats girded for war and proclaimed their need to defend liberty in words much like those of Republican soldiers going off to protect liberty by fighting the Confederacy. A good example of this is the speech given in Ohio during that state's 1863 gubernatorial election by Indiana Congressman Daniel W. Voorhees when rumors spread that the Democratic gubernatorial candidate, Clement Vallandigham, would not be allowed to assume office if he won the election. At the end of his speech Voorhees proclaimed: "Let American freemen . . . prepare for the conflict. Cowardice invites oppression. . . . I call on the Democracy of the nation . . . to rally with arms in their hands to the rescue of the principles of self government." Democrats in many parts of the Midwest had, in fact,

17. On flag presentations, see Wiley, *Billy Yank,* 28–30. For similar findings on community and the Founding Fathers, see Mitchell, *Vacant Chair,* 16–17, 25–29, 120. Mitchell has also expressed a number of interesting insights into self-control, manliness, and courage. I disagree with his tendency to see a northern manhood versus southern manhood, and his concept that passionate southern men were seen as being feminine by northern self-controlled males. There were multiple concepts of manhood in the North, even if the Republican version was predominant in the Union army. I would also contend that passionate men were not seen as feminine, but as dangerous. Their courage was seen as inferior because it lacked persistence. The opposite of a Christian man is not a Christian woman, it is a sinful male. Similarly, the opposite of a man of character is not a woman, it is a male without character. See Mitchell, *Vacant Chair,* 130; and Reid Mitchell, "Soldiering, Manhood, and Coming of Age: A Northern Volunteer," in *Divided Houses: Gender and the Civil War,* ed. Catherine Clinton and Nina Silber (New York: Oxford University Press, 1992), 46; Rodgers, "Dupes and Demagogues."

already begun to form militia-like mutual protection associations. In short, Democratic men felt compelled as citizens to prepare to fight under certain circumstances for their own version of the nation.[18]

The world in which most G.I. Joes were socialized in the 1930s and early 1940s was very different from that in which most Billy Yanks were raised in the 1850s. The mass political activities characteristic of the pre-election periods of the mid-nineteenth century were largely gone. Even participation in voting had dropped precipitously. The advent of universal female suffrage meant that males no longer were the sole representatives of family units in the public arena and that full citizenship was no longer exclusively male. The structure and nature of government were also changing. The invention of the government commission, the growth in the size and number of bureaucracies, and the growing dependence on the opinions of experts meant that more and more of the business of government was increasingly removed from the control of voters and their representatives. While neighbors and kin might still help each other out, there were now professional social workers, worker compensation programs, and numerous government welfare agencies extending from local government to the "alphabet soup" agencies of the New Deal to aid the sick, injured, and misfortunate. Except in some areas of the South, vigilantes and regulators were long gone—replaced by the institutionalized force of local and state police and J. Edgar Hoover's G-Men.[19]

18. Voorhees's speech was printed in the Sullivan, Indiana, *Democrat,* 13 October 1863. For background on Democrats avoiding enlistment and their dissent in the Midwest, see Rodgers, "Liberty, Will, and Violence"; Rodgers, "Republicans and Drifters"; Rodgers, "Northern Political Ideologies," 529–89; Frank L. Klement, *Dark Lanterns: Secret Political Societies, Conspiracies, and Treason Trials in the Civil War* (Baton Rouge: Louisiana State University Press, 1984); G. R. Tredway, *Democratic Opposition to the Lincoln Administration in Indiana, Indiana Historical Collections,* vol. 48 (Indianapolis: Indiana Historical Bureau, 1973).

19. For background on the developments noted here, see Robert H. Bremner, *From the Depths: The Discovery of Poverty in the United States* (New York: New York University Press, 1956); Michael B. Katz, *In the Shadow of the Poorhouse: A Social History of Welfare in America* (New York: Basic Books, 1986); Clarke A. Chambers, *Seedtime of Reform: American Social Service and Social Action, 1918–1933* (1963; paperback ed., Ann Arbor: University of Michigan Press, 1967); Michael E. McGerr, *The Decline of Popular Politics: The American North, 1865–1928* (New York: Oxford University Press, 1986); Glenn Porter, *The Rise of Big Business, 1860–1910,* 2nd ed. (Arlington Heights, Ill.: Harlan Davidson, 1992); Robert H. Wiebe, *The Search for Order, 1877–1920* (New York: Hill and Wang, 1967); Robert H. Wiebe, *Self-Rule: A Cultural History of American Democracy* (Chicago: University of Chicago Press, 1995); Alfred D. Chandler, Jr., *The Visible Hand: The Managerial Revolution in American Business* (Cambridge, Mass.: Harvard University Press, 1977); Guy Alchon, *The Invisible Hand of Planning: Capitalism, Social Science, and the State in the 1920s* (Princeton, N.J.: Princeton University Press, 1985).

With all of these changes, American society had come to be ordered by a new form of social organization that John Higham calls "technical unity." This new way of organizing society was an outgrowth of the Industrial Revolution and the large regimented, bureaucratic institutions it spawned. Higham defines this new organizational form as "a reordering of human relations by rational procedures designed to maximize efficiency." He also suggests: "Technical unity connects people by occupational function rather than ideological faith. It rests on specialized knowledge rather than general beliefs." Under technical unity, an American became a "participant," a kind of cog in the machine. According to Higham, this "participant" American valued his inclusive niche within the machine of society, while the "autonomous" American of the nineteenth century valued his freedom from restraint.[20]

Insights into the change from autonomous individual to participant individual can be found in the areas of business and the professions. In 1850, businessmen were evaluated largely on the basis of individual character. Personal moral qualities and the ability to perform a task were seen as being interlocked for the businessman, just as personal virtue and the ability to fight were for Civil War soldiers. These businessmen were entrepreneurs who created their businesses from scratch. Their businesses were rooted in and served a particular community. As the community grew, so did their businesses. In 1930, a corporate businessman was evaluated primarily on the basis of his expertise—his education, his professional certifications, his experience. Such a businessman often defined himself and his sense of self-worth in terms of his career and the expertise that made it possible. In fact, choosing a career became an important rite of passage for many Americans. They filled a niche within a preexisting, impersonal, national or international corporate structure that often moved them from place to place around the country. Their loyalty was to a company and to professional peers, not to a local community. Character, personal moral qualities, and one's role in one's community were no longer central to how one was seen or how one saw oneself.[21]

Conceptions of poverty show a parallel transition. In 1850, personal poverty was most often seen as the result of poor individual character, and poverty as a social problem was simply the sum total of individuals of poor character. Social problems were to be solved by the conversion

20. Higham, "Hanging Together," especially 19–28.
21. Burton J. Bledstein, *The Culture of Professionalism: The Middle Class and the Development of Higher Education in America* (New York: W. W. Norton and Co., 1976); Irvin G. Wyllie, *The Self-Made Man in America: The Myth of Rags to Riches* (New York: Free Press, 1954); Olivier Zunz, *Making America Corporate, 1870–1920* (Chicago: University of Chicago Press, 1990), especially 37–66.

of individuals to proper values and a work ethic. Just as the strength of the Republic was dependent on the virtue and will of its citizens, so, too, was putting an end to poverty and other social problems dependent on each individual doing his part. In 1930, many Americans thought that a person's poverty was the result of economic conditions and governmental policies that were beyond the individual's control. Proper management of the economy by experts and such innovations as workers' compensation and pension laws were the keys to ending poverty and other problems.[22]

Industrialization gave rise to a consumer society, mass production, advertising, and a restructuring of education that created conditions in which America's first youth culture was created. The existence of this pervasive youth culture was another factor that made the socialization process of young men in the 1930s dramatically different from that of young men in the pre–Civil War years. In 1850, most eighteen- or nineteen year-old males were farm laborers, artisan apprentices, or clerks who were basically apprentice businessmen. Their daily lives were integrated with those of the adult males with whom they worked and trained. Passage into the adult world required not only learning skills, but also the desire to show the qualities required of the adult male citizen. As Robert and Helen Lynd demonstrated in their famous study of Muncie, Indiana, there was a dramatic transition in "Middletown" between the 1890s and 1920s. The number of young people in high school increased dramatically, and the organic relationships of society gave way among teenaged males to the demands of an emerging youth culture. In her study of the development of the youth culture in the 1920s, Paula Fass has shown how youth peers mediated the transition of young people from the organic relationships they experienced as children within the family to the impersonal bureaucratic world within which they would live as adults. Within the youth culture, males and females of high school and college age were encouraged to reject parental values and to accept a relativistic point of view towards all beliefs and morals. The socialization that young people received within the youth culture taught them to value what Fass calls plasticity, a state of flexible beliefs that allowed one to conform to the latest youth fad and later in life to go with the flow of changes in corporate policy. Youth experienced new freedoms in their private social behaviors while at the same time becoming abject conformists to the peer norm of the moment. The values and conformity of the youth culture were useful for those who entered corporate bureaucracies that, as noted above, cared about the expertise of young men and

22. David J. Rothman, *The Discovery of the Asylum: Social Order and Disorder in the New Republic* (Boston: Little, Brown and Company, 1971); Bremner, *From the Depths*; Chambers, *Seedtime of Reform*.

women but not about their private lives. It also helped young men and women fit into a society that was making an overall transition from being dominated by the absolute values of Victorianism to being dominated by the relativistic values of Modernism.[23]

The clock as well as the youth peer group helped to create the regimentation of the new technical unity America. In *Work, Culture, and Society in Industrializing America,* Herbert Gutman demonstrated how the relaxed work rhythms embedded in seasonal changes gave way to the regimentation of the clock and the machine. Daily life and customs had to be adjusted to the industrial time the new society imposed. Workers had to be on time and work at a pace set by the needs of the machine with which they worked. In isolated pockets of America the older rhythms still existed in the 1930s and 1940s, but these places were not where most Americans lived. And when one left such a pocket, one quickly found oneself encountering and having to adjust to institutions organized around the clock. Among these institutions were the military services.[24]

Even though the army had its own highly structured ways from its inception, it nevertheless reflected the social structure and mentality of the society it protected at a given time in American history. In the Civil War, for instance, most of the lower officers who dealt directly with the men were often neighbors who had been elected as officers by their men as a sign of respect for their character and standing in the community. In many ways, the army reinforced its own hierarchy of command by encompassing to some degree the social structure of organic communities. By the time of the Second World War, the American military establishment had adapted many techniques from the scientific management of big business and embraced the characteristics of the new profession-

23. Robert S. Lynd and Helen M. Lynd, *Middletown: A Study in Contemporary American Culture* (New York: Harcourt, Brace and Company, 1929); Paula S. Fass, *The Damned and the Beautiful: American Youth in the 1920's* (New York: Oxford University Press, 1977); Daniel Walker Howe, "American Victorianism as a Culture," *American Quarterly* 27 (December 1975): 507–32. In setting up a contrast between the worlds of Billy and Joe, I am painting in broad strokes. Obviously, in some isolated areas of the nation things may not have changed dramatically. However, as Stephen Ambrose has pointed out, the vast majority of infantrymen who fought in Europe were high school graduates, and, presumably, this means they had been touched by the youth culture and much else described here. Stephen E. Ambrose, *Citizen Soldiers: The U.S. Army from the Normandy Beaches to the Bulge to the Surrender of Germany, June 7, 1944–May 7, 1945* (New York: Simon and Schuster, 1997), 14. On continuity and change in rural America between the Civil War and World War II, see Hal S. Barron, *Mixed Harvest: The Second Great Transformation in the Rural North, 1870–1930* (Chapel Hill: University of North Carolina Press, 1997), especially 7–16.

24. Herbert G. Gutman, *Work, Culture, and Society in Industrializing America* (1966; reprint ed., New York: Vintage Books, 1977), 3–78.

alism. More elaborate command and control, the systematization of weaponry for the National Guard and regular army units, the establishment of war colleges and specialty schools, and aptitude testing to efficiently allocate manpower were all part of an army that was quite different from the one of the 1860s and that reflected a society designed around technical unity. In World War II, men fought under officers who were complete strangers to them. The men who became officers were selected because of their IQs and their level of education in the civilian world. Once chosen, they were made into officers by putting them through the kind of training that would make them expert military managers. The American military was profoundly influenced by civilian industrial and management developments. The army, in fact, was in many ways like a large manufacturing plant: combat soldiers were like assembly line workers; their officers were like the foremen, engineers, and efficiency experts who ran the plant; and the President and Congress were like the chief executive officer and the board of directors of the company. Unlike the soldiers in the Civil War, the vast majority of people in the armed forces in World War II were not combat personnel, and women played important roles in the military. Service was no longer inextricably tied to male character or will, but was instead defined according to one's expertise.[25]

This concept of expertise outweighing male character is illustrated by the importance given to the training experience in World War II. In memoirs of the Second World War writers often credit their training or an intense concern for their comrades as the source of their ability to

---

25. Russell F. Weigley, *The American Way of War: A History of United States Military Strategy and Policy* (1973; paperback ed., Bloomington: Indiana University Press, 1977), 167–91, 504; Russell F. Weigley, *History of the United States Army,* enlarged ed. (Bloomington: Indiana University Press, 1984), 313–50; Stephen E. Ambrose, *Upton of the Army* (Baton Rouge: Louisiana State University Press, 1992), 85–135; Theodore Wilson, "Who Fought and Why? The Assignment of American Soldiers to Combat," in *Time to Kill: The Soldier's Experience of War in the West, 1939–1945,* ed. Paul Addison and Angus Calder (London: Pimlico, 1997), 284–303, 442–46; Edward M. Coffman, *The Regulars: The American Army, 1898–1941* (Cambridge, Mass.: Belknap Press of Harvard University Press, 2004), especially 142–201; Linderman, *World Within War,* 1, 187–97; Kennett, *G.I.,* 34–39; McPherson, *Battle Cry of Freedom,* 326–31. For an excellent account of a World War II officer taking command of a unit in which he knew no one, see the memoir: Charles McDonald, *Company Commander* (1947; reprint ed., Short Hills, N.J.: Burford Books, 1999). My analogy to working in a factory appears to have been made in the minds of some fighting men. In his chapter on how men coped with combat in World War II, Linderman lists several techniques, including conceptualizing what they were doing as a job. Linderman, *World Within War,* 48–55. For a nice overview of the proportion of support to combat troops (e.g., three to one in the European Theater of Operation), see Kennett, *G.I.,* 91–109.

perform courageously in the field. For example, in his well-known memoir, *With the Old Breed,* Eugene B. Sledge wrote that his experience on Peleliu in 1944 had taught him that: "A man's ability to depend on his comrades and immediate leadership is absolutely necessary. I'm convinced that our discipline, esprit de corps, and tough training were the ingredients that equipped me to survive the ordeal physically and mentally."[26] Training and comradeship could not prepare one totally for the horrors of combat, but they did help a great deal. In contrast to G.I. Joe, Billy Yank generally said little about training and unit cohesion as sources of the ability and courage necessary to stay in battle and perform his assigned tasks. This difference did not simply reflect the fact that Billy had very little training before encountering his first combat. Instead, Billy's courage and ability to perform were rooted in the qualities of manliness and character described above.

This is not to say that conceptions of manhood did not play a role in Joe's performance. Joe was conscious of his manliness, but the manliness of the World War II era differed from the varieties of the Civil War era described above and could not play the same role in combat motivation. An insight into Joe's manliness is provided by the authors of the *American Soldier,* who contend that certain aspects of manliness and courage are the same across time. For instance, men portraying weakness and cowardice as feminine would fall into this category. G.I.s made disparaging remarks about "acting like an old maid" or having "lace on your drawers." In this they were not unlike Civil War soldiers such as Henry Matrau, who stated: "Any young man who is drafted now and forgets his manhood so far as to hire a substitute is not worthy of the name of man and ought to be put in petticoats immediately." Or in the incident witnessed by Samuel H. Mattox, two deserters were forced to wear dresses about the camp as a sign of their cowardice. However, if there were some similarities over time, the social scientists who composed the *American Soldier* also suggested that courage and manliness had changed since even the time of the First World War. They contended that in the Second World War, "The general attitude was that everyone should do what he was assigned as well as he could, but it was not considered essential that the individual 'stick his neck out.'" In other words, despite some similarities in their concepts, G.I. Joe had a much more limited view than Billy Yank of what manliness and courage required. Billy had to embody the full range of manly and courageous character and republican virtue if the Union were to be preserved. By the time of the Second World War, the nation depended upon Joe to merely do the task assigned

26. Sledge, *With the Old Breed,* 156.

to him. Joe was essentially a cog with limited responsibilities in an impersonal machine.[27]

In fact, the impersonality of the World War II military machine is reflected in the term "G.I. Joe." The term "G.I." stands for "government issue" and was taken from initials printed on government commodities. The connotation is that one is a standardized product fashioned on an assembly line. It is dehumanizing. It connotes someone who is without agency and who is passively managed from above. Instead of being part of a community of men who define their beliefs and then defend them, a G.I. Joe is someone constructed by having expertise infused into him by a basic training designed by military professionals. His performance will be rooted in his expertise and training, not in his character and responsibilities to his community.[28]

One suspects that for the American soldiers of the Second World War, unit cohesion was not only psychologically important for enduring combat, but was also socially important for men who were cogs in an

---

27. Samuel A. Stouffer et al., *The American Soldier,* vol. 2, *Combat and Its Aftermath* (Princeton, N.J.: Princeton University Press, 1949), 131–35 (the italics appear in the original); Marcia Reid-Green, ed., *Letters Home: Henry Matrau of the Iron Brigade* (Lincoln: University of Nebraska Press, 1993), 97; Samuel H. Mattox to Father and Mother, 16 January 1863, Diary and Civil War Letters of Samuel H. Mattox, typescript, Vigo County Public Library, Terre Haute, Ind. Billy Yank was, of course, also part of a large organization, and he did sometimes grouse about regimentation by calling himself a machine or slave, but the organization he was part of was not so impersonal and bureaucratic a machine as Joe's army. Not only did Billy serve oftentimes with friends and relatives from home, but he also had, as Reid Mitchell has noted, personal feelings even for senior commanders that were unlike anything one would find among World War II soldiers. These feelings extended to the commander in chief. Although not an infantryman, marine pilot Samuel Hynes captured something about service in Joe's military when he wrote of his reaction to President Franklin D. Roosevelt's death in 1945:

> I remember hearing the news . . . The President is dead, and not feeling anything. I had seen him once, in the thirties . . . . But he wasn't a person; he was an institution of government . . . . I was surprised, I think, that he had died—institutions don't die. But his death would change nothing . . . . It meant nothing to me.

No Union soldier could have spoken of Father Abraham in such a detached manner. Reid Mitchell, "The GI in Europe and the American Military Tradition," in Addison and Calder, *Time to Kill,* 308; Mitchell, *Vacant Chair,* 39–54; Mitchell, *Civil War Soldiers,* 58–59; McPherson, *For Cause and Comrades,* 46–61; William C. Davis, *Lincoln's Men: How President Lincoln Became Father to an Army and a Nation* (New York: Free Press, 1999), 226–53; Samuel Hynes, *Flights of Passage: Recollections of a World War II Aviator* (New York: Penguin Books, 1988), 187.

28. For a discussion of the term "G.I." similar to the one presented here, see Paul Fussell, *Wartime: Understanding and Behavior in the Second World War* (New York: Oxford University Press, 1989), 69–72.

impersonal machine. Men needed to bond because there was no one to care about them. When Wayne Alford of the 6th Indiana Infantry Regiment fell ill during the Civil War, the unit's doctor who cared for him was his family physician from Indiana. When his illness grew worse, his father went in person to visit his son at the front. When Leon Standifer was wounded in France in World War II, the medical personnel who treated him were all strangers. His dad did not come to the front to see him. When Standifer recovered, he went to desperate lengths to return to his buddies in his old unit rather than be reassigned to a unit of strangers. All he had in the face of an impersonal army bureaucracy and hostile enemy forces were his training and his buddies, who were, perhaps, a kind of temporary organic unity that gave the soldier something on a human scale to hold on to while serving as a cog in a gigantic, impersonal, bureaucratic machine.[29]

The differences in experiences and motivations of Civil War troops and fighting men in World War II can be brought into even sharper relief by looking at the issue of patriotism. Some Civil War soldiers had little to say about politics or patriotism in their diaries and letters, but a remarkable number did include patriotic passages, comments on government policy, and much more. Wilbur Fisk of the 2nd Vermont Infantry Regiment wrote to his hometown newspaper: "Is the great experiment which our forefathers have made, and which has been our pride and boast so long, to be a failure after all? . . . Never! . . . Never in a war before did the rank and file feel a more resolute earnestness for a just cause, and a more invincible determination to succeed." Using a common metaphor of the time, Elijah Cavins of the 14th Indiana Infantry Regiment told his wife: "If it be the will of Him who holds the destiny of this Government in His hands, that my life should be sacrificed upon the alter [sic] of my Country's liberty, so let it be." Ohio soldier Owen J. Hopkins wrote to his girlfriend: "As to Standing By the old Flag, I promise to do so until death, under penalty of Forfeiting your Friendship and esteem, as well as that of the whole world. My lot is cast with the Glorious old Army of the Union so long as it Battles for Freedom and the Right, and the only compensation I ask is a grateful country Blessed with Freedom and Individual Liberty." Hundreds of other examples of patriotic and political statements can be found in the letters and diaries of Civil War soldiers. Such words were not empty rhetoric. Civil War soldiers often backed such florid statements with actions, as is especially evident in the case of the color bearers who proudly carried the

29. Skidmore, *Alford Brothers*, 285–87, 308; Standifer, *Not in Vain*, 186–203. Kindsvatter has interpreted Standifer's actions in a way similar to those presented here. He sees his desire to return to his unit as typical of World War II soldiers. Kindsvatter, *American Soldiers*, 132–33.

regimental flag into battle even though it made them prime targets of the enemy.[30]

One does not find this kind of overt patriotism very often in the letters, diaries, or memoirs of soldiers in the Second World War, and there is no counterpart to the bravado of the color bearers of the Civil War. When commenting in his memoir on his motivations, Robert Kotlowitz seemed to have no clear idea of what he was fighting for. He mentions wanting to please others, his hatred as a Jew for Germans, and even a "secret touch of patriotic fervor," which, however, he does not elaborate on and which seems less important than his ethnic identity and hatred of Germans. In his detailed and highly introspective memoir, Roscoe Blunt reveals little of a patriotic nature and, in fact, recalls not knowing what he was fighting for until he became outraged at the sight of German atrocities. Robert Leckie stated in his memoir that: "Without a cause, we became sardonic. . . . We had to laugh at ourselves; else, in the midst of all this mindless, mechanical slaughter, we would have gone mad." In addition to humor, he believed "the cult of the Marine" helped keep him going. William Manchester, also a marine, noted how men sacrificed their lives in great acts of bravery during the war and that he thought he fought for a just cause. Ultimately, however, he sees love for his buddies—unit cohesion—as the main factor in why men fought and died. Even the memoir of Audie Murphy, America's most decorated World War II soldier, contains no stirring patriotic passages. Murphy and those around him complain and whine incessantly and seem virtually devoid of any expressed patriotism. Murphy even notes that: "Monotony often achieves more than either pleading or patriotism. . . . to get out of our holes and relieve irritation by a slash at the enemy, we volunteer for dangerous patrols."[31]

The lack of patriotic statements by fighting men of the Second World War is widely recognized by scholars who have studied them. As Lee Kennett puts it: "Patriotic themes and talk of war aims are the excep-

30. Rosenblatt and Rosenblatt, eds., *Hard Marching Every Day,* 207; Barbara A. Smith, *The Civil War Letters of Col. Elijah H. C. Cavins, 14th Indiana* (Utica, Ky.: McDowell Publications, 1981), 24 (The original manuscript of this letter of 13 October 1861 is in the Elijah H. C. Cavins Papers, M 42, Indiana Historical Society); Otto F. Bond, ed., *Under the Flag of the Nation: Diaries and Letters of Owen Johnston Hopkins, a Yankee Volunteer in the Civil War* (Columbus: Ohio State University Press, 1998), 82. On color bearers, see Wiley, *Billy Yank,* 93–94. For especially good insights into the patriotism of Civil War soldiers, see McPherson, *For Cause and Comrades,* especially 98–116.

31. Kotlowitz, *Before Their Time,* especially 3–4, 17; Leckie, *Helmet for my Pillow,* 30; William Manchester, *Goodbye, Darkness: A Memoir of the Pacific War* (New York: Laurel, 1980), 289–92, 451; Audie Murphy, *To Hell and Back* (1949; reprint paperback ed., New York: An Owl Book, 2002), 125.

tions in G.I. letters. . . . Nor do there seem to have been many impassioned bull sessions on moral and patriotic themes. . . . And when Hollywood produced war films in which the heroes postured or declaimed, the G.I. audience would laugh and jeer." Still, Kennett and most other scholars claim the soldiers were patriotic. Stephen E. Ambrose, whose work encompasses both wars, insists that G.I.s were just as patriotic as Billy Yank but that the Joes just did not feel comfortable with patriotic talk. Reid Mitchell, an outstanding Civil War historian who has expanded his research to World War II, takes a similar position, contending that tough guy movies of the 1930s and early 1940s made men reluctant to express florid patriotism. Paul Fussell, a veteran as well as a historian of the war, contends that overt patriotic expressions simply were not popular after the horrors of World War I. Recently, Peter S. Kindsvatter has made a creative expansion on the view of the G.I. as patriotic but not prone to express it. He contends that if one compares the performance of soldiers in World War II with the breakdown of patriotic motivation among troops fighting in Vietnam after the Tet Offensive in 1968, one can see that patriotism, even if unexpressed, did exist and was a key motivational force in World War II.[32]

A major problem with the interpretation that G.I.s were just as patriotic as soldiers of earlier wars, including the Civil War, but were not capable of expressing it, is the World War II soldier's ability and willingness to engage in passionate and even florid praise of buddies and their sacrifices and acts of bravado for comrades. At the end of the war, Roscoe Blunt found himself deeply troubled by the prospect of being separated from his buddies. "These wartime relationships," he stated, "were akin to family love and were nurtured by months of shared deprivation and hunger, of sensitivity-shattering horror, crippling exhaustion and personal triumph." Perhaps the most emotional and heroic part of Audie Murphy's memoir is the passage concerning the death of his friend Brandon at the hands of Germans pretending to surrender. At first Murphy is in a state of denial: "For the first time in the war, I refuse to accept facts. . . . He can't be dead, because if he is dead, the war is all wrong; and Brandon has died in vain." When Murphy comes to his senses he turns into a one-man killing machine: "A demon seems to have entered my body. . . . I do not think of the danger to myself. My whole being is con-

32. Kennett, *G.I.,* 89; Ambrose, *Citizen Soldiers,* 13–14; Mitchell, "GI in Europe," 311; Kindsvatter, *American Soldiers,* 136–54; Fussell, *Wartime,* 129–43. A number of historians seem to take positions similar to that of Fussell. For examples, see Ellis, *On the Front Lines,* 282–320; Linderman, *World Within War,* 48–89, 263–99; Michael D. Doubler, *Closing with the Enemy: How GIs Fought the War in Europe, 1944–1945* (Lawrence: University Press of Kansas, 1994), 259–60. The social scientists who wrote *The American Soldier* also came to similar conclusions. Stouffer et al., *American Soldier,* 2:149–51.

centrated on killing." In analyzing the intensity of the World War II buddy bond, J. Glenn Gray developed the concept of "communal ecstasy" to suggest that dying for comrades in combat has similarities to true believers willing to be martyrs for their beliefs.[33]

Another problem with the unexpressed patriotism view is that it appears that those troops that were most aggressive and gung ho—the closest to Civil War units in motivation—were those that were best trained. One can see in Ambrose's *Band of Brothers* and Sledge's *With the Old Breed* that army airborne and marine rifle companies, which had more training, were instilled with a sense of superiority, had exceptional unit cohesion, and performed very well and very aggressively. Conversely, in the memoir of Charles Felix, a replacement sent to join a regular army unit, one does not find either impressive actions or motivations. As a replacement he is thrown in among strangers. In terms of training, Felix was an artillery replacement who was placed with an infantry unit even though he had no real training for such a job. Felix's attitude and that of many around him is quite similar to what Kindsvatter describes for the unpatriotic warriors late in the Vietnam War, including Felix's outrage over a gung ho lieutenant bent on doing his duty even if it is dangerous to Felix and the unit with which he is temporarily serving. Other units which did not have the extensive training and ego boosting of the marines and airborne seem to fall in between the extremes of the replacement and the elite troops. The overall impression is that the level of the motivation and performance of World War II troops was manufactured by the military and enhanced by comradeship, not created largely by patriotic fervor or the social and political milieu from which the men came.[34]

If the difference in the ability to express patriotism is not a convincing answer, how then does one explain why Billy Yank seems to have been so much more overtly and intensely patriotic than G.I. Joe? Two possible explanations seem to flow logically from the foregoing analysis. Billy Yank was raised in a world of moral absolutes, of organic relationships that entailed strong emotional ties, and strong ideological beliefs that intertwined with his sense of self. As we have seen, Billy's organic and ideological ties incorporated his company, his community, and his nation. Intense patriotic statements and an oft-stated willingness to die for his

---

33. Murphy, *To Hell and Back*, 177; Blunt, *Foot Soldier*, 259; J. Glenn Gray, *The Warriors: Reflections on Men in Battle* (1959; reprint ed., Lincoln: University of Nebraska Press, 1970), 44–51. For a thorough and insightful discussion of the importance World War II soldiers placed on comradeship, see Linderman, *World Within War*, 263–99.

34. Charles Reis Felix, *Crossing the Sauer: A Memoir of World War II* (Springfield, N.J.: Burford Books, 2002). For examples of the in-between units, see Murphy, *To Hell and Back*; Blunt, *Foot Soldier*; and McDonald, *Company Commander*.

nation were rooted in the certainties and emotional investment of the
Union soldier's world of absolute values and organic organization and ideological commitment. If he died, he died for those he loved and to preserve
a personal liberty for his heirs that his ancestors had fought and died to
hand down to him. G.I. Joe was raised in a world of relativistic values that
made it difficult for him to have or to express the kinds of powerful, emotional patriotism possessed by Billy Yank. It is interesting, however, that
while Joe might not break into eloquent praise of his country, he could be
quite intense and emotional in praising his buddies and the brother-like
bonds that existed between the men of a small unit within which unit
cohesion had created a kind of organic social organization. It may be that
Joe's willingness to die for his buddies and to praise them in high terms
and Billy's willingness to die for and to praise the Union are similar phenomena rooted in human-scale, organic relationships.

A second and, perhaps, more important reason for rhetorical differences in Joe and Billy has to do with their respective senses of their relationship to their nation. In addition to their emotional investment in the
nation, Civil War soldiers also saw themselves in a proprietary relationship to the country and its government. America was like a family business founded by their grandfathers and expanded by their fathers; now
it was up to them to preserve it and pass it on to their sons. Male identity was intertwined with the notion of responsibility and the necessity
of action. As outlined above, the need to protect and to act, whether
through politics, regulation, or military service, was an inherent part of
nineteenth-century male self-identity and republican ideology. As pro-
prietors their job was to define and nurture the family business. Thus,
they had a greater tendency to discuss politics and make patriotic statements. With so much of their identity wrapped up in responsibility to
family, community, and nation, the idea of self-sacrifice, including dying
for the nation, came naturally. Free men must be willing to die for liberty just as the Revolutionary Fathers had done.

Soldiers of the Second World War did not grow up in a society that
allowed them to think in proprietary terms. They tended to think in the
manner of workers on the assembly line. Discussing the big picture was
something for plant managers, boards of directors, and consultants, not
for them. They had limited roles to play, and their roles and those of others were defined by their training, their expertise, and their place in the
bureaucratic hierarchy. They did not live in the kind of relatively undif-
ferentiated and male-dominated society that produced the Billy Yanks.
Billy was taught by his political culture to be a proprietor responsible for
his nation. He was taught to believe that even his own individual character or will—his personal republican virtue—was inherently important to
the survival of the nation. A free nation was nothing more than a partnership of free men. Joe was taught that only experts knew how to run

the modern bureaucratic society of the 1930s and 1940s. Freedom was now as much freedom from want created by a managed economy as it was personal autonomy. Government and the army were no longer the sum total of the military-aged population, they were impersonal, bureaucratic entities that no one individual controlled. G.I. Joe simply was not qualified to comment on politics or patriotism. The nation was not dependent on his own personal character or will. The nation simply needed him to do the job he was trained for and nothing more. His sense of manhood required only that he do his assigned job whether it was in combat or supply. To be in the front lines putting one's life on the line, in fact, was no longer a mark of full citizenship and republican manhood. Instead, it meant one's IQ was too low to qualify one for any role in the machine except cannon fodder. Indeed, it was no longer necessary to be male to play a significant role in defending the nation. With the Rosie the Riveters in the war industries and women in all kinds of military positions from cryptographers to pilots ferrying bombers to England, America was no longer a nation solely dependent on fathers and sons for its survival.

These views of Billy and Joe are compatible with Higham's view of nineteenth-century Americans as "autonomous" and those in the twentieth-century technical unity as "participants." Liberty for autonomous Billy consisted of natural rights that must be guarded lest they be lost. For participant Joe, however, liberty meant something very different. Higham defines the participant's liberty as follows: "Not the absence of legal restraint but the capacity to share as widely as possible in the common good of the whole society makes us free and equal." Billy was a proprietor, an autonomous person who saw himself and those like him as collectively the masters of their communities and their nation. The liberty they fought for was that of the free individual who controls his government. When a Civil War soldier said he was fighting for the Union or for the preservation of the government, he was also, in essence, saying that he was fighting for his own personal, autonomous liberty. Personal liberty, community, Union, and government were all intertwined, and all were supportive of the autonomy of the individual adult male.[35]

The World War II soldier was a participant in a huge impersonal bureaucratic state. He was told by his commander in chief, President Franklin D. Roosevelt, that he was fighting for the Four Freedoms. As David Kennedy has noted, the Four Freedoms must be seen in the context of the New Deal. Two of the Four Freedoms—freedom from want and freedom from fear—have to do with material security. Such freedoms would have been incomprehensible at the time of the Revolution or the Civil War because freedoms were seen as natural rights. Such natural rights could not be given by any government, but a government could

35. Higham, "Hanging Together," 25.

take them away. Freedom from want and fear assume the existence of a leviathan state that can manage resources, the economy, and, ultimately, every individual's wealth and property. The other two freedoms of the Four Freedoms are the freedom of religion and the freedom of speech. Note what is not included among the Four Freedoms: freedom of assembly, freedom of association, and, most importantly, the right to live under a government created by the people and run by the elected representatives of the people. Higham seems to suggest that the participant concept was compatible with the state envisioned by either the Progressives or Socialists. The Four Freedoms, it would seem, could exist under a variety of forms of government, including an unelected one, and do not seem to assume a nation composed of autonomous individuals with a proprietorship relationship to the state.[36]

An interesting example and commentary on participant, materialist freedom can be found in Charles Felix's memoir in a passage concerning his thoughts at a time when he believed he might be about to die during a shelling. Felix's Portuguese immigrant parents had repeatedly told him how lucky he was to be in America and how poor people, such as a cousin of his age, were in Portugal: "All my life I had heard how much better my prospects were than his [the cousin's], everything better, better education, better food, better medical care, better jobs, better opportunities, a better life. . . . What good was it to live in the land of opportunity if they killed you at twenty-one?" Felix concluded: "America offered you much but it exacted too high a price—your life. My parents had made a terrible mistake coming to America." Felix never makes mention of personal liberty as one of the benefits of living in America. His conception of America revolves around a materialistic freedom from want and an opportunity for economic prosperity. In essence, the liberty Billy Yank fought for was significantly different from G.I. Joe's Four Freedoms, and the differences between the freedoms they fought for reflect the different societies and political cultures that existed in the 1860s and the 1940s. If liberty and the general relationship of the citizen to his country differed in these eras, it makes sense to suggest that the nature of patriotism may well have changed as well. Historians have tried very hard to demonstrate that G.I. Joe was just as liberty loving and patriotic as Billy Yank by contending they simply expressed themselves differently. While this explanation may be plausible, it is not as cogent as seeing the definition and nature of liberty and patriotism as having changed over time. In dying for his country Billy achieved the highest expression of republican virtue; he had proved himself worthy of the Fathers. For Joe achieving material success in a well-managed economy was the

36. David M. Kennedy, *Freedom from Fear: The American People in Depression and War, 1929–1945* (New York: Oxford University Press, 1999), 469–70.

expression of the patriotic participant citizen. This achievement is not reached by dying for one's country.[37]

The argument presented here is exploratory in nature. Its descriptions of soldiers and of society are painted in broad strokes. Doubtless many exceptions to the generalizations here could be made and other motivational factors suggested. Whatever the caveats, however, it does appear that Billy Yank was able to perform so courageously on the battlefield with so little training largely because of the way in which he had been socialized. He had been given a sense that every American male had to have the qualities of the autonomous, free men who had founded the country. He was a proprietor who in partnership with other males was responsible for his society both at the local and national levels. His self-identity and his place within an organic community of dense relationships led him to perform in battle and, if necessary, to die for liberty because that was what any free man deserving of his liberty would do. G.I. Joe did not have such a socialization experience. He was a participant in rather than a proprietor of society, who did not live in the dense organic relationships of Billy Yank. He needed basic training and the emotional bonding of unit cohesion to perform. Unit cohesion served as a substitute for the male identities and organic social structure of Billy's era, and allowed Joe to perform on the battlefield.

If these generalizations about Billy and Joe are accurate, they raise important questions for historians studying not only military history but also American society as a whole. For military historians this study suggests that extrapolating findings and ideas from the detailed studies of World War II soldiers must be done with caution because they can be misleading. Soldiers in different eras are not so alike as they might at first appear. For all American historians it suggests that concepts such as liberty and patriotism are quite malleable and change over time. Thus, comparing the courage of one generation to another is a rather tricky task because different generations may represent differing conceptions of bravery and patriotism. Finally, this study suggests that the organization of the social structure and the political system can influence how a citizen understands his relationship and obligations to society in very subtle ways that historians might not fully understand unless comparisons of different periods of American history are made. Urbanization, industrialization, and technological innovations represent just some of the obvious changes that took place between the Civil War and World War II. However, many other less obvious changes also took place between the America of 1861 and that of 1941. These more subtle changes can be more fully understood in a cross-comparative study such as the one presented here.

37. Felix, *Crossing the Sauer*, 52–53.

Captive Historians, Captivated Audience: The German Military History Program, 1945–1961

☆

James A. Wood

Abstract

From 1945 to 1961, former German officers, working first as prisoners of war and then as civilian employees of the U.S. government, produced roughly two hundred thousand pages of manuscript histories dealing with nearly every aspect of the Nazi war effort. This essay provides a general historiographical outline of their work and comments on the motivations, aims, and opinions of the authors. Taken together, these manuscripts provide telling insight into the experiences of German officers, both during and after World War II. Motivated by a desire to protect the reputation of the Wehrmacht, their cooperation with U.S. historical efforts produced a significant, influential, and arguably self-serving view of the war.

O N 8 May 1945—VE-Day—Allied forces turned from the destruction of the Third Reich to the occupation of its ruins. With the surrender of Germany, war weary Allied soldiers became reluctant governors and resigned themselves to the monumental task that yet lay ahead. It still remained to disarm the remnants of the German Army, arrest the surviving leaders of the Third Reich, attend to the displaced masses, and begin the redeployment of forces to other theaters, with some soldiers destined for home and others for the Pacific. Under the weight of these burdens, it is not surprising that the U.S. Army in May 1945 had no plan for a major historical project involving large numbers of captured Ger-

James A. Wood is a graduate of Wilfrid Laurier University and the University of New Brunswick. He is currently a Ph.D. candidate in the Tri-University Doctoral Program in History (Laurier-Waterloo-Guelph) and a research associate at the Laurier Centre for Military Strategic and Disarmament Studies.

man commanders and senior staff officers.[1] Before the turn of 1946, however, the U.S. Army Historical Division would embark on a program that was absolutely unparalleled in the annals of military history: a fifteen-year compilation of manuscript accounts dealing with every aspect of the Nazi war effort, written by former German officers working under the auspices of the U.S. Army.

When the German Military History Program was finally brought to a close in 1961, its chief German director, former Colonel-General Franz Halder, was awarded the United States Meritorious Civilian Service Award for "a lasting contribution to the tactical and strategic thinking of the United States Armed Forces."[2] That a man who served as Chief of Staff of the German Army from 1938 to 1942 should be so honored by the United States gives some indication of the significance of this program and its accomplishments. Between July 1945 and November 1961, former German officers, working first as prisoners of war (POWs) and then as civilian employees of the United States government, turned out roughly two hundred thousand manuscript pages that are now held by the U.S. National Archives and Records Administration. While many of these manuscripts were never translated into English, a wide-ranging selection of 213 translated accounts is readily available in the twenty-four-volume *World War II German Military Studies* series, edited by Donald S. Detwiler. The reports published in this series represent some 6 percent of the total German Military Studies collection, or roughly 16 percent of the manuscripts that have been translated into English.[3]

Beyond the staggering quantity of work represented in this collection, an even better indication of its worth may be seen in the subsequent use of these manuscripts in published historical accounts, such as the official history of the United States Army in World War II series. Every volume of the army "green series" dealing with American combat operations against the Wehrmacht (German Armed Forces) has made extensive use of these manuscripts, typically ranking them just behind captured documentary evidence in terms of their contribution to the reconstruction of events on the enemy side of the battlefield.[4] Other historical accounts have also made frequent reference to these manuscripts, beginning with popular and academic works published shortly after the end of the war and continuing to the present day. Titles ranging

1. Editor's Introduction, p. 3, to Donald S. Detwiler, ed., Charles B. Burdick, and Jürgen Rohwer, assoc. eds., *World War II German Military Studies,* vol. 1 (New York: Garland, 1979) (henceforth *WW2GMS*).

2. Ibid., 2.

3. Ibid., 3.

4. Every volume of the official history series includes a note on sources that recognizes the contribution of the German Military Studies manuscripts and describes briefly how they were used by the author.

from Cornelius Ryan's *The Longest Day* to *Decision in Normandy* by Carlo D'Este, *Brute Force* by John Ellis, and *Citizen Soldiers* by Stephen E. Ambrose, have all made use of these manuscripts in various capacities.[5] Finally, throughout much of the Cold War, these works represented one of the few sources available to Western historians that provided first-hand accounts of the war on the Eastern Front and thereby played an important role in shaping Western perceptions of the Soviet Union's Red Army in the immediate postwar era.[6]

The following essay is intended to provide a general historiographical outline of the German Military Studies manuscripts, as well as to comment on the motivations, aims, and opinions of the authors. Taken together, these reports provide telling insight into the experiences of German officers, both during and after the war. Reading them, it becomes possible to understand how German officers perceived their role in postwar Germany, and the ways in which they adapted themselves to the emerging Cold War between the United States and the Soviet Union. In 1945, it was by no means a foregone conclusion that former German officers, including many veterans of Normandy and the Ardennes, would offer even the slightest cooperation to their erstwhile enemy. The success of the U.S. Army in organizing this program therefore deserves elaboration and will here be explained in terms of the shared goals of the authors and their audience. From 1945 to 1961, the necessary motivation for former German officers to cooperate with the U.S. Army stemmed from the continuance of strongly anticommunist views among former German officers and a desire to overcome the tarnished reputation of the Wehrmacht, which the authors sought to disassociate from German leader Adolf Hitler, Nazism, and the SS. That the goal of opposing communism accorded well with American aims in Western Europe helps explain why former Wehrmacht officers were willing to cooperate with the U.S. Army. Their anticommunism, indeed, predated Hitler's rise to power in 1933 and persisted long after the passing of National Socialism. Their cooperation with the United States, in turn, facilitated their success in producing a significant, influential, and arguably self-serving view of the war.

5. Cornelius Ryan, *The Longest Day: June 6, 1944* (New York: Simon and Schuster, 1959); Carlo D'Este, *Decision in Normandy* (New York: Konecky and Konecky, 1983); John Ellis, *Brute Force: Allied Strategy and Tactics in the Second World War* (New York: Viking Press, 1990); Stephen E. Ambrose, *Citizen Soldiers: The U.S. Army from the Normandy Beaches to the Bulge to the Surrender of Germany, June 7, 1944–May 7, 1945* (New York: Simon and Schuster, 1997).

6. See Kevin Soutor, "To Stem the Red Tide," *Journal of Military History* 57 (October 1993): 653–58, for an in-depth study of how these manuscripts influenced American defense doctrine in Europe from 1948 to 1954.

During its early stages, the German Military History Program focused on providing narrative accounts of German operations against the U.S. Army in Western Europe. Within three years, however, the program began to shift toward studies of the German war on the Eastern Front. Brought on by increasing hostility between the United States and the Soviet Union, and intensifying after the Berlin Blockade crisis in 1948–49, this shift in emphasis resulted in a series of "lessons learned" reports written throughout the 1950s dealing with various aspects of the German war experience against the Soviets. Historical narratives of the war in the West were largely replaced during this period by an outpouring of "how to" manuals on fighting the Red Army. In order to understand the value of these works as an historical source, therefore, it must be borne in mind that throughout the program, manuscripts were written to serve the needs of the U.S. Army. As those needs changed in response to the emerging Cold War, so too did the selection of subjects. Former German officers were therefore able to justify their cooperation with a former enemy by their desire to fight the spread of Bolshevism. The manuscripts were one result of this entente and reflect the complementary goals of the German authors and their American audience.

Although the U.S. Army Historical Division determined the selection of topics, the views expressed in these manuscripts remained those of the authors. This has led to one of the more serious criticisms leveled at the German Military Studies manuscripts as an historical source:

> The work of the Historical Division also had its darker side. The seemingly apolitical, factual work fostered the myth of the professional, apolitical Wehrmacht. Finding themselves in a difficult situation, the German generals saw a chance for rehabilitation. Franz Halder, the former Chief of the General Staff and prominent survivor of the military resistance, served as the ideal "doyen" for the program, guiding it between the verdict of guilt and the verdict of professionalism. His plan was simple: to present the Army High Command as Hitler's victim, an instrument misused in the pursuit of a criminal policy. . . . The High Command and its military achievements were thus separated from the political sphere, propagating the myth of the blameless Wehrmacht and separating it from the crimes of the SS.[7]

The authors of these reports were not disinterested parties. Demonstrating the common failings of memoir accounts, including what might be described as "selective memory syndrome" among the authors, the collection as a whole is marked by the biases that one would expect from the losing side of a catastrophic war. This was particularly true in post-

---

7. Rolf-Dieter Müller and Hans-Erich Volkmann, eds., *Die Wehrmacht. Mythos und Realität* (München: R. Oldenbourg Verlag, 1999), 17 (author's translation).

war Germany, where, in 1945, the notorious "stab-in-the-back" myth of World War I had begun to re-emerge, this time asserting that the German High Command had been responsible for Germany's defeat. Through a combination of indecisiveness, cowardice, and the attempt to assassinate Hitler on 20 July 1944, the new "Hitler myth" asserted that the German officer corps had "squandered the opportunities for conquest that Hitler's military genius had provided."[8] Disarmed, imprisoned, and stripped of all influence in society, former German officers found the prevalence of this attitude among the German people profoundly disturbing, but given their current predicament, they had few avenues by which to counter the "defamation" of the Wehrmacht.[9] Cooperation with the historical efforts of the U.S. Army provided one.

By committing their views to paper, the German officer corps had the last word on the Wehrmacht's performance in World War II and used it to the best of their abilities. The resulting body of work therefore came to be characterized by the absence of war crimes (with the exception of those committed by the Red Army), an unquestioning admiration of the professional skill of the German soldier, and an explanation of the loss of the war that is almost invariably linked to Allied material strength and/or the interference of a certain Austrian corporal.

Historians who question this highly favorable image of Wehrmacht professionalism and dissociation from the crimes of the SS have therefore advised caution in the use of these manuscripts. Historian John Sloan Brown, for example, attributes much of the "current inflated image of Hitler's armies" to the uncritical use of the German Military Studies manuscripts by English-speaking authors in the immediate aftermath of World War II.[10] That being said, these manuscripts can add immeasurably to our understanding of the Second World War, provided that one is willing to consider the motivations, beliefs, and attitudes of their authors alongside the purposes of the U.S. Army in soliciting their views.

★ ★ ★ ★ ★

In 1954, the U.S. Army Historical Division in Europe published an index to the German Military Studies manuscripts.[11] This *Guide to Foreign Military Studies* organized the collection into seven categories,

---

8. Jay Lockenour, *Soldiers as Citizens: Former Wehrmacht Officers in the Federal Republic of Germany, 1945–1955* (Lincoln: University of Nebraska Press, 2001), 6, 132. See also Ian Kershaw, *The "Hitler Myth": Image and Reality in the Third Reich* (Oxford: Oxford University Press, 1989).

9. Lockenour, *Soldiers as Citizens,* 131.

10. John Sloan Brown, "Colonel Trevor N. Dupuy and the Mythos of Wehrmacht Superiority: A Reconsideration," *Military Affairs* 50 (January 1986): 16.

11. U.S. Army, Europe, Historical Division, *Guide to Foreign Military Studies, 1945–1954* (Karlsruhe: Historical Division, U.S. Army, Europe, 1954).

reflecting, in large measure, the evolution of American interest in these accounts. First in the collection, the European Theater Historical Inter-rogations, or ETHINT-Series, includes eighty interview transcripts recording the comments of high-ranking German officer POWs on a broad range of questions relating to the Nazi war effort. While these interviews were being conducted, other German officers held prisoner by the U.S. Army were asked to provide written responses to questions posed by American historians. In 1946, these responses were designated the A- and B-Series manuscripts. The majority of these works provide narrative accounts of German operations against American forces in Western Europe. A fourth group of manuscripts, the D-Series, was begun in late 1946 and deals mostly with German operations in other theaters, such as the Mediterranean and the Eastern Front. After the summer of 1947, the German Historical Program became divided into two main areas of concentration. One field of study, represented by the C-Series, continued to provide narrative accounts in support of the official history of the United States Army in World War II. The second group included manuscripts written for the purpose of providing specialized didactic reports based on German war experience for the benefit of the U.S. Army and other federal agencies. This instructional approach was first repre-sented in the T-Series and then continued on a much larger scale in the P-Series, which was carried on until the close of the program in 1961.[12]

The origins of the ambitious German Military History Program in the summer of 1945 lay in the efforts of the U.S. Army Historical Section in Europe to collect information regarding enemy actions in that theater of the war. This information was to be used in support of the Historical Sec-tion's production of a comprehensive narrative account of the war in Europe as requested by the War Department. Knowledge of enemy oper-ations was of vital importance to this effort, and was considered particu-larly significant to any historical reconstruction of the planning and execution of German-initiated offensives, such as those at Mortain and in the Ardennes. Historical Section officials were keenly aware of the need to incorporate this information into their work in order to provide a balanced view of the battlefield and a more complete history of the war in general.[13]

While there was much interest in finding out what, exactly, had hap-pened on "the enemy side of the hill," many in the Historical Section were not inclined toward the idea of asking the Germans themselves. In his memoirs, the former chief of the Historical Section, S. L. A. Marshall,

---

12. A complete listing of the German Military Studies manuscripts held in the U.S. National Archives and Records Administration (NARA), College Park, Maryland, together with an author index, is reproduced in volume 1 of *WW2GMS*.

13. Kenneth W. Hechler, "The Enemy Side of the Hill: The 1945 Background on Interrogation of German Commanders," *WW2GMS*, 1:1.

recalled that his colleague, Colonel Dr. Hugh M. Cole, initially did not support the idea of conducting historical interviews with German prisoners of war. "Doc Cole flatly opposed me on this," Marshall wrote, "it was our one big disagreement. He accepted the reasoning and the theory. His objection was on the purely practical grounds that our work was already overextended, and I was proposing that we practically double our research effort."[14] For Marshall, however, the potential gains to be had by such an approach were well worth the effort. As a historian assigned to cover the Pacific theater in 1943, Marshall had pioneered the Army's use of the "interview after combat" to reconstruct a battle's sequence of events.[15] He now sought to apply this same method to the German side of the battlefield. Others, however, doubted that the captive German officers would willingly cooperate with such a program, or that their testimony could be regarded as sincere and historically reliable.[16] One contemporary critic of the program nicely summarized opposition to the interview approach when he referred to a particularly cooperative German prisoner as "a filthy Nazi who cannot be trusted farther than you can throw a piano."[17]

With such opposition duly noted and ignored, Colonel Marshall went ahead with the idea and sent Major Kenneth Hechler to conduct a series of interviews at the prisoner-of-war enclosure in Bad Mondorf, Luxembourg.[18] Its prisoners included some of the highest-ranking German officers and Nazi officials to survive the war, many of whom were likely to face trial in the near future on charges of war crimes. Among the prisoners were such infamous former denizens of higher German headquarters as Reichsmarschall Hermann Göring, Grand-Admiral Karl Dönitz, Field Marshals Wilhelm Keitel and Albert Kesselring, Colonel-Generals Alfred Jodl, Joseph "Sepp" Dietrich, and Johannes Blaskowitz, along with a host of lower-ranking general officers. Ordered by Colonel Marshall to "get what you can in a week or ten days and then come back," Hechler proceeded to accumulate a mass of interview transcripts that became the founding basis of the ETHINT-Series.[19]

The first interview in this series was with General of Artillery Walter Warlimont, previously the Deputy Chief of Staff at OKW (German Armed Forces High Command) Operations Headquarters. The interview con-

14. S. L. A. Marshall, *Bringing Up the Rear: A Memoir,* ed. Cate Marshall (San Rafael, Calif.: Presidio Press, 1979), 153.
15. Stephen E. Everett, *Oral History Techniques and Procedures* (Washington: Center of Military History, United States Army, 1992), 6.
16. Hechler, "The Enemy Side of the Hill," 3.
17. Ibid., 89.
18. Marshall, *Bringing Up the Rear,* 154.
19. Hechler, "The Enemy Side of the Hill," 15.

firmed, at least for Hechler, the potential for new insights to be gained by this approach:

> My eyes widened as I saw for the first time what had taken place "on the other side of the hill." Each response opened a new vista: Hitler alone thought we would land in Normandy . . . . The other Germans thought it would be closer to [the] Pas de Calais. . . . German intelligence had penetrated our radio signals to the French resistance . . . . [Field Marshal Erwin] Rommel was not on hand on 6 June 1944 because it was his wife's birthday and he went home to Stuttgart.[20]

Not every German officer proved as cooperative as Warlimont, whose fluent English and marriage to an American predisposed him toward his captors. But further interviews continued, adding new details and filling in gaps, providing a more complete account of the overall course of the war.

Important as this information may be, any evaluation of the ETHINT transcripts as an historical source needs to take into account that the German prisoners had virtually no written documents or maps at their disposal during the interviews.[21] Despite the fact that these discussions were not seeking to elicit thoroughly researched and authoritative personal accounts, documents such as unit war diaries and maps would have been of great assistance to both the interviewers and the prisoners at Bad Mondorf. Unfortunately for the Historical Section, nearly all relevant documents were in the possession of the war crimes authorities and remained there until after the Nuremberg trials ended in September 1946. At best, the interviewer was sometimes able to provide the prisoner with a map drawn by U.S. Army intelligence officers during the war, but these often proved a poor substitute. Most of these maps had been drawn while the fighting was still in progress and as a result could provide only an estimate of German positions on the battlefield. In a few cases, ETHINT interviews showed American estimates to have been partially or completely inaccurate, such as when SS Colonel-General Dietrich pointed out that U.S. Army intelligence officers had completely misinterpreted the movements of his Sixth SS Panzer Army north of Liège during the Battle of the Bulge.[22]

The ETHINT-Series manuscripts were, therefore, only as good as the interviewees, and the accounts often produced wild inaccuracies of their own. Reichsmarschall Göring, for instance, was particularly hard-pressed to come up with accurate factual details. When asked if the German High Command had foreseen the use of Mulberry harbors during

20. Ibid., 32.
21. Ibid., 74.
22. SS Colonel-General Joseph "Sepp" Dietrich, *Sixth Panzer Army in the Ardennes,* MS# ETHINT-16, p. 8, NARA; Hechler, "The Enemy Side of the Hill," 111–12.

Categories of German Military Studies Manuscripts

ETHINT The European Theater Historical Interrogations were conducted at Bad Mondorf, Luxembourg, in the summer and fall of 1945. The series includes 80 interview transcripts. The interviews in the ETHINT-Series deal with a wide range of topics relating to the German war effort.

A The first series of written reports by German officer POWs. The A-Series includes all manuscript accounts completed and translated before mid-1946. Most consist of written responses to questionnaires submitted by the U.S. Army Historical Section, European Theater.

B When a systematic listing of studies was made in mid-1946, all manuscripts on hand but not yet translated were assigned to the B-Series. Manuscripts continued to be added to this series until July 1948. The bulk of these manuscripts consist of narrative histories of German units on the Western Front.

C The C-Series was begun in July 1948 as a continuation of the B- and D-Series. These studies were intended for use as source material for the official United States Army in World War II Series.

D The first D-Series manuscripts were written at the Garmisch prisoner-of-war enclosure between December 1946 and July 1947. Most of these studies concern German operations in the Mediterranean theater and the Soviet Union.

P This series was begun in July 1948 and includes manuscript studies dealing with subjects that were of immediate, practical use to the U.S. Army and other federal agencies. The bulk of these studies concern German operations on the Eastern Front.

T Each T-Series manuscript was completed by a committee of former German officers. The series was begun in July 1947 at the Neustadt Historical Division Interrogation Enclosure. Only 49 of the 120 team studies planned for this series were completed.

the Allied landings in Normany, he replied "Oh, sure, of course we knew that you had a lot of funny equipment which we thought you might use to build artificial ports."[23] In another instance, Hechler caught himself bickering with the Reichsmarschall over whether or not the Luftwaffe (the German Air Force) had successfully bombed the Remagen bridge after it was captured by the U.S. 9th Armored Division.[24] The argument went on for half an hour, even though Hechler knew from the reports of American engineers that attacks by German dive bombers had missed their mark.[25]

The results of this first round of interviews led ultimately to the expansion of the program, but time constraints limited the number of interviews that could be conducted by the Historical Section before the prisoners at Bad Mondorf were transferred to Nuremberg. This problem was overcome by submitting questions to selected German officers and having them prepare written responses. In some cases, the Historical Section submitted a list of specific questions to be answered point by point, while in others, prisoners were simply asked to write on a general subject. By the end of 1945, this approach resulted in a substantial collection of work, which was later incorporated into the A- and B-Series manuscript collections.

The usefulness of these written reports won further acceptance for the program within the Historical Section. In October 1945, Colonel Cole became fully convinced of the program's merits after the submission of a lengthy report on the Ardennes offensive, which later proved useful to him in writing the U.S. Army official history of the Battle of the Bulge.[26] In the last months of 1945, both Cole and Marshall took a greater interest in the historical interrogations program, which underwent an expansion largely as a result of their patronage.[27] In January

23. Hechler, "The Enemy Side of the Hill," 51; for the twenty-one-page interview with the cited statement on pp. 2–3, see *An Interview with Reichsmarschall Hermann Goering: From the Invasion to the Ruhr; Eastern vs. Western Fronts; High Level Strategy,* MS# ETHINT-30, *WW2GMS,* vol. 2.

24. *Interview with Reichsmarschall Hermann Goering,* MS# ETHINT-30, *WW2GMS,* 2:14.

25. Hechler, "The Enemy Side of the Hill," 52; Charles B. MacDonald, *The Last Offensive,* United States Army in World War II series (Washington: Office of the Chief of Military History, United States Army, 1973), 228.

26. The report that convinced Colonel Cole was SS Generalmajor Fritz Kraemer, *Operations of the Sixth Panzer Army (1944–1945),* MS# A-924, NARA. See also Hugh M. Cole, *The Ardennes: Battle of the Bulge,* United States Army in World War II series (Washington: Office of the Chief of Military History, United States Army, 1965), 680–81.

27. Hechler, "The Enemy Side of the Hill," 168; Marshall, *Bringing Up the Rear,* 153–59.

1946, the Operational History (German) Section was established and continuation of the program authorized by the War Department.[28]

That winter, a search began for other high-ranking German prisoners of war to assist with the program, although finding an individual prisoner in the camps during this period often proved to be an exercise in frustration. No one had bothered to keep a list of high-ranking German POWs. As a result, it was usually necessary to send a list of names throughout the camps, where the prisoners were then ordered to fall out in ranks and listen while the names of wanted generals were shouted out.[29] It is not difficult to imagine the problems inherent to this approach. Sometimes, a questionnaire was circulated among the prisoners, although in this case it was necessary to emphasize that the scope of the program was limited to the Western Front and that the Historical Division was interested only in operations occurring between June 1944 and May 1945.[30]

Initially, German officers engaged in historical work were gathered and housed at a camp in Oberursel, Germany, where they shared the minimal facilities available with other prisoners of war. While the search of other prisoner-of-war camps was underway, the program continued to expand under the direction of the Historical Section, now officially redesignated the Historical Division. In June 1946, this organization gained complete control and exclusive use of a U.S. Third Army prisoner-of-war camp at Allendorf, Germany.[31] Here the prisoners were divided into working groups corresponding with American campaigns in Normandy, Northern France, the Ardennes, the Rhineland, Southern France, and Central Europe. At Allendorf, the Historical Division was able to improve working conditions and grant the prisoners certain privileges as a reward for their cooperation. It also provided the prisoners with a venue for making additional requests of their captors, and in some instances those prisoners who made the most frequent demands were referred to as "resort guests in the first, second, and third tax brackets."[32]

The manuscripts written by German officers at Bad Mondorf, Oberursel, and the Historical Division Interrogation Enclosure at Allen-

28. Ellinor F. Anspacher, Theodore W. Bauer, and Oliver J. Frederiksen, *The Army Historical Program in the European Theater and Command, 8 May 1945–31 December 1950,* Occupation Forces in Europe series (Karlsruhe: Historical Division, European Command, 1951), WW2GMS, 1:221–22.

29. Hechler, "The Enemy Side of the Hill," 159–60; Anspacher et al., *Army Historical Program,* 52.

30. Anspacher et al., *Army Historical Program,* 52.

31. Ibid., 222.

32. Alfred Toppe, *The Story of a Project: The Writing of Military History at Allendorf and Neustadt (1946–1948),* MS# C-042, WW2GMS, 1:21–23.

dorf were designated the A- and B-Series of the German Military Studies collection. The division between these two groups is largely an artificial one. In mid-1946, the first major effort to index the collection resulted in the 145 manuscripts already translated into English being designated the A-Series. This series was then closed, and all remaining untranslated accounts were assigned to the B-Series, to which new manuscripts continued to be added until July 1948. By the time it was closed, the B-Series included some 850 manuscripts, representing the longest and most varied collection in terms of both reliability and subject matter.[33]

In general, most of the manuscripts in the A- and B-Series are narrative histories of German actions on the Western Front, ranging from division to army group level, written by commanders or senior staff officers within those formations. The collection includes both operational histories and responses to specific questions by U.S. Army historians. The overwhelming majority of these manuscripts deal with German operations against American forces, and as a result, accounts of the Normandy breakout and the Ardennes campaign figure prominently in the collection. Similar to the ETHINT-Series, most A- and B-Series manuscripts were prepared without the benefit of captured maps or documents. In all cases, it is necessary to check names and dates in these manuscripts against more reliable accounts. Provided that this warning is heeded, these reports can offer excellent operational narratives and are invaluable in recreating an overall sense of the German experience on the Western Front.

The unifying element in the manuscripts on Western Europe in the ETHINT-, A- and B-Series is the prevailing sense of hopelessness experienced by those faced with overwhelming Allied air superiority. This impression is readily observed in accounts of the Normandy campaign and grows stronger as the war progresses. There is also a sense of awe present in these accounts at the material strength of the Western Allies. Some have interpreted this to mean that American, British, and Canadian soldiers were themselves reliant on unlimited quantities of arms and munitions to batter their way across Europe.[34] Judging from the manuscript accounts, it certainly seems clear that the Germans did not expect much from their enemies prior to the Allied invasion of Normandy in June 1944. Nazi propaganda had inured them to the belief that the armies of democracy would be no match for their battle-hardened

---

33. Detmar H. Finke, "The Use of Captured German and Related Records in Official Military Histories," in *Captured German and Related Records: A National Archives Conference,* ed. Robert Wolfe (Athens: Ohio University Press, 1974), 68.

34. See Max Hastings, *Overlord: D-Day and the Battle of Normandy* (New York: Simon and Schuster, 1984); and Ellis, *Brute Force,* for two well-known examples of this school of thought.

Wehrmacht. As the campaign wore on, however, these same manuscripts go on to express a grudging admiration for the Allied soldier, who often proved himself much more adept and certainly more determined than the Germans had expected. While there is ample evidence in these manuscripts that the German authors held the professionalism of their Wehrmacht in the highest regard, one does not necessarily conclude from reading these accounts that they considered their enemies to be second-rate soldiers after they fought them.[35]

This is an interesting finding, given the weight of importance that some historians of the "Wehrmacht adulation" school of history have assigned to the opinions of former German soldiers. Authors such as Trevor N. Dupuy and Martin van Creveld make frequent reference to the German Military Studies collection in their highly favourable evaluations of German combat effectiveness in World War II.[36] In defense of this point of view, however, Dupuy made the following comments regarding the opinions expressed in *Overlord* by Max Hastings: "I reject totally the argument which at least one historian has made that we won the war only because of overwhelming numerical superiority, and despite poor performance. We were good! We were not as good as the Germans, but we can be proud of American performance against the best army in the world."[37] Dupuy arrived at this conclusion in consultation with the German Military Studies manuscripts, a conclusion that generally reflects the views expressed in those accounts. Hastings, on the other hand, scarcely mentions these works at all, and instead bases much of his analysis on memoir accounts and his own interviews with German veterans conducted long after the end of the war.

Where the A- and B-Series manuscripts do follow the expected pattern is in their explanation of Germany's defeat. With the "Hitler Myth" and the reincarnated "stab-in-the-back" theory then holding sway in Germany, the onus was on German officers to absolve themselves of responsibility for losing what had begun as a highly successful war. Not surprisingly, their accounts railed against the prevailing view of the war, professing their inability to counteract Hitler's frequent and often disastrous decisions. Here particular reference is often made to the numerous

35. Generalmajor Rudolf Freiherr Von Gersdorff, *The German situation estimate and strategy during the three phases of the campaign in Normandy and Northern France to mid-September 1944,* MS# B-122, WW2GMS, 12:20, 21, 28, 32.

36. Trevor N. Dupuy, *A Genius for War: The German Army General Staff, 1807–1945* (Englewood Cliffs, N.J.: Prentice-Hall, 1977); Martin van Creveld, *Fighting Power: German and U.S. Army Performance, 1939–45* (Westport, Conn.: Greenwood Press, 1982).

37. Trevor N. Dupuy, "A Response to 'The Wehrmacht Mythos Revisited,'" *Military Affairs* 51 (October 1987): 197.

occasions when the Führer issued his infamous "stand-fast" orders. Major-General Rudolf Freiherr von Gersdorff, for example, was fairly explicit in his criticism of high-level interference with German Army operations in the West: "The useless consumption of our forces on the Invasion Front and the unbelievably high toll in men and equipment [resulted from the] stern and idiotic orders issued by our High Command to hold the line at any cost."[38] Von Gersdorff and other manuscript authors argue that Hitler, by allowing entire divisions to be encircled in "fortress" positions, and by forbidding the use of defensive withdrawals, was responsible for the devastating losses suffered at Cherbourg, at Falaise, and in the Ruhr.

One often gets the impression from these manuscripts that high-ranking German prisoners of war were taking advantage of an opportunity, offered to them by their captors, to let off steam in the wake of a crushing defeat and commit their many frustrations to paper. They decried the "defamation" of the Wehrmacht in postwar Germany and pointed to their 1934 oath of obedience to the Führer in explaining their powerlessness to counteract Hitler's foolish decisions. It is also possible to find evidence in these reports that the impending war crimes tribunals weighed heavily upon what was written in these manuscripts. For example, the clearly stated purpose of a manuscript by Lieutenant-General Hans Speidel, entitled *Beck against Hitler: The Attitude of the Army High Command Toward Hitler,* was to serve as a defense of certain German generals indicted for war crimes.[39] Major-General von Gersdorff, meanwhile, wrote a manuscript entitled *The Truth About Katyn,* refuting an untrue allegation by the Soviet delegation at Nuremberg that the Germans had massacred thousands of Poles in a wooded area near Smolensk during the early stages of the war.[40] The inescapable conclusion indicated by these reports is that even after 1945, when the magnitude of Germany's crimes should have been dawning on the authors, they steadfastly refused to examine their own roles in supporting the state that perpetrated these crimes.

The von Gersdorff account of the Katyn massacre also demonstrates that German officers engaged in the early stages of the historical program sometimes allowed their attention to drift away from the Western

38. Von Gersdorff, *German situation estimate,* MS# B-122, *WW2GMS,* 12:31.

39. Generalleutnant Dr. Hans Speidel, *Beck Against Hitler, A sworn statement regarding the Army High Command's attitude towards Adolf Hilter,* MS# A-870, 15 pp., *WW2GMS,* vol. 24.

40. In *The Truth About Katyn,* MS# A-917, *WW2GMS,* vol. 19, Generalmajor von Gersdorff recounts his experience as the German general staff officer responsible for investigating the mass murder of Polish officers in the Katyn Forest by the Soviets in April 1940.

Front. The first significant collection of manuscripts dealing with other theaters of the war is represented in the D-Series. Following the success of the A- and B-Series manuscripts, the War Department recommended that the German history program be expanded to include other fronts. On 7 December 1946 the Historical Division sent a detachment to the prisoner-of-war camp at Garmisch, Germany. There they established an outpost to handle non-European Theater, or "NONET" projects. Many of the prisoners held at Garmisch were Eastern Front veterans who had managed to avoid capture by the Red Army during the final stages of the war.[41] Between December 1946 and July 1947, these prisoners wrote a series of 317 manuscripts concerning Wehrmacht operations in theaters ranging from North Africa to the Soviet Union. Also included in this series are a number of theoretical works on naval and air warfare and the operational problems of higher headquarters. Manuscript accounts of the war in the East, OKW reactions to the Allied landings in North Africa in 1942, the organization of Naval Group West in France, and a first-hand account of the German rescue of former Italian leader Benito Mussolini in 1943 stand out as notable examples from the D-Series collection.

As a group, D-Series manuscripts were often written in haste and are described as being perhaps less reliable than other collections.[42] Many take the form of individual narratives or reports of personal experience, and the series as a whole seems to lack specific direction. As one former inmate of Allendorf has pointed out, while studies written at the main Historical Division enclosure "followed a clearly established pattern, the procedure at Garmisch was apparently determined by what the individual contributor wanted or was able to write about."[43] While these issues certainly warrant caution on the part of the historian, it must be added that there are very definite advantages to the approach taken at Garmisch, where the authors wrote on subjects chosen by themselves rather than ones assigned to them by the Historical Division. These manuscripts provide telling insights into the experience of German field commands that are simply absent in accounts written from the perspective of OKW staff officers. The D-Series reports are not written, however, from the perspective of the common soldier. Although the authors were certainly closer to events on the battlefield than their counterparts at OKW Headquarters, most were Army or Waffen-SS divisional commanders, whose average rank was major-general.

The manuscripts written at Garmisch are also significant because they mark the beginning of a turn toward German studies of the war on

---

41. Toppe, *The Story of a Project,* MS# C-042, *WW2GMS,* 1:33–34.
42. Finke, "The Use of Captured German and Related Records," 68.
43. Toppe, *The Story of a Project,* MS# C-042, *WW2GMS,* 1:33.

the Eastern Front. While earlier manuscripts in the ETHINT-, A- and B-Series tend to focus on providing historical narratives of operations in the West, the D-Series manuscript projects were "co-ordinated with War Department intelligence requirements . . . and [were] not written primarily for historical purposes."[44] After the D-Series historical narratives, the German Military Program leaned increasingly toward providing a series of "lessons learned" accounts of the war against the Soviet Union. Manuscripts in the D-Series itself may be regarded as a transitional phase of the program—they provided a useful source of intelligence on the Red Army by examining the war on the Eastern Front, though not yet with the declared intention of providing the reader with the "lessons" of the campaign.

This changing focus of the program was largely the result of worsening relations between the United States and the Soviet Union. Throughout 1946, the year leading up to the establishment of the D-Series, there was growing alarm in Washington regarding Soviet foreign policy in Eastern Europe, the Far East, and northern Iran.[45] Soviet leader Joseph Stalin was also mistakenly believed to be sponsoring leftist insurgents in the Greek civil war.[46] In response, U.S. President Harry S. Truman had begun taking an increasingly hard-line stance toward communist expansion, and although he had not yet formally announced his policy of containment, the Soviet Union was clearly emerging as a perceived threat to the Western democracies. Faced with a change in the international situation, the U.S. War Department responded by turning to German Eastern Front veterans for intelligence regarding this new enemy. It was a task for which the vehemently anticommunist former German officers considered themselves ideally suited, offering a chance for continued, albeit indirect, opposition to the Soviet Union.

In eight months of work, German prisoners at Garmisch produced ninety-five manuscripts dealing directly with combat on the Eastern Front. In many cases, these accounts are marked by the exact sorts of prejudice one would expect from committed Nazis. In *The Fighting Qualities of the Russian Soldier,* for example, Colonel-General Dr. Lothar Rendulic describes how Russian character and racial heritage were manifested on the battlefield. From his and other reports, which are heavily influenced by National Socialist ideology, the Red Army emerges as an overwhelming horde of backward peasants pressed into

44. Anspacher et al., *Army Historical Program,* 81.

45. Michael H. Hunt, *Crises in U.S. Foreign Policy: An International History Reader* (New Haven, Conn.: Yale University Press, 1996), 120–21.

46. Ibid., 121.

service, lacking initiative and offensive spirit but stubbornly tenacious when backed into a corner.[47] While Rendulic's discussion of "Slavic endurance of suffering" mixed with Mongol "inclination toward cruelty" may not be of much use to historians seeking to understand the operational history of the war in the East, such accounts speak volumes in explaining how the Germans understood the Red Army and the German veteran's hopes of safeguarding postwar Germany and Europe against the continuing menace of communism. The war was over, but former German officers had not surrendered their beliefs. It was therefore fortunate in terms of preserving their thoroughly discredited world-view that one aspect of Nazi ideology—virulent anticommunism—accorded well with contemporary American aims in Western Europe.

The last D-Series manuscripts were completed after the Garmisch and Allendorf camps were closed and the inmates transferred to a new Historical Division establishment at Neustadt, Germany. This move was carried out to allow for the continued employment of former German officers upon their impending discharges from prisoner-of-war status. On 30 June 1947, all Historical Division prisoners were granted their discharges, though 401 of the 767 were retained as either permanent or temporary staff at Neustadt.[48] Former officers of the German General Staff, as members of what was legally a "criminal organization," were retained at the camp as "civilian internees," while other writers voluntarily continued work as paid employees.[49] At Neustadt, the work begun at Allendorf and Garmisch was continued, although work on the D-Series manuscripts was now limited to the completion of unfinished accounts. Once these were complete, the series was closed. At the new camp, the Historical Division continued to assign priority to B-Series accounts dealing with campaigns on the Western Front.

Although the Western Front narratives took precedence at Neustadt, this did not fully overshadow the work begun by German Eastern Front veterans at Garmisch. After the D-Series was closed in July 1947, a new T-Series was begun in order to continue where the Garmisch work left off, producing a collection of team studies dealing with complex organizational histories and campaigns outside Western Europe. While these works continued to suffer from a lack of documentary evidence to assist the authors, the team approach taken in this series seems to have compensated for this to some degree.[50] Unfortunately, since this program required considerable coordination of working groups at a time when

---

47. Generaloberst Dr. Lothar Rendulic, *The Fighting Qualities of the Russian Soldier,* MS# D-036, *WW2GMS,* 19:2–3.
48. Anspacher et al., *Army Historical Program,* 56.
49. Toppe, *The Story of a Project,* MS# C-042, *WW2GMS,* 1:34.
50. Ibid., 1:51.

many of the prisoners had just been released from internment status, only 49 of the 120 group projects begun in the T-Series were completed. Others were simply cancelled or submitted as individual contributions to other manuscript groups.[51]

The T-Series manuscripts tend to be much more comprehensive than the works produced at Garmisch. While many of the D-Series reports are only twenty-five to fifty pages long, the T-Series includes a number of multivolume works several hundred pages in length. Although there are a few works on the North African and Italian campaigns and an organizational study of the German Army High Command, detailed narratives and technical reports from the Eastern Front clearly dominate this series. These include operational histories of the Battle of Moscow, the Citadel offensive, and the collapse of Army Group Centre. The last of these three manuscripts outlines German defense measures in the East, where it was found that infantry outposts serving as triggers for armoured counterattacks offered the best means of countering Red Army offensives.[52] The lessons-learned approach is even more readily apparent in the technical reports of this series. These include detailed descriptions of defense tactics against Soviet breakthroughs, the operations of encircled German forces, the effects of climate and terrain on combat in European Russia, and the nightmarish logistical problems encountered on the Eastern Front.

The T-Series manuscripts presented the United States with an opportunity to learn from German experience in the last war—timely advice given the continuing drift toward a new one. In March 1947, Truman formally announced his containment policy, pledging American support to "free peoples who are resisting attempted subjugation by armed minorities or by outside pressures."[53] Stalin, in response, tightened his hold over the Eastern European Communist parties and withdrew his representatives from Marshall Plan negotiations, as he believed that the United States was attempting to use its economic strength to weaken the communist position in Eastern Europe.[54] Europe was now divided into two ideological camps, and the greatest fear was that the Soviets would use force to expand their sphere of interest.

In the event of a Soviet advance into Western Europe, the authors of the T-Series reasoned that the U.S. Army would find itself in a position similar to that of the Wehrmacht during its long retreat from the Soviet

---

51. T-Series Manuscripts in "Complete Listing by George Wagner of German Military Studies," *WW2GMS*, vol. 1.

52. Generalmajor Peter von der Groeben, *The Collapse of Army Group Center*, MS# T-31, pp. 68–71, NARA.

53. Hunt, *Crises in U.S. Foreign Policy*, 156.

54. Ibid., 125.

Union. According to this less-than-optimistic scenario, the invading Red Army would overwhelmingly outnumber Allied forces in Europe, just as it had outnumbered the Wehrmacht and forced the Germans onto the defensive after 1943. In 1947, however, the U.S. Joint Chiefs of Staff entertained no illusions of being able to defeat the Red Army until after the arrival of reinforcements from across the Atlantic. Current planning held that in the event of a Soviet attack, Allied land forces would initially withdraw to Italy, the Iberian peninsula, or the British Isles while the U.S. Air Force conducted a strategic nuclear offensive against Soviet cities.[55] Perhaps dissuaded by the fact that the Wehrmacht had ultimately suffered a crushing defeat in the last war, not to mention the staggering costs of maintaining an army overseas, the U.S. Army was not prepared at this time to defend Western Europe along the lines suggested by former German officers. The U.S. rejection of a forward defense policy in Europe did not preclude the use of these lessons at the tactical level, however, resulting in a proliferation of reports commenting on all aspects of the war on the Eastern Front. Nor did it dissuade the authors in their belief that by proclaiming the soldierly virtues of the Wehrmacht in the last war, they could recover the reputation of the German Army while simultaneously guarding against the Red menace.

In the first week of August 1947, General Lucius D. Clay, the American Commander in Chief in Europe, informed the Historical Division that he could no longer justify the costs of the project and that the U.S. Army was no longer responsible for the detainment of civilian internees. Instead, former German officers held at Neustadt were to be handed over to the civilian authorities for denazification trials, which were intended to rid Germany of authoritarian influences by punishing former Nazis and removing them from all positions of civil responsibility.[56] On 15 August, Clay further ordered that the German History Program be brought to a close by 31 December 1947.

Luckily, however, the T-Series had by this time succeeded in drawing attention to German Military Studies manuscripts from outside the Historical Division. This development was fortunate given the uncertainty regarding the future of the program in 1947. Two days after Clay issued his directive, the Historical Division received a request from the Undersecretary of the War Department asking for the preparation of a study of German Army's supply organization.[57] This presented the chief

---

55. Soutor, "To Stem the Red Tide," 661–62.
56. Anspacher et al., *Army Historical Program*, 58–59.
57. Ibid., 62. This study was completed in 1951 as a twenty-eight-volume study by Generalmajor Alfred Toppe et al., *Problems of Supply in Far-Reaching Operations,* MS# T-8, NARA, and covered all aspects of supply problems arising from the unique conditions on the Eastern Front.

historian with an opportunity to explain to the Undersecretary that the continued employment of German writers by the Historical Division depended on the decision of General Clay in regards to this issue. Consequently, in a high-level conference in Washington a week later, the War Department stressed the practical importance of the program and asked that every effort be made to have it continued.[58] Three days later, Clay received the following message from the U.S. Army Chief of Staff, General of the Army Dwight D. Eisenhower:

> In the absence of adequate German records, the reports by these German commanders of their operations are proving to be not only reliable, but the only information we will ever have as to what occurred on the German side. This is our one opportunity to prevent our own military history from being one-sided.[59]

The Chief of Staff went on to request that the project be extended past the original deadline. General Clay responded by extending the program by six months, setting the final date for completion to 1 July 1948.[60]

While the first message from Eisenhower to Clay stressed the historical importance of the German Military Studies manuscripts, another cable sent by the Chief of Staff on 19 November 1947 revealed a more practical motive for continuing the program. Here Eisenhower requested a shift in the "emphasis [of] the interviews . . . from the historical coverage of German operations to the study of special subjects of interest and value to the various staff divisions of the Army and to the service schools."[61] In accordance with this request, former German officers employed by the Historical Division were directed toward the production of reports that were of immediate practical use to the U.S. Army.

Notwithstanding the support of Eisenhower and the War Department, it still remained for the Historical Division to arrive at some form of agreement with the civilian authorities regarding denazification procedures. The key here was to find some legal justification for the continued employment of a writing community populated by former Nazis. In September 1947, the discovery of a legal loophole solved these problems by allowing the Historical Division to pay former German officers as "ordinary labour" until after their denazification trials. Those trials, as it happened, were to be conducted at a special tribunal established in Neustadt, which eventually acquitted 186 of the 205 defendants.[62] Of the

58. Anspacher et al., *Army Historical Program*, 62.

59. Dwight D. Eisenhower, *The Papers of Dwight David Eisenhower, The Chief of Staff*, ed. Louis Galambos et al. (Baltimore, Md.: Johns Hopkins University Press, 1978), 9:1908 n. 1.

60. Anspacher et al., *Army Historical Program*, 64.

61. Eisenhower, *Papers of Dwight David Eisenhower*, 9:1908–9 n. 1.

62. Toppe, *The Story of a Project*, MS# C-042, *WW2GMS*, 1:58.

19 convicted, only 4 received sentences that would interfere with their work for the Historical Division. Meanwhile, the Army imposed a security classification that forbade newspapers covering the proceedings from making any reference to the Eastern Front studies being completed at Neustadt, fearing that this sort of publicity might produce an unfavourable reaction in the Soviet Union.[63]

Not surprisingly, denazification trials failed to present a serious obstacle to historical work at Neustadt. While work on the B- and T-Series manuscripts continued through 1947, planning was underway for the continuation of the program after Clay's deadline for the closure of the Neustadt camp. On 8 December, the Historical Division was authorized to receive requests from the Department of the Army and its agencies for special historical studies by former German officers, who would be contracted to prepare the required studies in their own homes.[64] On 30 June 1948, the Neustadt camp was closed and the final phase of the German History Program began.

As of 1 July 1948, a Control Group was established to administer the German side of the program. Former Colonel-General Halder, who had been the German Camp Director at Neustadt, was placed in charge of this group, which was initially located at Bad Königstein near Frankfurt and later moved to Karlsruhe, Germany. For these efforts Halder later received the United States Meritorious Civilian Service Award.[65] Widely respected within the former German officer corps, Halder was considered indispensable to the program for a number of reasons. Not only was he able to secure the cooperation of former German officers who might otherwise have hesitated to assist the Americans after their release from internment, but he was also firmly committed to the new direction taken by the program. From March 1947, and perhaps even earlier, Halder had been openly declaring his willingness "to co-operate [with the Historical Division] in order to support the occupying power, insofar as possible, in its historic mission of combatting bolshevism."[66] Under his leadership, the Control Group was assigned responsibility for translating Historical Division requests into German and then selecting the individuals best qualified to provide the answers.

After the establishment of the Halder Control Group, projects assigned to former German officers fell into two distinct categories: C-Series historical narratives and P-Series reports on subjects relevant to current military concerns. The C-Series furthered the work of the D- and B-Series by supporting the efforts of the Historical Division in the pro-

63. Anspacher et al., *Army Historical Program,* 74.
64. Ibid., 84.
65. Editor's Introduction, *WW2GMS,* 1:7.
66. Toppe, *The Story of a Project,* MS# C-042, *WW2GMS,* 1:30.

duction of the United States Army in World War II series. Works in the P-Series focused on providing detailed information and practical lessons from the Eastern Front for the intelligence and training purposes of the U.S. Army.[67] After 1 July 1948, these two collections, along with a limited number of T-Series reports, were the only manuscript serials being produced by the German Historical Program.

The C-Series represents some of the most historically reliable works produced by former German officers, as it became possible after 1948 for the Historical Division to provide the authors with better access to relevant maps and captured documents. Even at this stage, however, significant gaps existed in the available documentary evidence, due to the destruction of records in the field during the war, neglect and vandalism after VE-Day, and the loss of several important archives which fell into the hands of the Soviet Union during the final collapse of the Third Reich.[68] The C-Series eventually included 139 historical narratives from all German theaters of the war. Among these were commentaries by Kesselring on the Mediterranean war, reports by Field Marshal Gerd von Rundstedt on operations in the Soviet Union, and a series of manuscripts on the Italian campaign that were used extensively in U.S. Army official histories of operations from Sicily to the capture of Rome. The most notable achievement of the C-Series, however, was the reconstruction of the OKW War Diaries by Helmuth Greiner and Percy Schramm. These works represent a particularly valuable contribution to the historiography of the Second World War and later facilitated the publication of the definitive German edition of the OKW War Diary.[69]

Had it not been for Stalin's decision at the end of June 1948 to impose a blockade on Berlin, the C-Series might have continued for some time as the pillar of the German Historical Program. As it happened, however, beginning in the first month of the blockade the Historical Division was bombarded by requests from the Department of the Army and other federal agencies for studies of German and Soviet operations on the Eastern Front. The result was a succession of P-Series manuscripts dealing with topics from the organization of the Soviet High Command down to detailed tactical studies of combat in Russian forests and swamps. This shift toward providing reports that were of practical military value paralleled developments in the Cold War, including the adoption of a forward defense policy in Europe whereby the United States committed itself to the defense of its allies in the North Atlantic Treaty Organization (NATO).

67. Anspacher et al., *Army Historical Program,* 93.

68. Hugh M. Cole, *The Lorraine Campaign,* United States Army in World War II series (Washington: Historical Division, Department of the Army, 1950), 617.

69. Editor's Introduction, *WW2GMS,* 1:8; the OKW War Diary studies are duplicated in *WW2GMS,* vols. 7–11.

By the time the Korean War broke out in 1950, "approximately 90 percent of the efforts of the Operational History (German) Branch [was] directed toward securing tactical, strategic, and operational reports, and 10 percent was devoted to campaign histories."[70]

The resulting collection of works in the P-Series, although written with the needs of the U.S. Army in mind, made a lasting contribution to the Western historiography of the Soviet-German war. Due to the lack of information on this subject throughout much of the Cold War era, P-Series manuscripts were used extensively in two of the U.S. Army Historical Series volumes, *Moscow to Stalingrad* and *Stalingrad to Berlin,* by Earl F. Ziemke. P-Series and other manuscripts dealing with the Eastern Front have also contributed to a number of published works by Western authors, such as *Soviet Partisans in World War II* by John A. Armstrong.[71] The difficulty is that these manuscripts invariably tend to present a one-sided view of the war from the German perspective. They do, however, provide a more balanced account than the published memoirs of some former German officers, such as those by Heinz Guderian and Erich von Manstein, which have been accused of presenting a particularly warped and self-serving view of war in the East.[72] Nevertheless, given the prevailing situation in Europe, the writing of historical accounts for the U.S. Army provided former German officers with much more than an opportunity to present the U.S. Army with lessons on fighting the Soviets— it allowed the authors to present the last war as a crusade against Bolshevism rather than a ruthless war of expansion.

In many respects, P-Series reports present views similar to those encountered earlier in D- and T-Series accounts. The most striking difference between these earlier works and the P-Series manuscripts is that the latter reports adopt a decidedly instructional approach to their subjects. Titles include *German Armored Traffic Control During the Russian Campaign, Night Combat, Small Unit Actions During the German Campaign in Russia,* and *German Antiguerrilla Operations in the Balkans.* Each of these training pamphlets includes a disclaimer by the Historical Division warning its readers of the prejudicial opinions held by the authors. This warning is well warranted, as many of the racist and Social-Darwinist views presented in earlier works are reproduced, and

---

70. Anspacher et al., *Army Historical Program,* 100.

71. John Alexander Armstrong, ed., *Soviet Partisans in World War II* (Madison: University of Wisconsin Press, 1964); Earl Frederick Ziemke and Magna E. Bauer, *Moscow to Stalingrad: Decision in the East* (Washington: Center of Military History, United States Army, 1987); Earl Frederick Ziemke, *Stalingrad to Berlin: The German Defeat in the East* (Washington: Office of the Chief of Military History, United States Army, 1968).

72. David M. Glantz and Jonathan M. House, *When Titans Clashed: How the Red Army Stopped Hitler* (Lawrence: University of Kansas Press, 1995), 1.

even intensified, in the P-Series manuscripts. Hitler remains responsible for the loss of the war and the Soviet soldier still suffers from a disgraceful lack of character or other redeeming qualities. German military professionalism, as always, remains highly regarded by the authors, perhaps even more so than in earlier works due to the fact that these old German soldiers were now being approached for advice rather than explanations. Given the political emasculation of former Wehrmacht officers in postwar Germany, the writing of historical manuscripts gave voice to the continuing anticommunism of the authors. While their views were often self-serving, the authors were also motivated by a desire to continue serving the German people—even if it meant assisting their occupiers.[73] At the same time, the frequently stated racial prejudices of the authors bear witness to the persistence of an ideology that should have died with the Third Reich.

While questions regarding the historical accuracy of the German Military Studies manuscripts remain, the U.S. Army clearly listened to what these authors had to say. So, too, did the historians who wrote the official history of the United States Army in World War II and the Army Historical Series accounts of the war on the Eastern Front. In the early 1950s, nineteen German Military Studies manuscripts were published by the Department of the Army and distributed throughout U.S. Army schools and staff colleges for training purposes.[74] The U.S. Army also solicited from General Halder a 257-page analysis of the *Field Service Regulations FM 100-5 (1950)* manual, asking for possible suggestions as to how current military doctrine might be improved.[75] In the latter half of the 1950s, the German Historical Program slowly declined in importance as the proliferation of U.S. nuclear weapons in Europe rendered many lessons from the last war obsolete.[76] The program was finally terminated in 1961 after a decade and one-half of useful service. During this time, former German officers produced more than twenty-four hundred manuscript accounts. These works have influenced the historiography of the Second World War in innumerable ways, and continue to have an impact upon the writing of military history today.

The manuscripts also provide telling insight into the authors' perception of their roles, both during the war and after 1945. Given the disarmament of Germany, assisting the U.S. Army became one of the few avenues by which former German officers could continue to defend the

73. Lockenour, *Soldiers as Citizens*, 73.

74. The nineteen studies, as published by the U.S. Army, are reproduced in *WW2GMS*.

75. Generaloberst Franz Halder et al., *Analysis of U.S. Field Service Regulations*, MS# P-133, NARA.

76. Soutor, "To Stem the Red Tide," 682.

Fatherland against the menace of communism. Writing historical manuscripts also provided an opportunity for the authors to counteract the postwar "defamation" of their beloved German Army by insisting upon the professionalism of the Wehrmacht, which they believed might have won the war had it not been for Hitler's meddling. Sixty years later, the success of their efforts may be judged, at least in part, by the fact that the "Hitler Myth" of 1945 now seems entirely foreign amid the preponderance of literature reflecting the influential views of former German officers working under the auspices of the U.S. Army Historical Division. That the authors were willing to cooperate with the United States, and that their views were given voice at all, testifies to the complementary aims of both the authors and audience from the very earliest stages of the Cold War.

United States Commission on Military History

Founded in 1972, the United States Commission on Military History is the official American representative to the International Commission on Military History. It arranges for American scholars to present papers at the International Commission's annual colloquies, where representatives from more than thirty nations gather to present formal papers and to exchange ideas and information on research topics and resources.

Application for Membership
$30 per year
(additional $2.00 fee for checks drawn on a foreign bank)

NAME_____

ADDRESS _____

CITY_____ STATE _____ ZIP_____

HOME PHONE_____ EMAIL_____

Mail to: Dr. Hans Pawlisch, 121 W. Lanvale Street
Baltimore, MD 21210–2699

Victims or Victimizers? Museums, Textbooks, and the War Debate in Contemporary Japan

☆

Roger B. Jeans

Abstract

This essay addresses a widespread misperception in mainstream thinking about Japanese views of their World War II record. Popular works, such as Iris Chang's *The Rape of Nanking*, tend to speak of a monolithic Japanese view of the war today. This article, through an analysis of the exhibits and descriptive literature of Japanese "war" and "peace" museums as well as recent struggles over how to depict Japan's wartime record in school textbooks, disagrees. Rather than a unified "Japanese" view of the war, the reality is a struggle in which conservatives and right-wingers duel with moderates and leftists over the "correct history" of the war.

SCHOLARLY reviews of *The Rape of Nanking,* by the journalist and freelance writer Iris Chang, have made clear it is half-baked history.[1] The title refers to the murder and mayhem Japanese Imperial Army troops engaged in for weeks after they took the Chinese Nationalists'

---

1. See, e.g., Masahiro Yamamoto, *Nanking: Anatomy of an Atrocity* (Westport, Conn.: Praeger, 2000), and the reviews by Joshua A. Fogel, *Journal of Asian Studies* 57, no. 3 (1998): 818–20, and Mark Eykholt, *China International Review* 6, no. 1 (1999): 70–73.

Roger B. Jeans, Jr., is professor of history at Washington and Lee University, where he teaches East Asian history. He is the author of *Democracy and Socialism in Republican China: The Politics of Zhang Junmai (Carsun Chang), 1906–1941* (1997); editor of *Roads Not Taken: The Struggle of Opposition Parties in Twentieth-Century China* (1992); co-editor of *Good-Bye to Old Peking: The Wartime Letters of U.S. Marine Captain John Seymour Letcher, 1937–1939* (1998); and author of a number of articles and papers on modern East Asian history. He is currently working on a book about the relationship between the U.S. government and Chinese "third forces," 1949–54.

The Journal of Military History 69 (January 2005): 149–95 © Society for Military History ★ **149** capital in December 1937. In writing about this horrific event, Chang strives to portray it as an unexamined Asian holocaust. Unfortunately, she undermines her argument—she is not a trained historian—by neglecting the wealth of sources in English and Japanese on this event. This leads her into errors such as greatly inflating the population of Nanjing (Nanking) at that time and uncritically accepting Tokyo War Crimes Tribunal and contemporary Chinese figures for the numbers of Chinese civilians and soldiers killed. What particularly struck me about her argument was her attempt to charge all Japanese with refusing to accept the fact of the "Rape of Nanking" and her condemnation of the "persistent Japanese refusal to come to terms with its past."[2]

Having read Ian Buruma's The Wages of Guilt,[3] I suspected that, where Japanese museums and textbooks were concerned, the story might be more complicated than Chang realized. Hence, I have gathered English-language materials from two types of Japanese museums: those that ignore the cruelties Japanese inflicted on others during World War II in favor of a concentration on the Japanese nation's own sufferings— the Japanese as the real victims of the war notion—and those that have made some effort, however slight, to acknowledge the pain and death Japanese brought to other Asians as well as Western prisoners of war (POWs). Perhaps one could term the former true "war" museums and follow some Japanese in calling the latter "peace" museums—although in Japan they also are known as "aggression" museums, since they acknowledge Japan's wartime actions.[4]

In drafting this article, I have focused on the Yasukuni Shrine's war museum (the Yushukan), the Chiran Peace Museum for Kamikaze Pilots, and the recently founded Showa Hall (Showa-kan), on the one hand, and the Hiroshima Peace Memorial Museum, the Nagasaki Atomic Bomb Museum, the Osaka International Peace Center, and the Kyoto Museum for World Peace at Ritsumeikan University, on the other. In addition, I have included some discussion of the Japanese Network of Museums for Peace. Finally, I have offered a brief history of the controversy over Japanese textbooks' treatment of Japan's World War II record, with

---

2. Iris Chang, The Rape of Nanking: The Forgotten Holocaust of World War II (New York: Penguin Books, 1997), 12.

3. Ian Buruma, The Wages of Guilt: Memories of War in Germany and Japan (New York: Farrar Straus Giroux, 1994).

4. T. R. Reid, "Japan Marks Day of Defeat by Facing Up to the Truth," International Herald Tribune, 15 August 1994, 5. According to one Japan specialist, there are more than one hundred museums and exhibition sites in Japan dealing with the war, the defeat, and world peace. Kerry Smith, "The Showa Hall: Memorializing Japan's War at Home," Public Historian 24, no. 4 (2002): 35.

emphasis on the nationwide struggle in 2001 over the adoption of a new middle-school history textbook.[5]

"War" Museums

1. *Yasukuni Shrine War Museum (Yushukan)*

The Yasukuni Shrine (*Yasukuni Jinja*) occupies a twenty-four-acre compound in Tokyo. According to its English-language brochure, it was first known as the Tokyo Shokonsha. It was founded in Kudan, by command of the Meiji Emperor, in 1869, that is, when the new regime was scarcely six months old. It was designed for worship of the "divine spirits" of those who died for the Japanese empire. In 1872, the army (war) and navy ministries took control of it, but by the end of World War II in 1945, the Home Ministry (*Naimusho*) was in charge. In 1879, the Meiji Emperor gave it a new name, the Yasukuni (meaning, ironically, "peaceful country") Shrine. During the decades from the founding of the Meiji through the end of World War II, 2,500,000 spirits were enshrined, with records of their names, dates, sites of death (which must have been murky for the closing months of World War II), and native places.[6]

The shrine is very closely associated with the imperial family. In April and October, a messenger visits the shrine to read an imperial message to the deities. Both Hirohito and his Empress visited the shrine on the occasion of its centenary in October 1969, followed by the Crown Prince, Princess, and their son Hiro in December of the same year. Other evidence of imperial interest includes an autographed poem by the Meiji Emperor in the main hall; brocades given by him when he visited for the first time in January 1874; a Japanese sword he donated; and the imperial symbol, the chrysanthemum crest, inscribed on the "Divine Gate."

Each year, hundreds of thousands of people visit to pay homage to their relatives, friends, and countrymen who died in the war and now are

---

5. I have made no effort, however, to compare Japanese textbooks to those of other countries. In an e-mail to the NBR Japan Forum list dated 16 May 2000, Charles Burress of the *San Francisco Chronicle* rightly points out the necessity of such comparative studies.

6. "Yasukuni Jinja," English-language brochure, n.p., n.d.; John Nelson, "Social Memory as Ritual Practice: Commemorating Spirits of the Military Dead at Yasukuni Shinto Shrine," *Journal of Asian Studies* 62, no. 2 (2003): 450–51. There are no bodies or ashes at Yasukuni. Instead, the names are recorded in more than two thousand folders. Katherine Tolbert and Doug Struck, "At Japan's War Shrine, Wounds Unhealed," *Washington Post*, 28 July 2001, A14. A scholar of religion who has studied the shrine states 2.46 million war dead are enshrined there. Nelson, "Social Memory," 446, 450. The Home Ministry was eliminated in 1947 as part of the Occupation reforms. Jane Hunter, comp., *Concise Dictionary of Modern Japanese History* (Berkeley: University of California Press, 1984), 63.

deities at the shrine. Including other visitors, the shrine welcomes as many as eight million people each year.[7] Many of these are veterans and their relatives, who tend to visit on 15 August, the anniversary of the end of the war.[8]

In the words of a recent study, the shrine glorifies prewar and wartime State Shinto, the imperial cult, and wartime sacrifice in the name of the emperor. As a result, the shrine's museum has been described as representing the nation's spirit.[9] Hence, one would be very surprised to find any acknowledgment therein of the sufferings inflicted on others by the Japanese military during the war.

On a more personal note, I have been interested in the Yasukuni Shrine for more than twenty years. Although I was familiar with it as the final resting place for the spirits of kamikaze pilots, it was the enshrinement, in October 1978, of Tojo Hideki and Japan's other war criminals that really stimulated my interest. The shrine has remained a recurring story in the Western press ever since, thanks to the perennial issue of whether Japanese prime ministers and cabinet ministers should visit it as private citizens or as governmental officials.[10]

In April 2002, it resurfaced in the press ("The Yasukuni Dilemma Again") because of a surprise visit by Prime Minister Koizumi Junichiro. As usual, there were vociferous protests from China and Korea. There were signs the government might be weary of the issue, for the press reported it had charged an "informal advisory body" with studying plans to construct a new "place of mourning" open to both Japanese and foreigners.[11] Perhaps as a result, in August 2002, Koizumi did not visit the Yasukuni Shrine, but instead attended a small, formal ceremony with the Emperor (Akihito) outside the Imperial Palace moat.[12]

Fascinating as the shrine is as a Japanese political, military, and religious institution, this is not the place to attempt a lengthy study of it.

---

7. English-language and Japanese-language brochures, both entitled "Yasukuni Jinja," n.p., n.d.

8. For a report on their visits in 2002, see Doug Struck, "Increasingly, Japanese Look Back in Anger," *Washington Post,* 16 August 2002, A15, A17.

9. Ellen H. Hammond, "Commemoration Controversies: The War, the Peace, and Democracy in Japan," in *Living with the Bomb,* ed. Laura Hein and Mark Selden (New York: M. E. Sharpe, 1997), 111.

10. The controversy may be traced to Nakasone Yasuhiro's decision to be the first prime minister to visit the shrine (on 15 August 1985) in his official capacity. For a brief history of this controversy, see Nelson, "Social Memory," 456–58.

11. "The Yasukuni Dilemma Again," *Japan Times* (online), 26 April 2002. The newspaper opined the shrine was "clearly not an appropriate place for the prime minister of a nation that has forever renounced war to visit." On Koizumi's 2001 visit, see Tolbert and Struck, "At Japan's War Shrine," A13–14.

12. Struck, "Increasingly, Japanese Look Back in Anger," A15.

Our object is the shrine's museum, the Yushukan, and the issue of whether it recognizes, in any way, the evil done by Japan in the war.

One of the oldest museums in Japan, the Yushukan was constructed in 1882, thirteen years after the shrine itself. Two years earlier (1880), the museum had already received its name, which is based upon the classics of the Chinese Warring States period. As explained in the museum's English-language brochure, *yu* means to "study under" and *shu,* "to be under a teacher"; hence, Yushukan means "the hall to study under and commune with a noble-minded soul."[13] It holds a collection of articles that had belonged to the Yasukuni *kami* (deities) since the Meiji Restoration, as well as ancient and modern weapons. "These are displayed," according to the English-language brochure, "in reverence and honor of the kami of Yasukuni Jinja." After the museum was damaged in the 1923 earthquake, it was abandoned. In 1931, a new building was opened. With defeat in 1945, the Yushukan again was closed. Not until 1986, after repair and restoration work, was it reopened to the public.

In the early 1990s, correspondent Ian Buruma called the Yushukan a "very odd museum." Until 1992, when the Kyoto Museum for World Peace opened, he explained, it was the only museum in Japan that dealt with the entire history of World War II. The Peace Museum in Hiroshima was limited to that city's history, while the Chiran Peace Museum for Kamikaze Pilots stuck to the history of that element in the war story. The weapons displayed in front of the Yushukan, that is, on "sacred ground," and the museum's collection testify to its glorification of the war and the centrality of the emperor system.[14]

As for the contents of the museum, in the first room there is a large oil painting of Emperor Hirohito visiting the shrine in the 1930s. The myth that Japan's goal, in invading first China (July 1937) and then Southeast Asia and the Southwest Pacific region (1941 on), was to "liberate" Asia from the white man is reinforced by the display of gifts from Burma's Ne Win and Indonesia's Sukarno. The captions and text, comments Buruma, are "straight wartime propaganda." The history booklet on sale in the bookshop uses the term "Greater East Asian War," which was banned during the American Occupation of Japan (1945–52).[15] That

13. English-language brochure, "Yushukan," n.d., p. 2. For a brief and informative discussion of the museum, see Nelson, "Social Memory," 454–56.

14. Buruma, *Wages of Guilt,* 219–22; Kerry Smith, "The Showa Hall," 35. On the "sacred ground" in front of the museum, there are an old machine gun, howitzer, torpedo, and tank. Nelson, "Social Memory," 454. There is even a stone monument to the military police, the Kempeitai, which Buruma calls "the Japanese equivalent of the SS." Buruma, *Wages of Guilt,* 221.

15. On 15 December 1945, the occupation authorities banned the term "Greater East Asian War," replacing it with "Pacific War." Saburo Ienaga, *The Pacific War: World War II and the Japanese, 1931–1945* (New York: Pantheon Books, 1978), 248.

war, the booklet asserts, was not an invasion but "a holy war to liberate the world from Communism." And yet, Buruma argues, the museum is less about glorification of the war than about self-sacrifice,[16] making its message very similar to those of the Chiran kamikaze museum and the Showa Hall.

Buruma's conversation with a young priest was of a piece with the exhibits. Referring to the "Greater East Asian War," the priest argued: "We had no choice. It was purely a matter of national survival. . . . the idea was to liberate Asia. The Asian people are still grateful."[17] He then went to the heart of the Yushukan's purpose. It was not an "educational museum," he maintained, but (in Buruma's words) "a place to preserve the relics of people enshrined at Yasukuni." Nevertheless—perhaps because of all the changes in the 1990s in how Japan viewed the war (textbooks, "peace" museums, public opinion)—he conceded it should become a "proper war museum." Under Buruma's questioning, however, he backtracked and made clear the museum's status as part of a religious shrine would still trump "history":

> The thing is, as soon as you bring historians in, you run into prob-
> lems, you get distortions. As a shrine, we must think of the feelings
> of the spirits and their families. We must keep them happy. That is
> why historians would cause problems. Take the so-called war of inva-
> sion, which was actually a war of survival. We wouldn't want families
> to feel we are worshipping the spirits of men who fought a war of
> invasion.[18]

In the fall of 1986, I also visited the museum. At that time, there were no exhibits concerning Japanese wartime aggression. Nor was there an English-language brochure, although there was a detailed and well-illustrated Japanese-language one (using the term "Greater East Asian War"). Instead, the Yushukan was a true "war museum," for its exhibits glorified that conflict, albeit with that particular sense of pathos Ivan

---

Later revivals of "Greater East Asian War" worried those who opposed attempts by some Japanese to shirk Japan's war responsibility. Ienaga, for example, referred to the term as an "odious name." Ibid., 253–54. And yet, as an American historian has pointed out, the ban had an unfortunate and unforeseen consequence. Use of the term "Pacific War" in effect excluded Asians—who had suffered the most—from the very name of the conflict (as they had been barred from any significant role in the occupation). This "semantic imperialism" (as this historian calls it) helped Japan to forget what it had done to other Asians. John W. Dower, *Embracing Defeat: Japan in the Wake of World War II* (New York: W. W. Norton, 1999), 419.

16. Buruma, *Wages of Guilt*, 219–23. An American scholar terms this ethos of "self-sacrifice" a "sanctimonious perspective of victimization." Nelson, "Social Memory," 454.

17. Buruma, *Wages of Guilt*, 223–24.

18. Ibid., 224.

Morris identified years ago in his book on the "Japanese hero."[19] For example, just as at the Chiran Peace Museum for Kamikaze Pilots, outside the Yushukan there is a statue of a "mother" (unlike the Chiran one, this one includes three children).[20]

The postcards sold in the museum shop drove home that heroic portrait of war, with their pictures of a fighter aircraft, a Kaiten torpedo, a locomotive used on the Thailand-Burma Railway (a perfect opportunity for recognition of the Japanese brutality that led to the deaths of thousands of Allied POWs and conscripted Asians),[21] a tank, an artillery piece, and a model of a coastal defense warship. Nor was the display of warmaking equipment limited to World War II, for samurai swords and helmets were also to be found in the exhibits.

Wondering if anything had changed, in the fall of 2000 I wrote to the museum soliciting their latest pamphlets, and staff in the shrine office very kindly sent me English and Japanese brochures on the Yushukan. The new publications are in color, in contrast to the 1986 black-and-white version. However, the biggest change from 1986 might well be that the shrine now has a website.[22] The brochures, however, continue to use the term associated with conservatives and the right wing, the "Greater East Asian War." The new brochure also contains new illustrations, for example, a photograph of Admiral Yamamoto Isoroku (the caption calls him *mikoto*, a term applied to kami and meaning "August one"), famous as the man who planned the attack on Pearl Harbor (although he did not lead it but watched over it from his flagship in the Inland Sea); a mural depicting a kamikaze attack; a rising sun flag; and an "Oka," a rocket-propelled special-attack flying bomb, with the imperial crest (chrysanthemum) on the fuselage, flown (or guided) by a human pilot. This suicide plane was a symbol to American sailors, who dubbed it the "idiot bomb," of the profligate waste of young Japanese lives.[23]

19. Ivan Morris, *The Nobility of Failure: Tragic Heroes in the History of Japan* (New York: New American Library, 1975). During my 1986 visit to the Yushukan, I was particularly moved by the memorabilia of a kamikaze pilot who was half-Japanese and half-French. It was painful to think how intense the pressure must have been to prove himself 100 percent Japanese by volunteering to become a Special Attack pilot.

20. Japanese-language brochure, "Yasukuni Jinja," n.p., n.d.

21. In 1979, survivors of a Japanese construction unit who had worked on the railway purchased the locomotive and donated it to the shrine. It was a memento of their dedication to an arduous project, albeit one others bitterly recall as the "death railway." George Hicks, *Japan's War Memories: Amnesia or Concealment* (Aldershot, U.K.: Ashgate Publishing, 1997), 63–64.

22. Http://www.yasukuni.or.jp.

23. English-language and Japanese-language brochures, both entitled "Yushukan," n.p., n.d. The English one is paginated. For a biography of Yamamoto, see Hiroyuki Agawa, *The Reluctant Admiral: Yamamoto and the Imperial Navy* (Tokyo: Kodansha, 1982). On the Oka ("Cherry Blossom"), see Morris, *Nobility of Failure,* 276–81.

The current brochures reveal no interest in the suffering imposed upon others during Japan's fifteen-year quest for imperial glory. Instead, each exhibition room in the museum is described as a display of "articles belonging to the kami who sacrificed themselves" during some particular war or incident, including the Manchurian Incident (dated 1931–34 rather than 1931–32) and the China Incident (dated 1937–45 instead of 1937–41). While only one room is devoted to the China war, which led to the deaths of millions of Chinese (according to one estimate, three million soldiers and eighteen million civilians[24]), the war against the United States and its allies (1941–45) merits three rooms. The third room of these includes those who died while carrying out Kaiten human-torpedo operations, that is, suicide attacks. Another room focuses on those kami who sacrificed themselves before and after the "Greater East Asian War," including the "Martyrs of Showa" and those interned in Siberia (by the Soviets) and "elsewhere" (those who died in Allied prison camps following the war?). Showa was the name of Emperor Hirohito's reign (1926–89); hence, "Martyrs of Showa" probably referred to the radical nationalists who called for a "Showa Restoration" in the early and mid-1930s, that is, reforms designed to replace political parties with imperial rule. The exhibits also include the uniform and decorations of General Anami Korechika, the minister of war who wanted to continue the war even after the atomic bombs and the Soviet intervention in August 1945, a stance that undoubtedly would have brought untold numbers of Japanese as well as Allied soldiers to early graves.[25]

In August 2002, a press report made clear the museum's message had not changed. The newly renovated museum, it reported, attracted thousands of visitors on 15 August, the fifty-seventh anniversary of the

24. Hsi-sheng Ch'i, "The Military Dimension, 1942–1945," in *China's Bitter Victory: The War with Japan, 1937–1945,* ed. James C. Hsiung and Steven I. Levine (Armonk, N.Y.: M. E. Sharpe, 1992), 179. According to another historian of modern China, "Precise and reliable figures do not exist." Lloyd E. Eastman, "Nationalist China during the Sino-Japanese War, 1937–1945," in *The Cambridge History of China,* vol. 13, part 2, *Republican China, 1912–1949,* ed. John K. Fairbank and Albert Feuerwerker (Cambridge: Cambridge University Press, 1986), 547 n 1. Having written that, he goes on to provide a range of figures for Chinese deaths in the war. Ibid.

25. English-language brochure, "Yushukan," n.p., n.d. In August 1945 the army was determined, until the emperor intervened, to fight a decisive battle in Japan. Despite arguments Japan was finished, the army still had 2,250,000 men, the navy had 1,300,000, and ten thousand planes were standing by for use in kamikaze attacks. Mikiso Hane, *Modern Japan: A Historical Survey,* 2d ed. (Boulder, Colo.: Westview Press, 1992), 335–36. For a convincing account of the end of the war, based in part on cryptanalysis materials, see Richard Frank, *Downfall: The End of the Imperial Japanese Empire* (New York: Random House, 1999; Penguin Books, 2001).

end of the war. The exhibits explained how U.S. President Franklin D. Roosevelt "force[d] resource-poor Japan into war" to revive the U.S. economy (badly hurt by the depression). That, the exhibit continued, was proof of American "hostility toward Japan." The exhibits also criticized the U.S. policy of unconditional surrender at the same time as they glorified the special attack forces. Unsurprisingly, there were no references to "comfort women," Asian and Western women dragooned by the Japanese military into serving as sex slaves for Japanese troops. Nor are there any mentions of massacres or other war crimes. Young Japanese, the press report concluded, had mixed reactions to the "historical slant." Sometimes, commented one, "it was necessary to see the Japanese side as well."[26]

In late October 2002, the museum directors declined to be interviewed and refused to divulge the source or amount of the renovated museum's cost. The editor of the exhibits, a historian at the National Institute of Defense Studies, explained the museum's omission of sensitive matters such as Unit 731 (the Japanese Army organization in Manchuria that carried out biological warfare experiments on live human beings), by insisting the "debate over what really happened is still under way. Therefore, we shouldn't take this matter up in a museum."[27]

2. Showa Hall (Showa-kan)

At the same time that "peace" or "aggression" museums were appearing in various cities in Japan (see below), in August 1994 the national government allotted $120 million for a huge new war museum in Tokyo that would "portray World War II as something Japan should be proud of." At first to be called the "War Victims Peace Commemoration Prayer Hall," it was to be built near the Yasukuni Shrine and managed by the Japan Association of Bereaved Families (*Nihon Izoku-kai*).[28]

The Showa Hall is the newest Japanese museum concerned with the war, having finally opened in late March 1999. As reports in the newspaper *Asahi Shimbun* and on NHK television news made clear, however, it is not a "war museum" in the sense of exhibiting weapons and the like.[29] It

26. Struck, "Increasingly, Japanese Look Back in Anger," A15, A17.

27. Howard W. French, "At a Military Museum, the Losers Write History," *New York Times,* 30 October 2002, A4.

28. Reid, "Japan Marks Day of Defeat," 5; *Muse: Newsletter of Japanese Network of Museums for Peace* 2 (December 1999): 2. For a recent and detailed study of the museum, see Smith, "Showa Hall." As he points out, the hall is different from the Yushukan, for while the latter is private, the hall was built and is funded by the national government. Ibid., 37.

29. Earl H. Kinmouth to H-Net list for Asian History and Culture, "National War Museum," 3 April 1999.

commemorates the sufferings of Japan's civilians but does not mention the causes of the war or the atrocities committed by the Japanese military.[30]

The plan for the museum was first presented to the Ministry of Health and Welfare in 1979 by the Japan Association of Bereaved Families, but implementation was delayed because of political controversy.[31] Critics immediately protested the new museum's location near the nation's leading shrine to Japan's war dead.[32] Ironically, even the Yasukuni Shrine opposed the new museum, protesting the fact that the new museum ignored the shrine's role in commemorating the war dead. Furthermore, shrine leaders worried that since the new museum was a public one, it might have to apologize for the war, an action shrine officials opposed.[33]

In 1995, it was reported that the project, meant to commemorate the fiftieth anniversary of the end of the war, was bogged down in political controversy over the issue of what it should exhibit. A spokesman for the Ministry of Health and Welfare, which was in charge of the project, decided the museum should focus on daily wartime items, such as boots and clothes, that "are really within the sphere of our ministry's work." As an American reporter quipped, although the museum would have a great collection of boots, the history of the war is "less about Japanese soldiers' footwear than about whom they stepped on."[34]

Historians Hosoya Chihiro, Hata Ikuhiko, and Fuyuko Kamisaka, members of the commission advising the government on the museum, then all resigned, claiming the government planned to use the museum to justify Japan's road to war. It was extremely unusual for members of such bodies to quit, and their departure left the commission without any historians. For its part, the government backed away from controversy, dropping, for example, plans for an exhibition about the Nanjing Massacre.

At this point, veterans organizations counterattacked and argued critics misunderstood the museum's purpose. As the chairman of the Japan Veterans' Association put it, ignoring the nearby Yasukuni Shrine, "The original purpose of the museum was to pay tribute to the souls of the war dead, by displaying their belongings. That way, their children can live with pride." Another supporter of the new museum added that

30. Brief dispatch from Tokyo in the *Washington Post,* 29 March 1999.

31. Kinmouth, "National War Museum"; Ellen H. Hammond, "Politics of the War and Public History: Japan's Own Museum Controversy," *Bulletin of Concerned Asian Scholars* 27, no. 2 (1995): 56. See also her article "Commemoration Controversies," 100–21.

32. Nicholas D. Kristof, "Japan's Plans for a Museum on War Mired in Controversy," *New York Times,* 21 May 1995, 4.

33. Hammond, "Politics of the War," 59.

34. Kristof, "Japan's Plans," 4.

critics were trying to "hijack" the project. They wanted to use the museum to expose Japanese war atrocities, he protested, but its original aim was to be a "memorial hall for the war dead."[35]

Construction finally began in late October 1996. Funded by the national government, it was to be operated by the Japan Association of Bereaved Families and built right next door to the latter's headquarters in the Kudan Kaikan. It was reported the museum would follow the association's line, that is, the Japanese were victims, first of a Western encirclement and then of incendiary and atomic bombings. In short, the museum would focus on the sufferings of Japanese civilians and soldiers in the war.[36] Noting he was aware of the "so-called history recognition" debate concerning the museum, Kakihara Yoji, the Ministry of Health and Welfare official in charge of the project, insisted the museum had one objective and that was to "collect, preserve, and exhibit information about Japanese life during and after the war," and especially to describe the hardships experienced by families of the war dead. In 1995, a special panel had concluded that at that time it would be "too difficult to objectively exhibit facts relating to the war." When originally planned in 1979, the museum was to be for the children of soldiers who died in the war. However, the 1995 panel decided the museum should narrow its aim to describing the "painful and hard life of the Japanese, especially the families of the war dead."[37]

The opposition to the museum continued to argue, though, that it also should describe Japan's aggression against Asia and the Allies. Nishikawa Shigenori, leader of a group of thirteen organizations that had filed a lawsuit to stop the groundbreaking, declared: "This is a national museum, but it does not touch on the history of the war—it does not state that this was a war of aggression. This museum offers only a one-sided view of the war."[38] The museum was important, Ishikawa continued, because schoolchildren who would visit it would get what he termed an "unbalanced" impression of Japan's role in the war. In addition, many Japanese academics (so much for Iris Chang's criticism of "the Japanese") signed petitions castigating the museum for ignoring Japanese atrocities, such as the Nanjing Massacre.[39]

As Professor Kerry Smith of Brown University pointed out, however, the Showa Hall is not "simply a renamed War Dead Peace Memorial

35. Ibid., 4; Hammond, "Politics of the War," 59.

36. Sebastian Moffett, "Past Perfect: Calls to Rewrite Recent History Gain Strength," *Far Eastern Economic Review,* 21 November 1996, 28; Hammond, "Politics of War," 57; Mary Jordan, "Japan Moves Ahead on War Museum in Face of Criticism of Its Limits," *Washington Post,* 31 October 1996, 7.

37. Jordan, "Japan Moves Ahead," 7.

38. Ibid.

39. Ibid.

Hall." Although local chapters of the Japan Association of Bereaved Families participated in its establishment, earlier plans to include memorials to fallen soldiers, exhibits on wartime and occupation-era suffering, and discussion of the tragedy of war and the necessity of peace were scrapped, and the Showa Hall ended up focusing very narrowly on civilian experiences at home during the conflict. As Smith puts it, "I can only begin to imagine what the curators went through trying to come up with exhibits that would offend the fewest possible observers; this may be all that was left."[40] Hence, according to television and press coverage of its opening, the museum avoids any "historical view" and "simply lines up its objects by year and category."[41] This led one Japanese visitor to remark there was "nothing at the core of the exhibit."[42]

What does the museum look like to visitors? It is housed in a rather striking, modern-looking multistory building. Unlike the Osaka and Kyoto peace museums (see below), in 2000, it did not have an English guide (by 2002, one was available, although all exhibits in the hall were described only in Japanese). It did have a very colorful twelve-page Japanese version, sent to me by one of my former students, Kuwayama Miki, an exchange student from Rikkyo University. In line with its mission to concentrate on the sufferings of the Japanese, however, the brochure says nothing about the Japanese record abroad during the years from 1931 to 1945. It also has a website, but again no English version.[43] Since it is exclusively devoted to the sufferings of Japanese civilians during the war, perhaps the museum directors—unlike those of the Osaka and Kyoto peace museums—do not think it necessary to tell non-Japanese about their approach and exhibits. Or perhaps, in light of the controversy over its founding, they would prefer not to draw attention to it from abroad.

Willamette University maintains an English-language website which briefly describes the museum and also contains pictures of a number of its posters. The museum, it notes, is an interactive one located in the Kudanshita section of Tokyo and dedicated to depicting the lives of "ordinary" Japanese during the war and early postwar years. "As much as anything," the site explains, "the Showakan may want to remind us that war is not only between governments and countries, but happens to

40. Kerry Smith, "Showa Hall," H-Net list for Asian History and Culture, 13 April 1999 (hereafter, Smith, "Showa Hall," [1999]).

41. Kinmouth, "National War Museum."

42. Smith, "Showa Hall," 54.

43. Http://www.showakan.go.jp; Smith, "Showa Hall," 50 n 40. In 2002, the hall's website was still exclusively in Japanese. Ibid. A staff member at the museum told Ms. Kuwayama that "information clerks" might understand English, so I could call them for further information about the museum. Kuwayama Miki, Tokyo, to author, [n.d.] August 2000.

people." The museum, it continues, contains exhibits, posters, still photographs, and numerous artifacts. Moreover, the site adds, much material is stored on a server and can be accessed from computer stations on the fifth floor. "Ironically," the site concludes, "it is located just down the street from the Yasukuni Shrine, the memorial to the Japanese war dead."[44]

When the *Washington Post* briefly mentioned the opening of the Showa Hall in late March 1999, I posted an inquiry on the H-Asia net. Among the responses was a wonderfully thorough and helpful one by Professor Kerry Smith, who had just spent an afternoon at the museum. After a detailed description of the building (seven stories, windowless, and "unobtrusive") and the location, he noted that the museum (although he adds the brochure never calls it a "museum") limits its coverage to the hardships experienced by the Japanese between 1935 and 1955. Hence, despite the inclusion of Showa (referring to the era from 1926 to 1989) in its name (Showa Hall), in truth it deals with only a small segment of that period.

Moreover, there is no attention to the sacrifices of the Japanese military in the war, though Smith argues "they are everywhere implied." Instead, the hall is all about the experiences of "families and children left behind by those killed in the war." In the entire museum, he points out, there are only two displays that "directly connect the exhibits to developments outside of Japan, or explicitly to the Japanese military." One is a collection of letters from soldiers to their parents and the other, displays of *sennimbari* (thousand-stitch belts). Although the museum's brochure states that the museum's mission is to provide opportunities for later generations to learn about the hardships of the war, he notes, the exhibits seem to make the greatest impact on those who lived through the war at home.[45]

As in the case of the Chiran kamikaze museum (see below), the exhibits take the high road and emphasize the "shared purpose, total commitment and self-sacrifice" of the war period. They make it seem, noted Smith, that those values were shared "equally and voluntarily by the citizenry," and portray the war years in a "nostalgic light." Just as in the case of the Chiran museum's portrayal of the kamikaze pilots, the videos and other images, according to Smith, are "more often than not of smiling people happily committed to the task ahead of them," whether farming or dispatching one's children to the countryside to escape the bombing. This, Smith notes, would be entirely normal for wartime propaganda, but the Showa Hall presents it as valid history. In other words,

44. Http://www.willamette.edu/~rloftus/showakan.htm.
45. Smith, "Showa Hall" (1999). The Sennimbari were "embroidered by a thousand female hands to give strength to the pilots who wore them." Buruma, *Wages of Guilt,* 225.

the hardships of the war are presented without any explanation of why they occurred. Smith's conclusion, after visiting the hall, makes it clear that this museum will not be joining the ranks of the "peace" museums any time soon. The exhibits, he argues, "lead one to conclude that the war itself wasn't so bad, but losing it was."

Smith left the hall looking for bright spots. At least, he reasoned, it was better than the proposed Memorial Hall. Moreover, he opined, the presence of reference and resource rooms suggest the exhibits are "not meant to end discussion but to promote it." The "Hall's silences," he concludes, might spur efforts to "fill in the gaps" in public memory of the war years.[46] One can only hope that the "peace museums" (discussed below) will play a greater role in that process than right-wing groups, such as the Society for the Creation of a New History Textbook mentioned by Smith (and described below).

The Showa Hall struggle made it clear that, in Japan, one ministry backed by powerful lobbies for the war dead and their families could stymie the elected national government. Hence, in 1995, the Murayama Tomiichi administration chose not to struggle with the Ministry of Health and Welfare any longer about the focus of the museum, but instead to launch a rival project, the Japan Center for Asian Historical Records (*Ajia rekishi shiryo sentaa*). This new project, to be administered by the cabinet secretary's foreign policy consultation office, was to exhibit a more comprehensive history of the war than the Showa Hall and, most importantly, recognize the suffering caused by Japan during the war. Far from being a small and inexpensive project, it was to take ten years to complete and cost one billion dollars. Again, however, the Japanese bureaucracy threatened to derail a war project. In mid-April 1995, the two leading historical associations within Japan expressed their fear that the cabinet secretary's office would subvert Murayama's intent. Hence, they appealed for support from historians abroad to compel the government to stick to its original approach.[47]

The center did indeed open in late 2001. However, the return of the Liberal Democratic Party to power in 1996 undermined the original intention of giving the center the task of broadening studies of the war to include other Asians. In 1999, it was denied independence when it was subordinated to the Japanese National Archives. In addition, the cabinet directed the center not to extend its scope to gathering research materials outside Japan, explaining that (in the words of an American

---

46. Smith, "Showa Hall" (1999).

47. Kazuki Iguchi, chairman of the Society of Japanese History, and Masanori Nakamura, Chairman of the Historical Society of Japan, to H-Asia Net, 13 April 1995; Smith, "Showa Hall," 46–47.

historian) "it would be too difficult to guarantee the veracity of documents held anywhere else."[48]

Meanwhile, Japanese peace activists criticized the Showa Hall. As one activist declared following a visit to the new museum, real history, especially Japan's aggression in World War II, had not been exhibited in the museum. The exhibits, he complained, do not show the misery of war and the reality of Japan's aggression against Asian countries. Much taxpayer money had been wasted, and, in a crowning insult, he pronounced the huge museum "ugly."[49] Nor did Japan's "peace" museums ignore the Showa Hall. In September 1999, for example, the Osaka International Peace Center hosted a talk on the new museum.[50]

The peace activists did not limit themselves to criticism, though. Beginning in 1992, the year plans for the Showa museum became public, they launched a movement to found a public peace museum in the nation's capital. In 1998, a report was submitted to Tokyo Governor Ishihara Shintaro. However, the museum plan was rejected due to insufficient funds and, according to the Japanese Network of Museums for Peace, the pressure of right-wingers. The activists immediately launched a movement to collect signatures on a petition calling for the establishment of a public peace museum in Tokyo. In addition, one author launched plans to create a private peace museum in Tokyo that would be, in the words of the peace network newsletter, "against the Showa museum that is nationalistic." By May 2000, he had collected twenty million yen of a projected goal of one hundred million yen.[51]

3. The Chiran Peace Museum for Kamikaze Pilots[52]

Although the Chiran museum is called a "peace museum," the Japanese Network of Museums for Peace (discussed below) clearly has its doubts. In an e-mail, the head of its International Exchange Section and editor of its newsletter noted that there are two views about this "very controversial museum." "If it glorifies the past," she wrote, "it cannot be called a peace museum," although she concedes there are those who deny it treats the past in this way.[53]

It is true a wooden sign outside the museum professes peace:

48. Smith, "Showa Hall," 56. The center's website (which I accessed on 13 July 2004) is http://www.jacar.go.jp/f_e.htm. Ibid., 56 n 52.
49. *Muse* 1 (July 1999): 2; *Muse* 2:2.
50. *Muse* 2:7.
51. Ibid. 3:8–9.
52. This is the English translation used by museum authorities in their brochures. Literally, the translation should read, "The Chiran Special Attack Peace Museum" (*Chiran Tokko Heiwa Kaikan*).
53. Yamane Kazuyo, Kochi City, e-mail to author, 14 September 2000.

We [the Japanese] are grateful to receive life through their [kamikaze pilots'] noble sacrifice. . . . We are grateful our country is on the way to prosperity. And we are grateful Japan is at peace today. . . . We believe that [the kamikaze pilots] wished for the restoration of peace and prosperity.[54]

Visitors to the museum approach the building by walking through a garden containing a small shrine dedicated to Kannon, the Buddhist goddess of mercy. When journalist Ian Buruma visited the museum, he received a leaflet noting that the museum was "founded to preserve the true facts of World War II on record and to contribute to true peace on earth."[55]

Is it really a "peace" museum, though? Based on what I have been able to find out about the museum,[56] it does "glorify the past" and hence does not fall into the same category as museums that belong to the "peace network." Located on the southern tip of Kyushu in Kagoshima Prefecture (an hour's bus ride south of Kagoshima), the museum is not private, like the peace museum in Kyoto discussed below, but was opened in 1975 (it took two years to complete) by the government ("a dull modern building"). Moreover, it was built on the site of a former kamikaze air base used for suicide missions to Okinawa. Amid the stone lanterns of the Kannon shrine sits a "silver suicide plane" (actually, a North American Texan rather than a Zero!).[57] Near the plane is a heroic statue of a kamikaze pilot in full flying kit standing on a pedestal. A picture of this statue appears on the front cover of museum brochures, in

---

54. Buruma, *Wages of Guilt,* 225.

55. Ibid. According to one of the museum's leaflets, the Heiwa-Kannon Temple was the first commemorative object on the site. It was built in 1955 with donations from all over Japan "to provide spiritual consolation." The leaflet differs slightly from Buruma's recollections. Instead of saying "to contribute to true peace on earth," it reads "to contribute to eternal peace on earth" by preserving the memorabilia of the kamikaze pilots.

56. In October 2000, a museum staff member kindly sent me two brochures. Moreover, it has a website (http://www2.gol.com/users/myhrman/ chiran.htm). For an interesting paper by a Japanese student who, in the course of her research, paid repeated visits to the Chiran museum, see Mako Sasaki, "Who Became Kamikaze Pilots, and How Did They Feel Towards Their Suicide Mission?" *Concord Review,* reprinted at http://www.tcr.org/kamikaze.html (see pp. 11, 14).

57. Buruma, *Wages of Guilt,* 219, 225. Buruma says the museum was established in 1985, but one of the museum brochures says 1975. According to a museum brochure, in 1942 the air base began as the Tachiarai Joint Service Flight Training School, established to train "volunteer student personnel as cadet officers for special maneuvers." When the war situation worsened in 1945, the school became the southernmost special attack base on the Japanese mainland. Today, the brochure adds, it is the "principal site" where the deceased kamikaze pilots are commemorated. For identification of the planes on display in the museum, see http://www2.gol.com/users/ myhrman/chiran.htm.

---

local tourist booklets, and on a banner a former student of mine purchased at the museum. The latter also contains a picture of the "silver suicide plane" as well as a sad poem.[58] Moreover, on the grounds of the museum, there is a statue of a Japanese mother.

The museum itself mainly contains memorabilia of kamikaze pilots. There is no question but that the exhibits are moving. The displays include thousand-stitch sashes (just as in the Showa Hall), torn uniforms, and parts of destroyed suicide planes raised from the ocean floor. Most importantly, the displays include letters and diaries left behind by the pilots. Although moved by the latter, journalist Ian Buruma also was troubled by emphasis on the cheerfulness of the pilots and the "romance of glorious death." It was "disturbing," he wrote, "to see how it [the romance of glorious death] is held up as a thing of beauty in the Peace Museum today." What Buruma saw, instead, was "the tragedy of wasted lives," "ghastly poignancy," and "underneath the merriment . . . a feeling of despair and barely contained hysteria." Buruma seemed almost angry when he contemplated the "cloying sentimentality that is meant to justify their self-immolation":

> they were made to rejoice in their own death. It was the exploitation of their youthful idealism that made it [the kamikaze endeavor] such a wicked enterprise. And this point is still completely missed at the Peace Museum today.[59]

He was harshly critical of the whole atmosphere at the museum:

> For the phony ideals and the saccharine poetics are still part of the atmosphere of the place. The streets lined with cherry blossoms leading to the museum; the blurbs about "beauty in the laughing faces"; the stuff in the museum guide about this being a "hall of tears"; the ghastly oil painting [which is reproduced in the large museum booklet], three meters by four, of a dead pilot being lifted to heaven from his burning plane by six white-robed [definitely Asian] angels; and most important of all, the denial that the suicide missions were an utter waste of life which only prolonged the war. Instead, the death of thousands is imbued with bogus significance: the young men died for peace and prosperity, their sacrifice was a noble example of patriotism [60]

58. The banner, entitled in Japanese "Souvenir of a Visit to the Special Attack Museum in Chiran," was given to me in the 1980s by Joel Bassett, Washington and Lee class of 1984. According to one of the museum brochures, the bronze statue of the pilot was unveiled in 1974, a year before the museum itself opened its doors.

59. Buruma, *Wages of Guilt,* 225–27. A Japanese student who visited the museum later wrote, "The photographs were extremely inspiring in a sense, since in none of them were the pilots showing an expression of fatigue, or regret. Most of them were smiling." Sasaki, "Who Became Kamikaze Pilots," 14.

60. Buruma, *Wages of Guilt,* 227.

Finally, Buruma seemed horrified when he told of Mr. Matsumoto, a "local civil servant in charge of the museum," passing all this along to a group of three hundred schoolchildren. After Matsumoto's talk, filled with "noble stories of sacrifice, of bravery, of pure, selfless sentiments and beautiful ideals," he admitted to Buruma that "some people" (the peace network activists!) might criticize him for "idealizing the war or promoting militarism," but he denied he did so. "War is bad, very bad," he insisted in his concluding remarks to the children. "We must never go to war again."[61]

Later, Buruma asked Matsumoto why the children would conclude that war was bad if the pilots were "so heroic and their ideals so pure?" Because, Matsumoto replied, the Special Attack Forces' pilots "sincerely believed in peace." Matsumoto and the museum founders, Buruma concluded, were not "bloodthirsty men, nor were they apologists for the war. But their faith in the ideals upon which war propaganda has always been based—sacrifice, sincerity, the sacred cause—was too deep to shake."[62]

To return to our main theme, what of the museum's exhibits? Was there any recognition of the harm done to others by Japan's aggression, of which the kamikaze effort was the last gasp? The answer will not surprise those who have followed the discussion this far. An examination of two museum brochures reveals that, with the rather incongruous exception of a British flag on the wall in the room devoted to the "history of war," there are no exhibits that would qualify this museum as a real "peace" museum, that is, one recognizing Japan's aggression. Instead, it glorifies one aspect of the war, the sacrifices of the kamikaze pilots.[63] This, of course, accounts for the unease with which the Japanese Network of Museums for Peace newsletter editor greeted my inquiry. Meanwhile, according to a museum leaflet, the number of visitors increases each year; on 3 May each year, for example, many visit Chiran for a special memorial service for the war dead. As a result, the town has plans to expand the museum.

It is inconceivable, frankly, that such a museum would acknowledge "the other's" war dead, any more than Arlington National Cemetery would have monuments to the dead of our enemies in all the wars of the

61. Ibid., 227–28.
62. Ibid., 228.
63. In this emphasis on "sacrifice," the museum resembles the postwar best-seller composed of letters by university students killed in the war, *Kike—Wadatsumi no koe* (Listen—voices from the deep). As one historian put it, the book "perpetuated an image of sacrifice that came perilously close to the imagery the militarists had promoted. These were pure young men. Their deaths were noble. . . . It was their deaths, rather than the deaths of those they might have killed, that commanded attention and were truly tragic." Dower, *Embracing Defeat*, 198–200.

Republic. As one American visitor said, "This is a memorial, and many Japanese visitors are openly showing their grief."[64]

"Peace Museums"

In the early to mid-1990s, as the fiftieth anniversary of the end of the war approached, the beginnings of a new Japanese attitude toward the war were made manifest in the appearance of several new museums. Known as "aggression" museums and "peace" museums, they were built in Osaka, Kyoto, Kawasaki, Saitama, and Okinawa, that is, away from the national capital.[65] According to the Western press, they may represent a "long-awaited shift in public willingness to face the wartime past."[66] They present Japan as an aggressor in the war and describe its brutal treatment of other Asian peoples.[67] In addition, the atomic bomb museums in Hiroshima and Nagasaki added exhibits making it clear the bombings did not take place in a vacuum but were the result of Japan's wartime aggression (see below).

In contrast to the "war" museums, these "peace" museums pay attention to the Japanese as victimizers as well as victims. Several of these museums belong to an organization called the Japanese Network of Museums for Peace, with headquarters in Kochi City.[68] Established in November 1998, it publishes a newsletter called *Muse* that is full of information concerning the activities of its member museums.[69] The newsletter makes it clear that criticism of Japan's war record is easier in private museums. "[T]here is more freedom of expression," it explained, "in private peace

64. Http://www2.gol.com/users/myhran/chiran.htm.

65. Smith, "Showa Hall," 38. This geographical distance is reminiscent of the idea in China that the further from Beijing, the freer things are. The Okinawa Prefectural Peace Museum was opened much earlier, i.e., in 1975, three years after the United States returned the islands to Japanese control. Ibid., 36.

66. Charles Burress, "Grafting Peace on the Roots of War," *San Francisco Examiner*, 2 August 1992, 14.

67. Reid, "Japan Marks Day of Defeat," 5; T. R. Reid, "Japan's WWII Self-Image Conflict," *Washington Post*, 6 August 1995, A22.

68. The website for the Kyoto Museum for World Peace (http://www.ritsumei.ac.jp) contains a list of museums that belong to the "peace network," including the Hiroshima Peace Memorial Museum, the Osaka International Peace Center, the Kawasaki Peace Museum, the Peace Museum of Saitama, the Takamatsu Civic Culture Center/Peace Memorial Museum, the Nagasaki Atomic Bomb Museum, and the Okinawa Prefectural Peace Memorial Museum.

69. As of December 2003, ten issues of the newsletter had been published. The editor, Ms. Yamane Kazuyo, very kindly sent me issues numbers 1 and 2. Number 10, with news of the various "peace" museums, may be found on the web by doing a net search on the organization's name: Japanese Network of Museums for Peace.

museums."[70] Hence, it is important, it asserted, to create peace museums that are independent and "free from a national policy and prejudice."[71]

In September 2000, the organization expressed concern about "the present nationalistic trend of Japan."[72] The first article in the second issue of the newsletter carried the headline "Right-wingers are Getting Powerful in Japan." There is a "tendency of neo-nationalism in Japan," the article begins. Neo-nationalism and "militarism" are getting powerful, the newsletter complains, and those who lived through the war are passing away.[73]

This network coordinates and reports on "peace" activities in and outside Japan. It is antinuclear, idealistic about "peace," does not care for the U.S.-Japanese alliance, and probably could be described as leftwing. However, one cannot help but admire it, for it is dedicated to shedding light on Japan's brutal wartime invasion of its neighbors in Asia. It also opposes the rising-sun flag (*hinomaru*) and the national anthem (*Kimigayo* ["His Majesty's Reign"]). These symbols do not represent peace culture, the newsletter charged, but war culture.[74]

Its own museums are not completely free from prejudice, though. The peace museums in Hiroshima, Nagasaki, Osaka, and elsewhere rejected a Dutch exhibition on the Japanese occupation of the East Indies, explaining that it "isn't fit for the aim of the peace museum." Unfortunately, this also put a stop to Japanese plans to hold an exhibition in the Netherlands on the atomic bombing, for, as the newsletter wrote, it was difficult for Hiroshima and Nagasaki officials to ask the Dutch to host such an exhibition after they had just turned down the Dutch show.[75]

Let us now take a look at four of the peace museums.

1. Hiroshima Peace Memorial Museum

One of the members of the network is the Hiroshima Peace Memorial Museum (founded in 1955), which in the past has been a bastion of the idea the Japanese were the real victims of the war. In 1995, there was still consensus in Japan that U.S. use of the atomic bomb was inexcusable, regardless of Japan's atrocities in Asia and the South Pacific. As the mayor of Hiroshima (hardly a disinterested witness) put it, "We cannot and will not deny Japan's aggression, that Japan did evil. But that does

70. *Muse* 2:3.
71. Ibid.
72. Yamane Kazuyo, Kochi, Japan, e-mail to author, 14 September 2000.
73. *Muse* 2:1, 6. The newsletter estimated that those who experienced the war would all be gone in ten years. *Muse* 3 (June 2000): 7.
74. *Muse* 1:5.
75. *Muse* 3:4.

not justify an atomic bomb. It is too cruel. It is inhumane to argue that anything justifies nuclear weapons."[76]

The struggle to revise the Hiroshima museum's exhibits to include some background regarding the use of the atomic bomb went on for years. In 1987, a group called Peace Link was formed from a coalition of Christians, antinuclear activists, and minorities who suffered from discrimination. It petitioned the city government to include the history of Japanese aggression in the museum. Right-wing nationalists, such as the Japan Patriotic Party, countered with rallies around Peace Park, with trucks with loudspeakers blaring patriotic songs. Hence, the peace activists' petition was rejected, although one participant noted the Hiroshima municipal government had been opposed to the idea of an "aggressors' corner" anyway.[77]

That request for an "aggressors' corner" was triggered by junior high school students from Osaka, who embarrassed museum officials by asking about Japanese responsibility for the war. No doubt prodded by their (left-wing?) teachers, they wanted to know what led to the dropping of the atomic bomb on Hiroshima. They also demanded acknowledgment that some of the victims had been Korean slave laborers. Both of the students' requests were turned down.[78]

When a foreign correspondent asked the director of the museum, in the early 1990s, why requests to add an "aggressors' corner" were rejected, the director explained that students came to the museum and tried to argue that Japanese had also committed war crimes, but, he insisted, "they don't know what they are talking about. They just repeat what their left-wing teachers say." Young people should be taught about the war, he agreed, but that was not the job of the museum. Echoing the priest at the Yasukuni Shrine (quoted above), he argued the Hiroshima Peace Memorial Museum was "not really intended to be a museum. It was built by the survivors as a place of prayer for the victims and for world peace." If people didn't think about "human solidarity and world peace," he concluded, then "we just end up arguing about history."[79]

76. Reid, "Japan's WWII Self-Image Conflict," A22. In April 1998, Hiroshima established another organization, the Hiroshima Peace Institute, as a research unit of Hiroshima City University. A survey of its website and the contents of thirteen issues of its newsletter, Hiroshima Research News, reveals only one reference to the events that led to the use of the atomic bomb. Under "Background," the institute acknowledged, "Japan has inflicted, by its colonialism and militarism, an enormous amount of grief and hardships upon peoples in Asia and the Pacific in its drive for modernization. Hiroshima has to fully recognize the seriousness of this fact." Http://serv.peace.hiroshima-cu.ac.jp/English/menuframe2.htm.

77. Buruma, *Wages of Guilt*, 106–7.

78. Ibid., 107.

79. Ibid., 107–8.

The passage of a few years made a big difference at Hiroshima, as elsewhere in Japan, when it came to incorporating the history of Japanese aggression in museum displays. Whether or not it was due to the influence of the peace museum network, even the Hiroshima museum now has made room in its exhibits for the admission that Hiroshima did not occur in a vacuum and that Japanese were victimizers as well as victims.

Previously, its exhibits had contained little, save a very brief reference to the Japanese attack on Pearl Harbor in December 1941, as background for the war that ended in the atomic bombings. However, in mid-1994, as the fiftieth anniversary of the end of the war approached, a new annex was opened with fuller coverage of Japan's aggression, including a display on the Nanjing Massacre that included a provocative photograph of Hiroshima residents celebrating Nanjing's fall with a lantern parade.[80] The caption for the photograph is rather startling, in light of the museum's history to that point: "Hiroshima's citizens celebrating with a torchlight parade. In Nanjing, however, Chinese were being massacred by the Japanese Army."[81] According to an American correspondent, this new annex, popularly known as "aggression corner," "helps to explain to people why the United States felt it necessary to use the atomic bomb."[82]

As Hiroshima's mayor admitted in 1995, "We ourselves were overwhelmed by the terrible damage of the atomic bomb. But we found that people around the world were not necessarily sympathetic. We realized it was necessary to see ourselves not only as victims of the war but also as perpetrators."[83]

In late July 2000, a dispatch in the *New York Times* confirmed the exhibits at the Hiroshima Peace Memorial Museum had been expanded to pay more attention to the war prior to 1945, in particular the record of Japanese military actions and war crimes in Asia.[84] In late August of the same year, this news was seconded in a report from Hiroshima by a correspondent for the *Christian Science Monitor*:

> In recent years, city bodies that run the museum and park have spent time examining their own country's responsibility for the gross rights abuses prior to 1945. One multilingual panel prominently displayed in the museum explains: "Japan, too, with colonization policies and wars of aggression inflicted incalculable and irreversible

80. Hicks, *Japan's War Memories,* 87.

81. Reid, "Japan's WWII Self-Image Conflict," A22.

82. Reid, "Japan Marks Day of Defeat," 5. For a description of the part of the exhibit explaining the U.S. decision to use the bomb, see Hicks, *Japan's War Memories,* 87.

83. Reid, "Japan's WWII Self-Image Conflict," A22.

84. Perri Klass, "To See Japan, Try Rail Pass and Ryokan," *New York Times,* 23 July 2000, 18.

harm on the peoples of many countries." Another says: "Hiroshima was dealt a severe blow by the atomic bomb, but Japan, too, inflicted great damage."[85]

When one adds to this the news that Peace Park administrators have at last permitted an association of Koreans to move inside the park a memorial to the thousands of Koreans killed in the atomic blast, then one can only conclude Hiroshima has moved a long way from the days when only Japanese war dead were commemorated. Previously, park administrators had forced the Koreans to build the memorial, a reminder of how Koreans in Japan were mistreated during the war as enslaved workers, outside the park.[86]

The *Christian Science Monitor* correspondent was surely right when she argued, "By increasing public acknowledgement of the past actions of their government, and of their forebears' frequent acquiescence in these actions, Hiroshimans have actively changed from passive victims of the bomb into more morally robust survivors."[87]

2. Nagasaki Atomic Bomb Museum

In the early 1990s, Nagasaki Peace Park (established in 1955) practiced the same sort of denial its counterparts in Hiroshima clung to until 1994. When builders discovered the foundations of a prison where Korean and Chinese prisoners had died in the war, next to the Peace Park, a group of Nagasaki citizens argued for preservation of the site, to (in the words of a correspondent) "show that the Japanese were not just victims, that the bomb was dropped for a reason." With the support of the Nagasaki mayor, though, the conservatives were able to bury the idea (literally, under a parking lot).[88]

Like Hiroshima, though, Nagasaki has changed with the times. A new museum that opened at Nagasaki in time for the fiftieth anniversary of the atomic bombing deals "extensively with Japan's wartime role."[89] It devotes a corner, for example, to a chronological chart of Japan's expansionism.

The tug-of-war between those who wanted fuller treatment of Japan's record and those who wanted to downplay it, however, continued. The original exhibit included a photograph of a woman being mistreated by

85. Helena Cobban, "Looking at Hiroshima: Tough, Touching," *Christian Science Monitor,* 23 August 2000 (web version at http://www.csmonitor.com/durable/2000/08/23/p9s1.htm, p. 2).
86. Ibid.
87. Ibid., 2–3.
88. Buruma, *Wages of Guilt,* 251. Both Hiroshima and Nagasaki were the sites of slave labor camps during the war. Ibid., 285.
89. Reid, "Japan Marks Day of Defeat," 5.

Japanese troops in Nanjing, but, because of protests, this was replaced by a photograph of refugees fleeing Nanjing—although there was no caption explaining the reason for their flight. Even this ambiguous coverage was protested, the argument being that the Nanjing Massacre and the atomic bomb were separate issues.[90]

3. Osaka International Peace Center (Kokusai heiwa Sentaa)

This three-story, modernistic museum, nicknamed "Peace Osaka," opened in 1991 in the country's second largest city, right next to its most famous sight, Osaka Castle. Begun in 1981 as a research library, the museum is a joint project of Osaka City and Osaka Prefecture. According to its director, it was the result of efforts by conscientious scholars and groups, including organizations concerned with human rights, peace, women's issues, and veterans and the bereaved:

> There are persistent voices in this country ceaselessly arguing that there is no need to expose past crimes now that so much time has passed. But we believe we are not merely attempting expiation, but that these facts are something which, in the name of human dignity, the older generation must communicate to the younger generation who will survive us.[91]

In 1992, a Western reporter was extravagant in his praise, writing that the museum was the pioneer and its exhibits might "help alter the way the world thinks of Japan and the way many Japanese think about themselves." He credited the museum with exposing what many Japanese consider the country's "darkest hour of shame," the atrocities committed by the Japanese military in Asia during the war. However, he complained, "virtually no foreign news organization noticed the opening of the museum, which might be the first public institution to provide a high-profile, detailed accounting of Japan's stark aggression during the war."[92]

Its opening was covered in the Japanese press, which quoted its director as claiming it was the "first institution of its kind." It garnered the headline "Peace Osaka's Important Inquiry: Exhibits Indict the 15-Year War" in the country's largest paper, the *Yomiuri Shimbun*. Meanwhile, the *Mainichi Shimbun* called it "very distinctive in that it portrays Japan as an aggressor."[93]

Although Japanese readers of newspapers and books have long known about Japan's aggression, the Osaka museum has placed it on permanent display and added new material as well as some shocking

90. Hicks, *Japan's War Memories,* 87.
91. Burress, "Grafting Peace," 14.
92. Ibid. The museum's modernistic design is described as consisting of "randomly jutting peaked roofs and diverse geometric shapes of glass and concrete."
93. Ibid.

images. Photographs of Chinese victims have stunned even the well-read. According to an Osaka librarian,

> The fact that Japan was an aggressor, I know that well by reading books and so on. It did not surprise me. But this is the first time I have ever seen those photos. . . .To tell the truth, I didn't want to see the reality of the cruel and miserable war. But I think it is our obligation to be conscientious and know about it.[94]

I first learned of the existence of the Osaka International Peace Center from Ian Buruma's 1994 book, *The Wages of Guilt.* The center was characterized, he noted, by "vigorous pacifism." Its goal, he continued, was clearly to "change the image of wartime Japan from that of a victim to that of an aggressor." And, he added, it was not funded by the national government, but by the Osaka prefectural and municipal governments.[95]

Intrigued by Buruma's assertion that the Osaka museum emphasized Japanese aggression, I went to the worldwide web to see what I could find. All that turned up was a very short description, which included a reference to an exhibit that presented "damage caused by Japan to the Asia-Pacific region during 15 years (1931–45) of hostilities in the region."[96] Curious to learn more about this exhibit, I wrote to the museum and received a very kind response from Mr. Tsunemoto Hajime, a staff member. He included two brochures, which I have combed for details of the exhibit.

After briefly dwelling on the sufferings of the Japanese people in general and Osaka in particular, the first brochure declared: "At the same time, we shall not forget that Japan was responsible for the great hardships suffered by the peoples of China and other Asian-Pacific region [sic], the battlegrounds of the fifteen-year war which ended on August 15, 1945, and the peoples of Korea and Taiwan under Japanese colonial rule."[97]

It is clear, however, the center does not exclusively focus on the story of what Japanese did to others; perhaps it is unreasonable to expect a museum to dwell solely on its own people's "sins." This did not escape notice by the Western press. The other half of the museum, one reporter wrote, is "Japan as victim." The museum, for example, covers the Tokyo raid of March 1945. It also reports on the fifty air raids on Osaka, with replicas of the bombs, a diorama and photos of the city

94. Ibid.
95. Buruma, *Wages of Guilt,* 229–30.
96. Http://www.gsquare.or.jp. The term "Fifteen-Year War," it has been asserted, is favored by Japanese leftists and liberals. Buruma, *Wages of Guilt,* 48.
97. Osaka International Peace Center, "A Guide to the Exhibition," n.d.

under attack, wartime newsreels, interview tapes with eyewitnesses, and a replica of a bomb shelter.[98]

Thus, the center devotes much effort to a depiction of Osaka's sufferings as well as an amorphous appeal for "peace." The center, the brochure explained, was "conceived in memory of Osaka's wartime victims" and "as an instrument to set forth new, regional support for the cause of peace."[99] At least two of the three films regularly screened in the center's auditorium concern Osaka, to wit, "Osaka in a Sea of Fire" and "Burned Up Osaka" (the third one is entitled, "Tale of Sixteen Jizo"). There also is a "video area,"[100] where one can view documentaries, movies, animations (this is Japan, after all) about "war and peace," wartime newsreels, and taped interviews with witnesses (presumably all Japanese) "relating their wartime experiences." According to a foreign correspondent, a colorful drawing by a child shows people fleeing and the head of a baby flying through the air trailing blood. However, he added, "care was taken to show that this happened as the result of a war that Japan started."[101] Moreover, the center's library contains foreign books about the war.

According to the museum's first brochure, there are three exhibition rooms, the first (A) on the "Osaka Air Raid and the Daily Life of the People" (complete with reproductions of U.S. incendiary and other bombs), the second (B) on the "Fifteen-Year War," and the third (C) on "Aspiration for Peace." There also is a fifteen-minute videotape entitled, "Chronology of the Fifteen-Year War," as well as exhibits labeled "Prologue" and "Epilogue."

The brochure's section on the "Fifteen-Year War" bluntly stated that the conflict "taught us many things. The most important is that there is no such thing as a good war."[102] As for the exhibit on the "Fifteen-Year War," according to the brochure it presents "facts" about the conflict. Sensibly, since it is attempting to inform the Japanese public about the "facts" of Japan's aggression, it includes displays on China, Korea, and Southeast Asia. According to a foreign correspondent who toured the museum, this room included exhibits on the Nanjing Massacre, the chemical warfare unit, and comfort women. The explanations were sim-

98. Burress, "Grafting Peace," 14.

99. Osaka International Peace Center, "A Guide to the Exhibition." The prospectus also recalls Hiroshima, Nagasaki, Okinawa, and, more broadly, the "countless number[s] of Japanese people [who] lost their precious lives, became wounded or fell to illness."

100. Ibid.

101. Buruma, *Wages of Guilt*, 230.

102. Ibid., 230–31.

ple, he was told, to avoid presenting wartime propaganda and to impress middle-school students with the "cruelty of war."[103]

The exhibition on the war, however, has not completely escaped the notion of the Japanese as the main victims of the conflict. In addition to the emphasis on suffering by Osakans, it also includes exhibits on the "Manchurian and Mongolian Development Corps Detained in Siberia," "The Pacific Region (Why the Suicidal Attacks?)," and Okinawa,[104] Hiroshima, and Nagasaki. The latter, it explains, shows the "terror produced by the atomic bombs" dropped on the two cities. In short, five of the eight exhibits focus on the sufferings of the Japanese. Rather jarringly—what does it have to do with the "Fifteen-Year War"?—there also is an exhibit "depicting the horror of the Auschwitz concentration camp."[105] Perhaps Auschwitz was included as part of the museum's "peace" orientation. As one would expect, perhaps, there is no mention of the Emperor Hirohito.

Mr. Tsunemoto sent a second brochure as well, which led off, rather surprisingly, by declaring Japan "won World War I." More surprisingly, in view of the contretemps in 1982 over the use in Japanese textbooks of the word "advance" rather than "aggression" when describing the war with China, the brochure relates that Japan "attempted to advance into China."[106] In the section of the brochure on Osaka, the U.S. attacks on Japanese cities are described as "indiscriminate bombings, with total disregard for private houses or factories." There is no attempt to analyze why such savage attacks were made on Japan. In describing the soldiers who went off to war, though, the brochure does note people thought the "war of aggression" was a "holy war."[107]

In the description of Exhibition Room B on the "Fifteen-Year War," this second brochure is much franker than the first brochure about Japanese crimes against other Asians. Many Japanese, it claimed, did not know until after the war how much "the people of China and various areas in Asia and the South Pacific suffered from the Japanese invasion." Japan, the brochure continued, "is said to have waged gas and germ warfare," and carried out "repeated indiscriminate bombing" of Shanghai, Nanjing, and Chongqing. In response, an anti-Japanese movement "naturally escalated." The Japanese military, however, "mercilessly attacked

103. Ibid., 230.
104. The exhibits do make clear where the blame for many Okinawan deaths rests, though, for they mention the tens of thousands of Okinawan civilians whom the Japanese army ordered to commit suicide rather than surrender. Burress, "Grafting Peace," 14.
105. Osaka International Peace Center, "A Guide to the Exhibition."
106. On the dispute over the use of the word "advance," see Hicks, *Japan's War Memories,* 43.
107. Osaka International Peace Center brochure (no title), n.d.

even the unresisting people." The brochure then cited the military policy of *sanko,* that is, "kill all, burn all, and destroy all." The Nanjing Atrocity, it continued, was a "typical example of that action." These facts, the brochure declared, are "verified" in (the rather oddly named, in English translation at any rate) *Supplementary Reader for Rabble's* (*sic*—the Masses'?) *United Front Movement to Save the Country* (which, it added, was published around 1937) as well as "present textbooks in China."

The English-language version of the video accompanying the China exhibits also is frank about Japanese actions, noting,

> The Japanese troops carried out atrocities called in Chinese "san-guang"—literally, "three types of light"—that is, plunder all, exterminate all, and reduce all to ashes. The invaders occupied Nanjing on December 13, 1937, and massacred, it is said, tens or hundreds of thousands of Chinese people. The Chinese troops, while withdrawing deep into the interior, bravely resisted the aggressors.[108]

As for Korea, the brochure continued, Japan annexed that country in 1910, and thereafter its suppression of Korean independence movements was "nothing if not brutal." Moreover, it mobilized the Korean people for war. The brochure was tactful when it came to the "live" issues of forced imprisonment, slave labor, and Koreans forced by the Japanese Imperial Army to become comfort women. Those issues, it declared, "must wait for their resolution in the future."[109]

In dealing with the end of the war, though, the brochure could not help alluding to the "victim" viewpoint when it declared that atomic bombs were dropped on a Japan that "no longer possessed the power to resist." However, as Edward Drea argues in "Intelligence Forecasting for the Invasion of Japan: Previews of Hell," Japanese forces in the homeland at the end of war were far stronger than earlier American estimates had reported, thanks to mass mobilizations during 1945. Between 1 January and 10 July 1945, Japanese troop strength in the homeland doubled from 980,000 to 1,865,000. Moreover, the Japanese were preparing thousands of planes, boats, and Kaiten torpedoes for suicide attacks against American invasion troops. In short, the Japanese clearly still possessed "the power to resist."[110]

Most devastating for the museum's image among Asian victims of Japanese aggression, perhaps, was that it permitted its hall to be used, on 23 January 2000, for a meeting entitled, "The Biggest Lie in the Twentieth Century: Complete Verification of the Massacre in Nanjing," at

---

108. Burress, "Grafting Peace," 14.

109. The exhibits also provide lists of Koreans forced to adopt Japanese names. Ibid.

110. Edward J. Drea, *In the Service of the Emperor: Essays on the Imperial Japanese Army* (Lincoln: University of Nebraska Press, 1998), chapters 10, 11.

which the Nanjing Massacre was denied. The peace center declined to cancel the meeting even though, on 18 January, the Chinese government asked the Japanese government to ban the meeting.[111] The Osaka museum belongs to the Japanese Network of Museums for Peace, but the latter's newsletter seemed at a loss as to how to report this meeting. Hence, it simply noted "there were voices of criticism for allowing such a meeting where the historical fact of the Nanjing Massacre was denied."[112]

4. Kyoto Museum for World Peace, Ritsumeikan University

The best known of the peace museums today is Kyoto Museum for World Peace at Ritsumeikan University (a private school), a ten-minute walk from the Golden Pavilion and Ryoanji (with its famous rock gardens). According to the press, the museum occupies a "handsome new building" on the outskirts of the campus. Displays include wartime artifacts, such as wartime diaries, and high-tech virtual reality exhibits, including a "chilling" demonstration of what would have happened if an atomic bomb had been dropped on Kyoto.[113]

Unlike the Yasukuni Shrine's museum, writes a correspondent who visited both museums, the Kyoto museum is a secular institution "without obligations to anyone's sacred spirit." There were no "relics," he continued, no "sacred grounds," and no "paeans to sacrifice," although, he added, pacifism did not lack its own "air of religiosity." Its goal, like that of the Osaka museum, is to tell about Japan the aggressor rather than Japan the victim. The correspondent found the Kyoto museum more informative than the Osaka one, for it focused on the regimentation of daily life, the suppression of free speech, and nationalist propaganda. In short, it was more political.[114]

In 1992, its director recalled, the university opened the museum as a "spot for learning peace" open to the community. Since its founding, he noted, 170,000 people have visited the museum, including students from primary, middle, and senior high schools as well as citizens. The latter have formed a group, "Friends of Peace," that provides volunteer guides for visitors. It is, he continued, the only "comprehensive peace

---

111. Muse 3:2. It should be remembered the Osaka museum was a prefectural and municipal rather than a national one.

112. Ibid., 3:3.

113. Reid, "Japan Marks Day of Defeat," 5; "Greetings of Director," http://www.ritsumei.ac.jp. The museum was not always the leader among the "peace" museums. In 1992, a Western reporter asserted that the Osaka Center was the "pioneer and leader in both scale and prominence." Burress, "Grafting Peace," 14. When the Kyoto museum was being planned, the curators went looking for wartime diaries. For one case in which a diarist was harrassed by other Japanese for his honesty about his actions during the war, see Buruma, *Wages of Guilt*, 133–34.

114. Buruma, *Wages of Guilt*, 229.

museum owned and steered by a university." It has tried to "send peace messages to the community," he explained, in cooperation with other domestic and foreign peace museums, such as the Hiroshima Peace Memorial Museum and the Nagasaki Atomic Bomb Museum.[115]

The Kyoto museum is a member of the Japanese Network of Museums for Peace, and its activities are reported in the network's newsletter.[116] In contrast to the Osaka center, the Kyoto museum maintains a complete website. In fact, the website is superior to the museum's printed guide in one way, and that is the inclusion of interesting wartime photographs.[117]

A former exchange student at Washington and Lee University from Kansai Gaidai visited the museum, at my request, and collected materials. Her comments were perceptive. The museum, she noted, adopted a left-wing point of view. However, she added, "I rarely see any information about . . . WWII written in Japanese like this museum shows." She also viewed a museum video about people's daily lives during the war and commented: "It emphasizes . . . how people were forced to sacrifice their food, clothes, and other belongings for the country. The view was quite different from my history textbooks and classes."[118]

The first exhibit hall makes clear who was responsible for the war and resultant suffering in Japan. "In World War II," the display asserted, "Japan attacked the nations of Asia and the Pacific. As a result, America responded with air raids on Japanese cities. These were not independent events. They arc all part of World War II in the Pacific."[119] The museum, like the other peace museums, also prefers to see the war as a continuum, and hence does not separate it into a China phase and a Pacific phase with different names, as did the wartime militarists (and the Yushukan today). Instead, it calls it the "Fifteen-Year War."[120]

The standing exhibit consists of three areas, each with several sections. Area one deals with the "Fifteen-Year War." According to the printed guide, the leaders of the Japanese Army pushed the nation into a "devastating drive against the peoples of the Asia-Pacific region that

115. "Greetings of Director," http://ritsumei.ac.jp. The site displays a photograph of the director but does not give his name (perhaps out of fear of the right wing?). The museum opened in May 1992, eight months after the Osaka International Peace Center. Burress, "Grafting Peace," 14.

116. See, for example, the report printed in *Muse* 3:2–3.

117. Http://www.ritsumei.ac.jp. The museum guide is entitled *Kyoto Museum for World Peace* (Kyoto: Ritsumeikan University, 1995). I am grateful to a former Washington and Lee University exchange student from Kansai Gaidai, Okano Kaori, for sending it to me.

118. Okano Kaori, Kanazawa, Japan, letter to author, June 1997.

119. Reid, "Japan Marks Day of Defeat," 5.

120. Ibid.

lasted for 15 long years."[121] Kyoto itself directly contributed to this aggression in Asia, for it was home to the army's 16th Division, which participated in the capture of Nanjing.[122] However, the guide misses the opportunity to comment on the Nanjing Massacre and the 16th Division's role in it.

The university itself played a role in the war. As the director explains in the museum's website, during the war Ritsumeikan was "militaristic."[123] Since the campus was in the Hirokoji area just outside the palace grounds, in 1928 a special security squad, called the Ritsumeikan Kin'eitai (Imperial Court Police Unit), was organized and charged with guarding the Imperial Palace in Kyoto. The museum's exhibits include a booklet designed to prepare Ritsumeikan students for service in the Kin'eitai and a banner, presented to the unit by Emperor Hirohito, containing the Chinese characters for Kin'eitai. Furthermore, on the web, there is a photograph of the Ritsumeikan Kin'eitai participating in the parade celebrating the fall of Nanjing in December 1937.[124] Again, there is no comment on what that "fall" meant to Nanjing residents.

Following revocation of student deferments in 1943 (the Government Mobilization Order), three thousand Ritsumeikan students were dispatched to the front.[125] Later students drew less glorious duty, with a great number of them assigned to war plants.[126] About five hundred Ritsumeikan University students, for example, were sent to work at the Toyokawa Naval Munitions Plant, which was eventually bombed.[127]

When describing the onset of the "Fifteen-Year War" in 1931, the guide is forthright. Japan "invaded" Manchuria, it asserts. Subsequently, the guide continued, Japan used the Marco Polo Bridge Incident in 1937 as a "pretext" to launch "all-out war" against China.[128] In describing the weak Japanese antiwar efforts, the museum even includes American leaflets and antiwar booklets and newspapers.[129]

The museum is honest about Japan's colonization efforts as well. Ritsumeikan University, it notes, expelled quite a few students from the Japanese colonies of Taiwan and Korea.[130] For Japanese school children who might have only the vaguest of ideas concerning the extent of

---

121. *Kyoto Museum for World Peace*, 2.

122. *Kyoto Museum for World Peace*, 3.

123. "Greetings of Director," http://www.ritsumei.ac.jp.

124. *Kyoto Museum for World Peace*, 7; http://www.ritsumei.ac.jp ("Japanese on the Home Front" section of the standing exhibit).

125. "Greetings of Director," http://www.ritsumei.ac.jp.

126. Ibid.

127. *Kyoto Museum for World Peace*, 6.

128. Ibid., 3.

129. Ibid., 8.

130. "Greetings of Director," http://www.ritsumei.ac.jp.

Japan's wartime empire, there is a map showing Japanese expansion during the war. Even before the war, it noted, colonial subjects in Taiwan and Korea were forced to assimilate Japanese culture, take Japanese names, learn Japanese in school, and always use the Japanese language. Once war broke out, those colonial subjects were forced to support it. Males were drafted and sent to the front lines, or mobilized in other ways to support the war. Some were shipped to Japan. At a time when the Japanese government has dragged its feet about recognizing that the Japanese military enslaved Asian and Western females as "comfort women," the museum guide is clear. Many women, it noted, were "forced into sexual slavery as 'comfort women' for military personnel."[131]

The museum also seems determined not to leave its visitors with any illusions concerning the Greater East Asia Co-Prosperity Sphere, a Japanese attempt to create an economically self-sufficient realm in which East and Southeast Asia countries would co-exist and prosper under Japanese rule, and the argument that Japan "liberated" the European colonies. The "Fifteen-Year War," the guide explained, began when the Japanese blew up a section of the South Manchurian Railroad in 1931 and blamed it on the Chinese as a pretext for taking over Manchuria. With the expansion of the war into the Pacific, Japan extended its territories and created puppet governments. In doing so, the guide lamented, "the Japanese Army often massacred civilians and tortured prisoners of war."[132] In the occupied areas of Asia, the Japanese military "forcibly suppressed resistance and destroyed villages and towns." The museum's display cases contain reproductions of whips, leg irons, and batons used to put down resistance in China.[133]

The museum does not shrink from mentioning one of the worst stains on Japan's record as a nation. It includes among its displays a military gas mask used by personnel in the "infamous" Unit 731 in Manchuria. This organization, the guide notes, "conducted germ warfare experiments and other abuses on live Chinese, Russians and Koreans, killing approximately 3,000." Unit 731 soldiers "completely dehumanized their victims," describing them as *murata* (logs). Next to the mask is a reproduction of a Unit 731 Uji-type germ warfare bomb.[134] In early 1993, the museum hosted a special exhibit on medical studies in Germany and Japan prior to 1945, while in late September 1994, it mounted a special exhibit on Unit 731, which featured two members of the unit.[135] Finally, the museum's website contains a photograph from the Ping-

131. *Kyoto Museum for World Peace,* 10.
132. Ibid.
133. Ibid., 11.
134. Ibid.
135. Ibid., 24–25.

tingshan Museum for Fellow Victims of War, in China, which was created by unearthing the remains of a Japanese Imperial Army massacre.[136]

The museum does not neglect Japanese suffering. It points out that fifty-five thousand men from Kyoto were killed during the war.[137] It emphasizes the American incendiary and atomic bombings, in which it claims some seven hundred thousand Japanese were killed, as well as the all-out struggle for Okinawa in 1945. It does not flinch from describing Japanese responsibility for the oppression and deaths of many Okinawa civilians, which surpassed the number of Japanese soldiers killed in the campaign. It also describes the suppression and torture at home, for example that carried out by the Special Higher Police.[138] It notes the daily hardships on the home front as well as the attempts at complete thought control of the population.[139]

Although it acknowledges that the United States dropped the atomic bombs to hasten the surrender of Japan and hold down American casualties, it cannot resist falling for the argument that the bombs were also used to end the war before the Soviets joined in, thus "ensuring that America would gain sole control of the occupied territories." The museum guide goes even further, boldly stating that the use of the atomic bombs "effectively became the first act of the Cold War that pitted the United States against the Soviet Union after World War II" (the Cold War, it is commonly agreed, did not begin until 1947). The museum also includes a section on the *Lucky Dragon* incident, in which members of a Japanese fishing boat crew suffered radiation poisoning when they strayed too close to U.S. hydrogen bomb testing grounds near Bikini Atoll in 1954. One of the chief missions of the museum is clearly its antinuclear stance, and hence this makes it a logical member of the Japanese Network of Museums for Peace to which the Hiroshima and Nagasaki museums also belong.[140]

Like the Osaka International Peace Center, the Kyoto museum rather jarringly introduces Auschwitz into its guide and displays. Below photographs of Hiroshima are etchings produced by a prisoner at Auschwitz. The displays also include a map showing the location of concentration camps in Europe as well as several items sent from Auschwitz and the Majdanek Concentration Camp in Poland.[141] Perhaps part of the point is to show what kind of people Japan was allied with during the war.

---

136. Http://www.Ritsumei.ac.jp ("Japanese Occupation and Rule" section, located under the standing exhibit heading).
137. *Kyoto Museum for World Peace*, 3.
138. Ibid., 4.
139. Ibid., 5–8.
140. Ibid., 13.
141. Ibid., 14–15.

As for the question of responsibility for the war, the museum makes clear Japan was on the side of the dictators. Japan, the guide noted, joined Fascist Germany and Italy "in its own attempt to establish a similar dictatorial empire." It accepts that Japan committed war crimes and includes exhibits from the International Military Tribunal for the Far East (more popularly known as the Tokyo War Crimes Trial), which is anathema for nationalists and right-wingers in Japan. It does not neglect the crimes. Displays include handwritten documents by Allied POWs brought to Japan as slave laborers, a photograph of the Bataan Death March in 1942, and a photograph of prisoners in the Changgi POW camp in Singapore.[142] In July 1993—exactly fifty-six years after the Marco Polo Bridge Incident that launched World War II for the Japanese—the museum mounted an exhibition of drawings of life in a Japanese camp done by Dutch POWs.[143]

Finally, the museum offers a section on "unresolved war responsibilities." "Many of Japan's responsibilities related to the Fifteen-Year War," the museum guide admits, "remain unresolved." They rightly note that those responsible for the use of poison gas in China and the Unit 731 experiments on live human subjects were never punished. In explaining that this was because "the American authorities decided it was not in their best interest to prosecute them," they leave the matter vague at best.

Many victims of Japan, the guide continues, have not received apologies or compensation, such as the thousands of Koreans and Chinese brought to Japan and forced to work in mines and other industries as slave laborers. It reminds readers of the notorious Hanaoka Affair, in which Chinese forced to work in a mine rebelled, and many were tortured and executed. It mentions that survivors and their relatives are now pressing for an official apology and compensation. "This," the guide comments, "is just one example of the great suffering Japan's war of aggression inflicted upon the peoples of Asia." Other victims, it added, such as comfort women, are scattered throughout the country and "awaiting justice."

Having focused on victims of the Japanese in its text, the guide then abruptly shifts gears and describes a display that focuses on a suit brought by victims of "illegal [American] bombing of civilians" in Nagoya.[144] Logically, this would have been a good place to mention cur-

142. Ibid., 14–16. The photographs of POWs on the Bataan Death March and inmates in the Changgi POW camp in Singapore also appear on the museum's website (see http://www.ritsumei.ac.jp). Those who abused prisoners at the Singapore camp, the site added, were tried as class B and C war criminals.

143. *Kyoto Museum for World Peace*, 24–25.

144. Ibid., 16–17.

rent suits by former American POWs. However, this might well be asking too much of a Japanese museum.

Perhaps in an effort to show that while Japan has erred, so has the United States, the guide ends with a section on the Vietnam War. The description of U.S. actions sounds eerily like those of Japan in World War II. The United States set up a puppet regime, it indiscriminately killed civilians and destroyed civilian buildings, it burned large areas of the countryside, and it also relied on aerial bombing (no doubt reminding the Japanese of their own destruction from the air). Making the parallelism complete, the guide reported that, as a result of America's involvement in Vietnam, an international war crimes tribunal was established with Jean Paul Sartre as presiding judge. In addition, there were waves of protest in Japan, the guide reported. It then credits a worldwide "strong antiwar tide" for ending the war.[145]

A foreign correspondent who visited the museum termed it "leftist" in its treatment of the postwar period. For example, an illustrated booklet for schoolchildren called the Vietnam War a U.S. "war of invasion" against which the Vietnamese, "thirsting for freedom and independence, struggled hard and were victorious." However, the point, the correspondent insisted, was not anti-Americanism, but that all wars were bad.[146]

The Struggle over Textbooks in Present-day Japan

Because of an ongoing fascination with Japan's record in World War II, as well as the implications of Japanese history textbooks for international relations in Asia, in recent years much has been published on these texts.[147] There is not space here to undertake a detailed study of Japanese school texts in modern times. Hence, what follows is a case study meant to demonstrate that, just as in the case of the museums, there is no one "Japanese" view of the war but rather a continuing struggle between opposing outlooks. Thus, this section focuses on a nationalist organization, dedicated to producing a "correct history" of Japan (especially its role in World War II), and the fervent opposition this group has provoked among many Japanese.

145. Ibid., 18–20.
146. Buruma, *Wages of Guilt*, 230.
147. For three recent publications, see Hicks, *Japan's War Memories* (several chapters on the textbook issue); Laura Hein and Mark Selden, eds., *Censoring History: Perspectives on Nationalism and War in the Twentieth Century* (Armonk, N.Y.: M. E. Sharpe, 2000) (four essays on textbook struggles in Japan); James J. Orr, *The Victim as Hero: Ideologies of Peace and National Identity in Postwar Japan* (Honolulu: University of Hawaii Press, 2001) (contains a chapter on "Narratives of War in Postwar Textbooks").

Introduction

Since the beginnings of modern Japan in the Meiji period (1868–1912), the central government has played a large role in education, including the approval, and sometimes even creation, of school textbooks.[148] After a "liberal" period during the American Occupation (1945–52), the central government reasserted its right to review and authorize school textbooks.

However, not all Japanese were content with this resumption of the Ministry of Education's authority over textbooks. In 1965, Professor Ienaga Saburo filed suit against the ministry's power over textbooks. After a lengthy struggle, in 1997 he lost his basic case, when the Supreme Court ruled against his argument that textbook certification was unconstitutional.[149] However, at the same time—demonstrating that the struggle over textbooks in Japan is not a simple, one-sided matter—the court ruled the government could not distort Japan's record in the war. Hence, the court deemed illegal the ministry's demand that a textbook author delete descriptions of Japanese wartime atrocities.[150]

The Society for the Creation of New History Textbooks[151]

By the 1990s, it looked as though the long battle to include the truth of Japanese wartime aggression in Asia in textbooks had been won. In 1995, a survey of the twelve most popular textbooks in Japanese schools

148. For an excellent analysis of Japanese textbooks from the beginning of the Meiji era through World War II, see John Caiger, "The Aims and Content of School Courses in Japanese History, 1872–1945," in *Japan's Modern Century: A Special Issue of Monumenta Nipponica Prepared in Celebration of the Meiji Restoration* (Rutland, Vt.: Charles E. Tuttle, 1968), 51–81. For an analysis of Japanese textbooks published from 1903 through 1943–44, see Harry Wray, "The Lesson of the Textbooks," in Harry Wray and Hilary Conroy, eds., *Japan Examined: Perspectives on Modern Japanese History* (Honolulu: University of Hawaii Press, 1983), 282–90. See also James L. McClain, *A Modern History of Japan* (New York: W. W. Norton and Company, 2002), 260, 262, 264, 465–66, 548–49, and 592–93.

149. For Ienaga's own rendition of his struggle, see his memoir, *Japan's Past, Japan's Future: One Historian's Odyssey,* trans. Richard H. Minear (Lanham, Md.: Rowman and Littlefield, 2001). See also his *Pacific War*, 254–56. For a description of the process of textbook review, see Irie Yoshimasa, "The History of the Textbook Controversy," *Japan Echo,* August 1997, 35.

150. Sonni Efron, "Japan's High Court Rules Government May Not Tamper with the Truth," *Washington Post,* 30 August 1997, A28.

151. *Atarashii rekishi kyokasho o tsukuru kai.* The name of this group also has been translated as Society for History Textbook Reform, Society for the Making of New School Textbooks in History, and Society for the Creation of a New History. Nelson, "Social Memory," 452 n 9; Smith, "Showa Hall," 40; John Nathan, *Japan Unbound: A Volatile Nation's Quest for Pride and Purpose* (Boston: Houghton Mifflin, 2004), 129.

showed they agreed Japan pursued a "war of aggression" as a "fascist state" (debatable) allied with Germany and Italy. They also included the Nanjing Massacre as well as Japan's use of poison gas and slave labor. The biggest break with the past was that questions on the war appeared on high school and college entrance examinations.[152] In the same decade, middle-school textbooks also mentioned the infamous Unit 731.[153]

A reaction from the nationalists was perhaps inevitable. Although their disagreement with textbook treatment of Japanese history and especially the war was broad, two issues particularly irritated them. After the 1982 Ministry of Education order that history texts should use "advance" rather than "invasion" to describe Japan's expansion into Asia during the war, the Chinese and Koreans protested. As a result, textbook review guidelines were revised to state that proposed texts should "show the necessary consideration for international understanding and . . . harmony in their treatment of the events of modern and contemporary history between [Japan and its] Asian neighbors."[154]

This outraged the nationalists. A professor of history at the University of Electro-Communications in Tokyo and founder of the Society for Creation of New History Textbooks, Nishio Kanji, labeled the ministry's action "diplomacy by apology" by a "diplomatically inept Japan." The "myth" that Japan had not apologized for its past, he wrote, was the "only way China and Korea can rock Japan's boat. That [1982] textbook incident was symbolic as an indicator of Japan's position in terms of diplomatic coordinates."[155]

The comfort women issue seems to have been the final straw for nationalists. In early August 1993, the Japanese government admitted

---

152. Reid, "Japan's WWII Self-Image Conflict," A22. In discussing Japanese commemoration of the air raids on Tokyo the night of 9–10 March 1945, Reid reported that the event included reminders that it was the Japanese who launched the war. Moreover, while the new municipal museum mounted a special exhibit on the Tokyo bombing, it also included film footage of Japanese troops attacking Chinese civilians and Chinese parents weeping over children killed by the Japanese in Chongqing and Nanjing. T. R. Reid, "Japan Assessing Past Role: Aggressor, Not Victim," *Washington Post*, 11 March 1995, A1, A24. According to an American historian, in 2001 the modern Japanese history section of the Japanese National Center Examination, which more than five hundred thousand Japanese took, included only two questions on the 1930s and 1940s. Earl Kinmouth to H-Japan@H net.msu.edu, "Japanese Textbook Revision," 24 January 2001.

153. Nicholas D. Kristof and Sheryl WuDunn, *Thunder from the East: Portrait of a Rising Asia* (New York: Alfred A. Knopf, 2000), 238.

154. Irie, "The History of the Textbook Controversy," 35–36. Irie argues the press reports concerning the replacement of "invasion" with "advance" were wrong. However, he also admitted that for several years the Ministry of Education had suggested that "advance" replace "invasion." Ibid.

155. Ibid., 36.

for the first time that women had been dragooned into prostitution by the government and military. Hence, textbook authors began including comfort women in their accounts.[156]

As a result of issues such as these, in December 1996 rightists, led by such figures as University of Tokyo Professor Fujioka Nobukatsu, founded the Society for the Creation of New History Textbooks. In its opening declaration, the society lambasted the interpretation of modern Japanese history in seven middle-school texts recently approved. The texts, the group claimed, labeled all Japan's modern conflicts "merely wars of aggression," considered the Meiji evil, and presented modern and contemporary Japanese history as "a condemnation of a history of crimes." As for the comfort women issue, it was dismissed as "a result of the facile self-denunciatory view of history they [the publishers] have adopted."[157] In propounding its message, it was clear the society had powerful friends. In Japan, that also meant it was well funded. In 2000, for example, it was reported the group raised 415 million yen ($332,000).[158]

The views expressed by the society were by no means new. For years, Fujioka had called for reform of the history curriculum. The view of Japanese history taught in the schools, he declared, was "masochistic" and "anti-Japanese." It was "dark history," the "Comintern view," and the "Tokyo War Crimes Trial view." In late June 1996, he wrote:

> The textbooks from the seven publishers that have passed the review process cannot by any means be called textbooks written for Japanese. The "indirect aggression" of foreign countries that begrudge Japan's prosperity has reached virtual completion in the field of history texts that form the framework for the nation's common store of knowledge. Using government funds to pay for textbooks so full of hatred against our own country and forcing them on schoolchildren represent a grievous violation of the people's right to education.[159]

156. Ibid., 37. Textbooks are changed every four years. Thus, it was April 1997 when the Ministry of Education announced new textbooks would include references to comfort women.

157. Ibid., 34.

158. Hiromitsu Inokuchi to H-Japan@H-net.msu.edu, "Economic Base of Japanese Revisionists," 21 March 2001. The dollar equivalent is based on an exchange rate of 125 yen. It was reported that prominent businessmen donated funds, took out paid memberships, and purchased copies of the society's publications.

159. Irie, "History of the Textbook Controversy," 34. One of Fujioka's three revisionist books on the war sold 250,000 copies in a few months in 1996. Moffett, "Past Perfect," 26, 28. For the fuzzy and illogical views of another leader of the society, see Nishio Kanji, "Rewriting Japanese and World History," *Japan Echo,* August 1997, 39–44; Howard W. French, "Japan's Resurgent Far Right Tinkers with History," *New York Times,* 25 March 2001, 3. In railing against what he terms the "Eurocentric viewpoint" of Japanese textbooks, Nishio revealed an abysmal ignorance of European his-

In commenting on Fujioka's view, a writer in a Japanese government journal missed the point. The question, he wrote, was whether the texts' viewpoint represented the authors' "loss of pride in their own country's history or merely the permeation of a pacifist view that innocently opposes war."[160] In fact, the question was whether the texts would contain the truth of Japan's invasion and occupation of Asia or whitewash that history.

One of the most worrisome aspects of the society's activities was its link with the *manga* (comic book) star Kobayashi Yoshinori, who became one of the founders of the society. That meant the Right had gone mainstream after decades of marginalization. Kobayashi's 1998 *manga, Sensoron* (A theory of war), which called the Nanjing Massacre and the enslavement of comfort women fictitious, sold almost a million copies.[161] In one of his many provocative statements, he wrote that the Nanjing Massacre, comfort women, and Unit 731 had become the contemporary *fumie* (brass tablets with a cross that suspected Christians in seventeenth-century Japan had to stamp on to prove they did not belong to that faith.)[162]

The far right's views did not go unchallenged (as we shall see when we examine the 2001 textbook controversy). A Western reporter described Fujioka Nobukatsu and his "pals" as "Japan's equivalent of Holocaust revisionists."[163] Professor Obinata Sumio, a Japanese textbook author himself, put it better:

> Professor Fujioka often talks about "history to be proud of.". . . Unfortunately, the facts include some things that we can't be proud of. Is it wrong to teach about them? I don't think so. . . . Faithfulness to the facts naturally means inclusion of both the good and the bad. History education isn't ethics. and it's not a matter of saying, "Read this and be uplifted." The factual record includes some bitter parts,

---

tory (referring, e.g., to Europe before the fifteenth century as "nothing but a collection of savage tribes"). Nishio, "Rewriting Japanese and World History," 41.

160. Irie, "History of the Textbook Controversy," 35.

161. Ibid., 37–38; French, "Japan's Resurgent Far Right Tinkers with History," 3. On Kobayashi, see also the excellent discussion in Nathan, *Japan Unbound,* 123–37. In November 2003, it was reported more than 250 million copies of *manga* are sold each year. André Schiffrin, "In Japan, Books Are Windows to the World," *Chronicle of Higher Education,* 28 November 2003, B5.

162. French, "Japan's Resurgent Far Right Tinkers with History," 3. In November 2001, Kobayashi dropped out of the society, as a result of his discontent with what he termed his colleagues' "fawning acquiescence" to the American interpretation of the 11 September 2001 attacks on New York and Washington. Nathan, *Japan Unbound,* 242.

163. Donald MacIntyre, "Seoul Searching: Hot Potato," *Time Asia,* 21 February 2001, wysiwyg://13/http:www.time.com/time/asia/news/column/ 0,9754,1000070,00.html.

but they're historical facts, so pupils need to deepen their understanding of them.[164]

The 2001 Textbook Struggle

Predictably, the dawn of the new century brought renewed struggle between those who wanted the texts to give the unvarnished truth and those who thought revelations of Japan's wartime record made the texts "masochistic" and "imbalanced" (right-wing code words). In the fall of 2000, the former expressed alarm at the contents of seven social studies texts, which they claimed had returned to those of twenty years before. Four of the texts, for example, had replaced "Nanjing Massacre" with "Nanjing Incident." Fearing the gains of the 1980s and 1990s would be lost, they blamed the Society for the Creation of New History Textbooks, the Liberal Democratic Party, and the Ministry of Education itself for the backsliding in descriptions of the war.[165]

In mid-January 2001, two Japanese scholars published a point-by-point analysis of drafts of eight new middle-school social studies textbooks put forward for Ministry of Education approval as 2002 texts. The professors reported coverage of "comfort women" had been watered down (with only one of the texts using the term) and references to Japan's wartime use of the Three-Alls policy ("kill all, burn all, destroy all") in China reduced. In addition, the word "advancement" had replaced "invasion," references to Unit 731 had been omitted, and there were fewer references to Japanese colonization of other Asian countries. The Japanese Association of History Educators, the authors added, had demonstrated its concern about the textbooks in an appeal to the public.[166]

Although there were eight texts under consideration for approval by the ministry and adoption by the schools, it was the Society for the Creation of New History Textbooks' volume that proved the main focus of

---

164. Irie, "History of the Textbook Controversy," 38.

165. Yoshida Takashi, e-mail to H-Japan@H-Net.msu.edu, 30 September 2000, forwarding a statement by the Children and Textbooks Japan Network 21 (Netto 21) and several other organizations entitled "The Falsification of History Under the Guise of 'Self-Censorship' Has Been Forced onto Textbook Publishers," 12 September 2000. The group also provided a critical review of a textbook prepared by the Society for the Creation of New Textbooks. Ibid., forwarding a review by Tawara Yoshifumi, who was apparently associated with Netto 21.

166. Hiro Inoguchi and Yoshiko Nozaki, "Japanese Textbook Revision," forwarded to H-Asia@H-Net.msu.edu by Hiromitsu Inoguchi, 18 January 2001. Inoguchi is at the University of East Asia in Shimonoseki, while Nozaki teaches at Massey University in New Zealand.

protests. A few samples from the society's text were even broadcast on NHK and Asahi television.[167]

Many different groups (again giving the lie to Iris Chang's generalizations about "the Japanese") protested the society's textbook. A group led by Oe Kenzaburo, 1994 Nobel prize winner for literature, criticized the society's text for "watering down the infliction of damage on other nations and [for] the justification of Japan's invasion and colonial rule." China and Korea have criticized the texts, the group continued, but "the textbook issue is our own problem. Can we raise the Japanese of the future, who must live in international society, by such textbooks?"[168] Even some veterans of the China war protested.[169] Furthermore, on 13 March, eight Japanese historical associations jointly issued a protest. Three days later, seventeen prominent intellectuals, including Iriye Akira (a Harvard University history professor), entered the fray by delivering an appeal to the Japanese government.[170] Finally, ordinary citizens were not reluctant to voice their views.[171]

As in previous textbook disputes, the Chinese and Koreans also protested against the textbook. As the crisis spread in April 2001, Korea delivered a formal protest to the Japanese government.[172] On 3 April, the crisis came to a head when, after the Japanese government declared it

167. Earl Kinmouth to H-Japan@H-net.msu.edu, "Latest Textbook Flap in Japan," 5 March 2001.

168. French, "Japan's Resurgent Far Right Tinkers with History," 3.

169. Hiro Inokuchi, University of East Asia, Shimonoseki, e-mail to H-Asia@H-net.msu.edu, "Updates of Japanese Revisionist Textbook Issues," 3 April 2001. For interviews with veterans who oppose the war, see Howard W. French, "Japan's New Self-Assertion Troubles Veterans of WWII," *Asahi Shimbun,* 21 June 2001, 1, 6. See also the recent film (2001) about these veterans, *Japanese Devils: Confessions of Imperial Army Soldiers from Japan's War Against China.* For an interview with the director and one of the producers, see wysiwyg://1/http://www.asiasource.org/news/special_reports/japanesedevils.cfm. The question of veterans' views of the war is not a simple one, though, for some cling to the nationalist version of the conflict. French, "Japan's New Self-Assertion," 1, 6.

170. Inokuchi, "Updates of Japanese Revisionist Textbook Issues," 3 April 2001. For a translation into English of the 5 December 2000 appeal by Japanese historians, see the website of the Children and Textbooks Japan Network 21: http://www.ne.jp/asahi/kyokasho/net21/english_contents.htm.

171. For an example, see the criticism by a retired teacher reported in French, "Japan's New Self-Assertion," 6.

172. For descriptions of the Korean and Chinese opposition, see French, "Japan's Resurgent Far Right Tinkers with History," 3; "Teaching Sadistic History," *Korean Herald,* 22 February 2001, wysiwyg://6/http://www.koreaherald.co.kr; "Ministry Displeased with Japanese Textbook," Chosun.com, 3 April 2001, p. 1; Earl Kinmouth to H-Japan@H-net.msu.edu, "Latest History Textbook Flap in Japan," 5 March 2001; Hiro Inokuchi, "Updates of Japanese Revisionist Textbook Issues," 3 April 2001; Carol Gluck, "Japanese History Angers Koreans," BBC News, 1 March 2001, http://news.bbc.co.uk/hi/english/world/asia-pacific/newsid_1196000/1196403.stm;

would not yield to foreign demands and ban the new nationalist history textbook, the Ministry of Education approved it.[173] Moreover, it also approved a nationalists' middle-school civics textbook, which had gone relatively unnoticed by foreign scholars.[174] At the same time, though, the ministry announced 137 sections in the nationalists' history text had been revised because of what the press report called their "controversial content." Nevertheless, the Chinese and Koreans continued to protest, and even brought suit in a Tokyo court in an effort to halt sale of the society's textbook.[175] That did not stop South Korean hackers from causing the crash of a Japanese Ministry of Education website and also attacking the websites of the book's publisher and the Liberal Democratic Party.[176] The society itself may have anticipated the cyber assault, for a day after the recall of the Korean Ambassador to Japan in early April, it removed its website from the internet.[177]

Just as predictable as Korean and Chinese protests of Japanese textbooks was the society's reaction to that opposition. A week after the Koreans recalled their ambassador to Japan, society leader Fujioka Nobukatsu defended the group's text. The Korean protests, he declared, were "blatant interference by a foreign country." "All nations," he insisted, "have a right to interpret their history in their own way, and pass down that interpretation. I think that is a part of sovereignty." Reports of wartime Japanese atrocities, he claimed, were "wartime propaganda . . . just a rumor." The "Greater East Asian War" was fought to secure the independence of Asians, he argued. Critics of Japan's colo-

---

"Korean Protest at Japan History Book," BBC News, 15 March 2001, http://news. bbc.co.uk/hi/english/world/asia-Pacific/newsid_1221000/1221047.stm; "Korea Anger as Japan 'Ignores Atrocities,'" BBC News, 4 April 2001, http://news.bbc.co.uk/hi/english/world/ asia-pacific/newsid_1259000/1259906.stm.

173. "Japan Will Not Bow to Neighbors on Textbook," CNN.com, 4 April 2001, wysiwyg://3/http://asia.cnn.com/2001/WORL...apcf/east/04/04/japan. textbook/index.html.

174. Hiro Inokuchi, "Updates of Japanese Revisionist Textbook Issues," 3 April 2001.

175. "Japan Textbook Angers Neighbors," BBC News, 3 April 2001, http://news. bbc.co.uk/hi/english/world-pacific/newsid_1257000/1257835.stm; "Japan Will Not Bow to Neighbors on Textbook," CNN.com, 4 April 2001. Two examples of changes the publisher made, in response to the ministry's request, were to make clear Japan's annexation of Korea was carried out by force, and to remove the reference downplaying the scope of the Nanjing Massacre. Ibid. According to a report a month earlier, the authors of the text had already made the 137 changes. "Japanese History Gets Rewrite," BBC News, 5 March 2001, http://news.bbc.co.uk/hi/english/world-asia-pacific/newsid_ 1203000/1203063.stm; "Japan Textbook Angers Neighbors," 3 April 2001, p. 2; "S. Koreans Try to Halt Sale of Book in Japan," *Washington Post,* 11 May 2001, A36.

176. "Japan Textbook Angers Neighbors," BBC News, 3 April 2001.

177. Michael Mandelartz to H-Japan@H-net.msu.edu, "Japanese Textbook Issues; Websites," 10 April 2001.

nization of Korea, he continued, did not credit Japan's construction of roads, bridges, and other elements of an infrastructure.[178]

The views expressed in the society's textbook were indeed alarming.[179] As a result, a member of the Center for Research and Documentation of Japan's War Responsibility worried that there was (in the words of a press report) "a mood afoot in Japan to forget its misdeeds." "I think," he mused, "there's some kind of atmosphere that allows approval of this textbook."[180] In light of Japan's depressed economic situation over the past dozen or so years, one can understand his concern. As a foreign editorial put it, "People lack confidence and feel put upon. The Japanese may well be in a mood that is susceptible to a view of history that glorifies their past."[181]

It was at this point that the focus of the struggle over the nationalist text shifted from the national level (the Ministry of Education, the Japanese government, and the Korean and Chinese governments) to the local level in Japan. Although the Ministry of Education had the power to approve texts, the decision whether or not to adopt textbooks for classrooms lay in the hands of local authorities throughout Japan. According to a 1963 law, the district groupings of local boards of education choose which textbooks to adopt.[182]

If Japanese schools did not adopt the nationalist texts (one history and one civics text), then the dispute would be resolved, and the critics would have won—for the time being. Hence, in early April, as part of the struggle to influence the schools' decisions, twelve Japanese organizations issued a critique of the disputed texts. The grounds for opposition are familiar by now, including such nationalists' "hot-button" issues as the Japanese foundation myths (the notions that the Japanese emperor and people are descended from the Sun Goddess and hence are superior to other peoples); the emperor; Japan's colonization of Asia, especially Korea; "comfort women"; and the Nanjing Massacre.[183]

178. Doug Struck, "New Text Reopening Old Wounds," *Washington Post,* 18 April 2001, A14.

179. For an analysis of the contents of the nationalist textbook, see John Nelson, "Tempest in a Textbook: A Report on the New Middle-School History Textbook in Japan," *Critical Asian Studies* 34, no. 1 (2002): 129–48 (esp. 138–44 on the Pacific War). For society member Takubo Tadae's rationale for the society's text, see Doug Struck, "New Text Reopening Old Wounds," A14.

180. Ibid.

181. "Glory Be, New Textbook Calls Japan's Invasion a Liberating Experience," *Daily Telegraph* (London), SMH.com.au, 24 February 2001, wysiwyg://3// http://www.smh.com.au/news/0102/24/world/world12.html.

182. Irie, "The History of the Textbook Controversy," 35.

183. Statement drafted by Children and Textbooks Japan Network 21 and eleven other Japanese organizations, "Information on the Outcome of the Japanese Government Textbook Screening of the History and Civics Textbooks Developed by the

However, the society was the first to move on the local level. In June 2000 in one prefectural assembly and in March 2001 in thirty-two others, it backed passage of resolutions claiming current textbooks conveyed distorted views of history, hence (in the words of an American scholar) "implying the need for the corrective offered by the new [nationalists'] textbooks." In response, in March 2001 the members of an opposition group, the "Textbook Network" (Children and Textbooks Japan Network 21), introduced resolutions and appeals to local assemblies and disseminated leaflets pleading for support. In addition, the network organized one thousand lecture meetings opposing the nationalist text. The struggle peaked in late June, when the books were displayed and citizens were invited to pen comments about them.[184]

In the summer of 2001, the textbook dispute was at last resolved, and by means that demonstrate yet again the gross generalizations of those (like Iris Chang) who criticize "Japanese" for clinging to right-wing memories of the war. In mid-August, local school districts in Japan overwhelmingly rejected the nationalist text. Of 542 school districts, 532 (around 98 percent) refused to adopt the textbook. Only six state schools (for the disabled) and six private schools decided to use the text. This result, the South Korean foreign minister admitted, would (in the words of the press) "partly defuse the controversy."[185]

However, it was evident that although the battle had been won, the war would continue. The week before the text's opponents celebrated victory, more than five hundred people filled a hall in Tokyo dominated by a huge Japanese rising-sun flag to endorse what speakers called the government's "good move" in approving the textbook. In addition, Tokyo's governor and nationalist author Ishihara Shintaro voiced his support for the nationalists' textbook. Moreover, just when the textbook dispute that had riled up the Koreans and Chinese subsided, Prime Minister Koizumi Junichiro paid homage to Japan's war dead at the Yasukuni Shrine and once again stirred up a hornet's nest of protest in Asia.[186]

Members of the Japanese Society for History Textbook Reform," 3 April 2001, forwarded by Inoguchi Hiro, University of East Asia, to H-Japan@H-net.msu.edu, "Controversial Textbooks in [Japan]," 30 April 2001.

184. Kirk Madsen, Kumamoto Gakuen University, to H-Japan@H-net.msu.edu, "Local Textbook," 6 May 2001; "Most Japanese School Districts Reject Disputed Textbook," 16 August 2001, wysiwyg://9/http:// www.nytimes.com/2001/08/16/international/asia/16JAPA.html.

185. Doug Struck and Shigehiko Togo, "Japanese Schools Rejecting Textbook," *Washington Post,* 15 August 2001, A14; "Japan Schools 'Reject Controversial Textbook,'" BBC News, 15 August 2001, http://news.bbc.co.uk/hi/ english/world/aisa-pacific/newsid_1492000/1492802.stm; "Most Japanese School Districts Reject Disputed History Textbook," 16 August 2001, wysiwyg://9/http://www.nytimes.com/ 2001/08/16/international/asia/16JAPA.html.

186. The rally in Tokyo supported Koizumi's visit to the Yasukuni Shrine.

Making matters even worse, the historical approach in the renovated museum at the Yasukuni Shrine, according to one report, was "reminiscent" of that in the nationalistic textbook offered to and rejected by school districts in 2001.[187] Finally, the link between the nationalist textbooks and the right wing was worrisome. In October 2002, a right-wing extremist who tried to peddle nationalist history textbooks at the office of a member of Diet, ended up assassinating the lawmaker.[188]

Conclusions

It should be clear from the material presented above that while some museums in Japan (government operated and/or affiliated with Shinto) still prefer to emphasize Japanese sufferings while ignoring the catastrophe their country inflicted on the Asia-Pacific area during the years between 1931 and 1945, beginning in the early 1990s other museums (the so-called "peace" museums, operated by local governments or privately) have taken it as their mission to shed light on Japanese atrocities during the war.

The parallel and ongoing textbook story also is not a simple one, but one of struggle between those who would confront Japan's past, painful as it might be, and those who, driven by irrational patriotism, practice willful amnesia. After attending a discussion in mid-May 2000 on Japanese high school history textbooks' treatment of the war, an American reporter noted a gap in the audience between those who "felt the text books still do not do justice to Japan's war history" and those who felt "the foreign perception does not do justice to what's in the textbooks."[189] Hence, the struggle between the "two lines" goes on. As one report put it in April 2001, current textbooks rendered "fuller accounts of Japanese actions in the war, but have been slammed by the right for going too far."[190]

One hopeful sign, for Japanese determined to be candid about Japan's wartime actions, is that polls show public opinion does not support the nationalists and conservatives, in and out of government, who prefer to downplay Japan's war record (a conclusion also supported by

---

187. French, "At a Military Museum, the Losers Write History," A4.

188. James Brooke, "Rightist Confesses to killing Japanese Lawmaker, Police Say," *New York Times,* 27 October 2002, 15; Doug Struck, "Japan's Thuggish Right Wing," *Washington Post,* 2 November 2002, A18, A22. According to Japanese police estimates, in 1996 there were eight hundred active right-wing groups in Japan with a total membership of sixteen thousand. Moffett, "Past Perfect," 30.

189. Charles Burress, *San Francisco Chronicle,* "Japanese History Textbooks," e-mail to NBR Japan Forum, 16 May 2000.

190. "Japan Will Not Bow to Neighbors on Textbook," CNN.com, 4 April 2001.

the local districts' rejection of the nationalists' texts in 2001). In 1995, opinion polls showed most Japanese supported an official apology to Japan's victims in the war.[191] More recent surveys reveal Japanese believe two-to-one that the government has not done enough to apologize for the war or to assist its victims. Hence, Japan, writes the author of a recent book, "is coming around."[192] Most hopeful of all, the authors of a recent study of Asia have concluded, "For the first time, there is a debate in Japan about its past, and this is a debate that the nationalists can never win."[193]

In another encouraging development, a private organization called The Center for Research and Documentation on Japan's War Responsibility was founded in Tokyo in 1993. As of January 1999, it had published twenty-two issues of its journal, *Kikan sensoo sekinin kenkyuu* (Reports on Japan's war responsibility), on various wartime crimes, such as the comfort women and Unit 731. It also holds seminars on such issues.[194]

As a result of this article's examination of the peace museums, the textbook disputes of recent years, and the polls, one has to conclude that those who insist "Japan has amnesia" about its wartime record are indulging in gross generalizations. As a scholar at the East-West Center in Hawaii put it in the mid-1990s, "many American commentators minimize the activities of students, historians, journalists and others working to document and publicize Japan's record of wartime aggression."[195] Hence, I hope this article has demonstrated it is careless to write about "the Japanese" view of the war, when the struggle over museums, textbooks, the flag, the national anthem, the emperor, and whether Japanese government officials should visit the Yasukuni Shrine reveal, above all, a divided Japan.

As for which side in this Manichaean struggle will win the right to interpret Japan's role in the war (if either side does), historians are loathe to predict the future. Much could happen in the coming years (economic crises, wars, etc.) to influence the outcome of Japan's division

191. Reid, "Japan's WWII Self-Image Conflict," A22.

192. Kristof and WuDunn, *Thunder from the East,* 236. Polls taken in the early 1990s also supported the notion that the Japanese people, unlike their government, were ready to acknowledge Japan's war responsibility. Hammond, "Commemoration Controversies," 121 n 35.

193. Kristof and WuDunn, *Thunder from the East,* 256. For an excellent study of this debate during the postwar years, see Hicks, *Japan's War Memories.*

194. Yoshida Takashi, e-mail to H-Net list for Asian History and Culture, 16 January 1999; Yoshida Takashi, e-mail to H-Net/KIAPS List for Japanese History, 21 March 2000; John Dower and Mark Selden, "Report on Japan's War Responsibility," in Mark Selden to Steve Leibo, H-Asia@H-net.msu.edu, 18 January 2001.

195. Reid, "Japan's WWII Self-Image Conflict," A1, A22.

over its war ghosts. Perhaps Ian Buruma's conclusion in the early 1990s still holds true today. Although there had been changes in views of the war in Japan, he wrote then, the basic arguments of the two sides remained the same:

> On the one side was a vision of a Japan that had learned from its crimes and would never fight in another war again. On the other was a Japan that should be free once more to be a "normal" military power. As long as one side used historical sins to support its vision of peace, the other would deny them.[196]

As for who was winning, in January 2001 one Japanese scholar confessed he did not know. "It seems to me," he wrote, "that both groups are [a] minority in Japanese society. It seems each group is still fighting over the ignorant majority who are not particularly interested in WWII issues."[197] Others thought of the children. As one reporter wrote, "Surely the children who are the objects of instruction would like to have a clear explanation of this disagreement."[198] What seems certain is that the end of the recurrent or cyclic textbook disputes is not in sight, with the struggles every four years to select new texts for Japan's schools.[199]

196. Buruma, *Wages of Guilt,* 231–32.
197. Yoshida Takashi, "Japanese Textbook Revisions," 25 January 2001. Hence, according to a 2000 poll, in response to the statement, "The last war was unavoidable for Japan's survival due to the shortage of natural resources," almost one-third (31 percent) did not know. Brian Shoesmith to H-Asia@H-net.msu.edu, 10 March 2001.
198. Irie, "History of the Textbook Controversy," 38.
199. "Ministry Displeased with Japanese Textbook," Chosun.com, 30 April 2002, 1–2.

Review Essay

The Military History of Ancient Israel

☆

Rose Mary Sheldon

The Military History of Ancient Israel. By Richard A. Gabriel. West-port, Conn.: Praeger, 2003. ISBN 0-275-97798-6. Maps. Illustrations. Tables. Notes. Selected bibliography. Index. Pp. xv, 334. $79.95.

THE publication of Richard Gabriel's latest book provides an excellent opportunity for addressing some thorny issues in the field of the military history of the Bible. Gabriel has written a military narrative for the conquest of ancient Israel by the successors of Moses with an eye to logistics, tactics, manpower, fortifications, command and control, weapons and weapons manufacture, troop leadership, and military strategy. He is correct in saying that this is the first such book to appear in English. Only Jacob Liver's book, *The Military History of the Land of Israel in Biblical Times,* is comparable, but that work has yet to be translated from the Hebrew. On the surface, Gabriel's book will be convincing to military historians, but only those motivated by religious belief or who are completely unaware of the last half century of scholarship on the subject.

There is no more complex issue in Near Eastern studies than who the Israelites were, how they got into Canaan, and by what means they came to dominate the area. The great French biblical historian Roland de Vaux, in his book, *The Early History of Israel* (Philadelphia: West-

Rose Mary Sheldon is a professor of Ancient History at the Virginia Military Institute. She has spent twenty-five years writing and lecturing on the subject of intelligence in the ancient world. Her articles have appeared in the *International Journal of Intelligence and Counterintelligence, Small Wars and Insurgencies, Studies in Intelligence,* and *Military History Quarterly.* Her books include *Espionage in the Ancient World: An Annotated Bibliography* (McFarland, 2003) and *Intelligence Activities in Ancient Rome: Trust in the Gods, But Verify* (Frank Cass, 2005). Her next book will be on *Spies in the Holy Land.*

minster Press, 1978), described the emergence of Israel in Palestine as "the most difficult problem in the whole history of Israel" (p. 475) and he was not exaggerating. The easiest way to deal with this problem is to assume that the biblical texts present history accurately. This view has come to be known as the Conquest Model. The last half-century, however, has witnessed an intense dialogue—even polemic—on the topic as two other major reconstructions of the evidence have vied for center stage. As early as the 1920s, there was already a group of scholars in Germany who rejected the Conquest Model. Albrecht Alt and Martin Noth put forward what came to be known as the "Peaceful Infiltration Model" as an alternative to the largely American fundamentalist approach. The German school discarded the stories in Joshua entirely and concentrated on modern ethnographic studies of Middle Eastern pastoral nomads who wandered over long distances but eventually put down roots as peasants or townspeople. They compared this modern phenomenon to the biblical tradition of Israel's ancestors described in Genesis as wandering, tent-dwelling shepherds. In this view, the Israelites did not fight their way in through the Sinai, but rather were part of a natural process of settling down in one place that has been going on in this region for millennia. In this view, the Israelites did not need military reconnaissance; they were simply shepherds looking for better pasture.

Finally, in 1962, George Mendenhall of the University of Michigan, a student of the famous biblical archaeologist and historian William Foxwell Albright, published an article which rejected both the "Conquest" and "Peaceful Infiltration" models ("The Biblical Conquest of Palestine," *Biblical Archaeology* 25, no. 1 [1962]: 66–87). Mendenhall believed that Israel did not win against its neighbors because of better military weapons or superior military organization. He believed that Israelite victory came as a result of a religiously motivated internal revolution. His theory was based solely on an analysis of internal social developments in Canaan during the Late Bronze Age. The conflict was thus not between the nomads and the settled population but between the rural population and the rulers of the city-states. Mendenhall believed that there was a peasant revolt, united in its worship of the God YHWH. The new religious movement placed its faith in a single God who established egalitarian laws of social conduct and who communicated directly to each member of the community. The hold of the kings over the community was therefore effectively broken by the spread of the new faith. The Israelite conquest was accomplished without invasion or immigration, but occurred when a large number of Canaanite peasants overthrew their masters and became "Israelites." According to Mendenhall, the concept that the Israelites must originally have been nomads or a distinct ethnic group is mistaken. One of the differences between the three schools is that adherents to the Conquest Model like W. F. Albright and his students G. E. Wright and J. Bright argued that archaeology had demonstrated the essential historicity of the biblical narrative. They were the last mainstream scholars to do so. The Conquest Model has been all but discarded by remaining investigators except for biblical fundamentalists and military historians. J. Maxwell Miller and John Hayes's publication of *A History of Israel and Judah* (London, SCM Press) in 1986 provoked more than 50 pages of review articles in a leading journal, most of which questioned the working assumptions of the authors in their attempt to recreate the ancient Israelite past.

The problem with Gabriel's book, therefore, is entirely methodological. He accepts the biblical texts as reliable in spite of over a century of literary research showing them to be internally contradictory, unreliable, filled with more myth than history, and, most importantly, written much later than the events they describe. Gabriel has no choice but to follow the Conquest Model because without it there is no reliable military history to write. Because no reputable scholar in the last half century outside of religious schools used this model, Gabriel had to go back more than fifty years to the works of W. F. Albright and his students to bolster his arguments. Gabriel accepts the early scholarship uncritically. True scholarly research, however, can take nothing for granted, and the pivotal points of one's dependence upon earlier scholars should be accepted only after careful verification of their correctness. The uncritical adoption of the work of Albright and Yigael Yadin (about whom more later) is unfortunate. A simple glance at William G. Dever's book, *Who Were the Early Israelites and Where Did They Come From?* (Grand Rapids, Mich.: Eerdmans, 2003) or V. Philips Long's *Israel's Past in Present Research: Essays on Ancient Israelite Historiography* (Winona Lake, Ind.: Eisenbrauns, 1999) would provide readers with an overview of the complexities of modern research in this area. Avraham Malamat has spent as much time as any writer at grips with the military history of ancient Israel, and even he admits that the Old Testament is a literary creation written for purposes quite other than historical reporting. He describes it as an "ancient theoretical model" depicting the conquest of the Israelites.

Recent archaeological studies that undercut rather than support the historicity of the biblical traditions about Israelite origins have yielded conclusions that are startling to the uninitiated. The search for historical ancestors has failed; the Exodus did not happen as described; the violent, swift, and total conquest of Canaan never took place; the picture of judges leading tribes in battle against their enemies does not fit the data; David and Solomon existed in the tenth century BCE but as little more than "hill country chieftains"; and there was no golden age of a united kingdom, a magnificent capital, and an extended empire. This is disturbing news to most people. Rather than interpret these conclusions as historical nihilism, however, they should be seen as alternative under-standings of the material and as invitations to fresh new discussions.

Gabriel's contribution to the field is in looking at the battles with a tactician's eye and describing what he thinks *must have happened.* An author is entitled to do this, but what he then produces is a work of spec-ulation, not history. In the process of using his fertile imagination to rewrite the story, Gabriel is willing to discard most of the modern litera-ture on Near Eastern archaeology and literary criticism while claiming to follow the Old Testament. On the other hand, he has no problem dis-carding the biblical texts once they, too, prove inconvenient. It has seemed implausible to many commentators that an army in rags, travel-ing with women and children and the aged, emerging after decades in the desert, could mount an effective invasion. How could this unorganized rabble overcome the great fortresses of Canaan with their professional armies and well-trained chariotry. What could their training have been in military tactics? To answer this question, Gabriel conjures up previ-ous military training for the Israelites. He cannot explain how a small force of Israelites could be so effective, so he asserts that the Israelites seriously outnumbered the Canaanites. Gabriel likes to take numbers from biblical passages and extrapolate them to produce impressive "facts" about military forces, but what he creates are factoids. Ancient numbers are notoriously unreliable not only because of manuscript cor-ruption, but also because the biblical authors, with no access to the actual battle accounts, used numbers from other sources or simply made them up. No amount of multiplication or division based on an inaccurate base number will produce accurate statistics.

Despite Mordechai Gichon's claim in the Foreword that this book will produce "a new stimulus to Exodus studies," Gabriel produces not a single shred of new evidence. The problem with the Exodus story, as every serious scholar of the period knows, is that it has no independent corroboration whatsoever. Gabriel does not put much stock in archaeol-ogy, because he knows that a science that can find even the most mea-ger remains of hunter-gatherers and pastoral nomads the world over has not turned up a single trace of the 600,000 wandering Jews mentioned in Exodus (or even the 50,000 that Gabriel suggests). There is simply no evidence for an Exodus in the thirteenth century BCE. Gabriel once again presents the history of the Exodus as it *should have been.* He writes: "The truth is that the Exodus is a saga of a people equipped and familiar with weapons, led by experienced and tactically proficient com-manders, who were not Egyptian slaves, and whose military proficiency and operational capability improved greatly during the desert trek until, with remarkable clarity of strategic aim, they were able to achieve their ultimate objective of conquering the land of Canaan" (p. 60). Even if we accept this "Joshua as George Patton" model, Gabriel has left out a step.

The Bible says very clearly that none of the original group was allowed to enter Canaan, not even Moses. Only two original members entered the Promised Land: Joshua and Caleb followed by an entirely new generation of followers. Were they in a training camp in the Sinai for forty years? Practicing against whom? Bedouin?

In the same way that the archaeological evidence does not support the Exodus story, it does not support the story of the lightning campaign of conquest of Joshua. The total absence of archaeological levels showing destruction at key sites like Jericho, Dibon, and Heshbon in Transjordan and the absence of any possible occupational levels giving a context for such destruction is either ignored or rationalized away. The last person to try to salvage the Conquest Model was another of Albright's students, Paul Lapp, who did a survey of the archaeological evidence on the Late Bronze Age I levels at these sites. Lapp believed the stratigraphic evidence pointed strongly to the complete destruction of nearly all important cities in Canaan in the last half of the thirteenth century BCE ("The Conquest of Palestine in the Light of Archaeology," *Concordia Theological Monthly* 38 [1968]: 495–548). No archaeologist today would make such a statement because the matrix of destruction levels is much more complex. Israel Finkelstein has summed up the evidence in eloquent fashion in *The Archaeology of the Israelite Settlement* (Jerusalem: Israel Exploration Society, 1988, pp. 295–302). Gabriel mentions neither of these studies.

Not only has Gabriel totally disregarded the archaeological evidence, his reconstruction of events never deals with the obvious anachronisms of the biblical story itself. To give just one example, the tales of Gideon and the Midianites and David and the Amalekites both assume a large-scale use of camels for trade and military purposes. Nadav Na'aman ("The Conquest of Canaan," in I. Finkelstein and N. Na'aman, *From Nomadism to Monarchy: Archaeological and Historical Aspects of Early Israel* (Washington: Biblical Archaeology Society, 1994, p. 226) has pointed out that excavations from Iron Age sites throughout Israel reveal only a small number of camel bones, and that camels were domesticated in a long and gradual process that took several hundred years and reached an advanced stage only in the last third of the second millennium BCE. The widespread employment of camels in caravans and for war became common only with the appearance of the Arabs in the ninth century BCE (contra both Albright and Malamat).

Gabriel over and over makes the mistake of assuming that because a battle occurred in a place that exists in Israel today where the geography roughly correlates to the biblical description, then this proves that the battle took place as described at the time the Bible says it did. He never takes into consideration that a later author might have used these locations because they were the sites of subsequent battles fought there closer to the time of composition of the Books of Joshua, Judges, Deuteronomy, and Kings. And indeed, this brings up another complex issue that Gabriel sidesteps entirely—the essential unity and date of composition of the so-called Deuteronomic history. Martin Noth is the scholar generally credited with the idea that the books from Deuteronomy to II Kings were written as a "unified and self-contained whole," by someone he named the Deuteronomist (Dtr) historian. Noth theorized that Dtr was writing in the middle of the sixth century BCE using traditional material. He compares Dtr's mode of composition to that of Hellenistic and Roman writers who used older sources to compose a history of the distant past. Later redactors added to the history in what Noth called a series of "accretions." While some scholars have challenged his sixth century dating or modified his redactional theories, most now take seriously Noth's concept of the Dtr history. The three major schools of thought that have developed concerning the sources and the redaction of the Dtr history can be roughly divided into those who think it is pre-exilic (before 587 B.C.E.), exilic (587–538 B.C.E.) , and post-exilic (after 538 B.C.E.). Israel Finkelstein's book, *The Bible Unearthed* (New York: Free Press, 2001) brings together the archaeological and literary evidence to argue for a seventh-century date.

The problem with the authors who follow the Conquest Model is, therefore, that they have the historical context wrong. When Mordechai Gichon writes, "all agree that the Biblical narrative reflects exactly conditions and the material background of its age," he is wrong. Very few people these days would assert that the Bible describes reality on the ground in the thirteenth century BCE, and scholars like Philip F. Davies have pointed out that using the biblical narrative for the critical reconstruction of periods it describes rather than the period it was written in, is precarious and should only be attempted where there is ample independent data. The context for these stories is not the twelfth century BCE but the seventh. The literary texts we are working from were probably created by a historian writing half a millennium later, and the author was probably using military examples from his own day to explain the Israelite takeover of Israel. Gabriel never considers the possibility that the narrative might well have been composed *de novo* in the seventh century in the reign of King Josiah or later. He completely ignores the works of Keith Whitelam, Niels Peter Lemche, Thomas Thompson, Israel Finkelstein, or Philip R. Davies, who all argue for a late date of composition that completely discards the notion that the battles were based on eyewitness accounts. Reference to Lori L. Rowlett's *Joshua and the Rhetoric of Violence: A New Historicist Analysis* (Sheffield, U.K.: Sheffield Academic Press, 1996) will give readers an excellent summary of the state of the question and a discussion of the Josianic influence.

One might legitimately point out that the Israelite view of their own history portrays them as a marginal and oppressed people (whether of Canaanite origins or not) who entered Israel (or rose up from within) and became a people with a national consciousness who wrote the history of their own origins. There is no doubt that the Bible has given us some of the most memorable war stories in literature. The Israelites *themselves* chose to see their history as a continuous military conquest. Does this allow us, then, as modern historians to think we can write an accurate military history of them? Unfortunately not, since we are unable to corroborate their story. There is certainly reason to believe Israelite history included armed conflict with neighbors. Even Norman Gottwald, normally one of the opponents of the Conquest Model, has admitted "there is truth in the Conquest Model in that there was some military activity that occurred" (in Shanks, "Israel's Emergence in Canaan," *Biblical Archaeological Review,* October 1989, p. 26). Most historians would also agree, however, that the Dtr author was not working from eyewitness accounts.

Missing from Gabriel's narrative is all the literary, biblical form criticism, and archaeological scholarship from the 1970s to the present. Gabriel neither acknowledges nor comes to terms with the works of German scholars Alt, Noth, or Fritz, American scholars George Mendenhall, William G. Dever, Kyle McCarter, Lawrence Stager, Anson F. Rainey, or Baruch Halpern. The pages of the *Biblical Archaeology Review* have been filled with debates between these men, and none of them accepts the Conquest Model. Ironically, Gabriel takes information on the nomadic *Apiru* out of Norman Gottwald's book, *The Tribes of Yahweh: A Sociology of the Religion of Liberated Israel, 1250–1050 B.C.E.* (Maryknoll, N.Y.: Orbis Books, 1979), for example, yet completely ignores the fact that Gottwald's book is one of the greatest onslaughts against the Conquest Model in print.

Gabriel never considers the work of Israeli scholars like Israel Finkelstein, whose *Archaeology of Israelite Settlement* took apart the Conquest Model in 1988. The work of archaeologists who have done all the important survey work in the areas so crucial to the discussion of who the Israelites were, where they lived, how they fought, and who they fought against are also ignored. Surely the book of Judges should be assessed in the light of the writings of N. Na'aman, Y. Aharoni, A. Mazar, M. Kochavi, S. Bunimovitz, T. Dothan, and D. Usshiskin. Instead, Gabriel relies on Yigael Yadin, whose work and its political intent, have come under severe attack by N. Ben-Yehuda (*Sacrificing Truth: Archaeology and the Myth of Masada* [Amherst, N.Y.: Humanity Books, 2002]).

The most difficult problem confronting any scholar writing about the ancient world is the limited, fortuitous, and tendentious nature of the sources. The one source at our disposal in this case, the Bible, was not written as a history in our modern sense of the word, and therefore had another agenda entirely. There is virtually no agreed-upon opinion in academic circles as to whether the Bible qualifies as history, as to its date of composition, or the process it went through to reach its present form, but readers would not be able to tell this by reading Gabriel's book. In all fairness to him, it is extremely difficult to show the diversity of opinion within the space limits of a book (let alone in this review), but one can at least allude in the notes to alternative interpretations. Any honest assessment will come to the same conclusion: we will never have all the information we need to make even an informed guess about the historicity of the activities discussed in the Hebrew Scriptures.

Besides the methodological problems noted here, Gabriel's present work suffers from the same sins as his other books: monolingual sources, reliance on out-of-date secondary sources by popular authors, and no real understanding for the state of current research. There is a lack of consistency in citing sources. The article by A. D. H. Mayes on p. 18 cited as: 19 (1951), pp. 253–360 would send any interested reader on a wild goose chase; the correct citation is 19 (July 1969): 353–60. There are some howling examples of modern military terms being inserted anachronistically into past contexts. The use of the word "bureaucracy" for David's government (p. 229) is one. On page 231 David develops a "grand strategy." Terms like "citizen army," "sense of national direction," "national government," "defense institutions," "national security situation," (p. 170) are examples of Pentagon jargon that are anachronistic in an ancient context.

Gabriel is certainly not the only writer to chase the chimera of the Conquest Model, and he will not be the last, but such an approach constitutes a rush down the same intellectually sterile path. The extent to which textbook authors have clung persistently to the traditional approach and ignored current scholarship has been eloquently demonstrated by Jack Cargill in "Ancient History in Western Civ Textbooks," *History Teacher* 34, no. 3 (May 2001): 297–326. Writers are, of course, entitled to adhere to any point of view they desire and to bolster it with whatever evidence they can find. What they are not allowed to do is to discard seventy-five years of research because it is inconvenient to their theory and call the results history.

Review Essay

The "Military Revolution," 1955–2005: From Belfast to Barcelona and The Hague

☆

Geoffrey Parker

Abstract

Michael Roberts launched his celebrated "Military Revolution" idea in a lecture delivered at the Queen's University, Belfast, fifty years ago. To commemorate this event, and to reflect its continuing impact, Geoffrey Parker—himself a participant in the debate—reviews recent "special issues" of two journals, one published in Catalonia and the other in the Netherlands, devoted to the military history of early modern Europe.

FIFTY years ago, at the Queen's University, Belfast, Michael Roberts delivered one of the most influential Inaugural lectures ever given: "The military revolution, 1560–1660." He began with a modest disclaimer that he felt the topic of his own research to be too obscure.

> I concern myself with a small country, peripheral to the main centres of European development; its history neglected, and almost unknown to English scholars; its language untaught in our schools, and unblessed, I am afraid, by any very high priority in our universities. In these circumstances, the cultivation of Swedish history is bound to be something of a purely personal hobby; and that is one reason why I have felt it better not to take it as my subject for this lecture.

Instead, Roberts deployed his daunting knowledge of early modern European history (in many languages) to select four critical changes in the art

Geoffrey Parker holds Ph.D. and Litt.D. degrees from Cambridge University and is the Andreas Dorpalen Professor of History at Ohio State University. His *Philip II* (1978) has been through numerous editions and translations, and *The Grand Strategy of Philip II* (1998) won the Society for Military History's Samuel Eliot Morison prize. His other books include *The Army of Flanders and the Spanish Road* (1972) and *The Dutch Revolt* (1984). He has written, edited, or co-edited thirty books.

of war in the century following 1560. He reviewed in turn the "revolution in tactics" (the replacement of the lance and pike with firepower), the growth in army size, and the adoption of more ambitious and complex strategies, ascribing most of these transformations to the military innovations wrought by Maurice and William Louis of Nassau in the Dutch Republic in the 1590s, and by Gustavus Adolphus of Sweden a generation later. He then examined the impact of the new-scale warfare upon Europe's political and social development.[1]

Like so many Inaugural lectures, probably even this novel contribution would have passed into oblivion had Sir George Clark not singled it out for special praise as the new orthodoxy in his 1956 Wiles Lectures, published two years later as *War and Society in the Seventeenth Century*. For a quarter of a century, almost every work on early modern Europe that mentioned warfare included a paragraph or two that summarized Roberts's argument. Then, from 1976, a plethora of books and articles by various historians discussed the "military revolution" of early modern Europe, and in the 1990s strategic analysts began to compare it with the "Revolution in Military Affairs" which they perceived in the wake of the Gulf War. All of them took that 1955 lecture as their starting point.[2] The two items that form the subject of this brief review attest to its continuing importance.

The journal *Manuscrits,* published by the Universitat Autónoma of Barcelona, devoted almost its entire issue for 2003 to "New perspectives

1. Michael Roberts, *The Military Revolution, 1560–1660: An Inaugural Lecture Delivered before the Queen's University of Belfast* (Belfast: Boyd, 1956), quotation from p. 3. It has been frequently reprinted, most recently in *The Military Revolution Debate: Readings on the Military Transformation of Early Modern Europe,* ed. C. J. Rogers (Boulder, Colo.: Westview Press, 1995), 13–35. Later in 1955, he also delivered a complementary lecture, "Gustav Adolf and the Art of War," printed in Michael Roberts, *Essays in Swedish History* (London: Arnold, 1967), 56–81. For more on how Roberts came to choose "The Military Revolution" as the topic of his Inaugural in January 1955—he had originally planned to speak on historiography—see Geoffrey Parker, "Michael Roberts, 1908–1996," *Proceedings of the British Academy: Biographical Memoirs of Fellows* 115 (2002): 333–54.

2. George N. Clark, *War and Society in the Seventeenth Century* (Cambridge: Cambridge University Press, 1958). For a succinct review of writings on the Military Revolution in the 1980s, see Rogers, *Military Revolution Debate,* 4–5; for the expanding debate in the 1990s, see Clifford J. Rogers, "'Military Revolutions' and 'Revolutions in Military Affairs': A Historian's Perspective," in *Towards a Revolution in Military Affairs? Defense and Security at the Dawn of the Twenty-First Century,* ed. T. Gongora and H. von Riekhof (Westport, Conn.: Archon, 2000), 21-35. For one example of the article's impact, see I. A. A. Thompson, *War and Society in Habsburg Spain* (Aldershot, U.K.: Variorum, 1992), ix: "My interest in the historical study of war [was] inspired by Michael Roberts's seminal essay on 'The Military Revolution.'"

on the history of war."[3] The "dossier" contained six articles, three of them by British Hispanists. I. A. A. Thompson opened with "Towards a Profile of the Spanish Soldier," using surviving recruiting lists in Spanish archives to establish the demographic profile and geographic origins of over 3,500 Spanish soldiers who enlisted between 1575 and 1628. His data show that the typical recruit was not the "gentleman soldier" of literary legend but rather a man of humble birth in his twenties (median age = 22), living in a town of 5,000 inhabitants or more, probably a bachelor, unemployed, and born in Old Castile. The brief descriptions of the recruits included in many lists further suggests that most were of average size, with brown eyes and brown hair, with at least one scar on their face—and almost never bald! In "The Resilience of the Spanish Monarchy under Carlos II (1665–1700)," Christopher Storrs sought to explain the survival for thirty-five years of the far-flung possessions inherited by Carlos II despite every effort by his enemies, led by Louis XIV, to dismember them. Storrs identified a coherent defense policy at the centre and the careful use of scarce resources to maintain armies and navies as the principal explanations, assisted by effective diplomacy to mobilize allies and surprising strong loyalty to the ailing dynasty. Lorraine White, in "War and the Military Revolution in Seventeenth-century Iberia," examined the longest running war in the peninsula—between Spain and Portugal between 1640 and 1668—to test the various "Military Revolution" theories advanced by Michael Roberts, Geoffrey Parker, John Lynn, and David Parrott, and in the process provided (in text and tables) much valuable information on that forgotten conflict. In "Image and Military Propaganda in the War of Succession (1700–1713)," Cristina Borreguero Beltrán included several striking artistic compositions—tapestries, engravings, paintings, even playing cards—issued in support of the Austrian and French candidates to succeed Carlos II; she also reviewed printed propaganda, including poems, pamphlets, and that most neglected form of mobilizing popular support—the sermon. She also prints a sample of the (shorter) written polemics. Manuel-Reyes García Hurtado, "War and Propaganda at the End of the Eighteenth Century: José Felipe de Olivé y el Correo de Gerona (1795)," examined the items published in the first Spanish newspaper ever to appear with an expressly military orientation: it was published in the Catalan city of Gerona during the war between Spain and the new French Republic and, in part, sought to counter stories that appeared in the "military newspapers" published by the French armies just across the frontier. Finally,

3. *Manuscrits. Revista d'història moderna* 21 (2003): 13–191. All articles appeared in Castilian with a summary (often substantial) in English and Catalan. Copies of the volume may be ordered from the Servei de Publicacions of the Universitat Autónoma de Barcelona: sp@uab.es.

Antonio Espino López, who also edited this dossier, reviewed "Works about War During the Habsburg Period Published by Hispanists Between 1991 and 2000." He divided the works of over seventy authors into five sections: military sociology; the army; the impact of war; military architecture; and the culture of war. Like all the contributors to this dossier, these historians include women as well as men, and foreigners as well as Spaniards: clearly the field is flourishing.

Early modern war also occupied most of the pages in the last issue for 2003 of the Dutch historical journal *Bijdragen en Mededelingen betreffende de Geschiedenis der Nederlanden.*[4] It contains five articles, one of them a short overview by Jeroen Duindam of the traditional contempt shown by academic historians for those who study war and how, recently, this has changed—in part because the "Military Revolution" debate provided an issue with which scholars in other fields could engage. He also noted the centrality of the military history of the Netherlands to this debate. Michiel de Jong's article on "Military Reforms in the Dutch Army and the Growth of the Arms Industry, 1585–1621" made this connection explicit. He examined five key aspects of the "Military Revolution" introduced by Maurice and William Louis of Nassau: the increased use of firearms; the standardization of weaponry; the growth of the Dutch army; the increased importance of siege warfare; and regular payment for the troops. Taken together, these developments transformed the scale and nature of the industrial demands of the Dutch armed forces (the expanding fleet also required far more equipment) and this in turn led to rationalization and concentration among arms producers. The result was unprecedented standardization, advanced credit arrangements, division of labor, and the creation of an arms industry able to supply not only domestic but also foreign demand.[5] Olaf van Nimwegen, "The Dutch Army and the Early Modern Military Revolution," set the reforms of the Nassau cousins in a broader context, noting that they were forgotten as soon as the Dutch Republic made peace and demobilized its armed forces. He argued that only in the 1670s did the Republic maintain a standing army of professional troops, so that the "Nassau tactical revolution" could become permanently embedded in their restructured army. Étienne Rooms, "The Salaries, Provisions and Quarters of the Royal Troops in the Spanish Netherlands, 1567–1700,"

4. *Bijdragen en Mededelingen betreffende de Geschiedenis der Nederlanden* 118, no. 4 (2003): 453–566. All articles are in Dutch, with English summaries at pp. 621–23. Copies of the issue may be ordered from the secretariat of the Koninklijk Nederlands Historisch Genootschap: knhg@xs4all.nl

5. This article is based on the first chapter of Michiel de Jong, *"Staet van Oorlog." Wapenbedrijf en militaire hervormingen in de Republiek der Verenigde Nederlanden, 1585–1621* (Leiden: Leiden University Press, 2002), which contains a much longer English summary.

surveyed the steady decline in the military effectiveness of the Spanish Army of Flanders as money from Spain gradually dried up after the 1640s, leaving the South Netherlands to provide their multi-ethnic defenders with pay, food, and lodging. Since they failed to find the necessary resources, only the intervention of Dutch and (after 1688) of British troops preserved the integrity of the state.[6] Finally, J. P. C. M. van Hoof, "New Methods, Strong Borders: Menno van Coehoorn's Building Plans and Contribution to Improving the Defense System," offered an important analysis of the remarkable fortification system designed by Coehoorn, the principal military architect of the Dutch Republic, between 1680 and 1685, and the way he implemented it between 1698 and 1702, modernizing existing fortifications and creating from them defensive "lines" to protect his country against the inevitable fresh onslaught of the French.

In January 1995, Michael Roberts observed with characteristic modesty, "It is a sobering thought that an obscure Inaugural in a provincial university should provide the pretext for forty years of debate. I can't help feeling that for once in my life I did *invent* something."[7] He would have been pleased and proud that, ten years later, the debate still continues.

---

6. This article too draws from a larger work: Étienne Rooms, "De materiele organisatie van de troepen van de Spaanse-Habsburgse Monarchie in de Zuidelijke Nederlanden, 1665–1700" (Ph.D. thesis, Vrije Universiteit Brussel, 1998), soon to be published in both Dutch and French. Note that his argument contrasts strongly with that of Christopher Storrs summarized above.

7. Letter from Michael Roberts to Geoffrey Parker.

Review Essay

War Stories

☆

Alex Danchev

Books mentioned in this article include:

Photo Nomad. By David Douglas Duncan. New York: Norton, 2003. ISBN 0-393-05861-1. Photographs. Pp. 464. $29.95/£19.95.

Don McCullin. Essay by Susan Sontag. Introduction by Harold Evans. London: Cape, 2003. ISBN 0-224-07118-1. Pp. 320. $32.00/£17.50.

The Eye of War. Edited by Phillip Knightley, Sarah Jackson, and Annabel Merullo. Washington: Smithsonian Institution/London: Weidenfeld & Nicolson, 2003. ISBN 1-5883-4165-8/0-297-84311-7. Pp. 288. $39.95/£30.00.

Regarding the Pain of Others. By Susan Sontag. New York: Farrar, Strauss and Giroux/London: Hamish Hamilton, 2003. ISBN 0-3742-4858-3/0-241-14207-5. Pp. 132. $20.00/£12.99.

THERE'S no way around it," rues Michael Herr in *Dispatches*, the *Under Fire* of the Vietnam generation, "if you photographed a dead Marine with a poncho over his face and got something for it, you were *some* kind of parasite. But what were you if you pulled the poncho back first to make a better shot, and did that in front of his friends? Some other kind of parasite, I suppose. Then what were you if you stood there watching it, making a note to remember it later in case you might want to use it? Those combinations were infinite, you worked them out, and they involved only a small part of what we were thought to be. We were

Alex Danchev is Professor of International Relations at the University of Nottingham, U.K. His most recent work includes a biography, *Georges Braque* (New York: Arcade; London: Hamish Hamilton, 2004), and an edited collection, *The Iraq War and Democratic Politics* (London and New York: Routledge, 2004). A shorter version of this article appeared in the *Times Literary Supplement*, 21 May 2004.

called thrill freaks, death-wishers, wound-seekers, war-lovers, hero-worshippers, closet queens, dope addicts, low-grade alcoholics, ghouls, communists, seditionists, more nasty things than I can remember. . . . And there were plenty of people who believed, finally, that we were nothing more than glorified war profiteers. And perhaps we were, those of us who didn't get killed or wounded or otherwise fucked up."

War photography is a lethal line of work. Peculiarly vulnerable to sniping of all sorts, its professional credentials, ethical cargo and political kinesis are subject to incessant questioning, and self-questioning. Is it a craft or a calling? A document or a statement? Does it verify or prettify? Sensitize or anaesthetize? Does it side with remembering or forgetting? Intervention or abstention? Does it leave the world as it is or seek to change it? Does it speak to moral scruple? What does it have to say?

"Patrol went up a mountain. One man came back. He died before he could tell us what happened." War is hell. Photography is tourism. The war tourist beats even the sex tourist in the exploitation stakes. "What passing-bells for these who die as cattle?" In the age of the military-industrial-media-entertainment network—James Der Derian's MIME-NET—where can we turn? We can turn to the old verities, trapped with a new light-fingered light-source: the ejaculatory force of the eye, as Robert Bresson put it, through a view-finder. Camera obscura. Leica aperta. Nikon icon. The pity is in the poetry. In a culture saturated by MIME-NET, war photography is the new war poetry. The passing-bells are plangent still. They are rung by the photojournalist. Don McCullin, an aesthete with combat fatigue, is Wilfred Owen incarnate—Owen who carried photographs of the dead in his wallet—the haunted witness, attending the roll-call in his darkroom. "It was like *All Quiet on the Western Front*. Men marching through the mist. Men I'd seen killed came up out of the mist of war to join me." Photographs are prophecies in reverse, as Roland Barthes remarked. Men at arms are shot and shot again. They bleed, reminiscent, in black and white. Contortionists, they practise composition. (McCullin, master of the frame, is partially colour-blind.) The visual lexicon of war is as well-learned, and as searing, as the verbal one; the strategy is the original shock and awe. Abraham Lincoln in his first inaugural address spoke of "the mystic chords of memory, stretching from every battlefield and patriot grave, to every heart and hearthstone, . . . when again touched, as surely they will be, by the better angels of our nature." After McCullin, the war photographer bids to be a better angel. Poet or parasite?

The basic issues are as old as war photography itself. When Roger Fenton, one of the founders of the Royal Photographic Society, was sent to the Crimea in 1855 to record what happened there, he was given strict instructions: no dead bodies. A century and a half later, the British and the American governments are plainly very nervous about images of dead bodies from Iraq—our dead, that is, not theirs—so much so that those images are now effectively banned from transmission on U.S. television. More surprisingly, such restrictions do not appear to have been as cramping as might have been expected. In an impassioned argument with her earlier self, *Regarding the Pain of Others,* Susan Sontag contends that we need images to make something real (a paradox, but only a superficial one): *to bring it home to us,* as the saying goes, more appropriately than we know. "A photograph can't coerce," she concludes a brilliant pendant, and homage, in *Don McCullin.* "It won't do the moral work for us. But it can start us on the way." Its force is not necessarily a function of the realism or naturalism of the images, still less of their X rating. "Realism" in war photography is a genre, rather like the "hard-boiled" mystery novel. Naturalism is a false nose. The pain of others may be exposed in the darkroom; but it is only a fleeting glimpse. Robert Capa touted his celebrated sequence of the D-Day landings in 1944 as "a cut-out of the event which will show more of the real truth of the affair to someone who was not there than the whole scene". And yet, for all the truth-serum tropes of documentary authenticity, the unholstered instantaneity of the hand-held camera, the off-centre, out-of-kilter blurred vision, there has been a certain sanitization of our wars as purveyed by our war photographers—a sanitization of the battlefield in particular but that tendency seems to owe more to self-censorship (or self-control) than to external imposition. The deputy director of BBC News has recently offered an interesting cultural explanation for this phenomenon: "our Anglo-Saxon sensibility," he suggests, has meant a pronounced reluctance to scrutinize the dead, above all British dead, and a chronic aversion to the close-up. If there is a Western way of warfare, as some commentators believe, perhaps there is also a Western way of war photography.

André Friedmann, who became Robert Capa, was actually a Hungarian, but something of an honorary Westerner by the time he claimed the mantle of "the world's greatest war photographer." Capa's way was dangerously simple. "If your pictures aren't good enough," he would say, "you're not close enough." Capa (meaning shark) led a voracious life, but getting closer eventually got him killed by an antipersonnel mine on the Red River Delta in Indochina in 1954. David Douglas Duncan, whose autobiographical assemblage *Photo Nomad* is a present to himself on his eighty-seventh birthday, is a rare survivor. His coverage of the Korean War in 1950 for *Life* magazine was later acclaimed by Edward Steichen as "the highest tide that combat photography has achieved". David Douglas Duncan's formula is at once homely and profound. It is set out in his book like a creed:

> Be close—Be fast—Be lucky
> Easy
> Always remember
> Be humane
> Never close-ups of the dead
> War is in the eyes

The classic war photographers (photographers of the classic wars) have all been portrait photographers *in extremis*. They sought the whites of the eyes, and tried to fathom what they found there. Wilfred Owen wrote to his mother of "the very strange look" he had seen on soldiers' faces at Étaples in 1917: "an incomprehensible look, which a man will never see in England. . . . It was not despair or terror, it was more terrible than terror, for it was a blindfold look, without expression, like a dead rabbit's. It will never be painted, and no actor will ever seize it. And to describe it, I think I must go back and be with them." A number of war photographers, including Don McCullin in his time, have surely felt the same impulse.

The problem of the communicability or incommunicability of suffering is nested in atrocity, and irreducibly in war. "Was it not noticeable at the end of the war that men returned from the battlefield grown silent—not richer, but poorer in communicable experience?" Walter Benjamin's observation in "The Storyteller" (1936) could apply to any war. Normally photographers take portraits. War portraits are not taken but frozen-seized—as if wrung from the very soul of the subject. These portraits lay claim to being the most immediate and the most profound communication of incommunicable experience available to us. They are nameless and numberless, but they are all face, and the face has the same look. David Douglas Duncan calls it the Thousand Yard Stare. It tells of the untellable. These photographs speak in their fashion of the unspeakable. Not coincidentally, two of them feature on the cover of *The Eye of War* and *Don McCullin*. There is no more eloquent war story. For Benjamin "the storyteller is the figure in which the righteous man encounters himself." There are many jobbing war photographers. There are doubtless some skunks. There are some storytellers too.

War photography has generally traded under the name of photojournalism. "Don't keep the label of surrealist photographer," Capa admonished Henri Cartier-Bresson. "Be a photojournalist. If not you will fall into mannerism. Keep surrealism in your little heart, my dear. Don't fidget. Get moving!" Ever since the founding of the legendary Magnum agency by Capa, Cartier-Bresson, George Rodger and David "Chim" Seymour, in 1947, it has been clear that the photojournalist could have a style, a point of view, even a sense of mission. Sontag writes of the "ethically weighted" mission of the Magnum photographer—something like humanitarian intervention—and one of its chief exponents, Philip Jones Griffiths, a war photographer who refused the label of war photographer in Vietnam, has spoken feelingly of the values of "concerned" photography which continue to animate that international collective. When all is said and done, however, there is a no-nonsense air about photojournalism, in keeping with Capa's admonition; a professional focus on the story; an all-too-human interest in the scoop. Photojournalists ply their trade on assignment. They are not sovereign. In short, a photojournalist is not an artist. There is no time, they seem to say, and no such affectation.

But of course the binary divide is as blurred as Robert Capa's professional signature. The best photographers have been led into temptation by the disasters of war. Don McCullin himself has described how he contrived one of his most famous images, an image at once memorable and memorious. The photograph is invariably captioned "A dead North Vietnamese soldier and his plundered belongings, Hue, 1968." It might have been *Nature morte.* McCullin: "I saw a whole bunch of [American] soldiers vandalizing his body for souvenirs. I thought there's got to be something I can say about this. So I put these things together, I put them there to make the picture. It was the first time I thought I could justify it. And I don't have any shame about doing it. It wasn't the dead soldier that is the statement, it was the family photographs, the wallet. I was making a still life."

War photography was for much of its history synonymous with combat photography. The scope of the former was defined by the possibilities of the latter, practically and politically. The age of miniaturized mechanical reproduction was also the age of declared wars, identifiable fronts, and set-piece battles in faraway places—the age of the fearless photojournalist, concerned and unconcerned, redeemed and unredeemed, mixing it with the best of them, "down the close darkening lines . . . to the siding shed." Now the old wars are over, more or less, and the old breed has gone. In an age of terrorism and tribalism, obliteration and occupation, war too has been brought home. No man's land migrates, from Lower Manhattan to Babylonia itself. As if to ape Don McCullin, war photography has turned to still life and landscape. The finest practitioners in the world today conduct a kind of autopsy. Gilles Peress traces the bones, the most reliable witnesses to atrocity. Simon Norfolk fixes the afterburn, using a wood and brass field camera, with tripod, magnifying glass to focus, and blanket over the head. Stupendous images slowly form on negative plates. They contain few people but many remains.

No man's land is never quiet. Somewhere a camera is clicking. The dead are ever returning. Moral life flickers in the angel's eye.

Book Reviews

☆

Bruce Vandervort, editor
Virginia Military Institute

Jerusalem Besieged: From Ancient Canaan to Modern Israel. By Eric H. Cline. Ann Arbor: University of Michigan Press, 2004. ISBN 0-472-11313-5. Maps. Illustrations. Tables. Notes. Bibliography. Index. Pp. xviii, 410. $29.95.

At least three millennia of history, probably more, its stones often marred by the blood of those certain that their beliefs were given by God and strengthened by the vicissitudes of history. This is the story of Jerusalem, a city sacred to three monotheistic religions and a place often resembling a ship beaten by winds and waves in a perilous sea. Eric Cline, the author of an interesting book on the battles of Armageddon, now gives us a fascinating account of the history of the city from the beginning to the present. The heart of Jerusalem is the Temple Mount. For the Jews it is the place where Abraham took his son Isaac as a sacrifice to God, where David placed the ark of the covenant, and nearby where the Temple of King Solomon and later Herod's Temple stood. For the Muslims it is the place where the Dome of the Rock, the third most sacred location of the Muslim religion, stands and from where the Prophet of God, Mohammed, ascended to heaven. The place, like the rest of the city, also has vestiges and memories of the Christian religion. No surprise then that wars have been waged for centuries for possession of the Rock and of the city as a whole.

Neither the wealth of the surroundings, which is minimal, nor the strategical location of the city, which is also relative, explain the depth of the attachment to the city and the ferocity of the different believers. Its importance is grounded on religion and the myths and symbols stemming from the beliefs in a God, theoretically identical to all, but enemy to those who worship Him according to different historical traditions.

Cline handles skillfully, and sometimes fascinatingly, the intricacies of the subject, although his book, like all books, has its pitfalls. His persistent tendency to read the present into the past is distracting and not always convincing, as for instance when he compares the Apostle Paul's visit in 58 A.D. to the Temple Mount to Ariel Sharon's visit about two thousand years later (p. 111). Although a topic like Jerusalem is inextricably mixed with the present, it would have been much more effective to take up the comparison with the past when dealing with the nineteenth and twentieth centuries. Also, the flow of the narrative is broken by too many details in places, especially in the account from the Roman times to the nineteenth century. Matters would have been simplified by paraphrasing the too frequent quotations.

These are minor criticisms for a book which is always interesting even if Cline clearly looks at the topic from the Jewish viewpoint. Still, he tries to remain impartial and candidly admits that after the Jews' expulsion in the seventh century, Moslems took over soon after and governed the city for the next 1,300 years, except for a brief period at the time of the Crusades. In spite of all that, I doubt that Cline's account will satisfy Muslims or anybody else for, as he states, "the histories of Jews, Christians, and Moslems in Jerusalem are inextricably intertwined, and no one of them can be dented without doing violence to the whole nexus" (pp. 162–63).

Antonio Santosuosso
University of Western Ontario
London, Ontario, Canada

Early Riders: The Beginnings of Mounted Warfare in Asia and Europe. By Robert Drews. New York: Routledge, 2004. ISBN 0-415-32624-9. Maps. Illustrations. Notes. Bibliography. Index. Pp. x, 218. $90.00.

Horse riding marked a decisive turning-point in the development of warfare comparable to the invention of firearms, the military use of airplanes, and, finally, nuclear power. Cavalry fought in armed conflicts for over two and a half millennia.

In the Introduction (Chapter 1) of this learned book the author surveys previous research. In Chapter 2, "Horsemeat," on the evidence of horse bones found at prehistoric human settlements, Drews rightly concludes that while in the Eurasian steppe and its neighboring regions horse meat was staple food, it remains unclear whether the horses butchered were wild or domesticated. Domestication must have been achieved early in the third millennium B.C. but, to my mind, research is faced with the problem of how domesticated horse-herds could be controlled by people who had not mastered the art of riding.

Chapter 3, "Speed," deals with the evolution of horsemanship. The earliest evidence for the riding of horses comes from the Near East and dates from around 2000 B.C. Good riding began in the eleventh or tenth century B.C. with the use of bronze-bits. Chapter 4, "Control," focuses on the evolution of various devices, such as saddles and bits, allowing a better control of the horse. In the first millennium evolved the difficult technique of the so-called "Parthian shot" in which, in feigned retreat, the rider shot his arrows backwards. Secure on his mount, he could also suddenly transform himself from archer into hand-to-hand warrior, able to charge with a devastating effect. In Chapter 5, "Plunder"—which in my view is the most interesting part of this fine book—the author argues that the aim of the mounted steppe-warriors was not territorial conquest but plunder, a view with which I disagree. To cite but western examples, Huns, Avars, and Hungarians did settle in the territories they had conquered. However, I would subscribe to Drews's unorthodox view that the Scythians and Cimmerians were not the migrating nations that, based on classical sources, conventional research makes them out to be. No reference is made to pastures, the size of which determined the cavalry's size and the radius in which it could operate.

The relatively short 6th chapter, "Iranian Empires," deals with the role of cavalry in the Median and Persian empires principally in the sixth century B.C. The concluding Chapter 7, "Hoplites and Horsemen," focuses on the emergence of the heavily armed foot soldiers who, in the author's view, in the fifth century B.C. ended the dominance of riders on ancient battlefields.

This is a short text, a mere 148 pages, followed by 47 impressive pages of supportive notes. The publisher showed much ingenuity in producing a book as user-unfriendly as possible. The font is small, the spacing of the lines too narrow and the presentation of the notes is a nightmare. They are grouped at the end of the book, their numbering begins anew with each chapter, and the running heads give no indication of the pages of the main text. The price of $90.00 is outrageous.

Denis Sinor

Indiana University
Bloomington, Indiana

Joan of Arc: The Warrior Saint. By Stephen W. Richey. Westport, Conn.: Praeger. 2003. ISBN 0-275-98103-7. Maps. Illustrations. Appendixes. Notes. Selected bibliography. Index. Pp. x, 175. $34.95.

Joan of Arc remains a lively topic, which is served enthusiastically by authors that can be identified as the "Johannic" school. This group's common agenda focuses on "the Maid of Orléans," whose brief appearance in history occurred at a dramatic and critical moment during the last phase of the Hundred Years' War between Lancastrian England and Valois France. Though volumes have been written on Joan of Arc, her influence on events—particularly on the war—remains controversial. With his book, *Joan of Arc: The Warrior Saint,* Mr. Stephen W. Richey raises the standard of those "Johannicists" who sense there is an inadequate recognition of the Maids's *military role—not just as a "warrior" but as a "military leader."* Richey picks up where one of the best modern Johannic historians, Frances Gies, in her *Joan of Arc, The Legend and the Reality* (1981), takes issue with Édouard Perroy, a renowned French historian of the Hundred Years' War. The objective is to counter Perroy's assertion (made in his *La Guerre de Cent Ans,* first published in 1945) that Joan "did not lead" the troops. He characterizes her role more as a cheerleader.

The clearly structured book identifies key questions concerning Joan's military career: "what" she did and "how" she did it. Joan's often-told story is summarized and supported by the usual primary references. Though numerous military historians praise Joan's role in her particular phase of the Hundred Years' War, Mr. Richey develops his own rationale to explain her performance as a warrior. His fundamental observation is that the English partial occupation was on precarious grounds, but the French were demoralized and psychologically paralyzed in defending the strategically important city of Orléans in 1429. Only Joan provided the required charismatic leadership to resist. In doing so, she was "essential" to the ultimate French victory in the war. The author insightfully enumerates "the lucky circumstances" that allowed Joan to exploit her martial skills, which he speculates were derived from her innate intelligence and self confidence.

Joan's initial successes are emphasized, where she bravely placed herself in the midst of fierce combat, and exhorted French troops assaulting fortified posts. Her performance enabled this teenage peasant girl to be recognized in French war councils, where she projected herself as a person of action, urging aggressive attacks and rapid exploitation of every tactical gain. Her persona dominated the raising of the siege of Orléans, securing the Loire valley, and conducting the march to Charles VII's coronation at Reims. Tragically, Joan did not live to see the ultimate French victory. Her successes took place over a few months in 1429, and were followed by reverses later in the year. She was captured in 1430, and burned in 1431.

The author's argument encounters difficulty when he takes up Joan's failure before Paris in September 1429. For Joan's military career, Paris was one inspirational assault too far. Without the French possessing a serious siege train, the expectation was that the citizenry would rise to aid the besiegers. This assessment is not shared by all military historians, and many are convinced that an anti-Burgundian uprising in Paris was unlikely. In true Johannic tradition, the author blames Joan's failure at Paris upon Charles VII's indifference and the king's preference for obtaining a rapprochement with the duke of Burgundy. After the Paris repulse, Charles VII disbanded the army associated with Joan's victories.

Events after Joan is no longer central to them are quickly reviewed. After some criticism of Charles VII's initial, frustrated attempts to win the Burgundians away from their English alliance, the author admits that the eventual 1436 Treaty of Arras was another of the Hundred Years' War's several key turning points.

This book will be welcomed by those attracted to Joan of Arc's remarkable story and who want to see repeated declarations that Joan was a military leader. The evidence is convincing that Joan possessed a tactical leader's awareness to promote aggressive action in combat, and that her credibility required her sharing the risks with her soldier companions. However, it remains questionable that she grasped the need to adapt tactical schemes to varied operational challenges, or had the patience for logistical preparation, thus hindering the author's thrust to define Joan as a military genius.

Joan's military career occurred during what could more accurately be described as the "War for the Survival of Charles VII of France," which spans 1422 to 1453. Remarkably, Providence seems to have been with Charles before Joan, when others shielded the young dauphin from many daunting threats. He continued to be well served after Joan's era with a remarkable new military establishment. Descriptions of battles and campaigns prior to and during Joan's time hardly explain the decisive victories that brought Charles VII his sobriquet, *"le roi très victorieux."* For centuries, Johannic lore and various nationalistic movements have found it useful to disparage Charles VII and his court. Those curious as to how the Valois monarch prevailed might seek clues in *Charles VII,* by Malcolm Vale, an English scholar of the Hundred Years' War and medieval Europe. This work, not included in the bibliography of the book being reviewed here, would provide balance to an otherwise scholarly presentation.

Albert D. McJoynt   Xenophon Group, *Société de l'Oriflamme*
Mount Vernon, Virginia

Art of War. By Niccolò Machiavelli. Translated, edited, and with a commentary by Christopher Lynch. Chicago: University of Chicago Press, 2003. ISBN 0-226-50040-3. Maps. Illustrations. Notes. Glossary. Bibliography. Index. Pp. xlv, 262. $25.00 (hb).

Machiavelli's *Art of War* is structured as a dialogue between a famous soldier—Fabrizio Colonna from Rome—and a number of Florentine gentlemen on how to manage war and military affairs in general. It is always hard to translate an author distant from us in time, space or cultural background, and in Machiavelli's case, the task is especially formidable, since we are dealing with a gap of five centuries, another continent, a different mindset, and an archaic language. For these reasons, if it is sometimes hard for an Italian to understand Machiavelli, the problem increases tenfold when a foreigner tries his hand.

Christopher Lynch's translation of Machiavelli's famous treatise on war is the first in English since Ellis Farneworth's classic rendering of 1775 (revised for modern readers in a 1965 edition of the book by Neal Wood). Lynch has also gone to considerable trouble to try to make *Art of War* relevant for modern readers, providing an introduction and a commentary whose purpose in large part seems to be to draw lessons from the great Florentine's book that can be applied by soldiers and statesmen today. This might be assumed to be the great strength of this new translation, but, unhappily, this quest for relevance sometimes gets in the way of accuracy in rendering the text into English and too often ends up drawing conclusions from the thought of a Renaissance man that are anachronistic and ahistorical. First, the problems with the translation itself. While Old Nick's archaic Italian clearly constitutes a major hurdle for the modern translator, Lynch's effort easily could have been improved by searching out a greater range of cognates for Italian terms. For example, he almost invariably uses the word "attack" for *affrontare, assaltare, assalto, combattere, offendere, offesa, urtare,* although each of these words possesses a number of different meanings. This often has the effect of making the translation dull and repetitive, not to mention detracting from its accuracy.

The author's "Introduction" and final "Interpretative Essay," where he attempts to make Machiavelli's military thought relevant to the present day, betray a troubling lack of familiarity with Italian cultural history. Thus, when he writes on p. xxv of the Introduction, "I have concluded that the aging condottiere [Colonna] is a self-consciously restrained version of Machiavelli himself," readers *au courant* with Italian (and/or ancient) culture will need to remind themselves that the dialogue as a medium for speaking one's mind is as old as Plato, and was used in Italy up to the first half of the nineteenth century. In a typical dialogue, there are at least two speakers, usually a main character who presents his own—that is to say the author's—ideas about a certain topic, while the other participants normally limit themselves to asking appropriate questions.

There are a number of instances in this edition of *Art of War* where the author seems determined to stuff Machiavelli into a recognizable (and relevant) modern mold, even at the risk of substantial distortion. There is, for example, the matter of Machiavelli's religion (or lack thereof). Lynch calls him an atheist. Our concept of atheism, however, is a by-product of the post-Kantian age. Lynch would have been much closer to the mark by labelling Machiavelli an anticlerical, which he certainly was, along with most of his fellow Florentines. But, the author's most dubious assertions come in the realm of military thought. Thus, Lynch avers (p. xxxi) that "His [Machiavelli's] strategic thought is generally lauded for being 'modern'— that is to say Clausewitzian." This argument needs to be read along with another statement on p. 179, where we are given the impression that the author has discovered something in Machiavelli that other readers have missed: "I implicitly defend Machiavelli . . . by challenging . . . critics to pay even closer attention to exactly what Machiavelli said and to take even greater pains to discern what he might have meant." The ultimate problem here is that, even were this kind of "modern" reading of Machiavelli's military thought possible, which seems to me extremely doubtful, theory and practice are clearly two different things. The great theorist Clausewitz, for instance, was defeated the one time he commanded troops in the field, and historical evidence shows Machiavelli to have been an incompetent military commander.

The author's knowledge of the history of the period he is writing about also leaves something to be desired. On p. 191, he states: "The very notion— let alone the actual existence—of an impersonal state in whose name a professional armed force could serve would not be born till the time of Thomas Hobbes." This is all very well, but what about Renaissance Venice and its army? Venice was a Republic, just like Florence, and so impersonal a state that everyone—Italian, Slav, or Greek—could easily and proudly call himself a subject of Saint Mark. Again, on p. xxviii we read: "no rapid change took place: gunpowder technology had been around for centuries by Machiavelli's day and it would be more than another century before gunpowder brought about fundamental changes on the field of battle." But at the same time, Lynch's "Interpretive Essay" informs us that artillery played a major role in the battle of Ravenna in 1512, and that major changes took place in the field of fortifications in Machiavelli's time. Not having a sure handle on the early modern "Military Revolution," one of the hottest topics in military history circles today, is a serious drawback in this edition.

We may also wonder what readers are supposed to think when the author refers to the East as Asia. On page xxxii, we find the "non Western militaries" the Romans went up against described as "the Numidian horsemen of Africa and the Parthian military of Asia, by which Machiavelli meant regions including modern Iraq, Iran and Afghanistan." The uneducated reader will have the impression that Asia equals Iraq, Iran, and Afghanistan (curiously enough, areas where the U.S. military is involved at present). This is not just inaccurate, but also misleading. In fact, what our Roman ancestors called Asia had nothing to do with the present one, being instead today's Middle East. Nor were the Parthians Arabs. They had become steeped in Hellenistic culture in the wake of Alexander the Great's conquest of the area, and their style of warfare had nothing to do with the military comportment of today's Afghanis or Iraqis.

Another, more glaring, example of the author's misleading way of thinking can be found on pp. xxxii and xxxiii, where he has Machiavelli amalgamating "crucial elements of the non-Western armies with essential elements of the ancient Roman and Greek armies to establish an entirely new kind of army led by commanders who judiciously alternate between the Western and the non-Western ways of war," followed a few lines later by the observation that "The US military has often hewn to the model of the 'Western' or Clausewitzian war of annihilation. The emphasis has been on achieving decisive victories by fighting big and (when possible) short conflicts such as the Persian Gulf War. . . . But dating back to the hit-and-run methods of both Washington and Nathaniel Greene during the Revolutionary War and all the way up to the Special Operation Forces currently in use in the war on terrorism the American military has shown its willingness and ability to fight the 'other' kind of war. What would be the consequences and requirements— military, moral and political—of such integration? Few writers can be of more use than Machiavelli when it comes to grappling with such urgent and fundamental military questions." Any average reader's conclusion would be that although Machiavelli is dead, Professor Lynch has managed to acquire the secret of his war-winning theories and is angling to parlay his knowledge into a consultancy at the Pentagon. This is a bit like saying that someone who knows Julius Caesar's *De Bello Gallico* would be the best person to direct the fight against today's British Army. This reviewer's advice to English-language readers: Don't throw out your Farneworth.

Ciro Paoletti

Ostia-Rome, Italy

The Duke of Alba. By Henry Kamen. New Haven, Conn.: Yale University Press, 2004. ISBN 0-300-10283-6. Maps. Illustrations. Notes. Short bibliography. Index. Pp. 204. $30.00.

Twenty-one years after an Anglophone historian produced the first scholarly biography of the third duke of Alba—the most famous, and notorious, of Spain's soldiers of the early modern period (W. S. Maltby, *Alba: A Biography of Fernando Alvarez de Toledo, Third Duke of Alba 1507–1582* [Berkeley: University of California Press, 1983])—it has been left to another English-speaker to re-evaluate his life and career. Though Kamen modestly directs this relatively short study to the general reader, this is no mere derivative biography of the great duke. The author has carefully reviewed many of the available published collections of primary materials from Europe's archives that pertain to Alba's life in the service of Emperor Charles V and his son Philip II of Spain. In addition, he has explored further in a number of manuscript depositories in Spain (Simancas, the Alba family archive, and other archives in Madrid) and elsewhere in Europe (Geneva, Vienna, and London), uncovering fresh material. Combining this with recently published secondary sources, Kamen has provided new insights into Alba's long and distinguished career (including some major events in which he played only a minimal or indirect role), and has corrected a number of the recent and not so recent misapprehensions about his life and times. Of the book's seven chapters, the two dedicated to affairs in the Netherlands (along with two of the three maps, though these are too small to provide sufficient detail to illustrate the text) and to the most notorious period of Alba's career, contain a number of insights and challenges to conventional wisdom. There is, however, one area where the author apparently sees no need for re-evaluation. The emphasis of the penultimate chapter on the logistical and disciplinary problems of the last campaign in Portugal diverges from Kamen's ampler coverage of strategy and tactics in Alba's military activities elsewhere. If, like others (though not Maltby), Kamen believes the 1580 military campaign was unimportant "because no great events were experienced" (p. 193), this belies the significance the author reveals that his protagonist attributed to the conquest (p. 153). Nevertheless, the final chapter more than makes up for this unexpected shortcoming. In it Kamen engages in a succinct and masterful reassessment of aspects of Alba's character, beliefs and achievements, reminding us that while he did not participate in most of the famous military events of his time, nor take part in a full-scale battle, he was "[f]ar more than merely a general, he was also an active creator of Spanish military power" (p. 157). Throughout, the biography is superbly documented by numerous quotations taken from the duke's and his contemporaries' letters and accounts. If only for this reason, this book will be a key source not just for students of early modern European and military history, but also for academics and researchers of the period.

Lorraine White   University of Wollongong
Wollongong, New South Wales, Australia

Fighting for Identity: Scottish Military Experience c. 1550–1990. Edited by Steve Murdoch and A. Mackillop. Leiden, The Netherlands: Brill, 2002. ISBN 90-04-12823-9. Illustrations. Glossary. Notes. Index. Pp. xliii, 303. $130.00.

The military conflict that began in 1642 and ended with the decapitation of Charles I in 1649 is the cockpit of British historiography. The label for these campaigns changes nearly every decade. The Great Rebellion became the Puritan Revolution, which begat the English Revolution, then the English Civil War, and then the British Civil Wars. Today the era is known most widely as the War of the Three Kingdoms. The conscious rejection of an Anglo-centric interpretation of these wars reflects the growing national self-consciousness of Scots, Welsh, and Irish. Interestingly, though, the United Kingdom's military forces, though often organized into national regiments, are an integrated *British* army, and have been for the most part since at least the 1600s.

Bundelskoenig Steve Murdoch and Andrew Mackillop have fashioned a book that contributes to the raging debate over "Britishness." This volume also sheds light on the nature of nationalism. In particular, the authors take aim at the "currently fashionable postures of romantic nationalism" (p. xx). The broad chronological scope of this work enables these more macrocosmic questions to be tackled.

As for the contributors, we hear new and intriguing voices such as Heather Streets, Aonghas MacCoinnich, Alison Cathcart, and Joachim Migglebrink. The editors season their roster with distinguished scholars such as Arthur Williamson (who sets this tome squarely in the middle of the "British" debate), Alexia Grosjean, Edward Furgol, Dauvit Horsbroch, and Alasdair Mann. And the editors should be commended for crossing the Tweed and recruiting the foremost historian of logistics in the Civil War period, Peter Edwards.

Two themes dominate: the dynamics of the society of Scottish soldiers over nearly a half millennium, and the forging of their identity at home and abroad. Murdoch salvages James VI and I's military reputation. Furgol provides an insightful and well-informed account of the campaign that for all intents and purposes made Scottish ascendancy in the 1640s a reality. Grosjean reveals the significance of the shifting allegiance (and hence self-identity) of Cranstoun's regiment in the Interregnum period. The Scots-Dutch brigade's demise is explored by Migglebrink.

The Gaelic and Highlander "military consciousness" makes up the second section of the book with essays from McCoinnich, Cathcart, Mackillop, and Streets, carrying the analysis through the Victorian era. The volume concludes with essays on equipping and arming the Covenanters, and the use of the printing press by the latter forces. Horsbroch's essay is particularly suggestive because it bridges the self-consciousness of the Covenanter with the perceptions held by the Scot fighting in the service of the British Empire.

Once London had tamed the British Isles, an integrated Britain looked abroad to manifest its power, in overseas adventures and Empire. The center then disengaged "from any further, systematic attempt to generate an uniform British military identity" (p. xlii). *Fighting for Identity* is a step forward in the methodology of writing military history because it applies the theory of disengagement to military consciousness and the identity of the warrior.

Mark C. Fissel   Augusta, Georgia

Princes, Posts, and Partisans: The Army of Louis XIV and Partisan Warfare in the Netherlands (1673–1678). By George Satterfield. Leiden, The Netherlands: Brill, 2003. ISBN 90-04-13176-0. Maps. Illustrations. Notes. Bibliography. Index. Pp. xvi, 344. $134.00.

George Satterfield has pulled off an unusual feat in the field of the history of warfare: he has written a genuinely original book that will enhance our understanding of military campaigning and strategic thinking in the late seventeenth century. Military historians of this era have been by and large fixated upon the great set-pieces of sieges and battles, *grande guerre*, but Satterfield has eschewed such an approach and buried himself in archival material to present a clear picture of *petite guerre*. In doing so he has given clarity to what otherwise seems to be a story of one siege after another in the Spanish Netherlands during the Dutch War; indeed, Satterfield's chapter (1) summarising the Dutch War in the Netherlands must now rate as the clearest thing written on the course of this conflict. *Petite guerre* might be conceived rather narrowly, as war-by-raid and ambush involving anywhere from a dozen to several hundred men; but by expanding the concept to include large-scale raiding and blockading of strong-points involving up to several thousand troops, Satterfield manages to explain just how closely related were *grande guerre* and partisan warfare of all shapes and sizes. He takes us through dozens of expeditions, sometimes, frankly, in rather self-indulgent detail. Yet this relentless and well-marshalled material produces a cumulative understanding that helps explain why some sieges took longer than others and why Louis XIV opted to attack one fortress over another at a particular time. Satterfield's argument that by 1676 the French king and his high command had developed an unprecedented understanding of the need to integrate *grande* and *petite guerre* in order to wear down their opponents' fortress garrisons has much to commend it, though this may underestimate the skill of both Maurice of Nassau and the high command of the Spanish army of Flanders in the 1590s and 1600s who were struggling under far greater logistical difficulties. Certainly, though, Satterfield's thesis is most convincing as an explanation for why the Dutch and Spanish were singularly unsuccessful in siege warfare in the 1670s while the French had one triumph after another. He also comes to eminently sensible conclusions about the material importance of *petite guerre* for the French war effort, engaging in the debate between this reviewer and John Lynn (his mentor) over the relative importance of contributions to the French military budget—even in the Netherlands where the French army was at its most organised in this regard, contributions accounted for only around 12 to 16 percent of military revenue in good years.

As a work of military history, then, Satterfield's book deserves high praise, and in an age when the mightiest army in the world is struggling to match its skill in waging *grande guerre* with success in *petite guerre,* it deserves to be studied in military staff colleges. But there are points of debate, and even weakness, which should be highlighted. Like John Lynn, Satterfield has an as yet underdeveloped understanding of the nature of the wider French polity and society, and he needs to sharpen his appreciation of aristocratic political culture and the motivation of regular French officers. On the matter of campaigning, with which the book is of course principally concerned, it should finally be stressed that Satterfield's arguments, if robust for the Dutch War, might break down for the period after 1688. In the Nine Years' War and the War of the Spanish Succession Louis and his generals were up against Allied commanders (including an older and wiser William of Orange) whose logistical support and skill was much improved from the 1670s. The integrated theatre strategy of blockades, raids and sieges during the earlier period could not be carried through on the same scale in the Low Countries by the French in Louis's later wars. Moreover, if the French did achieve, as Satterfield says, an "operational revolution" in the 1670s, most of the time they were unable to replicate such "joined-up" strategy in the Rhineland, northern Italy, Ireland, or Catalonia after 1688. This is, therefore, a book that is very much about the Netherlands in the 1670s, but it is no less valuable for it.

Guy Rowlands

University of Durham
Durham, United Kingdom

The British Navy and the State in the Eighteenth Century. By Clive Wilkinson. Rochester, N.Y.: Boydell & Brewer, 2004. ISBN 1-84383-042-6. Tables. Appendixes. Notes. Bibliography. Index. Pp. x, 246. $85.00.

Navies have always been expensive instruments of power. The long term funding required to maintain an effective seagoing force stretched eighteenth-century states to their limits, and in meeting the demand for funds navies transformed the states they served. John Brewer developed the concept of Britain as an advanced fiscal military state in *The Sinews of Power* of 1989. Clive Wilkinson applies these themes to specifics of naval administration, using the key question of why the Royal Navy fell short of expectation in the American War of Independence as his focal point. Wilkinson shows how the nation funded the Navy, and what the nation expected in return. With an excellent examination of the constraints of eighteenth century naval power, slow mobilisation, limited resources, and the uncertain durability of wooden ships he shows how narrow were the margins of success in the mid century wars with France. Naval expenditure was controlled by two processes, greater Treasury control and demands for greater accountability by a Parliament that dare refuse the service adequate funds.

In addressing the policies of the mid-century Admiralty Boards led by Anson, Egmont, Hawke, and Sandwich, Wilkinson uses the real strength of the battlefleet in ships ready for service as the key indicator of success. His conclusions will strike those who have made policy as eminently fair, and those who prefer their politicians to be venal, foolish, and flawed as a whitewash. No-one was really to blame for the massive structural problems inherent in the attempt to maintain the expanded wartime fleet of the mid century with inadequate infrastructure and poor construction methods. The roots of policy failure were many and deep. Instead key naval administrators did their best to address the issues. Lord Sandwich, bitterly attacked for his part in the loss of the American colonies by political opponents, was in reality highly competent. His attempt to rebuild the fleet with new, "scientifically" built ships that would be more durable and therefore cheaper in the long term, was only just starting to bear fruit when the needs of war interrupted. His predecessors had done much to upgrade the dockyard infrastructure and with Sandwich's policy in place, and much improved oversight of naval expenditure, the foundations were in place for the next round of global conflict, when an altogether more powerful fleet completed the recovery begun at the battle of the Saintes in 1782. Britannia ruled the waves because her pockets were deeper, and her need for sea power was greater than her rivals. But the mechanisms by which she ensured the money was effectively spent, and the fleet prepared for war have never been more clearly and incisively set out. Wilkinson's clearly written and thoroughly researched book joins those of Daniel Baugh and N. A. M. Rodger as a key text, engaging in the wider debates of the historical profession and ensuring naval history takes its proper place in any account of the development of the British state, and the loss of the American colonies.

Andrew Lambert

King's College London
London, United Kingdom

War in the Age of Enlightenment, 1700–1789. By Armstrong Starkey. Westport, Conn.: Praeger, 2003. ISBN 0-275-97240-2. Notes. Index. Pp. ix, 232. $67.95.

The "Age of Enlightenment" in the title of Professor Starkey's work is programmatic. It indicates the author's intent to trace the relationship between the ideas of the *philosophes* and their impact on social attitudes on the one hand, and the wars of their time on the other. His book does both less and more. It outlines and briefly comments on the reflections of

Voltaire, Robertson, Vattel, and other contemporaries on the history, laws, and morality of war, and their arguments concerning men's rights and duties—including the obligation of military service—in a just society. But a paragraph or two can hardly analyze their major theses, nor indicate the disagreements among them, and the compressed accounts of this side of the philosophes' readings of the modern world do not provide an adequate basis for a systematic exploration of their impact on military institutions, the place of war in foreign and domestic policy, and the conduct of operations. On the other hand, the book offers an overview of war in Europe and overseas at the time that goes far beyond tracing the links, positive and negative, between the moral and political theorists of the age and its military reality.

The book is divided into six chapters: "The Culture of Force," "The Military Enlightenment," "A Culture of Honor," "Fontenoy, 1745," the case study of one battle, which seems to me the strongest part of the book, not only because the author allows himself the space necessary for a thorough discussion of his subject; "Popular War," and "The Conflict of Cultures," this last a rapid comparison of conditions in Europe with those in the near and far East, Africa, and North America. Professor Starkey bases himself very largely on the secondary literature, which he employs to good effect as he moves rapidly from topic to topic, weaving a concise summary of a vast and complex subject. Specialists will not find anything surprising in his conclusions, for example that the Enlightenment influenced the growth of military education and—to some extent—of professionalization; that military reality was more complex "than the rococo battle portraits of the age might suggest;" or that "eighteenth-century technical developments contributed to the success of the French Revolutionary and Napoleonic armies." But the book has much to offer to graduate students and the general reader (though they, especially, would welcome a separate bibliography), and even the historian of war may find reading the author's succinct, thoughtful overview a profitable encounter with a clear, well-informed mind.

Peter Paret   Institute for Advanced Study
                                                     Princeton, New Jersey

The Frontier War for American Independence. By William R. Nester. Mechanicsburg, Pa.: Stackpole Books, 2004. ISBN 0-8117-0077-1. Maps. Notes. Bibliography. Index. Pp. 423. $34.95.

The French and Indian War. By Alfred A. Cave. Westport, Conn.: Greenwood Press, 2004. ISBN 0-313-32168-X. Maps. Illustrations. Notes. Annotated bibliography. Index. Pp. xix, 175. $45.00.

Two authors have recently taken up the subject of frontier warfare in eighteenth-century North America. William Nester's work concerns the American Revolution in the wilderness, while Alfred Cave gives an overview of the earlier French and Indian War. While Nester succeeds for the most part in describing what he holds to have been the key to American victory in the struggle for independence, Cave's brief study is a confusing jumble of sketches and essays marred by errors.

Cave's book is part of the Greenwood "Guides to Historic Events 1500–1900" series, designed to lead students "to a more sophisticated understanding of the events and debates that have shaped the modern world." This conceptually weak study fails to do so. Beginning with a cover illustration from the wrong war, Cave's brief overview of his subject reads like a dozen or so encyclopedia entries cobbled together, and is riddled with errors that ultimately ruin the book's credibility as a "resource for student research" (p. viii). To give but a few of many examples: several dates are wrong (one by as much as one hundred years, p. 6); George Washington was not a "civilian aide" in Braddock's Campaign (p. 8), nor was he "orphaned during his boyhood" (p. 117); James Wolfe was not a mere brigadier general at Quebec, nor was that campaign strictly a "naval operation" (p. 20); Edward Braddock was not born in 1695 (p. 101); and the British 23rd Regiment did not fight in America during this war (p. 21); and so on.

Following a sparse twenty-one page overview of the military events of the war, Cave provides five thematic chapters, and brief biographical sketches of key players. It is striking how much of the book is not directly related to the subject Cave claims to treat. His chapter on Native Americans, for instance, is an ethnohistorical treatment of Indians from 1492, the bulk of which does not address military issues or the middle of the eighteenth century. In another chapter entitled "Aftermath," more space is devoted to events leading up to the American Revolution than the subject at hand, while other essays seem to be only tangentially related to the struggle for North America between France and Great Britain. While several pages devoted to previous North American colonial conflicts and the challenges of using Indian allies are useful, Cave's volume is superficial and contains far too many errors to be reliable.

Nester provides a detailed and well-researched narrative of the "racial war without mercy along the frontier" that "paralleled and at times intersected" (p. 1) with the conventional war on the Atlantic seaboard. It was "at once genocidal and decisive" (p. 3), a war that Nester rightly claims the Indians lost. By frontier war, Nester not only means skirmishes and raids, but major battles as well. This conflict "involved two distinct elements. Large-scale campaigns were mostly fought by regulars or volunteers, but often accompanied by Indians who served as guides, scouts, and flankers. Small-scale raids were mostly composed of Indians and sometimes joined by white officers and volunteers" (p. 15). This frontier war in America was, he asserts, "more than a bloody sideshow." Rather, it "diverted huge amounts of men, money, supplies, and energies from the East Coast" (p. 21). Nester supports his claim of frontier importance by reminding readers that "the war's turning point [Saratoga], after all, took place on the frontier" (p. 21). This victory not only emboldened France to aid the American cause but also served to significantly cow northern Indians from supporting the British effectively for the rest of the war. The strength of Nester's detailed narrative of wilderness fighting is his emphasis on the role of Native Americans in it. Both the Americans and the British were for the most part wary of employing Indians against each other, though this position weakened by 1777. By 1779, reluctance to use Indians or fight them was gone, as shown by the Sullivan campaign against the Iroquois in New York, though Nester concludes that it only achieved temporary success.

While Nester's claim that the wilderness battle of Saratoga was decisive is reasonable, other assertions are more open to debate. That "Cornwallis never would have holed up [at Yorktown] had he not suffered . . . earlier defeats at Kings Mountain and Cowpens" (p. 2) is questionable. Nester's assertion that the frontier war also "accelerated the development of American nationalism" is a provocative one, as is his proposition that American "identity was forged in part by consciously contrasting it with 'savages,' who impeded the nation's destiny" (p. 21). Regrettably, Nester does not expand upon these questions. Rather, for the most part *The Frontier War* is a description of what appears to be every major and minor event in the American wilderness from 1775 to 1783 and beyond. The reader learns much about the trees, but the forest is often obscured by an overly detailed story. While this does make the book useful as a reference for an enormous amount of activity throughout the frontier area (as does the inclusion of five superb maps), it also leads to a tedious narrative. Despite these issues (and a number of factual errors concerning the South), Nester's study does make a compelling case for the importance of the wilderness campaigns of the Revolutionary War.

John R. Maass   Ohio State University
                                                                                        Columbus, Ohio

A Proper Sense of Honor: Service and Sacrifice in George Washington's Army. By Caroline Cox. Chapel Hill: University of North Carolina Press, 2004. ISBN 0-8078-2884-X. Photographs. Illustrations. Notes. Bibliography. Index. Pp. xxii, 338. $37.50.

The American Revolution has re-emerged as an area of vital scholarly interest in recent years, much of the best work coming from historians who have focused their research on the War for Independence. This new volume by Caroline Cox aptly fits this description. The author tackles certain vital issues relating to the Continental army, including the make-up and values of the common soldiery and officer corps; military justice and punishment; diseases and the practice of military medicine; death and burial of fallen troops; and rules and realities relating to prisoners of war.

Cox begins her investigation by discussing what she calls "the unthinking decision to divide the army into officers who were gentlemen and soldiers who were not" (p. 2). As such, the make-up of the Continental army reflected class attitudes in the colonies as well as the social composition of

European armies. The author then relates this basic social-economic split to each of the topics that form the core of her analysis. She discusses the fixation of officers on personal honor, even as soldiers dealt with far more fundamental matters of survival. She finds major differences in punishments meted out to soldiers (everything from floggings to running the gauntlet and, in extreme situations, execution) as compared to officers (from public or private reprimands to dismissal from the service). The same pattern held true in regard to the army's health, with ranking medical officers spending as much time haggling over who was in charge of what as actually providing treatment for the sick and wounded. In the delivery of health care, concludes Cox, "the needs of officers always took priority over those of soldiers" (p. 121). In matters of death and burial, the officers once again mattered the most. Rarely did anyone record the names of soldiers who died from some horrible disease or who lost their lives in battle. Officers, on the other hand, invariably represented "the named" among "the war dead" (p. 170) because society viewed them as legitimate exemplars of self-sacrifice. Whenever possible, fallen officers received decent, Christian burials. In the handling of prisoners, the officers again benefited from their higher status, both in living conditions while incarcerated and in exchange agreements. Because of their keen sense of gentlemanly honor, officers rarely sought to escape or break their parole arrangements. As for captured patriot soldiers, who invariably suffered in fetid circumstances (one need only to think of the British prison ship *Jersey*), they too had to consider whether "the honorable thing to do was to choose death rather than serve with the British" (p. 235). Most accepted death as the least obnoxious alternative, one of many "small steps" taken by lower status persons in the service "to protect and defend a more refined sense of dignity and honor than the world would allow them" (p. 249).

Cox has written a thoughtful, challenging book that reckons with major social assumptions and cultural constructions as they applied to Continental forces in Revolutionary America. Although few scholars will accept all of her findings, none should deny this book's significance. *A Proper Sense of Honor* represents a valuable addition to our ever expanding comprehension of the realities of fighting, as well as of those who fought, for independence during the American Revolution.

James Kirby Martin   University of Houston
                                                       Houston, Texas

New York State Society of the Cincinnati: Biographies of Original Members and Other Continental Officers. By Francis J. Sypher, Jr. Fishkill, N.Y.: New York State Society of the Cincinnati, 2004. Notes. Bibliography. Illustrations. Index. Pp. ix, 659. $200.00. Purchase from Treasurer, DeWitt Clinton, Jr., 15 Webhannet Harbor Road, Wells, Maine 04090.

Second Lieutenant Jonas Addoms and Captain Guy Young are at opposite ends of the 475 biographical sketches that Francis J. Sypher, Jr., revised with the assistance of the New York State Society of the Cincinnati Publications Committee from John Schuyler's *Institution of the Society of the Cincinnati . . .* (New York: 1886). The expansion from 234 biographies to those of 475 original members, eligible members who never joined and members who transferred membership from other states to the New York society is an enormously useful source for Revolutionary War era historians, New York State local historians, and genealogists.

Sypher does not claim to be "definitive" for every sketch. However, users will appreciate the identification of represented members, both wartime and postwar publications by the person being sketched, archives and library manuscript sources, secondary sources, and the location of identified portraits. In no other reference source will you find this amount of accurate and documented biographical material about regimental to company grade army as well as naval officers. A number of previous works confused, merged, and lumped together men with similar names and positions and this has led to faulty information being continued into later publications. This source should be added as a checklist for readers, researchers, and historians of local history, state history, and military history of late nineteenth-century America.

Besides military and postwar career information, researchers will appreciate information about bounty lands, pensions, and county line changes. Helpful information regarding military terms, variant name spellings of the times and the problems of the "Old Style" and "New Style" calendar terms as a result of the transition from the Julian calendar to the Gregorian calendar are explained.

I would recommend for future revision the use of the national and international *Niles Register* (1811–49) for obituaries of prominent members. William M. MacBean's compiled *Roster of Saint Andrew's Society of the State of New York with Biographical Data*, 4 vols. (New York: Saint Andrew's Society of the State of New York, 1911) is an overlooked source that identifies prominent Revolutionary era New Yorkers. A check of local history publications like the *Orange County Historical Journal* (New York) for recent sketches of officers is also a good approach for researchers. However, the New York Genealogical and Biographical Society, the National Archives New York Regional Office, the Society of the Cincinnati, Anderson House, Washington D.C. sources, and Columbia University's Rare Book and Manuscript library contributed their skills and resources to make this publication a stand out source. The privately printed book's high cost will limit the work to institutions, members, and specialists but it will be welcomed that the New York State Society of the Cincinnati carried out the project.

Alan C. Aimone

U.S. Military Academy Library
West Point, New York

Reading Clausewitz. By Beatrice Heuser. London: Pimlico, 2002. ISBN 0-7126-6484-X. Select bibliography. Notes. Index. Pp. xii, 238. £12.50.

The avowed purpose of Beatrice Heuser's book is to provide guidance for the reader who intends to tackle Carl von Clausewitz's *On War,* and also to describe the way in which his ideas have had an impact on the development of strategic theory. This is no easy task, particularly as Clausewitz died before he could revise *On War* to his satisfaction. Moreover, the complex and seemingly contradictory nature of Clausewitz's thought is best understood if one appreciates the milieu within which he lived, particularly the intellectual climate in which the Enlightenment gave way to the age of Romanticism. This context has been lost on many of Clausewitz's readers, and they have tended to see in selective elements of his work the confirmation of their own prejudices and concerns. As Heuser comments, many of Clausewitz's readers have looked for a telling quote when in fact he "mainly supplies philosophical reflections on the nature of war that are difficult to translate into simple, memorable prescriptions for action" (p. 12).

Heuser has sensibly structured her book. First, she takes the reader through the writing of *On War* and its reception during the nineteenth and twentieth centuries. There then follow sound analyses of Clausewitz's most important ideas: the primacy of policy, the paradoxical trinity, genius, the center of gravity, friction, and the nature of defense and offense. Heuser then examines two of the most important strategic theorists of the twentieth century, Sir Julian Corbett and Mao Zedong, describing Clausewitz's impact on their thinking. Finally, there is an analysis of Clausewitz's thought as applied to nuclear strategy, the Cold War, and the strategic problems of the twenty-first century.

One area in which Heuser's analysis falls short is in her interpretation of an earlier, "idealistic" Clausewitz writing about absolute war and a later, "realistic" Clausewitz writing about real war. In fact, Clausewitz's mature thought emphasized the absolute variant of war, which permits a rise to extremes in the abstract, to illustrate that war in reality has the opposite effect as it is the servant of policy. Real wars vary by degree, ranging in intensity from those of extermination to simple armed observation. Therefore, contrary to Heuser's view, the concepts of absolute war and real war are "mutually exclusive" (p. 43) in that one has no bounds while the other is constrained by political circumstance. The distinction between absolute war and real war should be clear but Heuser, like many before her, unnecessarily confuses the issue. This is unfortunate, particularly for the reader who is unfamiliar with Clausewitz.

Overall, however, Beatrice Heuser has done a fine job in producing a concise, well-written book that should be read in conjunction with the work of other Clausewitzian scholars, notably Peter Paret, Christopher Bassford, Azar Gat, and Antulio Echevarria. In this way, *Reading Clausewitz* will help to further the reader's understanding of a very complex, but also very rewarding, subject.

Stuart Kinross

University of Aberdeen
Aberdeen, Scotland, United Kingdom

Winfield Scott and the Profession of Arms. By Allan Peskin. Kent, Ohio: Kent State University Press, 2004. ISBN 0-87338-774-0. Maps. Illustrations. Notes. Bibliography. Index. Pp. xi, 328. $49.00.

This is the third Scott biography in five years. Each approaches the subject from a different perspective: Scott as *Agent of Manifest Destiny* (John S. D. Eisenhower, 1999), as seeker after military glory (Timothy D. Johnson, *Winfield Scott: The Quest for Military Glory,* 1998), and as leader in military professionalization. Each perspective is viable, but Eisenhower largely repeated the structure and judgments of Charles Winslow Elliott's *Winfield Scott: The Soldier and the Man* (1937), the only really scholarly biography before the 1990s. Manifest Destiny, either as idea or as the actual process of expansion, was little more than a gloss on Eisenhower's narration of Scott's career.

Johnson's research, documentation, and interpretive effort were much more complete. His Scott was the vain, irritable, self-aggrandizing "Fuss and Feathers" of legend. Yet Johnson went too far. While he credited Scott with great military ability, and gave a nod in the direction of Scott's work at military professionalization, *The Quest for Military Glory* seems a rather narrow peg on which to hang a career more than half a century long. Lust for glory cannot explain Scott's patient diplomacy with Britain, or in South Carolina during the Nullification Crisis. Nor does it explain the Anaconda Plan, Scott's prescient strategy for strangling the Confederacy through blockade.

Peskin has the advantage in sources, through his extensive use of internal Army correspondence preserved in the National Archives, and provides double the attention to the 1850s and 60s. Peskin suggests that Scott learned from the failure of his rigid, complex plan in the opening stages of the Second Seminole War in 1836, and showed far more flexibility in 1847. Though he still had difficulty, perhaps natural in an age of such limited communications, in maintaining control over tactical formations in battle, his appreciation of joint operations, logistics, and the need to conciliate local public opinion combined with his insight into the minds of his Mexican opponents to make him "truly the indispensable man" in that war (p. 191).

Peskin is critical of the character and extent of Scott's professional vision, arguing that it "was surprisingly narrow" (p. 120). But Peskin seems to view military professionalism largely in terms of manpower policy and technology: was the army to be composed of long-service regulars or citizen-soldiers, and would its tactics adapt to changes in technology? These are two of the great questions of American military policy, but they are not the sum of professionalism. Scott and his fellow "professionals" mistrusted the discipline and capability of citizen-soldiers, but their objective was to maintain a monopoly of command over the militia and volunteers, not to fight major wars with the Regular Army alone. The expansible army established in the reduction in force of 1821 did *not* "prove inadequate to preserve this professional monopoly" (p. 61): the principal tactical, operational, and strategic commanders of the war with Mexico and the Civil War were Old Army men and West Point graduates.

The limits of Peskin's vision are further evident in his exaggerated assessment of the impact of the rifle, "which spelled an end to Scott's cherished professionalism" (p. 218). Yet only a profession—an occupation dedicated to the in-depth study of its duties over long careers—could have adapted to the growing complexity of war. Indeed, such complexity was the root of military professionalism. Peskin has a far stronger case when he criticizes Scott for maintaining the Regular Army as an institution rather than dispersing its officers and noncommissioned officers to train the volunteers at the outset of the Civil War, but I wish Peskin had devoted more attention to how Scott's officers and men saw him, to how his example, and his support for professional institutions like the Military Academy, encouraged professionalization. Doing so would have provided a fuller picture of Scott's true impact, of the culture of professionalism he did so much to foster.

Samuel Watson   United States Military Academy
West Point, New York

Bulwark of the Republic: The American Militia in [the] Antebellum West. By Mary Ellen Rowe. Westport, Conn.: Praeger, 2003. ISBN 0-313-32410-7. Notes. Bibliography. Index. Pp. xii, 232. $69.95.

The traditional militia that existed from the colonial era into the 1850s was "a supremely localist institution," according to Mary Ellen Rowe, best understood when studied at local and state levels. Although powerfully populist and moved by majority opinion the militia was nonetheless constrained by law and embedded in the civil society from which it arose. The militia of colonial and early America moved westward where the "same system took shape . . . virtually unchanged" until the eve of the Civil War (p. xi). In its heyday, Rowe contends, the traditional militia defended local communities from hostile enemies, intrusive state and federal governments, and civil threats to the provincial status quo.

Rowe makes her case by examining the militias of Kentucky, Missouri, and Washington Territory from the 1790s through the 1850s, arguing that Kentuckians took their militia tradition (inherited from colonial Virginia) to Missouri and Missourians carried the institution to the territories of Oregon and Washington. *The Bulwark of the Republic* meticulously dissects militia affairs in the three locales, sometimes in war, notably in 1812 and 1846, but chiefly assesses Native American and internal threats to local safety and stability. Rowe demonstrates that local militia organizations, often in defiance of state or federal policy, were not vigilantes. Locals took care to elect officers, organize their units according to law, and adhere to conventional military procedure, although they were always ready to seek state and federal authorities' compensation once their unsanctioned actions came to an end. By the 1850s, as seen in Washington Territory, with Regular Army forces policing the Indians and the territorial and federal governments asserting centralized control, the traditional militia had lost its vitality and social purpose.

Rowe's work is notable for demonstrating that the traditional militia persisted well past the American Revolution, contrary to standard scholarly views, through the careful examination of county and state militia records and accounts. The only way that the militia, in whatever form it existed, can by assessed historically is to study it at the local, colonial, and state level. Rowe's research illustrates how deeply rooted the militia was in local affairs and how it remained a vital part of provincial America well beyond the 1780s. Rowe could strengthen her argument by moving beyond a tight focus on Kentucky, Missouri, and Washington Territory to make comparative observations with other states and territories. Recent studies suggest that Rowe's version of the militia was not a peculiarly sectional one, as she implies, but relatively widespread. Reliance on such works as Charles Skeen's *Citizen Soldiers in the War of 1812* (1999) would enhance this insightful study.

It is unfortunate that Praeger and its parent company, Greenwood Press, persist in selling useful monographs at such a high price. Their pricing is a disservice to both authors and their readers.

Jerry Cooper   Emeritus, University of Missouri–St. Louis
St. Louis, Missouri

Soldier-Artist of the Great Reconnaissance: John C. Tidball and the 35th Parallel Pacific Railroad Survey. By Eugene C. Tidball. Tucson: University of Arizona Press, 2004. ISBN 0-8165-2253-7. Map. Illustrations. Notes. Bibliography. Index. Pp. xvi, 226.

Pacific Railroad Reports represents one of the most important collective accounts ever assembled about the vast regions beyond the Mississippi River. These massive seventeen volumes, published between 1855 and 1861, exemplified the high quality of exploration and record keeping by an elite corps of army officers and their civilian colleagues. More important, the individual volumes offered vital scientific information on geology, ethnology, zoology, and botany, which was studied by American and European scholars for decades. The officers, many of whom received their scientific training at West Point, were ideally suited not only to protect the survey teams, but also to sketch scenes, compile data, and assemble specimens for study at the Smithsonian Institution.

Among the best documented of the surveys was the 1853 exploration of the 35th parallel across Oklahoma, the Texas Panhandle, New Mexico, and Arizona to Los Angeles. This venture eventually led to publications by commander Lt. Amiel Weeks Whipple, artist Heinrich Balduin Müllhausen, John Sherburn, Lt. David S. Stanley, and Lt. John C. Tidball. Although Tidball's "Report" has long been utilized by historians, a more polished account of his participation has recently been uncovered in the Beinecke Rare Book and Manuscript Library at Yale University. This "Itinerary" manuscript serves as the basis for this new book, and because it was written many years after the exploration, it contains more interpretive data than the original "Report." Through its pages we learn much more about the men of the expedition, their personal idiosyncrasies, their relations with various Indian tribes, and about Tidball's deeper thoughts.

The author has allowed Lt. Tidball to speak for himself at many junctures in this book, while simultaneously connecting the other men's published accounts into a broader and more coherent story. This technique is especially important for describing the initial two-thirds of the exploration because Lt. Tidball did not join the party until they had already reached the Zuni villages along the New Mexico–Arizona border. Tidball was stationed at nearby Ft. Defiance and had been instructed to take a twenty-five-man escort to join Whipple in the field.

Soldier-Artist of the Great Reconnaissance is organized around the day-to-day experiences of the Whipple Expedition. The author has meticulously examined the daily references of each of the record keepers and has compared their reactions to the phenomena encountered along the trail. He has also corrected their occasional mistakes and has clarified conflicting information. More important, the author has wisely placed the Whipple Expedition within the broader context of American expansion and the evolution of nineteenth century scientific thought. Like Pulitzer Prize winner William Goetzmann before him, he has interpreted government exploration of the first half of the nineteenth century within the proper framework of the United States Army's elite Corps of Topographical Engineers.

Persons looking for a lively account about exploration in the Southwest will be pleased with this well-researched and well-written book. Persons looking for a deeper understanding of the army's diverse scientific roles on the frontier will be even more pleased with this effort. It reminds current generations that the frontier army may not have always lived in glory, but it certainly contributed to a better understanding about the mysterious West.

Michael L. Tate

University of Nebraska at Omaha
Omaha, Nebraska

Days of Glory: The Army of the Cumberland, 1861–1865. By Larry Daniel. Baton Rouge: Louisiana State University Press, 2004. ISBN 0-8071-2931-3. Maps. Photographs. Notes. Bibliography. Index. Pp. xviii, 490. $44.95.

The author of several first-rate studies of the western campaigns, Larry Daniel here offers a history of the Union's principal western army (initially named the Army of the Ohio but renamed the Army of the Cumberland in the fall of 1862) from the beginning of the war to the fall of Atlanta when the army ceased to exist as a unified field force. Daniel makes it clear that he intended this work to be a counterpart to Thomas Connelly's two-volume history of the Confederate Army of Tennessee (*Army of the Heartland*

[1967] and *Autumn of Glory* [1971]), and like Connelly, Daniel focuses particularly on the competence (or, more aptly, the incompetence) of the army commanders.

One of the great strengths of this book is Daniel's attention to the impact of logistics on command decision making. Daniel shows clearly and in detail how dependent army commanders were on the capacity of the railroads, river transport, and mule trains to keep their armies fed and supplied. But Daniel's main focus (like Connelly's) is on the army's leadership. If Connelly's principal interpretive thrust was his sympathy for the long-suffering men in the ranks who bore the consequences of the army's inept leadership, Daniel asserts that the men in the ranks of the Army of the Cumberland were equally burdened. From the psychologically-shattered Robert Anderson, who was in over his head from the beginning, to George H. Thomas, who Daniel claims has been vastly overrated by his admirers, Daniel asserts that the Army of the Cumberland suffered under a series of, at best, second-rate commanders who were too often frozen by inertia or confused by their responsibilities. Daniel is incisive and often scathing in his assessment of the Army's leaders. Don Carlos Buell was "a maneuverer not a fighter," (p. 167) and his inaction was based on "his inability to grasp more than a single issue at a time" (p. 47); William S. Rosecrans was both overconfident and negligent, as well as "boisterous, opinionated, and brusque" (p. 182). Daniel's treatment of George H. Thomas is more complex. He depicts Thomas as often petty and sulking, but also concludes that during the Atlanta campaign he was a victim of "Sherman's prejudice" (p. 415). Stalwart on defense, he was slow to move, and Daniel concludes that Thomas was "competent but not brilliant" (p. 362.) The second echelon commanders fare much worse. Alexander McCook was "blundering" and "inept" (pp. 265, 286). and Gordon Granger was "short-tempered, crude, and at times a sadist" (p. 333). Indeed, of all the generals, in or out of the Army of the Cumberland, only Grant emerges undiminished.

Moreover, "bickering and intrigue" (p. 126) within the army, which included the murder of one general by another, undermined its efficiency. Just as Braxton Bragg faced mutinous conspiracy among the officers in his army, Buell, too, endured a near mutiny when twenty-one officers signed a petition to the government asking for his removal.

Daniel's commitment to thoroughness is evident in his determination to include a lot of detail, especially concerning army organization, which is certainly valuable but which also occasionally gets in the way of his argument. On the whole, however, this book achieves exactly what Daniel hoped it would in providing a thoughtful, authoritative, and comprehensive portrait of the Union's principal western army and its commanders.

Craig L. Symonds   U.S. Naval Academy
                                                                   Annapolis, Maryland

Union Jacks: Yankee Sailors in the Civil War. By Michael J. Bennett. Chapel Hill: University of North Carolina Press, 2004. ISBN 0-8078-2870-X. Illustrations. Notes. Bibliography. Index. Pp. xv, 337. $34.95.

This study of the enlisted men of the Union navy aims to avoid stereotypes and mythology and to present sailors as they really were. To do this, Michael J. Bennett, a lawyer and an independent historian, used letters, diaries, and journals of 169 common sailors. He also compiled statistical information on those who enlisted from April 1861 to April 1865. This involved selecting every twenty-fifth name from every rendezvous or recruiting report from all such stations that operated during the war. Published memoirs, books, and articles by and about sailors, the navy and the Civil War added to the documentation as did unpublished master's theses and doctoral dissertations. Subject files at the National Archives provided additional material on some topics. The author's goals were to present the social origins of sailors and why they enlisted; to recapture what it was like to adjust to, and interact with, new companions and a strange and sometimes deadly world of wood, metal, heat, guns, noise, and routine. This examination of the naval experiences that were common to most sailors also looks at the influence of such issues as war, race, religion, and monotony on their lives. Much of the best evidence comes from the writings of young men to whom everything was strange, new, and different. Bennett concludes that sailors shared few of the motivations that induced men to join the army. They had to learn much more than the soldier to become proficient fighting men, and they functioned in a harsher and more stressful environment with few opportunities for change. At the end of the war, many men left the navy angry about the treatment they had received as well as their lack of liberty, pay, and prize money.

The accuracy of the author's statistical sample will depend on future research. For some time to come it is apt to be the accepted scholarly standard. A wider use of Navy Department archives would have strengthened the documentation on some topics. As the author notes, most of the focus is on the experiences of white sailors in the blockading squadrons, where the majority of them served, and in the gun boats on the Mississippi River and its tributaries. There are only a few references to those who served in the cruisers and in the Pacific Squadron. The emphasis on shared experiences does not allow for examples of uncommon courage. The book contains an illustration of an event for which a sailor won the Medal of Honor, but the circumstance and the man are not noted in the text. Missing also are any references to the more than 300 Medals of Honor that were won by navy enlisted men during the Civil War. Nevertheless, this well written book is a valuable addition to the historiography on American sailors and on the Union navy during the Civil War.

Harold D. Langley

Emeritus, Smithsonian Institution
Washington, D.C.

West Wind, Flood Tide: The Battle of Mobile Bay. By Jack Friend. Annapolis, Md.: Naval Institute Press, 2004. ISBN 1-59114-292-X. Maps. Illustrations. Notes. Bibliography. Index. Pp. xiv, 308. $29.95.

The Battle of Mobile Bay, 5 August 1864, was certainly the most important naval engagement of the American Civil War. Other battles, like Hampton Roads between the *Monitor* and the *Virginia,* had been more spectacular; yet, the size of the naval forces engaged on both sides, the momentous consequences (the sealing up of the only major port still in Confederate hands on the Gulf of Mexico after the loss of New Orleans and Pensacola), and, last but not least, the direct confrontation between the first Admiral of the U.S. Navy and the only one of the Confederacy, all explains the outstanding importance of that battle.

Still, up to now, no full-scale book had ever been dedicated to the Battle of Mobile Bay. Now, Jack Friend has fulfilled the task of producing such a complete narrative, with a book that, if also addressed to general readers, will certainly be welcomed by scholars in the field as well.

The author states clearly the strategic (and logistical!) importance of the Mobile seaport. This importance did not escape the attention of the Union strategists (first of all, President Lincoln); therefore they started thinking about the capture of Mobile even before the fall of New Orleans. Jack Friend analyzes carefully the evolution of the Federal strategy, both from land and sea, against Mobile, and explains why several compelling reasons forced an almost continuous deferral of the operation.

The preparation of the attack (and the whole campaign) is also well covered—more, indeed, from the Union side: Confederate problems, like the excruciating difficulties of shipbuilding, the never-ending question of finding in time the necessary iron plates, the scarcity of coal and the difficulties of getting it, are only hinted at (and the last one all but overlooked). Yet, since the initiative of giving battle at Mobile Bay was from the Union side, the author might be right in not entering into such details.

The book discusses in broad terms (and with precision) the unfortunate decision by the Union authorities to withdraw the bulk of the military forces which should have cooperated with Admiral Farragut from the land side, by sending them to the ill-fated Red River Campaign, which almost ended in a military disaster for the Union and deprived the Admiral of the possibility of causing the fall of the city of Mobile together with the sealing of the bay.

The narration of the battle proper starts from page 161. This shows how complicated the preparatory phase had been, well analyzed by the author. The exposition of the battle is clear and concise; the only fault, according to this reviewer, is that, in narrating the sinking of the monitor *Tecumseh,* the book follows the old version, which attributes the responsibility for it to the rashness of Captain Craven, who had his ship cut across the torpedo field, to disaster.

Certainly, Captain Craven will never come back to give us his version; yet, in 1967, a maritime archaeological expedition, sponsored by the Smithsonian Institution and the U.S. Army Corps of Engineers, reached the remains of the *Tecumseh*. The divers discovered, under what had been the waterline of the ironclad, two big holes, caused certainly by perforating shots from the big Brook guns of the Confederate Water Battery. Therefore, a valid hypothesis is that the monitor did not run into the torpedoes because of the imprudence of poor Captain Craven, but because she lost her steering as a result of the two mortal shots she received. By the way, the entire question is discussed by this reviewer in his *History of the Confederate Navy* (pp. 324–25, and endnotes 66–67). But the author does not even note the existence of this book (which, incidentally, is listed by the publisher on the dust-jacket of *West Wind, Flood Tide*).

Yet, this is a minor fault. In the main, the book is good and useful and (what is also important) well written.

Raimondo Luraghi   University of Genoa
                                                                          Genoa, Italy

Reflections of a Civil War Historian: Essays on Leadership, Society, and the Art of War. By Herman Hattaway. Columbia: University of Missouri Press, 2003. ISBN 0-8262-1487-8. Notes. Index. Pp. xv, 254. $44.95.

Herman Hattaway's *Reflections of a Civil War Historian* collects essays from across his long and distinguished career. Some are addressed to fellow academics, others to a general audience. Some pieces are collaborative, but most were written solo. Almost all have been previously published. Hattaway forthrightly labels the collection a "late-in-career vanity piece" (p. xiii), but the book deserves wide readership, for it reminds us why Hattaway is considered one of the most distinguished students of the late T. Harry Williams. Many prominent Civil War scholars actually know very little about military history. Hattaway knows it well and writes it beautifully.

Hattaway's thirteen essays are in three sections. "Civil War Leadership" covers Stephen D. Lee; P. G. T. Beauregard; John Hunt Morgan; George H. Thomas; and Abraham Lincoln. "Society in Wartime" examines conflict within Christian churches; the relationship between state rights and local defense; and friction between the Lincoln administration and the United Kingdom. "The Art of War" has essays on balloons in the American military from the Civil War to World War I; the War Board, precursor to a true general staff; an overview of how Civil War armies were created, mobilized, and developed; and an analysis of how tactics evolved during the war.

Some of Hattaway's essays are printed versions of addresses to Civil War Round Tables or pieces written for popular magazines, based largely on secondary sources. They are well-written and by no means "light weight." For example, in "Stephen D. Lee and the Guns of Second Manassas," Hattaway unravels a complex controversy related to General James Longstreet's counterattack. Some essays come from papers presented at academic conferences, presaging Hattaway's subsequent monographs. In "State Rights and Local Defense," Hattaway outlines many of the ways the Confederacy benefited from localism. This was an important theme in his later collaborative work, *Why the South Lost the Civil War.*

Military historians will be particularly interested in two essays. "The War Board, the Basis for the United States's First General Staff," was originally published in *Military Affairs* in 1982. Here Hattaway and coauthor Archer Jones rescue from obscurity the important effort made by Secretary of War Edward M. Stanton, who in 1862 brought the heads of the various army bureaus together under retired Major General Ethan Allen Hitchcock. Although the Board did not last long, it gave Stanton crucial assistance early in his tenure and established important relationships that continued informally throughout the war. In "The Evolution of Tactics in the Civil War," Hattaway provides an overview of how West Point education and Mexican War memories combined with fortuitous circumstances at battles such as Shiloh, Antietam, and Fredericksburg to demonstrate the power of the defensive. He follows this with a survey of past and current writings concerning tactics, including Grady McWhiney and Perry D. Jamieson's controversial "Celtic thesis," which links ethnicity to a Southern propensity for the offensive, and assertions by Paddy Griffith and Earl J. Hess that historians have exaggerated the impact of rifles during the war.

Hattaway concludes with an epilogue that touches upon everything from Civil War Round Tables to Civil War reenactors, and from controversies over Nathan Bedford Forrest to Ken Burns's PBS extravaganza. It's a bit of a shotgun blast, but he hits his targets. Hattaway considers himself highly privileged to have made a living teaching and writing about the Civil War. This book, like his many other works, demonstrates how his career has benefited both the public and his chosen profession.

William Garrett Piston
Southwest Missouri State University
Springfield, Missouri

Soldiers of Peace: Civil War Pacifism and the Postwar Radical Peace Movement. By Thomas F. Curran. Bronx, N.Y.: Fordham University Press, 2003. ISBN 0-8232-2210-1. Notes. Bibliography. Index. Pp. xv, 228. $45.00.

With such vast expanses of the corporate media and the discipline of history devoted to the history of warfare, books about the history of peace are always welcome. Hence, Thomas F. Curran helps fill the gaping hole in the literature left by America's fascination with mass killing. *Soldiers of Peace* tells the story of "perfectionist pacifism" in the Civil War era. Primarily a narrative of the Universal Peace Union (UPU) and its leading light, Alfred Love, the book raises important questions about both the prospects and limitations for organized peace activists who confront the power of the military state. While Curran finds much to praise in the UPU, he argues that its very perfectionism limited its appeal.

Curran locates the origins of Civil War pacifism in millennialism and the general reform spirit of the antebellum period. Prewar movements had left figures such as Love, Adin Ballou, and Henry Clark Wright with a deep belief in the higher law of God's commandments and of their obligations as citizens in God's Kingdom. The demands of the war, especially conscription, forced such people to choose between the call of the President and the call of God. Believing that all killing was wrong, they chose the latter and embarked on a campaign of moral suasion to convince their fellow Americans to abjure violence. As the war heightened their commitment to nonresistance, it also brought them into contact with one another. Shortly after the close of hostilities, Love, Ballou and others organized the Universal Peace Union as a vehicle to spread peace through education. The UPU expanded its outlook beyond nonviolence, promoting a holistic vision of peace that linked it to racial justice, women's rights, justice for Native Americans, abolition of capital punishment, and other social justice issues. This linkage, Curran believes, represents part of the true significance of the UPU, admittedly a failed organization. It bridged the gap between nineteenth-century peace activists and twentieth-century organizations such as the War Resisters League.

Curran's book relates the story of the UPU in a lively manner and there are many insights that cannot be noted in a short review. The author might have focused more directly on the failure of the organization. He blames the perfectionists for sectarian views that "repelled many potential sympathizers" and for taking an "uncompromising position" that "narrowed the tactics they allowed themselves to enjoy" (p. 201). This conclusion, while certainly plausible, would be more convincing if argued more consistently throughout Curran might also have given more thought to changing definitions of masculinity and to how social movements work in general.

Overall, though, this slim volume is a valuable and much needed addition to the literature. As the country slides ever closer to a fully militarized society, there is much to learn from those in the U.S. past who stood against such a future.

James D. Schmidt
Northern Illinois University
DeKalb, Illinois

The Railroad and the State: War, Politics, and Technology in Nineteenth-Century America. By Robert G. Angevine. Stanford, Calif.: Stanford University Press, 2004. ISBN 0-8047-4239-1. Illustrations. Notes. Bibliography. Index. Pp. xvii, 351. $65.00.

In his revised Duke University Ph.D. dissertation, Robert G. Angevine offers a "more complete and more critical history of the relationship between the U.S. Army and the railroads throughout the nineteenth century" (p. xv). The vast literature on railroads and the military, he explains, leaves crucial subjects unexamined or only partially explored. Moreover, his approach allows him to analyze the army's response to technological change, the evolution of military thought, the beginnings of military-industrial cooperation, American political development, and numerous related and subsidiary themes. The author bases his volume on substantial research in primary and secondary sources.

Angevine begins his study with the army's participation in advancing transportation through the construction of roads, canals, and other public works during the early years of the new republic. The intense and shifting debate over the government's proper role in internal improvements always limited what could be done. With railroads seriously under way in the 1830s, army activity rose to a new and important level. As the nation's first and, for many years, premier engineering school, the United States Military Academy provided much of the professional staff required for surveying, building, and managing the emerging system. Around the same time, however, under the leadership of Dennis Hart Mahan and others, West Point began a significant transition away from civil engineering to concentrate on promoting military professionalism and the training which would advance it. During the Mexican War, the army's performance highlighted the positive results of the redirection. Consequently, the army's part in the spectacular railroad growth of the 1850s was much reduced from earlier decades.

Nonetheless, during the Civil War Ulysses S. Grant and his chief lieutenants worked out cooperative relations between the railroads and the army to transform the conduct of war. Moving troops and supplies with great speed and reliability, Union armies simultaneously launched continuing and devastating attacks upon Confederate railroads and other transportation modes. The new partnership continued in the Gilded Age, based on mutual advantage. The army and War Department became avid and valued supporters of transcontinental railroads and provided them with badly needed supplies, police forces for railroad settlements, and security against Native American attacks. In return, railroad executives often turned to army officers for advice and the land forces benefitted from relatively cheap and reliable transportation which advanced the military mission in numerous ways. Additionally, key officers received lavish gifts and lucrative investment opportunities from the grateful railroads. Although working well in the trans-Mississippi west, the partnership broke down in anticipating and preparing for the Spanish-American War.

The author systematically pursues and elaborately documents familiar themes which others have examined in a more cursory or piecemeal way. The richness of his provided detail is only suggested in the summary above. At times, he appears to have difficulty in developing his material in a fully coherent manner, as is exemplified by Chapter 6, and a number of his generalizations are unclear or open to question. Overall, Angevine's contribution rests more with his narrative than his analysis. Criticism aside, the author has written a useful monograph.

Paul A. C. Koistinen

California State University
Northridge, California

The Natal Native Contingent in the Anglo-Zulu War. By Paul S. Thompson. Scottsville, South Africa: Privately published, 2003 [1997]. ISBN 0-620-30298-4. Maps. Notes. Bibliographical essay. Pp. v, 179. $70. Can be obtained from the author at Thompson@ukzn.ac.za.

Most students of the Anglo-Zulu War will probably not be aware that black Africans made up more than half of the British army that invaded Zululand in January of 1879 and went on to fight the storied battles of Isandlwana, Rorke's Drift, and Ulundi. The British invasion force, under the overall command of Gen. Frederick A. Thesiger, soon to be Lord Chelmsford, totaled some 16,800 men, at least 9,000 of whom were Africans. Of these, a few, perhaps as many as 1,000, were dissident Zulus, warriors whose leader held a grudge against Zulu paramount chief Cetshwayo or who were out to avenge a slight directed their way by men of another Zulu regiment. The bulk of the large African component, however, was comprised of the Natal Native Contingent (NNC), men recruited from Africans resident in Natal, the province of South Africa adjacent to Zululand from which the British invasion was launched.

This is the force whose story Paul Thompson first told in a 1997 edition of the book under review here. He later returned to the subject and in 2003 has produced a revised and expanded version of his book that is sure to remain the definitive account of Britain's black allies in the Anglo-Zulu War for some time to come. Not that Thompson is likely to have much competition. As he points out in the Foreword to the book (p. v), the substantial literature on the Anglo-Zulu War contains very little about the NNC, for reasons that are "partly political, partly cultural." During the imperial era, Europeans were not interested in diminishing their own exploits by extolling those of their "native" levies. And, "In the wake of empire, the African had no desire to glorify them, unless they were feats of resistance." To many in the current generation of South Africans, Thompson says, the NNC represents "collaboration in colonial rule, egregiously incorrect politically and best forgot. It is fairly safe to say the new history textbooks for South Africa are hardly likely to mention the contingent at all."

Not only would this deny "many brave men their meed of praise and [distort] our appreciation of the past," Thompson writes (p. v), but it would scant the part played in the Anglo-Zulu War by the province of Natal. In 1879, Africans made up the vast majority of the population of that province, accounting for just under 320,000 of its overall population of 361,587. Many of these Africans, like the amaHlubi, amaNgwane, or amaQadi, were peoples who earlier had been driven from Zululand as a result of Zulu expansion, the Mfecane or "crushing," that began in the time of the great king Shaka in the 1820s and continued under his successor, Dingaan.

Most of these "displaced persons" were bitterly anti-Zulu, Paul Thompson tells us, and supported the British because they "had brought peace to a land ravaged by warfare, the source of which had been Zulu expansion" (p. 1). That the British, about to go to war against the 250,000-strong Zulu nation, should have tried to tap into this vast reservoir of manpower should not surprise us. Nor that there should have been so much local opposition to doing so, however short-sighted it might have been. Heavily outnumbered white farmers and town dwellers in Natal were not eager to see young blacks issued with guns, as army recruiters proposed doing. There was a widespread fear that black fighters were likely to turn their weapons on whites rather than Zulus. This issue lay at the heart of the interesting prewar debate among the white authorities as to how the African levies were to be organized and equipped. The British military wanted them to be organized along the lines of the British regimental system and to be issued, at least partially, with firearms. Civilian authorities, on the other hand, wanted the African contingent to retain its traditional military organization, the *amabutho* or age-grade system so many of them had brought with them from Zululand, and to be armed with their traditional weapons, principally the *assegai* or short stabbing spear. The military won this argument, however, and on 11 December 1878 orders were issued calling up 7,550 Africans to form the Natal Native Contingent. Seven thousand of the recruits were to serve as infantry, 250 as cavalry, and the rest as pioneers. The NNC units would be officered by members of the local white gentry, most of whom were not up to much, or by British officers on special service, who performed somewhat better.

The NNC fought in most of the campaigns and battles of the Anglo-Zulu War but perhaps the only aspect of its participation in the war that has attracted the attention of posterity is its role in the battle of Isandlwana, the great massacre which claimed the lives of 895 British soldiers and of at least 550 of their African allies. Paul Thompson has observed that the Zulus at Isandlwana "seemed especially determined to kill the men of the NNC" (p. 63). This targeting, plus the fact that many of the NNC fought without arms and, when they did have rifles, without sufficient ammunition, provoked a flight of part of the contingent at the height of the battle. Unfortunately, it is this flight of "cowardly blacks" (as Lt. Gonville Bromhead, alias Michael Caine, calls them in the film *Zulu*) for which the NNC at Isandlwana will be remembered, not the fact that two-thirds of its number perished in the battle or in its aftermath. Donald Morris, in his classic *Washing of the Spears* (New York: Simon & Schuster, 1972), wrote that "470 of their bodies were found in the camp and along the fugitives' trail [by which the British and their allies had tried to escape].The rest had vanished, but scores must have been hunted out in the kraals and crannies and killed far from the field" (p. 387).

In addition to providing readers with an account from the contingent's perspective of NNC participation in the epic battle of Isandlwana, Paul Thompson has recounted their service over the whole scope of the war in voluminous detail, backed up by sixteen clear, helpful maps. His account is based on a rich selection of contemporary primary sources: diaries, journals, letters, memoirs, government documents. This extensive research has enabled the author to conclude that the NNC was "indispensable" to the British victory in the Zulu War, not only for its service as "scouts and skirmishers, stalkers and harriers," but as line infantry and cavalry. "[I]n hand-to-hand combat and firing at close quarters, the men of the contingent showed that they were as ready to fight and die as their fellow colonists" (pp. 171–72). In spite of this, Thompson writes, up to now "so little has been said or written about the African soldier in the Anglo-Zulu War that he is virtually its unknown soldier" (p. v). If that should cease to be the case, it will be largely due to the efforts of Paul Thompson.

Bruce Vandervort   Virginia Military Institute
                                             Lexington, Virginia

Shame and Endurance: The Untold Story of the Chiricahua Apache Prisoners of War. By H. Henrietta Stockel. Tucson: University of Arizona Press, 2004. ISBN 0-8165-2414-9. Photographs. Notes. Bibliography. Index. Pp. xii, 191. $35.00.

Shame and Endurance describes the treatment of the Chiricahua Apaches by the United States government from 1886 to 1914. Beginning with the military campaigns of George Crook and Nelson Miles against Geronimo and his insurgent band, the author chronicles the controversial incarceration of these prisoners of war (a term that included not only warriors but also their families and those who served as Army scouts), first in Florida, then Alabama, and finally Oklahoma. Supported by numerous quotations from official documents and eyewitness testimony, the author purports to tell the "Untold Story of the Chiricahua Apache Prisoners of War."

The subtitle is misleading, since Stockel herself told the story in *Survival of the Spirit: Chiricahua Apaches in Captivity* (Reno: University of Nevada Press, 1993), a book over 120 pages longer than her latest work. While the earlier study concentrated on the impact of captivity on the prisoners' health, and did not provide as detailed a description of the circumstances surrounding their confinement, it was nevertheless a well-written and balanced account with a disciplined use of quotations. This is not the case with *Shame and Endurance,* which suffers from excessive and lengthy quotations connected by pontifical indictments of the alleged prejudices of the individuals cited.

Lieutenant Colonel Lummis Landon's report on the prisoners is included in the first chapter. This officer was responsible for Forts Pickens (Pensacola) and Marion (Jacksonville), Geronimo and his warriors being held in the former, their families, the latter. While the author describes him as "A naturally compassionate man" who was "protective of the Apaches, disregarding their bad reputation" (p. 13), she concludes: "Despite his knowledge of the Apaches' situation and his sincere sympathy for his newly arrived charges, he was a product of his education, military training, and upbringing as a white male in white America in the late years of the nineteenth century" (p. 14). Stockel based this conclusion on "Langdon's choice of words," which reflected "the dominant society's intellectual framework" (p. 14).

The author's pet phrase "language of colonialism" peppers the text. While much useful information can be gleaned from the documents frequently quoted, this reviewer preferred the more restrained approach taken in her earlier book. H. Henrietta Stockel is unquestionably an authority on the subject and those with an interest in the Chiricahua prisoner of war experience are well advised to consult her *Survival of the Spirit,* which is better and more skillfully written than *Shame and Endurance.*

Frank Kalesnik   Orange County Community College
                                        Middletown, New York

The People in Arms: Military Myth and National Mobilization since the French Revolution. Edited by Daniel Moran and Arthur Waldron. Cambridge: Cambridge University Press, 2003. ISBN 0-521-81432-4. Notes. Index. Pp. 268. £47.50.

If one had to pick a central concept that characterized European warfare in the nineteenth century the *levée en masse* would naturally come to mind. In the usual narrative, the French Revolution's ability to unleash and exploit the energies of its citizens swept away the armies of the *ancien régime,* who could not recover until they had, in a famous phrase, "rifled the armory of the revolution." To be sure, military historians have long pointed out the gross weaknesses of such an oversimplified view: the reliance of the French armies on the drill books and methods, and even many of the personnel of the monarchical army; the evolution of the French army under Napoleon into a bureaucratically efficient machine in which republican enthusiasm played a much diminished role; the effectiveness of militaries like the British which, once reformed, could fight the French on equal terms. Still, the idea of mass warfare characterized by a mobilization of soldiers from the entire population, and supported by nationalist ardor, remains a topic of interest to historians.

The People in Arms is a competent collection of essays on this subject. Not surprisingly, the focus is on France and secondarily Europe, although there are two essays on the idea of the *levée en masse* in China and Vietnam. The one American chapter, by John Whiteclay Chambers, deals more with American impressions of European events than with the American experience proper. This is unfortunate, perhaps, because the American model of mass citizen participation in warfare deserves more comparative analysis than it normally receives (some of the work of Stig Förster and his colleagues being a noteworthy exception). The Civil War, for example, seems to have had some effect on British thinking about voluntary citizen militias in the latter part of the century, and even the Revolution had its effect on European soldiers through men like Johann von Ewald.

The essays here explore different aspects of the myth of the people in arms. They highlight in different contexts the tension inherent between the ideological or mythic aspects of citizen service in war, on the one hand, and the administrative requirements of raising armies adequate for particular purposes on the other. Convincingly, if unsurprisingly, the authors all conclude that myth and reality rarely coincided, and for a variety of reasons. Unfortunately, the technological dimension is missing in much of this book: the *levée en masse* requires, after all, ways of war in which weapons can be mass-produced and soldiers trained with them in relatively short periods of time. They require too forms of warfare in which sheer numbers count for a great deal, something which is not always the case.

As in all collections, some of these essays are better than others. Arthur Waldron's piece on Chinese discovery of the French revolutionary experience, and the later translation of the French socialist Jean Jaurès's book on military service is a fascinating study of how history and military concepts move between continents. By itself, in fact, it makes a merely useful edited volume something more valuable.

Eliot A. Cohen   Paul H. Nitze School of Advanced International Studies
Baltimore, Maryland

Paths of Glory: The French Army, 1914–18. By Anthony Clayton. London: Cassell, 2003. ISBN 0-304-35949-1. Maps. Photographs. Appendixes. Bibliographical essay. Index. Pp. 238. £20.00.

Anthony Clayton, Senior Lecturer at the Royal Military Academy, Sandhurst, from 1965 to 1994, has enriched our knowledge of several fields of military history, particularly British and French colonial history, and has added to his list of metropolitan studies in his most recent book, *Paths of Glory: The French Army 1914–18.* This very readable volume appraises the performance of the French Army at the field level and follows its evolution, based on the most recent British and French sources. Written for the student of military history and informed general reader, the book serves as a corrective to many British accounts which give the impression that the British Army was the main army in the field on the western front in World War I and carried the brunt of the fighting throughout the war. It also corrects the skewed vision of the performance of the French Army in the Great War, as seen in light of the debacle of 1940. As Clayton notes, the French Army, though initially ill-equipped, ill-armed, and badly trained in modern tactics, nevertheless bore the brunt of the fighting through to 1917, and, after the mutinies of 1917, under the superlative leadership of two remarkable soldiers, Philippe Pétain and Ferdinand Foch, went on to play a decisive role in the final victory.

Clayton is particularly interested in the appraisal of French morale at the various stages of the war and shows that, even after the renewal of fighting spirit at the end of 1917, morale in 1918 was variable, which contributed significantly to the French soldiers' sense of *isolement,* or isolation, from the rest of French society. That tradition, continuing to World War II, was a cause of defeat in 1940. Also of interest to Clayton is the significant development of trench weaponry, improved artillery, new registering techniques and other more feted innovations such as tanks and airplanes, showing that World War I, especially in its later stages, was anything but technologically stagnant. He finds in Pétain's successive directives the foundation for the modernization of the French Army.

All of the horrors of trench warfare, including mud, lice, rats, rotting corpses, heat and frost, lack of sleep, and often food and water, and horrendous fear under shell fire, are detailed. After the mutinies of 1917 the French Army, which traditionally took less good care of its men than the British Army, also began under Pétain to improve the living conditions of the French *poilus* and, as a measure of raising morale, granted regular leaves, which, however, were withdrawn from time to time during the campaigns of 1918 under Foch.

The academic scholar might object that Clayton has not included a scholarly apparatus which footnotes his findings. Rather, he has written a substantive bibliographical essay, which evaluates recent key works in French and English, a helpful aid to the general reader and scholar alike. While the treatment of both the preparation of the French Army and its involvement in the campaigns of successive years is generally well handled, there is minimal coverage of the political-military environment which underpins French grand strategy. And the treatment of 1915 falls somewhat short in its appraisal of the strategy of Joseph Joffre, who, despite what he told the British, was still seeking a breakthrough in his great spring and fall offensives.

Overall, the author provides a convincing demonstration of the essential contribution of the French Army— in the words of Winston Churchill, "that sorely tried, glorious Army upon whose sacrifices the liberties of Europe had through three fearful campaigns mainly depended" (p. v). Clayton's volume is also the first comprehensive synthesis in English of the history of the French Army in World War I and, as such, will be helpful to the scholar, and of particular interest to the military history student and general reader.

Roy A. Prete Royal Military College of Canada,
Kingston, Ontario, Canada

Tommy: The British Soldier on the Western Front, 1914–1918. By Richard Holmes. London: HarperCollins, 2004. ISBN 0-00-713751-6. Maps. Photographs. Notes. References. Index. Pp. xxxi, 717. £20.00.

Mud. Barbed wire. Tragic and weary infantry machine-gunned in futile offensives. Incompetent and callous leadership. Lions led by donkeys. Fields of graves. And the ultimate ignominy: a lost peace. While Paul Fussell famously argued that the "uniquely awful" circumstances of the British war effort in northern France and Flanders defied rational explanation—that, in fact, it lay "outside history" proper (p. xviii)—Richard Holmes believes the contrary: that in British life, as in the memories of its survivors, the western front is a clearly discernible epoch, wholly understandable in historical terms. At the heart of this admirable tome are the papers, memoirs, and official unit histories of the participants.

There are many things that make this book an attractive piece of scholarship: its general even-handedness, its attention to detail, its illumination of obscure subjects, its effortless humanity. Indeed, one is as likely to learn about the special pleading of a young girl who asked Lord Kitchener to spare her pony during an early war requisitioning blitz (he did) as about the disposition of a division at the front (at full establishment of about 10,000 men, only 1,000 could be expected to be manning the parapet), the length of a communication trench (some as long as three miles), who received staff cars (divisional commanders and above), the social composition of the officer corps (by 1918, extremely heterogeneous), gas masks (effective, but never comfortable or easy to fight in), underground warfare (psychologically devastating), or about the development of new arms such as the Tank Corps (not entirely useful, but a harbinger of things to come) and Machine Gun Corps (extremely effective), to name only a few of the subjects on which Holmes sheds light. In the bigger picture, far from lambs led to the slaughter, the 1918 BEF had become a sophisticated fighting force, incorporating mixed platoons comprised of Lewis gunners, bombers, rifle bombers and riflemen. Without this evolution, which had had a painful teething period in 1916 and 1917, the victories of 1918 would have been impossible.

Holmes also weighs in on still emotionally sensitive subjects, including British generals (far less cavalrymen among them than hitherto thought; and the casualties they suffered were far heavier than in the Second World War), capital-courts martial (the benefit of the doubt usually went to the accused), and officer-man relations (extremely important, usually effective, and central to morale and discipline).

There are problems. Frustratingly, one soon realizes that even though the book bulges with 31 pages of endnotes, whether a sentence is documented or not is in fact purely at the whim of the author. On pages 545 and 546, for instance (there are many others), Holmes fails to provide citations for the passages mentioning Frank Crozier and the 2nd Royal Welch Fusiliers respectively. And the sources themselves are far from faultless. As Holmes is adamant that only contemporaneous sources will reveal the true "Tommy," not the memoirs or musings of the postwar authors (though plenty of these are cited), this is especially unfortunate. Censorship—both formal, by officers, and self-imposed, by the writer himself—prevented many letter-writers from speaking freely on a wide variety of subjects. Furthermore, because diaries were against King's regulations, they were often written up surreptitiously and hastily. Perhaps most damning, the majority of surviving documentation derives from the literate (and literary) class of officers and men, and not from the ordinary Tommy, many of whom remain in France, never wrote a letter beyond a few lines, and had they had the opportunity to write about their experiences in a free and unfettered fashion, I suspect, may very well have elucidated the experience of the soldiers at the sharp end in different ways.

Most perplexing of all, there is little recognition of the basic fact that, though estimates vary, troops spent a majority of their time on the western front well behind the lines. Much of this area was populated by French and Flemish shopkeepers, farmers and miners whose presence formed some of the soldiers' most powerful and enduring memories, as recorded in contemporaneous diaries and letters, as well as postwar novels and memoirs. True, Holmes, like Denis Winter, *Death's Men,* and John Ellis, *Eye-Deep in Hell,* before him, briefly discusses gambling, sports, theatrical troupes, and billeting, but this is all.

For troops for whom leave was rare, the towns and villages of northern France and Flanders became surrogate homes, complete with everyday domesticity, "pubs" (*estaminets*), women and children, a chance for social interaction beyond the regiment, an escape from army "bull"—in short a cultural and social phenomenon of the first order, with numerous yet largely ignored implications for the BEF. If there is one aspect of the campaign in France and Flanders that distinguishes it from other campaigns and deserves greater attention, it is surely this. This is a marvellous book, a joy to read and learn from, sure to be snapped up by Holmes's many admirers and a reading public craving insight into the western front. It is not, however, the final word.

Craig Gibson   Willowdale, Ontario, Canada

The Cross and the Trenches: Religious Faith and Doubt among British and American Great War Soldiers. By Richard Schweitzer. Westport, Conn.: Praeger, 2003. ISBN 0-313-31838-7. Photographs. Notes. Bibliography. Index. Pp. xxxiii, 311. $74.95.

Over the last few years we have come to learn a great deal about the lives of British soldiers in the First World War. Historians have explored subjects such as morale and discipline, relations between commissioned officers and other ranks, and the experience of battle. Fewer studies have appeared on their American counterparts, but nonetheless some interesting work is being done. However, the role of religion in both armies has been somewhat under-researched. Richard Schweitzer's *The Cross and the Trenches* is thus particularly welcome.

Schweitzer deals with a number of interesting issues concerning the religious history of the war, such as the reasons why the revival in faith that many anticipated did not occur. However, the book's subtitle—*religious faith and doubt among British and American Great War soldiers*—neatly captures his main focus. The core chapters deal with the experience of individuals. He has consulted a variety of sources, both published and unpublished, including a large number of manuscripts at the Imperial War Museum in London, as well as collections elsewhere, including the U.S. Army Military History Institute. Since it was rare for even devout soldiers to write very much about their faith, Schweitzer has had to work through a mass of writings, often picking up snippets of information on religion. In spite of the obvious drawbacks, this method, given the size of the sample Schweitzer has used, is surprisingly effective. It is a shame, therefore, that in his discussion of Field Marshal Sir Douglas Haig's religious faith, he relies on published sources rather than the British Commander-in-Chief's letters and diaries.

Schweitzer's ultimate conclusion is that "in sincere prayer or sacreligious defiance, the name of God was on the lips and in the writings of . . . soldiers and civilians more often than previously published accounts of their experience would lead us to believe" (p. 264). This is perhaps an exaggeration. British soldiers in particular were noted for their profanity. Many years ago, Eric Partridge and John Brophy, two British war veterans who collected and analysed soldiers' songs and slang, noted the number of songs that were parodies of hymns. Moreover, Schweitzer sometimes misreads his evidence. He quotes a British officer describing a Tommy "praying aloud 'with real fervour'" for God's help in getting a recalcitrant mule to move, which Schweitzer cites as an example of the way in which "God was worshipped in the ranks." However, this incident, taken from a book co-edited by your reviewer, is surely an example of the British sense of humour in action, or an example of the common practice of using blasphemy as a form of swearing. Either way it has nothing to do with the worship of God.

While this book is not the last word on the subject, it is a useful addition to the literature. *The Cross and the Trenches* contains some important insights into soldiers' attitudes to Christianity. Schweitzer provides a nicely nuanced picture that enriches our understanding of the culture of the ordinary British and American soldier on the Western Front.

Gary Sheffield

Joint Services Command and Staff College
Watchfield, Wiltshire, United Kingdom

Meuse-Argonne Diary: A Division Commander in World War I. By William M. Wright. Edited by Robert H. Ferrell. Columbia: University of Missouri Press, 2004. ISBN 0-8262-1527-0. Maps. Photographs. Notes. Sources. Index. Pp. xv, 174. $29.95.

Robert Ferrell, distinguished scholar and professor of American history, has recently written or edited a wave of books dealing with World War I. Having edited the diaries or memoirs of four young AEF soldiers and written a book on the collapse of the 35th Division in the Meuse-Argonne, he has now edited this volume, which presents and contextualizes the diary of Maj. Gen. William M. Wright, who commanded the 89th Division during the St. Mihiel and Meuse-Argonne offensives of 1918.

Although many AEF generals, and quite a few division commanders, wrote memoirs after the war, most notably Robert L. Bullard, Joseph T. Dickman, and John A. Lejeune, Ferrell notes that no *diary* of a division commander has ever been published. Wright's diary is particularly special because it has the ring of authenticity. It lacks sensationalism and self-aggrandizement; includes doubts, regrets, and changes of mind; and is filled with the kind of professional details that, although seemingly mundane, open a window into the thoughts and concerns of a competent, conscientious, and thoroughly professional U.S. Army division commander. Wright spent his days, and often his nights, visiting superior and subordinate commanders; organizing his staff and command post; considering who to promote, retain, and relieve; checking on his men up front; inspecting their clothing, rations, weapons, and tactical positions; and generally doing all he could to ensure their success in battle.

The book opens with a brief introduction by Ferrell, who describes Wright, a number of key subordinate commanders, and the division as a whole, the latter called "a marvelous group of men." The diary begins on 6 September 1918, the day Wright took command and just a week before the battle of St. Mihiel. On that day Wright noted that he "found the division in very good shape," a testimony to the leadership it had received from its former commander, Maj. Gen. Leonard Wood, who trained it in the U.S., and its then-acting commander, Brig. Gen. Frank L. Winn, the ranking brigadier. At St. Mihiel the division fought between the 2nd and 42nd Divisions, two of the AEF's best, and advanced creditably during its one long day of battle. Wright was generally pleased with his division's performance, as were his superiors (including Pershing), but he saw much needing improvement, too. After the battle, the 89th held the new line near St. Mihiel until mid-October, and Wright spent the time discussing lessons learned, inspecting his men, reorganizing, and retraining. When the division joined the Meuse-Argonne offensive, it was ready, and it did well as one of the spearhead units in the First Army's final push on 1 November. Eleven days later the war ended, and so does the diary. Throughout, Ferrell adds plenty of helpful explanation and contextualization.

Scholars of the AEF, and of military command in general, will be as interested in those subjects Wright addresses (the importance of logistics, ratings of senior AEF commanders and his own subordinates, his division's weaknesses), as in those he neglects (his own advancement; impressions of the French, British, and Germans; views on combat doctrine, tactics, and training; and his reaction to the death and maiming of thousands of his men). By exposing both, Professor Ferrell has added something significant to our knowledge of the AEF, and divisional command in the Great War.

Mark E. Grotelueschen   APO AE 09853

Collapse at Meuse-Argonne: The Failure of the Missouri-Kansas Division.
By Robert H. Ferrell. Columbia: University of Missouri Press, 2004. ISBN 0-8262-1532-7. Maps. Photographs. Notes. Sources. Index. Pp. xi, 160. $29.95.

Recent scholarship demonstrates that the American Expeditionary Forces was a largely ineffective army in 1918. It was impossible to field a force capable of independent engagements with European antagonists in eighteen months. The only independent campaign of any length, the Meuse-Argonne offensive, proved desperately difficult. Only after 1 November 1918, when the German army collapsed and began a general retreat, did the AEF achieve important gains. Most of the divisions were poorly trained and equipped. They lacked experienced commands and staffs, qualified junior and field-grade officers, and competent NCOs. They went into combat without sound operational plans.

Professor Ferrell's book lends significant support to this view. He chronicles the disastrous experience of the Missouri-Kansas National Guard Thirty-fifth Division, thoroughly describing its poor training, tensions with the regular army, logistical errors, and particularly its operational failure. In only four days of fighting on the left flank of the Meuse-Argonne sector (26–29 September 1918) the division suffered terrible casualties and after advancing about nine kilometers withdrew to a defensive line near its starting position. The next day the First Division relieved the Thirty-fifth. It was soon assigned to a quiet sector and saw no more action.

A notable part of the book is the account of the controversy that took place after the war between the critics and defenders of the Thirty-fifth Division. One of the latter was Captain Harry S. Truman, an artillery officer, who ever after blamed the regulars for the debacle in the Meuse-Argonne and even thought of abolishing West Point. Ferrell carefully documents the bravery of the men who fought. They deserved much better training than they received; their vicissitudes derived from the many difficulties that beset the entire army in the hasty mobilization of 1917–1918. Unpreparedness was the villain. All too many American servicemen and women, before and after the Thirty-fifth Division, fought courageously without the training they needed to fight well. Ferrell notes mordantly: "If the United States in 1917 had had a large, well-equipped, and tactically efficient army it is entirely possible that President Wilson's diplomacy could have brought peace without victory, which is what he and the nation desired" (pp. 128–29).

This excellent book is what one expects from its author, unsurpassed for his industry, competence, and honesty. It is most unusual that a scholar of his eminence would devote himself to such a valuable "small" history. His father, a veteran of the AEF, would have been proud.

David F. Trask   United States Army Center for Military History (Ret)
Ft. McNair, District of Columbia

***The "Casualty Issue" in American Military Practice: The Impact of
World War I.*** By Evan Andrew Huelfer. Westport, Conn.: Praeger, 2003.
ISBN 0-275-97760-9. Notes. Select bibliography. Index. Pp. xv, 244. $69.95.

In *The "Casualty Issue,"* Evan Andrew Huelfer adds a much-needed
and unique element to the existing scholarship on American military history between the world wars. For Huelfer, the high casualty rate among
American troops in the trenches in World War I left an indelible mark on
the young officers who led those troops. For decades thereafter, the likes of
George Marshall, George Patton, Omar Bradley, Mark Clark, and even Douglas MacArthur, searched for ways to limit similar casualty rates in future
wars.

High ranking commanders in the American Expeditionary Forces
believed they could win the war through open warfare, an operational concept which stressed the ability of masses of American riflemen to move
quickly and fire frequently and accurately. The killing power of the machine
gun, however, rudely awakened Americans on the battlefield to the realities
of modern, industrialized warfare. Huelfer cites the heavy losses at the Battle of Soissons in July 1918 in which the 1st and 2nd Divisions suffered
12,000 casualties. He puts blame for these horrific losses on poor planning,
inadequate education, and foolish tactics.

Younger officers in the AEF found the high casualty rates to be unac-
ceptable. When rising in rank following the end of World War I, they
sought to apply lessons from their experiences in trench warfare. The best
parts of Heulfer's book cover the sweeping attempts to transform the Army
into a force capable of winning wars with minimal loss of life. Although he
does not see the "casualty issue" as the dominant factor, he does convincingly argue that conserving lives was a contributing factor to the
Army's planning, doctrine, training, and procurement efforts during the
1920s and 1930s. American strategists planned for national wartime
mobilization as well as for quick and decisive campaigns during a future
conflict. Doctrinal development increasingly emphasized combined arms
operations to overcome the defensive advantages in firepower during
World War I. Training and educational programs inculcated Army officers
at all levels with the desire to minimize casualties. Lastly, the American
military sought new technological means to bypass, envelop, or annihilate
enemy forces without subjecting its own ground forces to heavy losses in
wars of attrition.

Huelfer makes good use of primary sources from the National Archives,
Carlisle Barracks, and West Point. His argument, however, could have been
strengthened with additional archival research. Collections at the Industrial
College of the Armed Forces, for example, include materials on logistics
planning during the interwar years. Likewise, holdings at the Dwight D.
Eisenhower Library, such as the papers of Eisenhower and of Henry Aurand,
contain evidence about the Army's mobilization planning process before
World War II. These omissions notwithstanding, Huelfer's book will prove

useful to anyone interested in American military history between the world wars.

David J. Ulbrich

Ball State University
Muncie, Indiana

Soldiers of the Pátria: A History of the Brazilian Army, 1889–1937. By Frank D. McCann. Stanford, Calif.: Stanford University Press, 2004. ISBN 0-8047-3222-1. Maps. Tables. Notes. Select bibliography. Index. Pp. xxvi, 593. $75.00.

Veteran Brazilianist Frank McCann seeks to present a solid historical foundation for understanding the military's role in Brazil's national development by explaining how it defended its institutional identity between 1889 and 1937. During this period, Brazil experimented with a decentralized republic after having deposed the monarchy and then imposed, in 1937, a short-lived civilian-led dictatorship. The military, and especially the Army, played a crucial role in these and most other critical political events throughout the period. McCann's extensive archival research and review of the growing volume of secondary literature leads him to conclude that the military's defense of national unity—the concept of "Pátria" or "motherland"—earns it the distinction of being the only truly national institution during this period.

McCann supports this argument by recounting in detail how the Army matured institutionally while honoring its commitment to Brazilian unity. It dutifully responded to a series of armed challenges to the agrarian-oriented regional elites whose effectiveness in governing decreased progressively in the face of growing urbanism and industrialism. With officers largely from the urban middle or lower middle classes, and soldiers and sailors often impressed off the street, the military struggled to assert the central government's authority in Brazil's vast hinterland. Although eventually victorious, its disastrous battlefield experiences—the product of poor leadership, inadequate planning, and, especially, logistical deficiencies—and then contact with German and French military experts engendered a spirit of reform. This generated core institutional values and a desire for national industrial self-sufficiency. By 1937, the Army's institutional strength made it the nation's foremost national political broker, supporting the onset of Getúlio Vargas's dictatorship in exchange for his commitments to the military's short-term rearmament and the nation's long-term industrialization.

Along the way, McCann's account also serves as a traditional institutional history imbued with personal histories of prominent officers and of institutional tensions produced by pressures for reform from both within and outside of Brazil. He delivers detailed accounts of the critical battles of Canudos, the War of the Contestado, and the 1922 uprising at Copacabana, as well as of minor uprisings that attested to the proclivity of troops at all levels to engage in political activism. He shows how the military struggled to improve its education, training, and armament even while hamstrung by a tradition of lax discipline and an unworkable conscription system.

This work deserves serious consideration by military historians and scholars of Brazil and civil-military relations in Latin America. McCann contributes to the debate on the Brazilian state's development by arguing that only in the 1930s did the military's institutional development endow it with the capabilities to perform a "moderating role" in society, and not earlier. McCann also disputes the argument that only after the 1964 coup did the military shift its focus from external threats to internal development. The post-1964 military professionally defended its institutional interests just as it had done during the period of McCann's study. Finally, he implies that the burdens of military government and then the adoption of the Constitution of 1988 have forced the military to redefine its role—finally relegating to society as a whole its role of defending the Pátria.

Richard Downes   Downes Technology Consulting
                                                         Miami, Florida

A Century of Valor: The First One Hundred Years of the Twenty-Eighth United States Infantry Regiment—Black Lions. By Col. Stephen L. Bowman, USA (Ret.). Wheaton, Ill.: Cantigny First Division Foundation, 2004. ISBN 1-890093-14-9. Maps. Photographs. Notes. Indexes. Pp. xxix, 432. $35.00 from the Foundation, which includes all shipping, handling and applicable taxes (Illinois residents).

This volume is a fine contribution to the regimental history genre, a field that is often overlooked by military history scholars. Frequently, officers of a particular regiment have written the history of their organization, more as a collective pat on the back than for any reasons of scholarship. These histories are sometimes long on the minutiae of a unit's comings or goings and short on the kind of critical analysis that would make them truly valuable to historians. This is unfortunate because the history of a regiment can tell us much about the evolution of the military experience.

Colonel Stephen Bowman is a Duke-trained historian and combat infantryman whose credentials for this kind of project are quite impressive. He was the director of the United States Army Military History Institute in the mid-1990s. He brings the historian's trained eye to telling the story of the 28th. In researching the history of the regiment, he made use of USAMHI's archive, in addition to a range of sources from the National Archives, the United States Army Center of Military History, and, most prominently, the growing archive of the First Infantry Division Museum in Wheaton, Illinois, an organization that helped fund his efforts.

In 1901, Congress authorized the creation of the 28th Infantry in response to the war in the Philippines. In World War I, the "Black Lions" were part of the 1st Infantry Division and fought well at Cantigny. In World War II they were affiliated with the 8th Infantry Division, but later they rejoined the 1st Division in Vietnam. Colonel Bowman covers all of the distinguished combat service of this fine unit and many of its peacetime experiences as well. His chapters are well organized and informative and his assertions are well supported with numerous citations. One senses that he is most comfortable narrating the Vietnam experiences of the 28th because he was in that war himself (with a different unit). Hence, the chapters on Vietnam are the most detailed and the best written. Each chapter of the book is well illustrated with useful maps. At the end of the book, Colonel Bowman has included a wide range of fascinating photographs that provide a nice visual sense of the regiment's journeys. *A Century of Valor* is clearly a significant contribution to the story of the United States Army in the twentieth century. Very few historians have taken the time and trouble to illuminate the experiences of one regiment, and Colonel Bowman's book is a good start in that regard.

Having said that, I believe the book could have been substantially better. There are no overarching themes stressed, nothing that ties the story together, or places the experiences of one group of Black Lions in perspective with others. The volume reads like an official history. While there is nothing inherently wrong with that, the human element gets lost. Bowman writes from the viewpoint of a colonel. There are flanking maneuvers, battalions going here and there, and officers are usually in charge of each situation. It makes for a fairly bloodless narrative. There are a few first hand accounts and they are the highlight of the book, but mostly Colonel Bowman narrates from the top down. In his note on sources he expresses regret that he did not have more first hand accounts available to him, but he must have had the opportunity to interview many living veterans of the 28th Infantry. I wish he would have made better use of that crucial human component because it would have made his book even stronger.

As it is, *A Century of Valor* is still a fine work of history. It will be of interest to anyone who served in the 28th Infantry as well as any scholar interested in the modern history of the United States Army.

John C. McManus   University of Missouri-Rolla
                                                         Rolla, Missouri

A Question of Loyalty: Gen. Billy Mitchell and the Court-Martial that Gripped the Nation. By Douglas Waller. New York: HarperCollins, 2004. ISBN 0-06-050547-8. Photographs. Source notes. Index. Pp. 439. $26.95.

Billy Mitchell was a controversial figure during his lifetime, and the decades since have not dimmed the controversy. Supporters hailed him then and continue to do so today as a courageous visionary who saw the future of war more clearly than his colleagues. Because he challenged traditional military thinking, he was silenced and then destroyed by hidebound surface officers. Detractors see a different Mitchell. To them he was an arrogant troublemaker who played loose with the facts and got what he deserved.

This new study of Mitchell, written by a senior correspondent for *Time* magazine, focuses on the climactic event that defined and ended the airman's career—his court-martial for insubordination in 1925.

Waller begins his story by recounting the events that led up to the court-martial, primarily the crash of the Navy airship *Shenandoah* in a thunderstorm over Ohio. Mitchell, who had been "banished" to Texas and demoted in rank to colonel after having served in Washington as a brigadier general, used the crash as justification to issue a stinging attack on senior officers in the Army and Navy. His press release accused them of "incompetency, criminal negligence and almost treasonable administration of the national defense." These were harsh words and retribution was swift. Mitchell was recalled to Washington for a court-martial.

Waller shows that the trial initially went Mitchell's way. His defense attorney, Congressman Frank Reid, understood that the trial was as much political spectacle as it was legal proceeding, and scored telling points. But then the Army brought in Major Allen Gullion to help the prosecution. Gullion was very capable and quickly began to turn the tide of the case by cleverly and clinically dissecting the testimony of Reid's witnesses. The climax came, however, when Mitchell himself took the stand.

Reading the trial transcript—and Waller's faithful recounting of it—is compelling. Bluntly, Mitchell's performance was an embarrassment. Gullion showed on point after point that Mitchell knew very little about naval aviation—especially of dirigible operations, which had generated his accusations in the first place. Moreover, Mitchell appeared surprisingly ill-informed about conditions within the Air Service.

Waller also discovered new and damning information about Mitchell's private life. A forgotten file in the Army's Inspector General (IG) papers recounts a 1920 incident that occurred between Mitchell and his first wife. During an altercation Mrs. Mitchell was shot in the chest—fortunately, it was not serious. She claimed that her husband shot her in a drunken rage; he claimed that she shot herself in a drunken stupor. (Waller claims that Mitchell had a serious drinking problem during this period.) The shooting incident was hushed up and no charges were brought—although the Army ordered Mitchell to undergo a psychiatric evaluation.

Despite this amazing new bit of information, Waller concludes that Mitchell was a great airman. The horrors of the trench carnage in the First World War convinced him that war must change and that the airplane must be the instrument of that change. Traditional surface officers in the Army and Navy refused to expand their horizons beyond acknowledging that airpower could perhaps play a useful role in assisting those surface forces. Mitchell's vision of the future was the more accurate. On the other hand, his method of expounding that vision was outrageous. He was guilty as charged.

Waller's discovery of Mitchell's IG file should give historians pause. Why did historians and biographers not discover these facts regarding Mitchell's personal life over the past seventy years? Are our research methods fundamentally deficient? Waller is a journalist, not a trained historian; yet he was able to ferret out key documents and facts that others could not. Perhaps it is time for us to go back to school.

Overall, this is an excellent and readable account of Mitchell's personal life and the court-martial that ended his career. But Waller covers not at all the very important subject of Billy Mitchell the air theorist. It was in this arena that Mitchell's star shone mostly brightly. For this story, the reader must return to the study by Alfred Hurley written forty years ago. It is time to update this aspect of Mitchell's life.

Phillip S. Meilinger   Northrop Grumman Corporation
                                                                      Arlington, Virginia

Imagining Flight: Aviation and Popular Culture. By A. Bowdoin van Riper. College Station: Texas A&M University Press, 2003. ISBN 1-58544-300-X. Photographs. Illustrations. Notes. Bibliographic essay. Index. Pp. xii, 206. $33.00.

Starting with the premise of technology as a captivating power, A. Bowdoin van Riper offers to chart the progress of aviation as reflected in popular culture. The engaging series of vignettes he offers suggests that the fascination aeronautics exercises on humans is due to the combination of god-like power it bestows, the ability to travel fast, and its very symbolism, an end in itself (pp. 4–6). Over six chapters, the author has chosen a thematic approach as a means to synthesize what would otherwise require an encyclopedia. "Imagining the Air Age" surveys the multiple promises and fears early aviation elicited, from women's liberation to war in the air. The culture of flying as embodied in "Pilots as National Heroes" shows how the implicit combination of fear and awe associated with aviation found its expression in the adulation of fliers. In a similar manner, "The Allure of Air Travel" makes clear that airline advertising was essential to convincing average travelers to become air passengers. The irony of turning an adventure, flying, into routine is not lost on van Riper, and he does a nice job of exposing this dichotomy. A similar approach is echoed in his closing chapter on the space program, thus echoing Howard McCurdy's point about the problems with NASA's culture of exceptionalism.

Van Riper's synthesis, although outstanding, is not without problems. For example, the chapter on "Death from Above" offers a good survey of the English literature on the subject. Yet it includes a discussion of 11 September 2001 which only lists military and novelized precedents. It is as if there had never been murder-suicides on commercial flights before, or these had never been covered. This is an unfortunate oversight, for elsewhere in his book, when discussing plane crashes, van Riper shows convincingly how important a role live coverage has played in raising our awareness of aviation tragedies.

The same wish for deeper analysis stems from his intriguing discussion of plane crash movies. Van Riper rightfully suggests that the stereotype of the passenger saving the flight relates directly to our psychological wish to master our fates. The many films he lists throughout his book tend to confirm this, but only in the conclusion does he touch on the central draw of such material (without specifying it). What attracts spectators is in fact the clichéd train wreck phenomenon: a morbid fascination prevents us from looking away.

Overall then, van Riper's selection of materials from such a wide array of sources is excellent. There are occasional misspellings of proper nouns, which would confuse a lay reader wishing to learn more. The tools of analysis, including the placement of aviation within wider popular cultural frames (from song to political campaigning), are generally limited. Perhaps a somewhat tighter focus would have done a better job of conveying van Riper's factual information. Nonetheless, his final point about aviation being a symbol of power, whether real or imagined, suggests a valuable base from which to teach students the fascination with aviation's technological sublime, or even to pursue advanced inquiry into its many facets.

Guillaume de Syon

Albright College
Reading, Pennsylvania

The Reader of Gentlemen's Mail: Herbert O. Yardley and the Birth of American Codebreaking. By David Kahn. New Haven, Conn.: Yale University Press, 2004. ISBN 0-300-09846-4. Photographs. Illustrations. Figures. Notes. Bibliography. Index. Pp. xxi, 318. $32.50.

It is perhaps fitting that the life of Herbert O. Yardley, an American pioneer in the secretive field of cryptology and the man who founded the United States's first permanent organization to intercept signals and break codes, has remained largely shrouded in mystery. Until now, Yardley has never had a biographer. Thanks to David Kahn, he will never need another. Just as Yardley revealed the secrets of American codebreaking in his 1931 bestseller *The American Black Chamber,* Kahn has laid bare the triumphs and failures of Yardley's life in this definitive biography of one of the most important figures in the history of American intelligence.

Kahn not only traces the fascinating arc of Yardley's life but also explains why it mattered. He argues that Yardley's principal contribution was to institutionalize codebreaking in the United States. As the leader of MI-8 in the War Department during World War I and of the Cipher Bureau jointly funded by the War and State Departments from 1919 to 1929, Yardley transformed cryptology from a black art into a science. In the process, he gave the United States a new source of intelligence that often provided information otherwise unobtainable. Yardley's greatest triumph was the Cipher Bureau's reading of Japanese diplomatic codes during the 1921 Washington Conference on the Limitation of Armament. The decrypted telegrams revealed Japan's willingness to accept the tonnage ratio for capital ships proposed by the United States and Great Britain. Their resolve bolstered, the U.S. negotiators waited until Japan agreed to the figure they had suggested. The efforts of Yardley and his codebreakers helped their government save millions of dollars and ease tensions in the Pacific.

As one might expect from the author of *The Codebreakers* and a leading expert on cryptology, Kahn provides valuable insight into the process of codebreaking. He details how Yardley and his staff attacked the codes of their primary targets—Japan, Great Britain, Mexico, Germany, and the Soviet Union. Although success against British and German codes was limited and interest in Soviet codes waned, the Cipher Bureau repeatedly broke the codes of Mexico and other Latin American nations, as well as those of Japan. Even more interesting is Kahn's discussion of how codebreaking has evolved. He explains that Yardley's success was due to his administrative and management skills during an era when cryptanalysis shifted from artisanal piece work to mass production and that Yardley's career paralleled the rise of intelligence as a significant factor in international affairs.

The book is exhaustively researched; it is based on more than twenty-five interviews and material from over thirty archives in five different countries and six different languages. It is also remarkably evenhanded. Kahn examines Yardley's flaws as well as his successes. He points out that Yardley was a better executive than cryptanalyst. He also notes that Yardley's greed distracted him from taking the steps necessary to ensure the future of the Cipher Bureau, such as recruiting, training, and developing new codebreaking methods. Anyone interested in the history of codes and ciphers, intelligence, or twentieth-century international relations will find this biography of America's first official codebreaker worthwhile.

Robert G. Angevine   Washington, D.C.

Detachment W. By Derek Richardson. Lincolnshire, U.K.: Paul Mould Publishing, 2004. ISBN 1-58690-012-9. Maps. Illustrations. Index. Pp. 232. £12, postpaid, or $22. Available from the author, 16 Fairford Avenue, Luton, LU2 7ER, U.K. Orders in the United States may be placed with EEF LLC, 25 Murray Way, Blackwood NJ 08012 to overcome any difficulties of currency availability, or electronically through Amazon.com.

Detachment W takes its name from the Vichy French 15th Military District unit assigned after April 1941 to supervise interned Allied soldiers and airmen found in the Unoccupied Zone. With the capitulation of French armies and the withdrawal of British forces at Dunkirk, many Allied servicemen were left adrift. Where the Germans successfully rounded them up as captives, lax security permitted some to escape. Marseille and, eventually, Lisbon represented the gateway to freedom and home. Once over the border into Vichy, the soldiers became subject to internment, not POW status. Time after time, British soldiers noted the lack of anti-British feeling on the part of the French—in contrast to the attitude of the Vichy government.

The United States assumed the role of protecting power for British interests, initially providing relief to indigent Britons in the south of France. Soon these responsibilities expanded to cover the successful evaders encamped in Marseille. The Rev. David Caskie, a Scots Presbyterian minister and refugee from Paris, soon joined the throng. Appalled by what he encountered, he received his superiors' approval to provide aid to the soldiers from the Seamen's Institute, just incidentally providing notice to the homeland of their survival. He was soon recruited to help organize their escapes from France.

The Italian occupiers of the Rhone valley assumed overall responsibility for holding Allied soldiers, delegating to the French the details of internee supervision. Repeated French assurances that the internees would be kept under close control and repeated escapes (often with the "assistance" of the supervisors) led to increasingly more severe incarceration conditions. The French initially sought to hold several hundred "guests" in the Fort Saint-Jean in Marseille, later in Saint-Hippolyte-du-Fort (Gard), and lastly Fort de la Revere (Alpes-Maritimes). Several British field officers among the internees assumed command of the group to organize the evasion and escape efforts.

The author makes exhaustive use of escapees' files in the Public Record Office, newspaper accounts, oral history interviews, and memoirs to provide details of the organization of escape, the support of sympathetic French and Spanish people, and the efforts from home. Airmen who had been shot down over France in 1940 evaded capture, returned home to fly again, and in a few cases were shot down a second time only to make their way to the Unoccupied Zone once again. Richardson explores the various methods used to communicate between the internees and home. Some involved subterfuge, others used the postal system. From an operational standpoint, the value of this work lies in the comprehensive coverage of the variety of evasion and communication techniques. Those responsible to train soldiers, and especially airmen, in "E&E" will find this a valuable resource.

Reviewer's disclosure: The reviewer offered the author the use of his consulting firm to facilitate orders from the United States where currency availability might adversely affect readers' ability to obtain the work.

Gene Fricks   Blackwood, New Jersey

Panzer Operations: The Eastern Front Memoir of General Raus, 1941–1945. By Erhard Raus. Compiled and translated by Steven H. Newton. Cambridge, Mass.: Da Capo Press, 2003. ISBN 0-306-81247-9. Maps. Appendix. Pp. xv, 368. $35.00.

Reconstructed from various sources, Erhard Raus's memoirs provide a fascinating look into mechanized warfare in an unforgiving environment. Edited and translated by Steven H. Newton, Raus's narrative concentrates on tactics and small unit action. A brigade commander with the 6th Panzer Division in June 1941, the Austrian-born Raus steadily rose through the ranks, ultimately commanding panzer armies after 1943 until unceremoniously sacked by Hitler in March 1945.

The German effort in the east became a war of "gigantic improvisation" forced upon the Wehrmacht as a result of the political and military leadership's "improper" conclusions regarding "strategy and military policy" (p. 1). In short, Raus attributes defeat in the east to insufficient knowledge regarding climate, terrain, and the general socioeconomic and political conditions in the east. Preparations for Barbarossa were therefore completely inadequate. Hence, commanders at every level had to improvise solutions to awesome problems from day one. Whether combating crippling summer dust or paralyzing subzero winter temperatures, German soldiers in the east accomplished what they did only through inspired improvisation.

Raus learned combat tactics under fire, yet he had an innate grasp of combined-arms warfare. As the 6th Panzer Division's commander, he decimated Soviet armor formations in the unsuccessful effort to relieve the Sixth Army at Stalingrad in late 1942. He was also a crafty officer, as his February 1942 "snail offensive" demonstrates. In that campaign, with meager assets Raus launched judicious surgical strikes against key villages to secure the Ninth Army's line of communication during the furious Soviet winter counter-offensive of 1941–42. As the German military situation deteriorated, he performed brilliantly on the strategic defensive. His dogged defense of Belgorod and Kharkov stabilized the front in 1943 at critical moments. Raus, however, should best be remembered for his creation of the "zone defense," with which he stymied Soviet attacks with minimal losses in 1944 at Lvov and then in East Prussia. Static but flexible, the zone defense greatly contrasts with his more famous contemporaries' mobile defense, which required yielding territory.

Although indeed satisfyingly "less self-serving" (p. xv) than the personal accounts of better-known generals, such as Heinz Guderian, Raus nevertheless takes a subtle stab at exonerating himself from complicity in Hitler's war of annihilation in the east. The German Landser, according to Raus, conducted himself impeccably on the battlefield, often honoring the vanquished Soviet enemy with prayers and military honors. The Red Army, of course, acted treacherously, mutilating the bodies of dead German troops and slaughtering civilians. He nevertheless praises his stealthy and adept opponents for their tenacity, endurance, and iron discipline, and denies that Red

Army commissars imposed a fanatic will to fight through fear. Instead, the commissars, by their "personal exemplification of the soldier and fighter" (p. 6), inspired their troops to fight to the bitter end.

Despite a liberal sprinkling of typographical errors and poor maps, this remains an informative and compelling account. It contains some jargon, but Raus provides sufficient whiffs of gunpowder to engross even the non-specialist.

David R. Snyder

Austin Peay State University
Clarksville, Tennessee

Harvest of Despair: Life and Death in Ukraine under Nazi Rule. By Karel C. Berkhoff. Cambridge, Mass.: Belknap Press of Harvard University Press, 2004. ISBN 0-674-01313-1. Photographs. Appendixes. Notes. Bibliography. Index. Pp. xiii, 463. $29.95.

Assessments of the Second World War in Ukraine are mostly fragmentary and dominated by accounts of attempted cooperation with the Nazi regime or collaboration in the murder of the Jews. Few writers have questioned the official Soviet stance, which regarded those left behind to the mercies of the occupiers as traitors. Rarely has this view been more effectively challenged than in Karel C. Berkhoff's history of daily life in the Reichskommisariat Ukraine. An associate professor at the Center for Holocaust and Genocide Studies of the University of Amsterdam, Berkhoff departs from the usual examination of politics and collaboration. By writing a territorial history, he uncovers a pitiless and brutal colonial policy that did not permit ordinary persons "to live their own lives with as little interference from grand sociopolitical events as possible" (p. 5). There is more to this than the Holocaust of the Jews and Roma and the mass murder of prisoners of war. In the countryside, after a short period of improved living standards, conditions steadily declined as the Nazis introduced violence and abuse to perfect the collective farming system. Nazi policy aimed to demolish industry and depopulate urban centers, and Kiev in particular was subject to a deliberate policy of starvation, resulting in a deadly, but wholly artificial, famine. Berkhoff argues that conditions in Ukraine were even worse than in the General Gouvernement of occupied Poland. Such claims are not backed up by comparative analysis, but there can be no doubt that conditions in the Reichskommissariat were horrific by any objective standard.

Harvest of Despair is primarily a history written "from the bottom up," and Berkhoff's most important findings concern popular culture, religion, ethnic identity, and political loyalties. He addresses social cohesion among ordinary people, finding social disunity and passivity. Civil society, here defined as "solidarity with strangers" (p. 310), did not exist. This is attributed to the years of Communist rule, which had atomized the population, rendering citizens "self-centered, distrustful, and apathetic" (p. 311). Additionally, the author investigates identities and mental outlooks. At the start of the war ethnic identity among Ukrainians was only vaguely defined. Thus nationalism and statehood elicited little interest. Also, expressions of anti-Russian sentiment and resentment for the prewar terror, which one might expect, are difficult to find. Deportations to forced labor, which plucked one million workers from the Reichskommissariat before its liberation, played an important role in the emergence of large numbers of partisans toward the end of Nazi rule. Nevertheless, the course of the Ukrainian partisan movement is torturous. In August 1943, for example, the Ukrainian Insurgent Army began a bloody campaign to cleanse Volhynia of its Polish population. Berkhoff's conclusions are bound to arouse controversy. However, none can fault his research. This study is the product of patient work in archives in Ukraine, Russia, Canada, and the United States. This Dutch author's command of Ukrainian, Polish, German, and English secondary materials is also impressive. The book is to be commended not least for its ability to shed light on the burgeoning historiographical debate about European societies under Nazi and Soviet rule. Military historians as well as East Central European and Russian specialists will find this work of immense value in assessing the wartime experience in Ukraine and its historical legacy.

Matthew R. Schwonek
Air Command and Staff College
Maxwell AFB, Alabama

An Officer and a Lady: The World War II Letters of Lt. Col. Betty Bandel, Women's Army Corps. Edited by Sylvia J. Bugbee. Lebanon, N.H.: University Press of New England, 2004. ISBN 1-58465-377-9. Photographs. Notes. Index. Pp. xxiv, 222. $24.95.

An Officer and a Lady includes excerpts from letters that Betty Bandel—among the first 440 women to attend Officer Candidate School at the First Women's Army Auxiliary Corps (WAAC) Training Center at Fort Des Moines, Iowa, in the summer of 1942, and who served as aide to Director Oveta Culp Hobby and as Chief Air-WAAC Officer—wrote home to her family in Tucson between June 1942 and August 1945. The letters are deposited in the Bailey-Howe Library (Special Collections) at the University of Vermont in Burlington, where Miss Bandel taught English from 1947 until her retirement in 1975.

Born in 1912, Betty Bandel was a reporter at the *Arizona Daily Star* in Tucson when she joined the WAAC. She was among the first women—the Pioneer 440—who arrived at Fort Des Moines on 20 July 1942, to begin six weeks of officer training. Having brought her typewriter, that first day she typed a letter to her mother: "We get along well. All these people look the earnest small professional type—schoolteachers, etc. No glamour girls, I can assure you. Some bright, some bossy. I am really having a wonderful time" (p. 7). Bandel and her colleagues advanced quickly to become senior officers and rose to the top of the Women's Army Corps administration during World War II. Fellow first OCS class graduates included Mattie Treadwell, who wrote the definitive official history, *The Women's Army Corps,* a volume in the United States Army in World War II series (Washington: GPO, 1954) and Charity Adams Earley, who wrote *One Woman's Army: A Black Officer Remembers the WAC* (College Station: Texas A&M University Press, 1989).

Bandel was among eighteen newly graduated officers assigned to WAAC headquarters in Washington, D.C., where she served as aide to Director Oveta Culp Hobby—"that most diplomatic of diplomats, and most forceful of leaders" (p. 35). Witty and entertaining, Bandel relates her travels accompanying Hobby across the United States to inspect WAAC units and in England to visit British women's military organizations. When, during a visit to the United States by Jean Knox, head of the British Auxiliary Territorial Service (ATS), Hobby and Bandel expressed at such length their "wonder over the state of the Englishwoman's shoes (they shine like old mahogany) that Knox got out her little box of polishes, . . . took off her coat, rolled up her sleeves, and gave us a lesson in how to polish shoes. Most amazing sight you ever saw—this faultlessly dressed, every-eyelash-groomed Englishwoman, with her eyes that look through you—solemnly polishing away at the Colonel's shoes as if she were playing a Bach concerto" (p. 40).

Bandel's letters are witty, detailed accounts of her experiences written during the formative years of the U.S. Women's Army Auxiliary Corps, which became the Women's Army Corps in 1943; but unfortunately and disappointingly this volume is not a documentary edition of her letters. Most scholars will find the transcription editorial policy disturbing: "The letters in this book have been excerpted from the very long originals. Due to the extensive editing of some of the letters, ellipses to indicate deleted text have been omitted as they would have distracted the reader without contributing to the narrative" (p. ix). Serious researchers would have preferred the ellipses along with editorial explanation, rather than not knowing where, what, and how much text in the original letters has been silently omitted. This reviewer compared several of the original (photocopied) letters that Bandel wrote during training at Fort Des Moines in 1942, and found that the printed version included random silent omissions ranging from one word, sentence, or paragraph to over two single-spaced typed pages. Scholars wishing to quote from the Bandel letters will need to see the original (or photocopied) document at the University of Vermont.

Nevertheless, the book is a welcome addition to the published letters and memoirs of women who served in the Women's Army Corps during World War II. It is a "must" for the library of anyone with an interest in the WAC during World War II or in the expansion of women's leadership roles.

Sharon Ritenour Stevens   George C. Marshall Foundation
                                           Lexington, Virginia

A Bridge Not Attacked: Chemical Warfare Civilian Research During World War II. By Harold Johnston. River Edge, N.J.: World Scientific Publishing, 2003. ISBN 981-238-153-8. Illustrations. Figures. Index. Pp. 261. $20.00.

A Bridge Not Attacked is a book one cannot help but like. Harold Johnston, a distinguished scientist, states his aim in the Preface to his book: "In this book, I tell novel true stories concerning highly talented civilian scientists in some unusual places during World War II, carrying out research on defense against poison gases" (p. vii). The result is a mixture: part memoir, part scientific record, part series of biographies of scientists the author worked with, part anecdotal accounts of the trials and tribulations they underwent.

Although one could wish for a tighter organization, the book is engaging and well written. Johnston does not neutralize his personality while describing his scientific achievements. He introduces the reader to a number of memorable individuals who are deftly sketched. Although the book is not a comprehensive history of the National Defense Research Committee (NDRC), it has the virtue of conveying the flavor of the experience of scientists who worked in Divisions 9 and 10 of the NDRC. While a graduate student at the California Institute of Technology (Caltech), Johnston joined a wartime chemical warfare project. His first assignment was to a laboratory where he handled extremely dangerous chemical agents, like phosgene. Later he was assigned to field testing. Johnston became a meteorologist who carried out measurements of the movement of gas clouds in various locations around the U.S.: the Mojave Desert, Mt. Shasta, and Stinson Beach, California; the Withlacoochee swamp area near Bushnell, Florida. The author also describes the chemical warfare tests carried out by Division 10 on San José Island, Panama. Due to health considerations, Johnston did not participate in these tests, which were designed to measure the effectiveness of chemical warfare agents in jungle conditions. The agents tested both by exploding ground bombs and by aerial drops were phosgene, hydrogen cyanide, cyanogen chloride, and mustard gas.

Johnston tells a harrowing story: the tragic death of Samuel Ruben, a promising scientist who was poisoned when phosgene accidentally escaped in a laboratory at the University of California at Berkeley. He also narrates a near miss which took place on Mt. Shasta. The Army wanted to use phosgene in its test area, arguing that the town of Shasta was a safe four miles down hill. The scientists foiled this project by mixing a chemical solution that gave off a distinct skunk odor. They then poured it over roads and trails leading from the test site to the town. The result: "The residents of the town below probably thought the skunk situation was the worst it had ever been" (p. 86). The Army canceled the project. Makes one think!

John Ellis van Cortland Moon   Emeritus, Fitchburg State College
                                        Fitchburg, Massachusetts

The Anguish of Surrender: Japanese POWs of World War II. By Ulrich Straus. Seattle: University of Washington Press, 2004. ISBN 0-295-98336-1. Maps. Photographs. Illustrations. Notes. Bibliography. Index. Pp. xx, 282. $27.50.

This book focuses on an important and neglected group of Pacific War combatants: Japanese prisoners of war held by the United States and its British Commonwealth allies. Its author is eminently qualified to tell their story. He grew up in prewar Japan, served as an Army Japanese language officer during the war, and later became first an interpreter at the Tokyo War Crimes Trials and then a career foreign service officer specializing on Japan. He bases his account on interviews with and memoirs of former Japanese POWs and the records of their interrogation and captivity stored in the U.S. National Archives.

Straus tells a tale of death and rebirth. In the first third of the book he explains why so few Japanese combatants surrendered and why so many regarded captivity as akin to death. The *Senjinkun* [Army Field Service Order] of January 1941 in effect "forbade . . . [being] taken as prisoners of war for any reason whatever" (p. 17). Strong nationalism, belief in Japan's superiority, severe discipline, and fatalism in the face of adverse battle circumstances made Japanese soldiers and sailors respect that order. Only one in three who became prisoners surrendered voluntarily. Driven by a sense of shame that shattered their sense of self-worth, those who did so misremembered or manufactured stories about their capture so as to make it seem unavoidable. In their own eyes and those of family and friends back home, they were dead.

Straus focuses in the second third of his story on those who coaxed and questioned the prisoners back to life. "America's secret weapons" (p. 89) were enlisted Army Japanese American native speakers and Caucasian Army and Navy officers trained in pioneering intensive language programs at the Universities of Michigan and Colorado, respectively. These interpreter/ interrogators broke down prisoners' reluctance to talk in ways one wishes their counterparts at Abu Ghraib and Guantanamo had emulated. Army Nisei played upon their subjects' shock at seeing fellow Asians in American uniforms and in some cases used their ties as former pupils or classmates to get prisoners to open up. Otis Cary, perhaps the most successful Navy interrogator, made them feel alive again and willing to cooperate by showing them that Americans honored their fighting men who had or might become POWs and by getting them to think and talk as patriots about a democratic Japan of the future.

Straus uses his last chapters to describe the prisoners' lives in captivity and their troubled rebirth after repatriation to postwar Japan. While uprisings roiled Allied-run stockades, peace generally prevailed in better-managed, more cross-culturally tolerant American POW camps. The author is particularly telling in describing returnees' struggles to come to terms with their former status in a society which continued to live under a *senjinkun* mentality.

This is a book meant for a scholarly audience focused on a war that ended nearly sixty years ago. But it has current relevance and is so gracefully written that it will appeal to anyone interested in prisoners of war or cross-cultural issues more generally. I chafed at Straus's occasional silence on sources and few factual errors. But I left the book feeling that its insights into Japanese thinking about war more than made up for those weaknesses.

Roger Dingman   University of Southern California
Los Angeles, California

Weapons Used Against U-Boats, vol. 2 of U-Boat Archive Series. Edited by Jak P. Mallmann Showell. Milton Keynes, U.K.: Military Press, 2002. ISBN 0-85420-076-2. Index and glossary. Pp. 123. £25.00.

German Naval Code Breakers. By Jak P. Mallmann Showell. Annapolis, Md.: Naval Institute Press, 2003. ISBN 1-59114-308 X. Maps. Photographs. Appendixes. Index. Pp. 160. $38.95.

Jak Mallmann Showell, the son of the senior diesel mechanic of *U-377* lost in 1944, has become a prolific author of books on the U-boat war and the German navy in general. His publications draw upon the extensive archives of the *U-Boot Archiv* in Cuxhaven and are characterized by numerous photographs, many of which have never been published. His descriptions of the technical details of the weapons and ships of the *Kriegsmarine* as well as the men who fought are well written and provide insights into the character of the war that complement more academic accounts. The author's U-Boat Archive Series provides a unique source for both the aficionado of the naval war of 1939–45 and the research historian. Based on the secret Monthly Anti-Submarine Reports, circulated to officers in the Royal Navy's Escort Forces, these reports provided information on weapons and developments in the Battle of the Atlantic. They must be used carefully in regards to the statistical information available at the time, but the inconsistencies, obvious propaganda comments, and omissions (e.g., the acoustic torpedo) are interesting and reveal how much of the antisubmarine research was kept secret from those fighting the U-boats. Using these highly classified reports, the author has gleaned from the few remaining copies, a collection of articles describing the weapons and techniques for fighting the U-boats. (Volume 1, *What Britain Knew and Wanted to Know about U-Boats,* was published in 2001.)

German Naval Code Breakers follows the author's usual format detailing the often overlooked history and achievements of the German Naval Radio Monitoring Service or *B-Dienst* (*Beobachtungs-Dienst*), supplementing the text with extensive photographs and helpful appendixes. Utilizing intercepted scraps of information on ship movements in the various theaters and battles, he demonstrates the importance of the role daily intelligence played in these operations. Although the German naval code breakers had been recognized as playing a significant role in the U-boat war and in the initial successes of the *Kriegsmarine* and the invasion of Norway, the publication of books beginning in the 1970s which revealed the "decisive" success of British and Allied code breaking in World War II (Ultra) overshadowed the contributions of *B-Dienst* (whose record, according to David Kahn's 1978 *Hitler's Spies,* was unmatched by any other German military or political intelligence service). Given the lack of any detailed monograph on the *B-Dienst* in English (as well as the paucity of German sources), the author has provided a useful and highly engaging study which should serve to point the way to a more detailed scholarly investigation of this subject. My only quarrel with this book is the lack of significant other sources that could provide a deeper context for the history of German radio intelligence, particularly its successes in direction finding, traffic analysis, and decryption. The assessment of German naval intelligence in my 1985 literature guide, *German Naval History,* includes a number of key works apparently not consulted by the author. Kahn, in particular, devotes a chapter in *Hitler's Spies* ("The Codebreaker Who Helped the U-Boats") to the leadership of Wilhelm Tranow in developing the *B-Dienst* and its contributions in the Second World War. Yet, Tranow is not even listed in Mallmann Showell's index. There are also other more recent books that might have provided additional perspectives, such as Kahn's 1991 *Seizing the Enigma: The Race to Break the German U-Boat Codes, 1939–1943: The Battle of the Atlantic and Signals Intelligence: U-Boat Situations and Trends, 1941–1945* (ed. by David Syrett, 1998); or, even more notably, the 1999 revisionist work of W. J. R. Gardner, *Decoding History: The Battle of the Atlantic and Ultra,* which suggests the dynamism of the U-boat war and a framework for re-evaluating the role of *B-Dienst* and Ultra.

Keith W. Bird   Kentucky Community and Technical College System
Lexington, Kentucky

The Battle for Ginkel Heath Near Ede 17 and 18 September 1944. By C. E. H. J. Verhoef. Soesterberg, The Netherlands: Aspekt, 2003. ISBN 90-5911-386-1. Maps. Photographs. Notes. Index. Pp. 124. $19.95. Available in the U.S. from ISBS, Portland, Oreg.

Seeking to provide clarity and historical record to the military conflict occurring near Ede, Holland, on 17–18 September 1944, C. E. H. J. Verhoef adds a well written, easy to read book to the field of Battle of Arnhem scholarship. The focus of this work is limited in scope, the struggle for control of Ginkel Heath, that critical piece of polder land that the British 1st Airborne Division labeled as Drop Zone "Y". This was where in the initial days of Operations Market and Garden nearly 2,000 paratroopers sought to isolate Arnhem and secure the eventual route of advance of British XXX Corps.

Mr. Verhoef opens his book by briefly outlining the strategic and operational settings for the airborne invasion and corresponding ground assault.

The initial military plan and the internal Allied politics surrounding its development are adequately described. Further, the author proffers the widely accepted reasons for the British defeat at Arnhem and dispels common misconceptions, setting the foundation for the remainder of the work. The subsequent four chapters cover in ample detail the action of British units tasked to defend the drop zone for follow-on forces and the quick and efficient initial German responses and defensive efforts that sought to isolate and defeat the airborne assault. The author rightly explains the success of those British units such as the 7th King's Own Scottish Borderers and the 21st Independent Parachute Company, which defended Drop Zone "Y" and allowed for the aerial deployment of the 4th Para Brigade. Mr. Verhoef, however, misses the point when he attempts to explain the subsequent failure of the 4th Para Brigade by attributing it to poor drop zone locations, late arrival, and loss of the element of surprise. In current military vernacular, the 4th Para Brigade was "fixed" shortly after departing Ginkel Heath by the hastily organized, yet highly effective German forces near Oosterbeek. These German defenses inflicted heavy casualties on the attacking British forces and prevented the 4th Para Brigade from accomplishing its supporting mission, focused on the isolation of the Arnhem road bridge.

This concise book is only 124 pages long but is riddled with highly detailed diagrams, maps, and rarely published photographs of operations surrounding Arnhem and Oosterbeek. Skillfully the author merges various primary and secondary sources with the operational unit histories of both British and German forces battling for Ginkel Heath. This book is recommended for Arnhem enthusiasts or those seeking detailed examination of particular units or personalities. Although contributing little to the overall scholarship on the Battle of Arnhem due to the lack of an original thesis and research, Mr. Verhoef's contribution represents the compilation of various sources of information into a concise, single document that can be used to supplement battle staff rides or research into this isolated, yet highly important portion of the battle.

Steven D. Rosson   Richmond Hill, Georgia

Dresden, Tuesday, 13 February 1945. By Frederick Taylor. London: Bloomsbury Publishing, 2004. ISBN 0-7475-7078-7. Maps. Illustrations. Notes. Appendixes. Bibliography. Index. Pp. xxi, 522. $16.00.

Readers should not be misled by the title of this massive work. Far from an account of two catastrophic days in February 1945, the book surveys the whole history of the city of Dresden from its thirteenth-century foundation to the recent turn of the century post-Communist years, a comprehensive overall story which Taylor has thoroughly researched and sets out vividly.

Obviously leading up to the great destruction of the British and American air raids, Taylor provides us with necessary reminders of several matters which in controversy and discourse over the raids have not been given the weight they deserve. Firstly, Taylor describes, in all its nastiness, the enthusiasm with which the vast majority of the citizens of Dresden welcomed and supported the Nazi government, and turned their eyes away from its increasing excesses, in particular the persecution of the Jewish members of the community. Secondly, he points out, well backed with detail, the fact that peri-urban Dresden did constitute a justifiable military target for bombing: numerous factories in the city's suburbs were engaged in manufacture related to military needs, and the city was a very important railway communication center for the Army's operations on the Eastern Front. As Taylor indicates, these were, however, not the targets for the bombers, and in some detail and with clinical detachment in three chapters he recounts the evolution of aircraft bombing theory, from the strategic to the frankly selective center-city fire-storming. Thirdly, Taylor reminds us of the aims of earlier Luftwaffe attacks on Britain, Hitler's and Goering's expressed desire in 1940 to see London turned into a huge conflagration, and the German policy of attacks on cultural centers such as Canterbury and Exeter.

Successive chapters give readers an interesting presentation on life in the interwar and Second World War years in the city, the coarse brutality of its regional Nazi administration, the city's narcissistic self-confidence that it would never be attacked, and the weakness of its antiaircraft defences. The best chapters in the book are those in Part 2, the early 1945 events leading to the war-weary decision to strike at Dresden, the Royal Air Force's operational plan and briefings, the accounts of the apocalyptic night provided by survivors, and the devastated state of the city after the British and later the American raids. One cannot read the descriptions of the fire storms without a profound sense of horror.

The work, admirable overall, is, however, not without blemishes. The author, a specialist in the German political right, devotes much space to the repulsive Nazi Gauleiter of Dresden, Martin Mutschmann, but makes no mention of a leading and honourable Dresden citizen in the opposition to Hitler, General Friedrich Olbricht, an opponent of Hitler from the outset, an active conspirator from 1943 onwards and one of the 20th July 1944 conspirators executed by the Nazis. The internal opposition to Hitler is dismissed in a few lines although material noting a Roman Catholic priest and a number of members from many walks of life is available and is interesting. The most reliable figures suggest over one thousand men were executed. In his description of the British domestic opposition to city bombing Taylor gives much credit to the Labour Member of Parliament, Richard Stokes, a critic of much less weight and importance than George Bell, Bishop of Chichester, who is not mentioned at all. Bell's repeated attacks on the policy cost him his otherwise excellent chances of becoming Archbishop of Canterbury. Nor is there any mention of the appeal that Dresden be spared in the *Manchester Guardian* of 12 February 1945. Taylor seems to suggest that the doubts in London about city bombing were a result of the effectiveness of Goebbels's propaganda but although this was a factor, domestic British criticism was at least as important in the later decision to end these attacks.

Taylor leaves open the question of justification for the raid. Also open to question should perhaps be the book itself, revisiting scenes of horror already well known. Any writer of history must of course record events and the truth as accurately as he can. But writers of history are members of the human race in which each individual has a duty to play a part, however small, in improving that race's lot. The book appears in a year in which Dresden's greatest architectural glory, the Frankenkirche, was restored to recreate the matchless prewar Dresden skyline, with contributions from peoples of the February 1945 attacking nations in a spirit of reconciliation. Readers might consider both questions; the work is thought provoking.

Anthony Clayton

University of Surrey
Guildford, United Kingdom

The Papers of George Catlett Marshall, volume 5, *"The Finest Soldier," January 1, 1945–January 7, 1947*. Edited by Larry I. Bland and Sharon Ritenour Stevens. Baltimore, Md.: Johns Hopkins University Press, 2003. ISBN 0-8016-7871-3. Maps. Photographs. Illustrations. Index. Pp. xxxii, 822. $85.00.

Volume 5 of the Marshall Papers possesses the same laudable features as its predecessors: selections from a variety of sources; meticulous attention to detail; and numerous helpful aids, including a chronology and excellent illustrations. This volume consists of 508 documents and covers the years 1945–46, and editors Bland and Ritenour Stevens have divided it logically by year into two periods. During 1945, Army Chief of Staff Marshall's primary concerns were the final stages of World War II and preparing the Army (and the defense establishment) for the postwar era. The day after he retired on 26 November, President Truman asked him to serve in a new and quite different capacity, as an emissary to China to try and resolve the factional conflict in that troubled country. Despite Marshall's valiant effort, by the end of 1946, his China mission had failed, and the Nationalist-Communist civil war finally ended in a Chinese communist victory in 1949.

Marshall's activities in 1945 were much more upbeat, and his correspondence reflects his optimistic outlooks. To be sure, he was genuinely anxious about the redeployment of troops in the Pacific; the timely discharge of other soldiers returning from Europe; and remembering America's military weakness in 1939, the need for a strong defense to help keep the peace after the war was over. But he also took time to write the bereaved parents as well as family and friends and to spell out his vision for the future in speeches to such disparate groups as the Academy of Political Science, Maryland Historical Society, Salvation Army, and the Women's Conference on Universal Military Training (which he favored). Moreover, in spite of Marshall's admission to Admiral Harold Stark in September 1945 that "I have never been busier," (p. 318), he still made clear how much he looked forward to retiring with his wife, Katherine, to their Leesburg, Virginia, and Pinehurst, North Carolina, homes.

Any time for leisure, however, was not to be. In the 1946 portion of Marshall's papers, the editors skillfully weave together the various strands that made up his China mission. Since we know the outcome, the China sections make for depressing reading, and Marshall himself realized from the beginning that his "chances of success were slim" (p. 398). Yet, he did everything in his power to persuade especially the Communist foreign minister, Chou En-lai, and the Nationalist leader, Chiang Kai-shek, to have their forces stop fighting and to agree to a democratic government and a unified army. Even though Marshall ultimately failed in his creative attempts to reconcile the two parties, he amply demonstrated the qualities of perseverance, determination, and diplomatic skill that made him such a great leader. These characteristics also stood him in good stead for his next assignment as secretary of state.

Rounding out the volume are an appendix giving the names of War Department officials and theater commanders during this time, beneficial maps and organizational charts, a glossary, and a list of Chinese names and places rendered in both Wade-Giles and *pinyin* spellings. The longtime editors have maintained the high standards of previous volumes, and readers and researchers can look forward to the next installment.

Alan F. Wilt

Iowa State University
Ames, Iowa

The Secret Annexe: An Anthology of the World's Greatest War Diarists. Edited by Irene and Alan Taylor. Edinburgh, U.K.: Canongate Books, 2004. ISBN 1-84195-443-8. Bibliography. Index. Pp. xix, 676. £25.00.

The Secret Annexe is a kind of lucky dip. It consists of extracts from some two hundred diarists, published in English, from the seventeenth century to the present. Translations are allowed, but are not favoured. A select few are made to work very hard, especially if they are on the side of the angels (Anne Frank, Victor Klemperer, Primo Levi). Anglo-American authors predominate, therefore, in a widely-gathered company ranging from Davy Crockett to Eleanor Coppola, Iris Origo to George Orwell. Many wars are represented, but not all. There is a heavy weighting towards the twentieth century; inevitably, perhaps, the First and Second World Wars receive most attention. The British bulk large—it sometimes seems as if they had more diarists on the ground than armoured divisions—contributing much of the most acute observation, chilling, droll, poignant, or downright eccentric. "The necessary supply of heroes must be maintained at all costs" (Siegfried Sassoon, 24 February 1917, quoting Sir Edward Carson). "The Marines have sent me a long questionnaire asking among other things if I am a chronic bedwetter. It seems that I am to get a commission there" (Evelyn Waugh, 22 November 1939). "I made a potato and leek soup for supper—then went fire watching. It was a beautiful evening. On the bridge I saw a girl warden (rather plain) being kissed by a Doughboy (a hidey-ho, a sweet and lo, a come and go boy). Lucky pigs I thought" (Barbara Pym, 14 April 1943). "Mrs Thatcher announces the surrender of Port Stanley in well-modulated tones. Film follows of the funeral of the commandos killed at Goose Green, the simple service and the youth of the wounded unbearable. A pilot of one of the Harriers talks about the effectiveness of the Sidewinder missiles. 'A bit of an eye-opener' is how he puts it. A bit of an eye-closer too. Not English I feel now. This is just where I happen to have been put down. No country. No party. No Church. No voice" (Alan Bennett, 15 June 1982).

The selection is not always as discriminating. Too many entries are trivial, disconnected, recondite, or simply uninteresting. The editors hope to provide a composite portrait of war. Neither the selection nor the organization is equal to the task. The entries are arranged day by day throughout the year—a factitious year—such that August 5, for example, contains fragments from that day in 1901 (David Miller), 1914 (Beatrice Webb and André Gide), 1940 (Count Ciano), 1942 (Weary Dunlop), and 1945 ("Chips" Channon). This is not so much a portrait as a grab-bag. Disorientation outbids delectation.

The Secret Annexe does not set out to be a work of scholarship. There is a brief and highly coloured introduction, and potted biographies of the diarists, but the diary entries themselves float free of any context. No mention is made of the editors or the translators of the editions used. No credit is given for editorial borrowings from those works. Frustrated readers may turn to *Witness to War* (Doubleday, 2004), edited by Richard J. Aldrich, to see what can be done with an anthology of war diarists by a scholar with a keen eye for the unconsidered trifle.

Alex Danchev
University of Nottingham
Nottingham, United Kingdom

Enola Gay and the Court of History. By Robert P. Newman. New York: Peter Lang, 2004. ISBN 0-8204-7071-6. Notes. Bibliography. Index. Pp. xv, 201. $24.95.

Robert P. Newman's latest entry into the historiographical debate over the atomic bombing of Japan is engaging, vivid, and, in important respects, convincing. At the same time, the book is partisan, contentious, and, in important respects, unconvincing. There is little in it that is new or surprising; Newman has aired most of his arguments in earlier articles and in a previous volume, *Truman and the Hiroshima Cult* (1995). But the book still has value as a lively and engrossing summary of the views of a leading scholar in the controversy over the decision to use the bomb.

Newman shows that the competing positions over using the bomb emerged within a short time after World War II. Paul Nitze and P. M. S. Blackett laid the foundations for what later became the revisionist interpretation by challenging the "official narrative." Nitze concluded in the 1946 report of the United States Strategic Bombing Survey that Japan would have surrendered by 31 December 1945 without the use of the atomic bomb, the invasion of Japan, or Soviet entry into the war. Blackett contended in a 1948 book that the United States dropped the bomb more to intimidate the Soviet Union than to defeat the Japanese. Newman demonstrates beyond reasonable doubt that Nitze's conclusions were not consistent with the evidence the Strategic Bombing Survey collected from high-ranking Japanese officials. He is equally persuasive in pointing out the flaws and distortions in the revisionist view of President Truman's decision. The best chapter in the book deals in an informed and discerning way with the morality of the bombing of Hiroshima and Nagasaki.

But Newman fails to employ the same analytical skills in his discussion of the traditional position on the use of the bomb; he turns a blind eye to the fallacies, or at least the uncertainties, of the "official narrative." Further, he does a serious injustice to scholars who stand between the polar extremes by lumping them, with the partial exception of Barton J. Bernstein, with doctrinaire revisionists. Worse, Newman occasionally applies a double standard in making his judgments. He is sharply critical of curators at the Smithsonian Institution, whom he claims "bought the Nitze-Blackett narrative in toto" (p. 98), for failing to conduct primary research in the records of the Strategic Bombing Survey in the process of planning the ill-fated *Enola Gay* exhibit in the early 1990s. But he is guilty of the same offense in a brief but highly opinionated discussion of a complex and controversial study of the effects of radiation on workers at nuclear weapons plants. Newman did not consult either primary sources or relevant scholarly literature before arriving at his conclusions; instead he relied heavily on a conversation with the scientist whose research was at the center of the controversy.

J. Samuel Walker   U.S. Nuclear Regulatory Commission
Washington, D.C.

Oppenheimer: Portrait of an Enigma. By Jeremy Bernstein. Chicago: Ivan R. Dee, 2004. ISBN 1-56663-569-1. Photographs. Notes. Bibliography. Index. Pp. 240. $25.00.

This short biography explores the complex personality of physicist J. Robert Oppenheimer, using materials and interviews collected by the author since the 1950s. Bernstein, a physicist and historian of the nuclear age, knew Oppenheimer personally as director of the Institute of Advanced Study at Princeton during the 1960s.

Each of the five chapters focuses on a specific period of Oppenheimer's life: his early childhood to the completion of his Ph.D. under Max Born at Göttingen, Germany; his pre–World War II years in California as a professor at Cal Tech and Berkeley; his leadership in the Manhattan Project as director of the Los Alamos Laboratory during the war; the 1954 Atomic Energy Commission hearing that revoked his security clearance; and his last years as director of the Institute for Advanced Study.

The author provides interesting insights into Oppenheimer's personal and professional relationships. Jean Tatlock, a serious girlfriend, Kathryn "Kitty" Puening, his wife, Frank, his brother, and Haakon Chevalier, a university colleague, were major influences in his personal life. Edward Teller, General Leslie Groves, Ernest Lawrence, and Lewis Strauss played key roles in determining the path of his career.

In the final analysis, this biography adds little new factual information but presents intimate glimpses into the life of this conflicted scientist who directed the production of the first nuclear weapons and was later victimized by the anticommunist movement that gripped the United States in the 1950s. It is a good introduction to Oppenheimer for neophytes and a nostalgic read for those familiar with his life.

Frank A. Settle   Washington & Lee University
                                              Lexington, Virginia

Observing Our Hermanos de Armas: U.S. Military Attachés in Guatemala, Cuba, and Bolivia, 1950–1964. By Robert O. Kirkland. New York: Routledge, 2003. ISBN 0-415-94784-7. Photographs. Appendixes. Notes. Bibliography. Index. Pp. xii, 178. $70.00.

The time period covered was a formative one for American (that is, *Norte Americano*) foreign policy in Latin America; basic Cold War strategies for the region were being worked out which would remain in effect for the duration. One such was the use of indigenous military forces as proxies to effect regime change in countries whose policies seemed communist inspired and threatening. The year 1954 saw the Central Intelligence Agency prompting the Guatemalan army to precipitate the overthrow of the government of Jacobo Arbenz Guzmán in Guatemala. The CIA attempted to mimic that success at the Bay of Pigs in Cuba in 1962 with disastrous results, partly because it thought it had a deeper understanding of the Cuban revolution than it really did. Finally, in 1964, the United States helped the Bolivian military execute a *golpe de estado* against the democratically elected, middle-class government of the *Movimiento Nacionalista Revolucionario,* even though the U.S. had helped establish that regime in the 1950s. These are the events around which Kirkland builds his analysis of the activities of U.S. military attachés.

The core of Kirkland's study is an analysis of U.S. military attaché activity and training within the Army and Air Force. His purpose is to assess the effectiveness of attaché reporting and its impact on policy formation in Washington. His methodology for the former is to examine attaché reports and for the latter to study relevant intelligence reports, National Intelligence Estimates, and the like. His conclusions are that attachés vary in their effectiveness, often based more on their individual experiences in the military than on the training provided, but that they usually fulfill the tasks assigned. The problem seems to be in the use to which their information is put in higher circles. This analysis would be of some interest to students of military institutional effectiveness.

Of much more interest to this reader are the narratives Kirkland provides of the actions of the attachés themselves in these sensitive places during these volatile times. The air attaché in Guatemala, Maj. Manuel Chavez, had superb access to the military there mostly because his Hispanic background enabled him to converse through the appropriate cultural filters. But, he was rotated to other duties before the coup and was recalled at the last minute: too late to provide the intelligence the United States could have used to manage the coup better. The attachés in Cuba dropped the ball on Fidel Castro; they underestimated his power and failed to impress Washington with the weakness of the Batista military. Col. Edward Fox, the U.S. air attaché in Bolivia, was so well connected in the Bolivian military as a close friend of the eventual coup-maker, General René Barrientos, that he could not provide objective analysis to his superiors. The serendipitous roles of individual players and their impact on the intelligence the U.S. had available turned out to be critical in the process of early Cold War interventions in Latin America. In these times of new preemptive policies in other, less amenable, parts of the world, Kirkland provides us with a small, but pointed lesson on the importance of good intelligence to decision making.

Blair P. Turner

Virginia Military Institute
Lexington, Virginia

NATO Divided, NATO United: The Evolution of an Alliance. By Lawrence S. Kaplan. Westport, Conn.: Praeger Publishers, 2004. ISBN 0-275-98377-3. Bibliographical essay. Index. Pp. xii, 165. $24.95.

This is a timely and insightful book, written by the dean of NATO studies. Larry Kaplan, University Professor Emeritus of History at Kent State and Emeritus Director of its NATO-EU Center, has written about the alliance since 1954. This is his tenth book on the topic, and the focus here is on West-West tensions. The thesis is that "old fissures" are reemerging among alliance members, particularly between the U.S. and its European partners. Internal troubles are more apparent today, in the absence of the traditional threat emanating from the U.S.S.R. and with the U.S. as the lone super-power, but Kaplan successfully shows that differences have existed since NATO's inception and tensions among members have always been present, though often muted. Intractable quarrels have been frequent and bitter, typically centering on the "transatlantic gulf" between U.S. and European nations over matters of military resources and differing worldviews.

The book succinctly and chronologically presents key events in alliance history, with roughly decade-long periodization, from NATO's 1949 founding through its 2004 expansion to twenty-six nations. Crises (such as Suez and Bosnia) and issues (such as *Ostpolitik* and *détente*) are given short, separate analyses of about three pages apiece. Throughout, the author returns to several major themes: repeated attempts by France to assert its position, expand its influence, and counter perceived U.S. hegemony; concerns among European nations over Germany (rearmament, NATO integration, unification); continual frustration among U.S. leaders over financial and military burden sharing; and repeated European attempts to build a separate military capability independent of NATO. The author consistently examines why U.S. strategic views often differ from other members, and why American leaders have routinely acquiesced to concerns from their junior partners. Kaplan continually explores and praises the tremendous NATO capacity for change, as time and again the Alliance struggles, then reinvents itself to confront new challenges. It is refreshing to read this broad historical perspective that stresses the cyclical nature of NATO internal crises.

A few minor errors detract. There are some transcription flaws with dates (pp. 72, 91, and 115), and occasionally the author does not distinguish between the timing of a NATO political decision and its bureaucratic manifestation (pp. 63 and 143–45). The term "out of area" is initially used to describe any world event outside NATO boundaries, even without formal alliance participation (preface, pp. 12 and 70). Under NATO parlance, as described at the 2002 Reykjavik Summit, the term more properly refers to formal, unified alliance military action in territories beyond those listed in Article 6 of the Atlantic Charter. The book also discusses the implications of several other NATO articles, and could benefit from an appendix listing the complete texts.

Overall, though, this book is exceptional for its clarity, purpose, and scope. It is highly recommended to international scholars, diplomats, and military professionals. The title is well chosen, for Kaplan uses his extensive knowledge to provide a long view, and he ends on an optimistic note: "Tensions and frictions were built into NATO by virtue of a free association of its component parts . . . [but] there is a mutual dependence that has kept the alliance together in the past and should continue to do so in the future" (pp. 148–49). Contentious issues persist, but, as one of his previous titles proclaims, NATO remains "the enduring alliance."

Kurt W. Schake

University of Illinois
Urbana-Champaign, Illinois

Cheating Death: Combat Air Rescues in Vietnam and Laos. By George J. Marrett. Washington: Smithsonian Books, 2003. ISBN 1-58834-104-6. Photographs. Map. Pp. xxii, 225. $27.95.

Apart from its literary merit, this memoir is of value in addressing a largely overlooked aspect of the Vietnam War: the creation by the U.S. Air Force of a specialized combat rescue force to recover aviators downed deep within enemy territory in Laos and North Vietnam. Based on long-range Sikorsky HH-3 and later HH-53 "Jolly Green" helicopters, so-called for their radio callsign, it saved hundreds of aviators from capture and death, facing enemy antiaircraft artillery and on occasion surface-to-air missiles in addition to the usual small arms and automatic weapons fire. The big helicopters were supported by HC-130 command-and-control and communications relay aircraft that served as aerial tankers for the helicopters and—the focus of the book—a dedicated force of piston-engined Douglas A-1 Skyraider attack aircraft flying under the "Sandy" callsign.

Helicopters proved too vulnerable for search operations and Sandys were responsible for locating survivors, supporting them with fire, serving as forward air controllers for flak suppression strikes, and providing fire support for the rescue helicopter. With a massive ordnance load, excellent low-altitude endurance and surprising maneuverability for so large an aircraft, the A-1 was perfect for the job, and a demanding job it was: In addition to the survivor, enemy activity, terrain and weather, Sandy Lead had to keep track of two helicopters (Jolly Greens committed in pairs with one in reserve), his wingmen, and supporting strike flights—the list is not exhaustive. Surely, there has been no more demanding job in the history of aerial warfare. In this reviewer's opinion, rooted in combat experience flying Jolly Greens in 1965–66 and 1975, the Sandy mission represents the limiting case in situational awareness, spatial orientation, and tactical judgment. For reasons that the reader will come to appreciate, not all A-1 pilots could handle the Sandy mission and only a minority qualified as Sandy Lead.

Marrett was an experienced jet test pilot before he was a Sandy, and he addresses his subject with aeronautical sophistication. His tour with the Thailand-based 602nd Fighter Squadron (Commando) ran for a year beginning in April 1968, encompassing a full range of strike missions in support of the so-called "Secret War" in Laos in addition to an impressive array of rescue missions. Marrett's first Sandy sorties were flown as a wingman on the 31 May–2 June mission to rescue Navy A-7 pilot Lieutenant Kenny Fields, callsign Streetcar 304, the biggest rescue mission of the war to date—thirty-nine hours and 189 combat sorties—and not without cost: Fields's wingman ditched at sea, two Sandys were shot down and one pilot captured, another Sandy was heavily damaged and a Jolly Green was abandoned in enemy territory. Marrett received his baptism of fire watching his element lead shot down early in the mission and Fields's rescue required fire support so close that he was wounded by cluster bomb pellets from an accurate F-4 drop just before being rescued. It is a dramatic story and well told, but by no means the end of the book.

Marrett takes the reader through his tour, repeatedly confirming the adage that flying combat consists of hours of boredom punctuated by seconds of terror, nor was the terror always caused by enemy guns: miserable weather, errors in judgment, matériel failure, and poor leadership inflicted their share of losses on Marrett's squadron and his clinical descriptions of each loss provide a catalog of all that can go wrong—and usually does—in aerial warfare. The roll of his fellow pilots lost in combat and the account of the fates of those who survived, and of those whom they rescued, adds poignancy. This is an honest, well-written and exceptionally well-informed account, conveying the airmanship and human reality of the Vietnam air war "Up North" as well as any I know.

John F. Guilmartin, Jr.   Ohio State University
                                                          Columbus, Ohio

Commandants of the Marine Corps. Edited by Allan R. Millett and Jack Shulimson. Annapolis, Md.: Naval Institute Press, 2004. ISBN 0-87021-012-2. Photographs. Notes. Bibliography. Index. Pp. xx, 580. $55.00.

This is military history at its best. For anyone with even a slight interest in the U.S. Marine Corps it is not just an invaluable reference, it is wonderfully readable, as well. Dipping into it almost anywhere is a pleasure, with new insights about Marines you thought you knew.

Twenty-seven essays, each by a different author (a few do double duty) describe each Commandant's tenure. Readers will appreciate the writing of Allan Millett, Ed Simmons, Brian Linn, Ron Spector, Jack Shulimson, Jon Hoffman, Joe Alexander, Merrill Bartlett, and Don Bittner, among others—a Who's Who of military writers at the top of their form. Each essay is intended to be a brief critical discussion focusing on the individual's years as Commandant. In some cases, one wishes for more pre-CMC biography, but virtually every piece is insightful and highly informed, as one would expect of writers of such high ability and involvement with the subject matter. There is surprisingly much that is new regarding the early Commandants, despite their being written of so often in the past. Nor are punches pulled: the notable shortcomings of Commandants Lemuel Shepherd and Robert Cushman, for example, are squarely faced.

General Robert Barrow's Commandancy, 1979–83, is the book's final essay, leaving readers wishing for accounts of later CMCs, too. Co-editor Millett explains that the historical dust takes time to settle and he is probably correct. It would be difficult to today write a balanced account of the leadership of Generals P. X. Kelly or Al Gray, with their controversial styles, political highs and lows, and shifts in Marine Corps philosophy. That lacuna is partially filled by Millett's excellent preface and introduction, in which he briefly limns the Commandants following Barrow, and traces the evolution of Headquarters Marine Corps, the latter an historical pleasure in itself.

As expected in a book by twenty authors, there is an occasional unevenness in the over-all high standard of historical evaluation. Millett's assessment of Wallace Greene, a still-underrated officer, and Simmons's study of Robert Barrow, are highlights, written with an authority and style that bring those twentieth-century Marine Corps giants to life. A weak link is the far too brief coverage of General Lou Wilson, another Marine icon whose contributions to the post-Vietnam Corps were immeasurable. The account of Wilson's tenure smacks of a late replacement for an essay that never materialized. Ron Spector's fine review of the Chapman years largely avoids the fascinating intramural in-fighting that led to his selection. The entry on General David Shoup, a notoriously difficult personality, is evenly- and well-done by Howard Jablon. Lieutenant General Victor Krulak's review of Lemuel Shepherd's Commandancy is jewel-like, reminding us that Brute, himself so close to being Commandant (see Chapman), has always been skillful with pen, as well as sword. That he was a player in the events he describes, an unmentioned point, adds verisimilitude and color to his account.

The generally outstanding writing is complemented by good notes and an excellent index. The tired reviewer's phrase, "an essential volume that should be on every serious historian's bookshelf" actually applies here. I have read the book twice and still return to savor this or that account. I suspect you will, too.

Gary Solis   United States Military Academy
                                                          West Point, New York

---

The School of the Americas: Military Training and Political Violence in the Americas. By Lesley Gill. Durham, N.C.: Duke University Press, 2004. Illustrations. Notes. References cited. Index. Pp. xviii, 281. $19.95.

The School of the Americas is less a history of this controversial military institution than a lengthy rationale for its closure and a complete overhaul of American foreign policy. According to the author, the school represents the "tip of a vast iceberg" that comprises American imperialism (p. 228). The school controls, through its courses of instruction and other more subtle means of influence, a Latin American military that is essentially an appendage of American might, or, as the author notes, given "the custodial duties of empire assigned to them by the United States" (p. 226).

Gill's first major error in *The School of the Americas* is her insistence that American power is the product of a monolithic construct. In terms of basic diplomatic and military history, she ignores the interagency rivalries and operational divisions that have blunted American policy throughout its history. More to the point, the author also dismisses much of recent American history in her work. From Gill's perspective Vietnam, Watergate, and the various presidencies of the past fifty years are largely irrelevant. What apparently matters is an America dominated by reactionary, "neoliberal" interests (pp. 35–36). The clumsiness of this model is ironic, given the constant drumbeat of criticism Gill aims at over-generalized U.S. policy identifying communism, narcotics, and terrorism as threats to American interests.

A second significant problem is the author's willingness to discount Latin America's participation in its own history. According to Gill, the hemisphere is composed of chess pieces that the United States moves according to its own whims. What the author ignores is a record that clearly indicates Latin American sovereignty despite U.S. hegemony. Peruvian participation in the School of the Americas, for example, peaked during the seventies at the same time that it openly pursued Marxist policies at home and open relations with the Soviet Union (p. 80).

In its failure to make a distinction between U.S. complicity in human rights abuses and the control it exerts over the issue, Gill's doctrinaire study does a disservice to an important topic. Clearly, both the United States and the School of the Americas have much to answer for in Guatemala, El Salvador, Colombia, and other nations plagued by violence. The extent to which lives have been shattered by state-sponsored terror are obvious and legitimate subjects of investigation. Unfortunately, Gill's tendency to smother the United States and Latin American militaries with blame prevents her from addressing the particularities of each case in an measured, historical manner. Again, and not without some additional irony, she subverts her own effort to hold these actors accountable.

Both scholars and the interested lay person would be better served by a number of works that have more precisely focused on the issues raised in Gill's book. Older studies by James Dunkerley and Michael McClintock set a superior standard for an audience interested in the mechanisms of military power and U.S.-Latin American relations. Similarly, newer scholarship by Robert H. Holden examining state-sponsored violence in Latin America is another highly useful resource.

Michael D. Gambone   Kutztown University of Pennsylvania
Kutztown, Pennsylvania

Navies in Modern World History. By Lawrence Sondhaus. London: Reaktion Books, 2004. ISBN 1-86189-202-0. Illustrations. References. Bibliography. Index. Pp. 336. $39.00.

Surveys of modern naval history seldom stray very far beyond the competition between dominant naval powers (Great Britain, the United States) and their competitors (principally France, Germany, Japan, and the Soviet Union). This book adopts a somewhat different approach. To highlight the variety of roles that navies have played in the modern world, Lawrence Sondhaus employs a series of case studies covering both great and minor powers since the end of the Napoleonic Wars. Each chapter examines a single navy over a period ranging from a decade to nearly a century. The focus throughout the book is on the evolution of naval policy and matériel in peacetime, but the author also examines how each of these services recruited, trained, and educated their personnel, and how well they met the challenges of war.

The book begins with overviews of the British and French navies during the nineteenth century, a period characterized by unprecedented technological advances. As the leading naval and industrial power of this period, Britain had little incentive to force the pace of naval innovation: its superior resources enabled it to meet all of the qualitative and quantitative challenges that emerged in these years. The French navy, on the other hand, embraced technology as a means to undermine Britain's predominant position at sea. During the 1840s–1890s, France repeatedly took the lead in applying new technologies to warship construction, forcing the British to respond with new designs of their own. The book next turns to the western hemisphere, with chapters on the United States and Confederate navies in the American Civil War, the Brazilian navy in the years 1822–31, and the Chilean navy from 1879 to 1892. The Latin American case studies are a welcome diversion into a region often neglected by naval historians. Fleets in these waters were small by European standards, but Sondhaus shows that they were nonetheless critical in shaping the region's history. Brazil's navy played a decisive role in its struggle for independence from Portugal and in the preservation of national unity in the years following. Chile's victory in the War of the Pacific (1879–84) brought significant territorial expansion and catapulted it to the front ranks of South American states. Its emergence as the leading naval power in the region in the early 1880s also raised serious concerns in the United States, which responded with its own naval buildup.

The twentieth century receives slightly less attention, but the focus here is more conventional. Sondhaus begins with Wilhelmine Germany's unsuccessful challenge to British naval supremacy from the turn of the century to the end of the First World War. This is followed by a survey of the Japanese navy from its victory over China in 1894 to its crushing defeat by the United States in the Second World War. The Cold War era is examined from the perspective of another challenger, the Soviet Union. Under the direction of Admiral Gorschkov, the Soviet navy assumed a prominent place in Soviet strategy and effectively contested the United States's command of the sea. The book concludes with a chapter on the United States Navy since 1991. Sondhaus is skeptical about this service's commitment to "transformation," noting that most technological breakthroughs in recent years were produced in European shipyards. In the absence of a peer competitor, he maintains that the United States has adopted a leisurely approach to warship construction and innovation, much like a previous hegemon, the British navy, during parts of the nineteenth century.

Each of these case studies offers a solid introduction to the navies under consideration, demonstrating the complex forces that guided their development, the range of activities they engaged in, and their ability to shape the fate of nations and empires. Taken together, they also provide a good overview of broad trends in naval technology, personnel and combat in the modern era. The case-study approach inevitably means, however, that some important topics are either pushed to the sidelines or overlooked altogether. The book does not, for example, examine the decline of British sea power or the rise of the U.S. Navy during the early twentieth century. Nor does it consider Allied naval operations against Germany and Italy during the Second World War. And with the exception of the two Latin American case studies, little attention is paid to minor navies and regional rivalries. These gaps will probably limit the book's appeal, but the author's unconventional approach ultimately succeeds because of the high quality of the individual case studies.

Christopher M. Bell   Dalhousie University
Halifax, Nova Scotia, Canada

The Machine in Neptune's Garden: Historical Perspectives on Technology and the Marine Environment. Edited by Helen M. Rozwadowski and David K. van Keuren. Sagamore Beach, Mass.: Science History Publications/USA, 2004. ISBN 0-88135-372-8. Photographs. Figures. Notes. Index. Pp. xxviii, 371. $49.95.

The engaging essays that constitute this work were first presented as papers at the third Matthew Fontaine Maury Workshop, convened in June 2001. Gary E. Weir, the co-founder with David K. van Keuren in 1997 of the first Maury gathering, pointedly honoring the U.S. Navy's "patron saint" of oceanography, contributes to this volume, which expands on his own excellent *An Ocean in Common* (College Station: Texas A&M University Press, 2001). The publication of the Maury III proceedings as *The Machine in Neptune's Garden* heralds a broad range of new research in the ocean sciences while it also, sadly, notes the premature deaths of two key players in this vibrant community: the book's dedicatee, Philip F. ("Fritz") Rehbock, and editor-contributor David van Keuren.

Within the last two years, reports from such estimable bodies as the Pew Oceans Commission and the U.S. Commission on Ocean Policy have raised public awareness—with an attendant level of urgency, even alarm—of the very real fragility of American territorial waters and, by extension, the oceans beyond. Though necessarily addressing the technological more than the environmental, the contributions to *The Machine in Neptune's Garden* nonetheless overlap in key areas, and certainly—as the subtitle promises— lend an important perspective on the increasing sophistication of human interaction with the world's oceans.

The book's title is derived from Leo Marx's pivotal work, *The Machine in the Garden: Technology and the Pastoral Ideal in America* (New York:

Oxford University Press, 1964), and its introduction by Keith R. Benson, Helen Rozwadowski, and David van Keuren proffers the thesis, collectively bolstered by the included authors' wide variety of study and research, that the cultivated "garden" of oceanographic knowledge, primarily and increasingly, has had technology to thank for its rich yield. Michael S. Reidy and Eric L. Mills write on nineteenth-century investigations of the oceans' tides and patterns of circulation through the application of unprecedented measuring devices and newly derived theories, setting the stage for their colleagues' ensuing essays on twentieth-century developments in ocean science, including Gregory T. Cushman's history of the international investigations of El Niño from the 1950s into the 1980s, Christine Keiner's study of the nearly contemporaneous project for the colossal Chesapeake Bay Hydraulic Model, David van Keuren's detailed tracing of the interplay of science and industry in the development and applications of ocean floor drilling, and Helen Rozwadowski's "might-have-been" account of the industrial/scientific dreams that fostered the promise of what the creation of "Scripps Island" could have brought to the ocean science community—and the realities that prevailed instead.

The intersections of marine and military sciences inform contributions such as Gary Weir's profile of naval oceanographer Columbus O'Donnell Iselin, and Kathleen Broome Williams's elucidation of the life and work of the pioneering "cultural interpreter" (Gary Weir's apt term) Mary Sears, who brought her scientific specialty to the aid of Allied amphibious operations in World War II. The early consideration by the scientific and military community of the atomic bomb as a "wonderful oceanographic tool" before their gradual subsequent understanding of the hazards of radiation makes for sometimes hair-raising reading in the essay by Ronald Rainger, and Vera Schwach's account of Norwegian fisheries acoustics between 1935 and 1960 offers the seeming twist of civilian commerce benefiting from wartime experience with Asdic antisubmarine detection equipment adapted for the peacetime "hunting" of fish. As this book appeared, it dovetailed, coincidentally, with an updating analogue evincing the continuing cooperative work in these fields: a July 2004 article in *International Defense Review* reporting on various navies and defense research establishments engaged in studies on the harmful effects of active sonars on marine mammals. The acknowledgements and references throughout *The Machine in Neptune's Garden* reveal the extensive cross-fertilization and high mutual regard that characterize this group of authors, and it is devoutly wished that researchers and interested readers alike might be assured of further published proceedings from future Maury workshops.

Gordon E. Hogg   University of Kentucky Libraries
                                                                      Lexington, Kentucky

Receive Your Own Copy of
The Journal of Military History

Enroll Me as a Member of the Society for Military History

Name _____

Address _____

_____

Membership dues: $50.00 per annum. Students $25.00 with professor's

signature and institution: _____

Add $10.00 for mail outside USA–Canada–Mexico. Make checks payable
(in US dollars only) to *The Journal of Military History*
or use Visa or MasterCard.

☐ Check   ☐ MasterCard   ☐ Visa   ☐ Am.Ex.

Card No.:_____

Expiration Date: ____ /____

Signature:_____

Gift Membership

Gift for   Name_____

Address_____

_____

From   Name_____

Address_____

_____

Membership dues: $50.00 per annum. Students $25.00 with name of
institution: _____

Add $10.00 for mail outside USA–Canada–Mexico. Make checks payable
(in US dollars only) to *The Journal of Military History*
or use Visa or MasterCard.

☐ Check   ☐ MasterCard   ☐ Visa   ☐ Am.Ex.

Card No.:_____

Expiration Date: ____ /____

Signature:_____

TEAR OFF

TEAR OFF

BUSINESS REPLY MAIL

FIRST-CLASS MAIL PERMIT NO. 1 LEXINGTON, VA

POSTAGE WILL BE PAID BY ADDRESSEE

THE JOURNAL OF MILITARY HISTORY
GEORGE C. MARSHALL FOUNDATION
PO BOX 1600
LEXINGTON VA 24450-9991

BUSINESS REPLY MAIL

FIRST-CLASS MAIL PERMIT NO. 1 LEXINGTON, VA

POSTAGE WILL BE PAID BY ADDRESSEE

THE JOURNAL OF MILITARY HISTORY
GEORGE C. MARSHALL FOUNDATION
PO BOX 1600
LEXINGTON VA 24450-9991

Military Power: Explaining Victory and Defeat in Modern Battle. By Stephen Biddle. Princeton, N.J.: Princeton University Press, 2004. ISBN 0-691-11645-8. Maps. Tables. Figures. Appendix. Notes. Index. Pp. xi, 337. $37.50.

In *Military Power,* Stephen Biddle, an associate professor at the Army War College, demonstrates a tremendous knowledge of the technical aspects of war. He restricts his analysis to conventional warfare, and excludes guerrilla and nuclear conflict. Biddle deals only with "middle-intensity" wars represented by recent conflicts in Afghanistan, the Balkans, and the Israeli-Arab wars, and with "high-intensity" wars represented by conventional wars between the great powers.

Biddle maintains that conventional warfare "will remain the central purpose for the majority of the U.S. military, and it will continue to occur between other parties in other parts of the world." In the war on terror, Biddle holds that—while attacks on terrorists will involve "counterintelligence and police work"—conventional warfare will still occur against states that harbor terrorists.

This is a legitimate argument. But by making middle-intensity warfare the centerpiece of his work, Biddle focuses on an element that, though indispensable, will not be our cardinal military task over the next few years. Our great challenge will be from terrorist cells that deliver sneak attacks against our most vulnerable targets, like office buildings, trains, and other places where defenseless people gather. To combat this threat, we must create small, guerrilla-like elements that can move so fast and so lethally that they can kill terrorists and partisans before they can get away. These forces are now being built, and will work in a network using instantaneous radio, TV, and computer communications to swarm around an enemy target on all sides, isolating it, and destroying it quickly.

Conventional wars against rogue states are going to be rare in the foreseeable future because no rogue state can stand up militarily to the United States, and few will try. American power was demonstrated by the inability of Iraq to restrain U.S. forces in any way in March-April 2003. Furthermore, U.S. precision-guided munitions conveyed by piloted aircraft and unmanned aerial vehicles (UAVs) have transformed conventional warfare fundamentally. Only the most demented ruler of a renegade state would dare to challenge the U.S., because its air forces can deliver devastating rocket and bomb attacks with pinpoint accuracy on any target anywhere.

Nevertheless, Biddle presents a scholarly and convincing analysis of the conventional warfare that dominated military conflict from World War I through the Korean War, and may occur in the future. He states an important, but often-unrecognized truth that "threat assessments based on the numbers and types of hostile weapons are likely to overestimate real capability for enemies with modern equipment but limited skills [such as the Iraqis under Saddam Hussein] and underestimate militaries with older equipment but high skills [such as the Communists in the Vietnam War]."

Biddle's greatest contribution is his careful analysis of two great battles of conventional warfare, the great German offensive, Operation Michael, on the Western Front in March and April 1918 in World War I, and Operation Goodwood, the attempt of the British army to break out of Normandy in a massive attack southeast of Caen on 18–21 July 1944.

Biddle shows that the Germans actually cracked a fifty-kilometer hole in the British front in 1918 but could not move their troops fast enough to achieve a decisive breakthrough. In Operation Goodwood, the British stacked up their armor on a constricted two-kilometer front. The resulting traffic jam prevented much of the armor from being employed, and the narrow front allowed the Germans to sweep the entire penetration corridor with enfilading fire from both flanks.

Biddle provides an immense quantity of details and statistics to back up his arguments. *Military Power* is an excellent source for any reader who wishes to understand the underlying realities of conventional warfare.

Bevin Alexander   Longwood University
Farmville, Virginia

War in the Twentieth Century: Reflections at Century's End. Edited by Michael A. Hennessy and B. J. C. McKercher. Westport, Conn.: Praeger, 2003. ISBN 0-275-97709-9. Tables. Figures. Notes. Selected bibliography. Index. Pp. 238. $67.95.

This varied collection offers both panoptic surveys and more detailed pieces. Of the latter, Lawrence Aronson's careful piece on the economic foundations of the Cold War alliance systems offers interesting contrasts of the situation in East and West. The latter system was more balanced, in part due to the crippling internal contradictions of communism, although, as Aronson points out, on the American side the economic foundations of the Western alliance were influenced by immediate considerations of national security. In the East, an economic iron curtain descended rapidly, long before direct Soviet political control was imposed. Gary Hess assesses U.S. presidential decision making and the deliberations of the National Security Council, concluding that Truman, Eisenhower, and Bush senior managed a better job than Johnson. Norman Hillmer's survey of Canadian peacekeeping focuses on domestic support, rather than the difficulties of the process. More generally, Donna Arzt discusses the development of radically new norms and subjects of international law with specific reference to the evolving convergence of human rights, humanitarian and refugee law: the state of the latter is presented as the chief barrier to full merger. Erik Goldstein offers a characteristically clear survey of disarmament, arms control, and arms reduction: the difficulties of the first have encouraged the others. Geoffrey Smith's wide ranging analysis of containment, disease, and American Cold War culture (*Life* disparaged Soviet bras among much else) suggests that the American containment culture excluded too many citizens "who slowly recognised that containment aimed at them as it did the Soviets" (p. 115). Drawing, as he acknowledges, heavily on two of his articles published in 1996, John Lynn provides a problematic account of watersheds in the evolution of war and military institutions that begins "As we face the new millennium, time takes the head seat at the intellectual table, and civilization discusses its future and its past" (p. 197). He makes a pertinent point about technology, but offers an overly simplistic account of war and institutions that would have profited from immersion in the literature on conflict in the Third World both before and after 1945. A more acute typology of conflict is provided by D. Cameron Watt, although the second 1958 on p. 40 is a typo for 1968. The topics covered by Watt include the criminalization of "aggressive" war, the disappearance of war at sea, civil conflicts, the increasing cost of weaponry, and abandonment of conscription, and the development of unusable weapons for threat rather than employment. Watt argues that war as such became criminalized, so that most conflicts were fought under conditions lacking any widely accepted legal basis. He links this to the role of measures against non-military populations. The introduction is an effective and well-annotated survey of subject and book, with a useful discussion of total war.

Jeremy Black

University of Exeter
Exeter, United Kingdom

Peacekeeping in the Abyss: British and American Peacekeeping Doctrine and Practice after the Cold War. By Robert M. Cassidy. Westport, Conn.: Praeger, 2004. ISBN 0-275-97696-3. Figures. Notes. Bibliography. Index. Pp. 284. $67.95.

Robert Cassidy takes a fresh look at the differences in the organizational culture of the British and U.S. armies, how this difference affected their respective approaches to peace operations in Bosnia and Somalia, and how it contributed to a more effective participation for one than for the other. The volume is strongly recommended for students of peace operations, as it is well crafted and draws on extensive primary sources and secondary research. It is lucidly written despite its ponderously laborious academic style.

The purpose of the book is to explain the British and U.S. "military strategic cultural preferences" for the use of force and to analyze how these preferences influenced doctrine and actions in Bosnia and Somalia. First, the British enjoy a rich tapestry of "peacekeeping" experience gained from policing their far-flung Empire from the reign of Queen Victoria through its dissolution following World War II, but even so this experience often has had to be relearned. The "cultural preferences" of this period are catalogued in such volumes as Colonel C. E. Callwell's *Small Wars: A Textbook for Imperial Soldiers* and Sir Charles Gwynn's *Imperial Policing.* Yet during World War II these concepts and their associated skills were overshadowed by the need for large conventional forces capable of fighting a very different conflict. Following World War II, the British Army was involved in no less than a dozen insurgencies. The learning curve was persistently steep in each of these conflicts, as the military leaders in place had gained their experience and military maturity in the fight against the Axis powers and little understood a coordinated civil-military response. They treated each new conflict with a conventional approach and struggled to adapt. Theater doctrines for Malaya (*The Conduct of Anti-Terrorist Operations in Malaya*) and Kenya (*A Handbook of Anti-Mau Mau Operations*) are classics, for instance, but each had to be written from scratch from the experience gained there. When General George Erskine, who had fought in Malaya, arrived to assume command in Kenya, he was amazed to find that personnel there were unaware of the Malayan doctrinal handbook. The troubles in Northern Ireland and the British response are yet another example of forgetting history. The culture of the British Army was only able to change when the officers who had fought in Malaya and the like rose to senior positions of responsibility and could exert an influence on changing the "cultural preferences" of the service. British Army performance in Bosnia reflected this hard-won adaptation.

In the second instance, the author takes a selective look at the U.S. Army in Somalia. In his treatment of this conflict he fails to develop the crucial point that the mission there changed from one of protecting the distribution of aid to a starving population to one of "nation building" in the vision of UN secretary-general Boutros Boutros-Ghali. The U.S. Marines, who are essentially a light infantry force and who have a long history of participating in small, politically charged conflicts, entered Somalia on 9 December 1992 as the key participant in a multi-country coalition known as the Unified Task Force (UNITAF). President Bush's special envoy, the skilled diplomat, Ambassador Robert Oakley, would oversee Lieutenant General Robert Johnson and his 28,000 Marines. Johnson announced that the operation would be strictly humanitarian and that his troops would use only sufficient force to protect themselves and the humanitarian relief organizations (HROs).

UNITAF was dissolved on 4 May 1993 with the departure of Oakley and the U.S. Marines having achieved their goal of getting food to elements of the starving populace, establishing a relatively secure environment in which to do so, and fostering local political institutions. The new entity, UN Operation in Somalia II (UNOSOM II), would be the vehicle for Boutros-Ghali's ambitious vision of "nation building" with the recently elected President Bill Clinton as its powerful sponsor. The military arm of UNOSOM II was nominally under the respected Turkish Lieutenant General Cevik Bir, but the U.S. commander, Major General Thomas Montgomery, U.S. Army, controlled U.S. forces. Oakley's replacement was Admiral Jonathan Howe, who had been deputy director of Bush's National Security Council. Unlike Johnson, who had had recent experience in managing coalition forces in Operation Desert Storm, Bir, Montgomery, Howe, and UN headquarters had developed no such skills for a coordinated civil-military response.

The situation began to unravel swiftly. Negotiations with warring elements were increasingly punctuated with firefights and a series of bloody exchanges culminating in the well known downing of two Blackhawk helicopters on 3 October 1993. Oakley was recalled to sort things out, Howe was marginalized, and U.S. forces were withdrawn over the next five months. Cassidy has selectively looked at this four-month period, 4 May to 3 October 1993, to make his thesis of "American military strategic cultural preferences" in Somalia. The 28,000 U.S. Marines under Oakley and Johnson exhibited a very different approach than the U.S. Army-centric UNOSOM II that the author examines. The contrast could not be more stark and certainly challenges the author's thesis in implying all U.S. forces have a dysfunctional approach to peace operations. Missing from the references are the important contributions on Somalia by Ambassador Mohamed Sahnoun, John Drysdale, Johnson, and General Anthony Zinni, USMC, former UNITAF Director of Operations.

Perhaps certain U.S. political and particularly U.S. Army leaders will eventually overcome the propensity to tackle peace operations with a heavy hand and will draw a more useful balance between force and the other available tools, but the irregular results to date portend a long journey to enlightenment. The author ably makes this point, that the officer corps of the U.S. Army must do some serious and innovative thinking about future war. As he also observes, change is a difficult process, but without it the U.S. Army will not be able to address future unconventional conflicts and peace operations successfully.

John P. Cann   Marine Corps Command and Staff College
                                                              Quantico, Virginia

Books Received

☆

Compiler: Blair P. Turner, *Virginia Military Institute*

General

Attack Aircraft and Bombers of the World. By Anil R. Pustam. Mechanicsburg, Pa.: Stackpole Books, 2004. ISBN 1-86176-197-X. Photographs. Glossary. Pp. 128. $24.95. A pictorial catalogue of aircraft types from the Greenhill Military Manuals series.

Combating Proliferation: Strategic Intelligence and Security Policy. By Jason D. Ellis and Geoffrey D. Kiefer. Baltimore, Md.: Johns Hopkins University Press, 2004. ISBN 0-8018-7958-2. Figures. Tables. Notes. Index. Pp. xxi, 287. $48.00. A critique of efforts to contain the proliferation of weapons of mass destruction with a focus on the shift in the Bush administration from nonproliferation to counterproliferation.

Compass: A Story of Exploration and Innovation. By Alan Gurney. New York: W. W. Norton, 2004. ISBN 0-393-05073-4. Illustrations. Figures. Notes. Bibliography. Index. Pp. 320. $22.95. A light and entertaining history of the mariner's most basic navigational tool from the lodestones and wind roses of the Middle Ages to the advent of gyroscopic machines in the early 20th century.

Force-Application Planning: A Systems-and-Effects-Based Approach. By Jay M. Kreighbaum. Maxwell Air Force Base, Ala.: Air University Press, 2004. Tables. Appendixes. Pp. xi, 115. Paper. Investigates how to improve current force-application methodologies; a thesis from the School of Advanced Airpower Studies.

The Gathering Biological Warfare Storm. Edited by Jim A. Davis and Barry R. Schneider. Westport, Conn.: Praeger, 2004. ISBN 0-275-98314-5. Illustrations. Tables. Notes. Index. Pp. 263. $39.95. Ten experts offer essays outlining the current biological warfare threat, focusing on terrorism and the state of U.S. defenses.

The Homeland Security Papers: Stemming the Tide of Terror. Edited by Michael W. Ritz, Ralph G. Hensley, Jr., and James C. Whitmire. Maxwell Air Force Base, Ala.: USAF Counterproliferation Center, 2004. ISBN 0-9747403-20-2. Tables. Figures. Notes. Pp. 264. Paper. A series of ten essays discusses a variety of issues of homeland security, from Colombian narco-terrorism to the effectiveness of first responders on the home front, in an effort to provide a thematic framework for future research.

The International Development of Space and Its Impact on U.S. National Space Policy. By Dale L. Hayden. Maxwell Air Force Base, Ala.: Air University Press, 2004. Notes. Bibliography. Pp. 42. Paper. The author argues that a multinational, diplomatic approach to space issues offers the most security for the U.S.; Airpower Research Institute Paper 2004-1.

Know Thy Enemy: Profiles of Adversary Leaders and Their Strategic Cultures. Edited by Barry R. Schneider and Jerrold M. Post. Maxwell Air Force Base, Ala.: USAF Counterproliferation Center, 2003, 2nd edition. ISBN 0-9747403-0-6. Figures. Notes. Pp. 325. Paper. A series of eleven essays discusses strategic problems involving some of the adversaries faced by the developed West in the early

21st century. Most are, not surprisingly, figures and organizations from the Middle East (Al Qaeda, Iran, Saddam, Qaddafi) but the list includes Kim Chong-il.

Living by the Sword? The Ethics of Armed Intervention. By Tom Frame. Seattle: University of Washington Press, 2004. ISBN 0-86840-519-1. Photographs. Appendixes. Notes. Index. Pp. 278. Paper. $24.95. The Anglican Bishop to the Australian Defence Force discusses the ethical issues involved with humanitarian and political interventions in the current international arena.

Neither Star Wars Nor Sanctuary: Constraining the Military Uses of Space. By Michael E. O'Hanlon. Washington: Brookings Institution Press, 2004. ISBN 0-8157-6457-X. Tables. Figures. Notes. Index. Pp. xi, 173. Paper. $16.95. The author argues it is in the United States's best strategic interest to maintain its current superiority by resisting the temptation to put more weapons in space.

No End in Sight: The Continuing Menace of Nuclear Proliferation. By Nathan E. Busch. Lexington: University Press of Kentucky, 2004. ISBN 0-8131-2323-2. Tables. Appendix. Notes. Bibliography. Index. Pp. xiv, 490. $40.00. An analysis of the state of nuclear programs among the traditional nuclear powers and newly proliferating states and of the debates over international policy to contain nuclear weapons.

The Origins of the Arab Israeli Wars. By Ritchie Ovendale. Harlow, UK: Pearson Education, 2004. ISBN 0-582-82320-X. Maps. Notes. Bibliography. Index. Pp. xxi, 375. Paper. £30.99. This fourth and updated edition of the 1984 history traces the conflict from its origins in Zionism and the "Arab Awakening" through the "road map" of 2002.

Resisting Rebellion: The History and Politics of Counterinsurgency. By Anthony James Joes. Lexington: University Press of Kentucky, 2004. ISBN 0-8131-2339-9. Map. Tables. Notes. Bibliography. Index. Pp. 351. $35.00. The author explores a variety of insurgencies, mostly modern ones, and the few successful (the U.S. in the Philippines) and many unsuccessful counterinsurgency campaigns. Success

depends on isolating the insurgents and supporting indigenous civilian reform movements. He concludes with a brief, not optimistic, note on the current U.S. effort in Iraq.

Samurai: The History of Japan's Noble Warriors. By Stephen Turnbull. London: Collins and Brown, 2004. ISBN 1-84340-207-6. Illustrations. Glossary. Appendix. Bibliography. Index. Pp. 256. £20.00. A lavishly illustrated, large-format history of the warrior elite of Japan with special attention to the "invincible military caste" and its practices, armor, and weapons.

Stranded in the Present: Modern Time and the Melancholy of History. By Peter Fritzsche. Cambridge, Mass.: Harvard University Press, 2004. ISBN 0-674-01339-5. Notes. Index. Pp. 268. $27.95. The author explores the early 19th century origins of what he argues is the West's modern conception of History, in which the past no longer serves as a reliable guide to modern life and History is seen as a "relentless, often painful movement away from the past into an uncertain future."

Symbol of Courage: A History of the Victoria Cross. By Max Arthur. London: Sidgwick & Jackson, 2004. ISBN 0-283-07351-9. Maps. Photographs. Appendix. Bibliography. Indexes. Pp. xxv, 686. £25.00. This is a compendium of brief biographical sketches of each of the 1,354 recipients of the U.K.'s highest award for valor, presented in order of the campaigns in which the medal has been awarded, from the Crimea to the Falklands, with indexes listing the recipients alphabetically.

Technology Challenges for Operationally Responsive Spacelift. By Kendall K. Brown. Maxwell Air Force Base, Ala.: Airpower Research Institute, 2004. Photographs. Glossary. Notes. Pp. 39. Paper. Airpower Research Institute Paper 2004-2.

Time-Critical Targeting: Predictive versus Reactionary Methods: An Analysis for the Future. By Gregory S. Marzolf. Maxwell Air Force Base, Ala.: Air University Press, 2004. Illustrations. Tables. Notes. Pp. 67. Paper. The author suggests that preemptive tactical air strikes at likely targets might prove a bridge method until more rapid reactive methods can be implemented; a thesis from the School of Advanced Airpower Studies.

United States Army Unit and Organizational Histories. Volume 1, *Pre-World War I*;. Volume 2, *World War I to Present.* By James T. Controvich. Lanham, Md.: Scarecrow Press, 2003. ISBN 0-8108-4595-4 AMD 0-8108-4595-4. Index. Pp. 1248. $240.00 for the 2-volume set. A massive compilation of sources for research on U.S. Army units from the Army Groups to the state militias. The first volume has entries for every state prior to 1917; the second focuses on the modern Army's organization down to the battalion level, including sources on forts and bases and local histories at the county level.

Whole World on Fire: Organizations, Knowledge, and Nuclear Weapons Devastation. By Lynn Eden. Ithaca, N.Y.: Cornell University Press, 2004. ISBN 0-8014-3578-1. Photographs. Tables. Charts. Notes. Index. Pp. xiv, 365. $32.50. The author argues that the destructive potential of fire storms pursuant to nuclear detonations has been dangerously overlooked because of institutional and organizational obsession with blast effect.

Before 1800

Four Anglian Kings of Northumbria (Or Four Yorkshire Anglo-Saxon Crowns). By Raymond E. O. Ella. Otley, U.K.: Old Yorkshire Publications, 2002. ISBN 0-9533762-3-0. Map. Illustrations. Pp. 27. £2.95. Reprint of a 1982 chapbook outlining the reigns of four Yorkshire rulers from the sixth, seventh and ninth centuries.

A Nation of Villages: Riot and Rebellion in the Mexican Huasteca, 1750–1850. By Michael T. Ducey. Tucson: University of Arizona Press, 2004. ISBN 0-8165-2383-5. Maps. Illustrations. Tables. Figures. Notes. Index. Pp. xii, 235. $39.95. A study of the century-long, almost continuous peasant uprisings along the Gulf Coast of Mexico and their impact on the Mexican independence movement and subsequent national strife in the 19th century.

*The Pulaski Legion in the American Revo-*lution. By Francis Casimir Kajencki. El Paso, Tex.: Southwest Polonia Press, 2004. ISBN 0-9627190-7-2. Maps. Photographs. Illustrations. Appendixes. Notes. Bibliography. Index. Pp. xiii, 407. This author's second volume on the exploits of the legion founded by the Polish commander, Casimir Pulaski, focuses on the officer corps and combat in South Carolina and Georgia.

Sea Raiders of the American Revolution: The Continental Navy in European Waters. By E. Gordon Bowen-Hassell, Dennis M. Conrad, and Mark L. Hayes. Washington: Navy Historical Center, 2003. ISBN 0-16-051400-2. Photographs. Illustrations. Glossary. Principal sources. Pp. 73. Paper. The three authors offer brief histories of the exploits of Lambert Wickes, Gustavus Conyngham and John Paul Jones during the American Revolution.

19th Century

Agent of Empire: William Walker and the Imperial Self in American Literature. By Brady Harrison. Athens: University of Georgia Press, 2004. ISBN 0-8203-2544-9. Notes. Index. Pp. x, 238. $34.95. How the career of the 19th-century filibuster in Mexico and Central America exemplified a peculiar type of American imperialism and inspired the literary subgenre of "mercenary romance."

*Brigadier General Tyree H. Bell, C.S.A. For-*rest's Fighting Lieutenant. By Nathaniel Cheairs Hughes, Jr., with Connie Walton Moretti and James Michael Browne. Knoxville: University of Tennessee Press, 2004. ISBN 1-57233-309-X. Maps. Illustrations. Notes. Bibliography. Index. Pp. xii, 346. $45.00. Biography of a Tennessee farmer who joined the militia and eventually became a brigade commander under the legendary Confederate general.

Charlestonians in War: The Charleston Battalion. By W. Chris Phelps. Gretna, La.: Pelican Publishing, 2004. ISBN 1-58980-166-0. Maps. Photographs. Appendixes. Notes. Bibliography. Index. Pp. 299. $22.00. The story of a battalion raised from a cross section of Charleston society for the city's defense and which also participated in the defense of Petersburg and Wilmington during the last stages of the Civil War.

Civil War in Kansas. By Roy Bird. Gretna, La.: Pelican Publishing, 2004. ISBN 1-58980-164-4. Illustrations. Selected bibliography. Appendix. Pp. 152. Paper. $12.95. The story of the bitter guerrilla conflict in Kansas.

Counterpoint to Trafalgar: The Anglo-Russian Invasion of Naples, 1805–1806. By William Henry Flayhart, III. Gainesville: University Press of Florida, 2004. ISBN 0-8130-2795-0. Maps. Illustrations. Tables. Notes. Bibliography. Index. Pp. xvi, 198. Paper. $24.95. Reprint of the 1992 story of the combined British-Russian invasion fleet ordered to Naples to present a southern threat to Napoleon's forces; the fleet was the tempting prize which drew the French to their defeat at Trafalgar.

The Last Stronghold: The Campaign for Fort Fisher. By Richard B. McCaslin. Abilene, Tex.: McWhiney Foundation Press, 2003. ISBN 1-893114-31-7. Maps. Photographs. Appendix. Index. Pp. 120. Paper. $16.95. How the successful Union assault on the Confederate coastal stronghold helped end the Civil War; from the Civil War Campaigns and Commanders Series.

Pale Horse at Plum Run: The First Minnesota at Gettysburg. By Brian Leehan. St. Paul: Minnesota Historical Society Press, 2002.

ISBN 0-87351-511-0. Maps. Photographs. Appendixes. Notes. Bibliography. Index. Pp. xx, 243. Paper. $17.95. The story of the First Minnesota Regiment's charge, which stopped the Confederate assault on 2 July 1863 and "saved the day for the Union."

Phantom Pain: North Carolina's Artificial Limbs Program for Confederate Veterans. By Ansley Herring Wegner. Raleigh: Office of Archives and History, North Carolina Department of Cultural Resources, 2004. ISBN 0-86526-314-0. Illustrations. Tables. Notes. Index to records. Bibliography. Index. Pp. x, 261. Paper. $15.00. This volume contains a brief discussion of amputation during the Civil War, but is mostly an alphabetical index of the records for amputees from North Carolina and so is a research tool for those interested.

To Live and Die: Collected Stories of the Civil War, 1861–1876. Edited by Kathleen Diffley. Durham, N.C.: Duke University Press, 2004. ISBN 0-8223-3439-9. Illustrations. Bibliographic essay. Index. Pp. xiii, 428. Paper. $22.95. Thirty-one contemporary pieces from magazines such as the *Atlantic Monthly* and *Harper's Weekly* from various authors, including Louisa May Alcott and Mark Twain, offer diverse views of the Civil War.

Triumph and Defeat: The Vicksburg Campaign. By Terrence J. Winschel. New York: Savas Beatie, 2004. ISBN 1-932714-04-9. Illustrations. Maps. Notes. Bibliography. Index. Pp. x, 219. Paper. $16.95. A reprint of the 1999 account of the siege and fall of the "Gibraltar of the Confederacy" from April to July of 1863.

Since 1900

America's Oil Wars. By Stephen Pelletière. Westport, Conn.: Praeger, 2004. ISBN 0-275-97851-6. Appendixes. Notes. Index. Pp. xi, 192. $34.95. A former CIA senior political analyst for Iraq offers a critique of the Bush foreign policy in the Middle East in particular and neoconservative ideology in general and places the current U.S. involvement there in the context of larger global economic and social conflict.

An American Rabbi in Korea: A Chaplain's Journey in the Forgotten War. By Milton J. Rosen. Tuscaloosa: University of Alabama Press, 2004. ISBN 0-8173-1400-8. Maps. Illustrations. Bibliography. Index. Pp. 127. $35.00. The author's son provides English translations of 19 articles written in 1950 and 1951 and originally published in the New York Yiddish daily, *Der Morgen Zhornal.*

Arnhem 1944: Operation Market Garden. By Stephen Badsey. Westport, Conn.: Praeger, 2004. ISBN 0-275-98284-X. Maps. Photographs. Illustrations. Index. Pp. 96. $35.00. Reissue by the Praeger Illustrated Military History Series of the original Osprey edition of 1993.

At Hitler's Side: The Memoirs of Hitler's Luftwaffe Adjutant 1937–1945. By Nicolaus von Below. Mechanicsburg, Pa.: Stackpole Books, 2004. ISBN 1-85367-600-4. Photographs. Notes. Index. Pp. 256. Paper. $19.95. This reissue of the 2001 English translation of von Below's memoir of his time as Hitler's adjutant for air force affairs from 1937 to 1945 offers eyewitness insights into decision making in the Third Reich..

Bagration 1944: The Destruction of Army Group Center. By Steven J. Zaloga. Westport, Conn.: Praeger, 2004. ISBN 0-275-98285-8. Maps. Photographs. Illustrations. Index. Pp. 96. $35.00. Reissue by the Praeger Illustrated Military History Series of the original Osprey edition of 1996.

The Battle of the Bulge: Hitler's Last Gamble in the West. By James Arnold. Westport, Conn.: Praeger, 2004. ISBN 0-275-98261-0. Maps. Illustrations. Index. Pp. 96. $35.00. Reissue by the Praeger Illustrated Military History Series of the original Osprey edition of 1990.

The Canadian Battlefields in Normandy: A Visitor's Guide. Waterloo, Canada: Wilfrid Laurier University, 2004. ISBN 0-9688750-4-1. Maps. Photographs. Appendixes. Pp. 152. Paper. $28.00 Cdn. This 60th anniversary commemorative double edition of Canadian Military History, 13 (Winter-Spring, 2004), offers a pictorial guide to the operations of the 3rd Canadian Division from D-Day to the end of August when it reached the Seine River.

CIA Spymaster. By Clarence Ashley. Gretna, La.: Pelican Publishing, 2004. ISBN 1-58980-234-9. Illustrations. Notes. Index. Pp. 350. $26.95. Biography of George Kisevalter, the CIA's most decorated case officer, who handled Pyotr Popov, the agency's first important Soviet asset, and Oleg Penkovsky, whose information about Soviet intelligence was critical to John F. Kennedy's handling of the Cuban missile crisis.

Con Thien: The Hill of Angels. By James P. Coan. Tuscaloosa: University of Alabama Press, 2004. ISBN 0-8173-1414-8. Maps. Photographs. Appendixes. Glossary. Notes. Bibliography. Index. Pp. xx, 360. $29.95. A captain in the 3rd Marine Division tells the story of the occupation of the important outpost along the DMZ in Vietnam from 1966 to 1969.

D-Day: Normandy Revisited. A Photographic Pilgrimage. By Richard Bougaardt. London: Chaucer Press, 2004. Photographs. Bibliography. Index. Pp. 192. $30.00. A photographic tour of the Normandy battle areas including historical pictures as well as contemporary ones.

D-Day 1944: Gold and Juno Beaches. By Ken Ford. Westport, Conn.: Praeger, 2004. ISBN 0-275-98267-X. Maps. Photographs. Illustrations. Bibliography. Index. Pp. 96. $35.00. Reissue by the Praeger Illustrated Military History Series of the original Osprey edition of 2002.

D-Day 1944: Omaha Beach. By Steven J. Zaloga. Westport, Conn.: Praeger, 2004. ISBN 0-275-98266-1. Maps. Photographs. Illustrations. Tables. Index. Pp. 96. $35.00. Reissue by the Praeger Illustrated Military History Series of the original Osprey edition of 2003.

D-Day 1944: Sword Beach and the British Airborne Landings. By Ken Ford. Westport, Conn.: Praeger, 2004. ISBN 0-275-98265-3. Maps. Photographs. Bibliography. Index. Pp. 96. $35.00. Reissue by the Praeger Illustrated Military History Series of the original Osprey edition of 2002.

D-Day 1944: Utah Beach and U.S. Airborne Landings. By Steven J. Zaloga. Westport, Conn.: Praeger, 2004. ISBN 0-275-98268-8. Maps. Photographs. Illustrations. Tables. Index. Pp. 96. $35.00. Reissue by the Praeger Illustrated Military History Series of the original Osprey edition of this year.

Dieppe 1942: Prelude to D-Day. By Ken Ford. Westport, Conn.: Praeger, 2004. ISBN 0-275-98281-5. Maps. Photographs. Illustrations. Bibliography. Index. Pp. 96. $35.00. Reissue by the Praeger Illustrated Military History Series of the original Osprey edition of 2003.

The Diplomacy of the New Order. By Arthur Stam. Soesterberg, The Netherlands:

Aspekt, 2003. ISBN 90-5911-436-1. Photographs. Bibliography. Index. Pp. 112. Paper. $19.95. In this brief analysis, the author argues that conflicting interests and designs doomed efforts to coordinate the efforts of the Axis powers in World War II: "It wasn't possible to form a 'Fascintern.'"

The Ebro 1938: Death Knell of the Spanish Republic. By Chris Henry. Westport, Conn.: Praeger, 2004. ISBN 0-275-98277-7. Maps. Photographs. Illustrations. Glossary. Index. Pp. 96. $35.00. Reissue by the Praeger Illustrated Military History Series of the original Osprey edition of 1999.

The Enemy Within: Hucksters, Racketeers, Deserters, and Civilians During the Second World War. By Donald Thomas. New York: New York University Press, 2004. ISBN 0-8147-8286-8. Photographs. Notes. Index. Pp. xvi, $29.95. An exposé of the racketeering activities of the organized criminal underground—both civilian and military—in Britain during World War II.

First to Warn: My Combat Experiences in the 1st Reconnaissance Troop, 1st Infantry Division, in North Africa and Sicily in World War II. By George J. Koch. Chicago: Cantigny First Division Foundation, 2004. ISBN 1-890093-15-7. Maps. Photographs. Illustrations. Index. Pp. xv, 201. Paper. $20.00. Memoir of a soldier in a mechanized scouting unit covering the assault on Oran in North Africa and Operation Husky in Sicily.

First Ypres 1914: The Birth of Trench Warfare. By David Lomas. Westport, Conn.: Praeger, 2004. ISBN 0-275-98291-2. Maps. Photographs. Illustrations. Index. Pp. 96. $35.00. Reissue by the Praeger Illustrated Military History Series of the original Osprey edition of 1998.

France 1940: Blitzkrieg in the West. By Alan Shepperd. Westport, Conn.: Praeger, 2004. ISBN 0-275-98279-3. Maps. Photographs. Illustrations. Index. Pp. 96. $35.00. Reissue by the Praeger Illustrated Military History Series of the original Osprey edition of 1990.

From Anzio to the Alps: An American Soldier's Story. By Lloyd M. Wells. Columbia: University of Missouri Press, 2004. ISBN 0-8262-1537-8. Photographs. Pp. xviii,

256. $29.95. World War II memoirs of a junior officer in the First Armored Division in North Africa, Italy, and Germany.

Gallipoli 1915: Frontal Assault on Turkey. By Philip Haythornthwaite. Westport, Conn.: Praeger, 2004. ISBN 0-275-98288-2. Maps. Photographs. Index. Pp. 96. $35.00. Reissue by the Praeger Illustrated Military History Series of the original Osprey edition of 1991.

God, Country, and Self-Interest: A Social History of the World War II Rank and File. By Toby Terrar. Silver Spring, Md.: CW Press, 2004. No ISBN. Illustrations. Notes. Bibliography. Indexes. Pp. xxxvii, 382. Paper. $9.95. The author offers a combined memoir of his parents, both of whom served in the U.S. forces in World War II, as a case study of how typical Americans coped with and survived the conflict.

The Grace of God in Action: God's Grace in One Man's Death March. By Pastor Valentine H. Derr. New York: Vantage Press, 2004. ISBN 0-533-14752-2. Pp. 97. Paper. $8.95. Brief memoir of an American GI captured at the Battle of the Bulge in 1944 and his subsequent POW experience in Czechoslovakia until his release by U.S. forces.

The Great Escape. By Paul Brickhill. New York: W. W. Norton, 2004. ISBN 0-393-32579-2. Maps. Photographs. Illustrations. Pp. 264. Paper. $13.95. Reprint of the 1950 classic story of Stalag Luft III which inspired the movie.

Guadalcanal 1942: The Marines Strike Back. By Joseph N. Mueller. Westport, Conn.: Praeger, 2004. ISBN 0-275-98270-X. Maps. Photographs. Illustrations. Index. Pp. 96. $35.00. Reissue by the Praeger Illustrated Military History Series of the original Osprey edition of 1992.

Guns of the Third Reich. By John Walter. Mechanicsburg, Pa.: Stackpole Books, 2004. ISBN 1-85367-598-9. Illustrations. Line drawings. Appendixes. Notes. Bibliography. Index. Pp. 256. $34.95. A study of the small arms used by the German armed forces during World War II.

Heart of the Storm: My Adventures as a Helicopter Rescue Pilot and Commander. By Col. Edward Fleming. New York: Wiley, 2004. ISBN 0-471-26436-9. Photographs. Glossary. Index. Pp. xi, 259. $24.95. Memoirs of a thirty-year career as pilot in the Air Rescue Service in the Air Force and the National Guard in both military and civilian operations.

Hitler's Stuka Squadrons: The JU 87 at War, 1936–1945. By John Ward. St. Paul, Minn.: Motorbooks International, 2004. ISBN 0-7603-1991-X. Photographs. Glossary. Appendixes. Bibliography. Index. Pp. 224. Paper. $19.95.The first volume in the Eagles of War series tells the story of the development of the famous German dive bomber and its operational history throughout World War II.

If Britain Had Fallen: The Real Nazi Occupation Plans. By Norman Longmate. Mechanicsburg, Pa.: Stackpole Books, 2004. ISBN 1-85367-599-7. Maps. Photographs. Note on sources. Index. Pp. 276. Paper. $19.95. Reprint of the 1972 analysis of the German plans for the invasion of Britain in World War II with a speculative discussion of the possible British response to a successful invasion based partly on a study of responses to occupation elsewhere.

If the Gods Are Good: The Epic Sacrifice of the HMS Jervis Bay. By Gerald L. Duskin and Ralph Segman. Annapolis, Md.: Naval Institute Press, 2004. ISBN 1-59114-819-7. Photographs. Notes. Bibliography. Index. Pp. xii, 268. $28.95. The story of how a British escort ship—a converted cargo vessel—took on the much larger German pocket battleship *Admiral Scheer* in November of 1940; the HMS *Jervis Bay* was lost, but the convoy was saved.

Impact Zone: The Battle of the DMZ in Vietnam, 1967–1968. By Jim Brown. Tuscaloosa: University of Alabama Press, 2004. ISBN 0-8173-1402-4. Map. Photographs. Glossary. Index. Pp. xi, 277. $29.95. Memoirs of an artillery man at both Khe Sanh and Con Thien.

Inside the Iron Works: How Grumman's Glory Days Faded. By George M. Skurla and William H. Gregory. Annapolis, Md.: Naval Institute Press, 2004. ISBN 1-55750-329-X. Illustrations. Index. Pp. xi, 225. $32.95. A combined memoir of its last CEO, Skurla, and corporate study of the famous combat aircraft manufacturer from the glory days before and during World War II to its takeover by the Northrop Corporation in 1993.

Inventing Anzac: The Digger and National Mythology. By Graham Seal. St. Lucia, Australia: University of Queensland Press, 2004. ISBN 0-7022-3447-8. Illustrations. Appendix. Notes. Select bibliography. Index. Pp. 232. $32.95. The author offers an analysis of how deliberate policies combined with informal social mechanisms to merge the myth of the Australian "digger—the independent citizen-soldier—with the official image of the Anzac armed forces.

The Iraq War: Hidden Agendas and Babylonian Intrigue: The Regional Impact on Shi'ites, Kurds, Sunnis, and Arabs. By Raphael Israeli. Portland, Oreg.: ISBS, 2004. ISBN 1-903900-90-5. Map. Notes. Bibliography. Index. Pp. x, 278. $27.95. The author offers an exposé of the Ba'athist regime and an analysis of the regional political and social consequences of the current war in Iraq.

Iwo Jima 1945: The Marines Raise the Flag on Mount Suribachi. By Derrick Wright. Westport, Conn.: Praeger, 2004. ISBN 0-275-98273-4. Maps. Photographs. Illustrations. Index. Pp. 96. $35.00. Reissue by the Praeger Illustrated Military History Series of the original Osprey edition of 2001.

Jutland 1916: Clash of the Dreadnoughts. By Charles London. Westport, Conn.: Praeger, 2004. ISBN 0-275-98293-9. Maps. Photographs. Illustrations. Notes. Select bibliography. Index. Pp. 96. $35.00. Reissue by the Praeger Illustrated Military History Series of the original Osprey edition of 2000.

Kaiserschlacht 1918: The Final German Offensive of World War One. By Randal Gray. Westport, Conn.: Praeger, 2004. ISBN 0-275-98289-0. Maps. Photographs. Index. Pp. 96. $35.00. Reissue by the Praeger Illustrated Military History Series of the original Osprey edition of 1991.

Kilroy Was There: A GI's War in Photographs. By Tony Hillerman. Kent, Ohio: Kent State University Press, 2004. ISBN 0-87338-807-0. Photographs. Pp. 79. $25.00. Sgt. Frank Kessler of the Army Signal Corps saved and stored hundreds of photographs of the campaign in Europe in World War II; after his death, his younger brother and the well-known author of the Navajo Mysteries edited them and supplied captions in this volume, covering events from D-Day to V-E Day including some grim photographs at Nordhausen concentration camp.

Kursk 1943: The Tide Turns in the East. By Mark Healy. Westport, Conn.: Praeger, 2004. ISBN 0-275-98283-1. Maps. Photographs. Illustrations. Index. Pp. 96. $35.00. Reissue by the Praeger Illustrated Military History Series of the original Osprey edition of 1993.

The Last Colonial Massacre: Latin America in the Cold War. By Greg Grandin. Chicago: University of Chicago Press, 2004. ISBN 0-226-30572-4. Maps. Illustrations. Glossary. Notes. Bibliography. Index. Pp. xviii, 311. Paper. $22.00. The author uses a case study of the Panzós massacre in Guatemala in May of 1978 to argue that U.S. Cold War policy in Latin America resulted in illiberal, militarized regimes in the region.

Late Thoughts on an Old War: The Legacy of Vietnam. By Philip D. Beidler. Athens: University of Georgia Press, 2004. ISBN 0-8203-2589-9. Pp. 213. $29.95 The author, a Vietnam veteran himself, offers a series of reflective essays on how Americans have dealt with—sometimes well and sometimes poorly—the legacy of the Vietnam war.

Lorraine 1944: Patton Versus Manteuffel. By Steven J. Zaloga. Westport, Conn.: Praeger, 2004. ISBN 0-275-98264-5. Maps. Photographs. Illustrations. Index. Pp. 96. $35.00. Reissue by the Praeger Illustrated Military History Series of the original Osprey edition of 2000.

Masters of Chaos: The Secret History of the Special Forces. By Linda Robinson. New York: Public Affairs, 2004. ISBN 1-58648-249-1. Maps. Illustrations. Index. Pp. xxii, 388. $26.95. A journalist tells the story of Special Forces from the period immediately following the Vietnam War to current operations in the Middle East.

Megiddo 1918: Lawrence, Allenby, and the March on Damascus. By Bryan Perrett. Westport, Conn.: Praeger, 2004. ISBN 0-275-98292-0. Maps. Photographs. Illustrations. Index. Pp. 96. $35.00. Reissue by the Praeger Illustrated Military History Series of the original Osprey edition of 1999.

Memory and Memorials: The Commemorative Century. Edited by William Kidd and Brian Murdoch. Burlington, Vt.: Ashgate, 2004. ISBN 0-7546-0735-6. Illustrations. Notes. Index. Pp. xii, 284. $89.95. A series of eighteen essays survey how the British, French, and Germans have used various forms of memorials, such as cemeteries, statuary, and film, to manipulate the memory of their war experiences of the twentieth century for particular political and social purposes.

Midway 1942: Turning Point in the Pacific. By Mark Healy. Westport, Conn.: Praeger, 2004. ISBN 0-275-98276-9. Maps. Photographs. Illustrations. Index. Pp. 96. $35.00. Reissue by the Praeger Illustrated Military History Series of the original Osprey edition of 1993.

Mons 1914: Britain's Tactical Triumph. By David Lomas. Westport, Conn.: Praeger, 2004. ISBN 0-275-98290-4. Maps. Photographs. Illustrations. Index. Pp. 96. $35.00. Reissue by the Praeger Illustrated Military History Series of the original Osprey edition of 1995.

None Braver: U.S. Air Force Pararescuemen in the War on Terrorism. By Michael Hirsh. New York. New American Library, 2004. ISBN 0-451-21295-9. Map. Photographs. Index. Pp. xxi, 297. Paper. $13.95. Reprint of last year's account by a journalist embedded with the 38th Expeditionary Rescue Squadron in Afghanistan during Operation Anaconda in 2002.

Normandy 1944: Allied Landings and Breakout. By Stephen Badsey. Westport, Conn.: Praeger, 2004. ISBN 0-275-98260-2. Maps. Photographs. Tables. Index. Pp. 96. $35.00. Reissue by the Praeger Illustrated Military History Series of the original Osprey edition of 1990.

Okinawa 1945: The Last Battle. By Gordon L. Rottman. Westport, Conn.: Praeger, 2004. ISBN 0-275-98274-2. Maps. Photographs. Illustrations. Index. Pp. 96. $35.00. Reissue by the Praeger Illustrated Military History Series of the original Osprey edition of 2002.

Operation Cobra 1944: Breakout from Normandy. By Steven J. Zaloga. Westport, Conn.: Praeger, 2004. ISBN 0-275-98263-7. Maps. Photographs. Illustrations. Index. Pp. 96. $35.00. Reissue by the Praeger Illustrated Military History Series of the original Osprey edition of 2001.

Operation Compass 1940: Wavell's Whirlwind Offensive. By Jon Latimer. Westport, Conn.: Praeger, 2004. ISBN 0-275-98286-6. Maps. Photographs. Illustrations. Bibliography. Index. Pp. 96. $35.00. Reissue by the Praeger Illustrated Military History Series of the original Osprey edition of 2000.

Pearl Harbor 1941: The Day of Infamy. By Carl Smith. Westport, Conn.: Praeger, 2004. ISBN 0-275-98272-6. Maps. Photographs. Illustrations. Appendixes. Index. Pp. 96. $35.00. Reissue by the Praeger Illustrated Military History Series of the original Osprey edition of 1999.

Peleliu 1944: The Forgotten Corner of Hell. By Jim Moran and Gordon L. Rottman. Westport, Conn.: Praeger, 2004. ISBN 0-275-98275-0. Maps. Photographs. Illustrations. Bibliography. Index. Pp. 96. $35.00. Reissue by the Praeger Illustrated Military History Series of the original Osprey edition of 2002.

Please, Jesus, Give me Three More Minutes to Live. By Dr. Harold Hammil. New York: Vantage Press, 2004. ISBN 0-533-14699-2. Illustrations. Pp. 274. Paper. $15.00. Memoir of a GI in the 34th Infantry Division in World War II, focusing on the Italian campaign.

Poland 1939: The Birth of Blitzkrieg. By Steven J. Zaloga. Westport, Conn.: Praeger, 2004. ISBN 0-275-98278-5. Maps. Photographs. Illustrations. Index. Pp. 96. $35.00. Reissue by the Praeger Illustrated Military History Series of the original Osprey edition of 2002.

Rattler One-Seven: A Vietnam Helicopter Pilot's War Story. By Chuck Gross. Denton: University of North Texas Press, 2004. ISBN 1-57441-178-0. Maps. Photographs. Glossary. Notes. Bibliography. Index. Pp. xii, 229. $27.95. Memoirs of an American helicopter pilot in Vietnam from 1970 to 1971 including his participation in operation Lam Son 719, an assault on the Ho Chi Minh Trail, which was the largest airmobile campaign of the war.

Rhetoric and Reality in Air Warfare: The Evolution of British and American Ideas About Strategic Bombing, 1914–1945. By Tami Davis Biddle. Princeton, N.J.:

Princeton University Press, 2004. ISBN 0-691-12010-2. Notes. Bibliography. Index. Pp. viii, 406. Paper. $19.95. Reprint of the 2002 critique of Allied strategic bombing doctrine which argued that the flawed doctrine was based on faulty assumptions about the impact of strategic bombing.

The Rhineland 1945: The Final Push into Germany. By Ken Ford. Westport, Conn.: Praeger, 2004. ISBN 0-275-98269-6. Maps. Photographs. Illustrations. Index. Pp. 96. $35.00. Reissue by the Praeger Illustrated Military History Series of the original Osprey edition of 2000.

Russia, America, and the Cold War. 2nd edition. By Martin McCauley. Harlow, UK: Pearson Education, 2004. ISBN 0-582-78482-4. Maps. Bibliography. Index. Pp. xxxvii, 186. Paper. £22.99. This text from the Seminar Studies in History series offers a summary of the high points of U.S.-Soviet conflict during the Cold War.

Sacrifice of the Generals: Soviet Senior Officer Losses, 1939–1953. By Michael Parrish. Lanham, Md.: Rowman & Littlefield, 2004. ISBN 0-8108-5009-5. Appendix. Index. Pp. xxviii, 477. Paper. $70.00. This biographical dictionary of some 1,000 senior Soviet officers lost in combat or captured, victims of purges, or lost by other causes from 1939 to 1953 yields insight into the issue of personnel loss in the Red Army during the Stalin era.

The "Sailjers," the Sea, and Sulfur Island: A Maritime Memoir of an Air Force Floating Unit in World War II. By George Hans Christiansen. Self-published, 1992. Previous title *Odyssey of the (212) Keiser.* No ISBN. Illustrations. Paper. Pp. viii, 242. $25.00. The story of a repair ship in the Air Force navy. Order from Dorothy Christiansen, 75 Beulah Dr., Raphine, VA 24472 (540-377-6449).

Secrets of a Century: The Influence of Espionage and Secret Agreements. By Johnson Parker. Lanham, Md.: Rowman & Littlefield, 2004. ISBN 0-7618-2795-1. Bibliography. Index. Pp. 236. Paper. $34.00. The author traces the impact of covert activities on such historical developments as the First World War, code breaking in World War II and U.S. involvement in the Cold War.

Shot at and Missed: Recollections of a World

War II Bombardier. By Jack R. Myers. Norman: University of Oklahoma Press, 2004. ISBN 0-8061-3619-7. Photographs. Pp. x, 309. $29.95. Memoirs of a B-17 bombardier in the Fifteenth Air Force based in Italy who flew 35 missions over Germany and Eastern Europe.

Small Wars Manual: United States Marine Corps 1940. Manhattan, Kans.: Sunflower University Press, 2004. ISBN 0-89745-112-0. Illustrations. Tables. Pp. xvii, 584. Paper. $28.95. Reissue of the classic manual, which was declassified in 1972 and first printed by Sunflower Press in 1988, and which is enjoying a renaissance among some military circles with the current war in Iraq.

The Smell of Kerosene: A Test Pilot's Odyssey. By Donald L. Mallick with Peter W. Merlin. Washington: NASA, 2003. NASA-SP 2003-4108. Photographs. Appendixes. Index. Pp. xi, 252. The career of a naval aviator who went on to test some 125 different aircraft beginning in 1957 with the National Advisory Committee for Aeronautics and then service with NASA ending in 1987.

St. Nazaire 1942: The Great Commando Raid. By Ken Ford. Westport, Conn.: Praeger, 2004. ISBN 0-275-98280-7. Maps. Photographs. Illustrations. Bibliography. Index. Pp. 96. $35.00. Reissue by the Praeger Illustrated Military History Series of the original Osprey edition of 2001.

Stalinism as a Way of Life. Abridged edition. By Lewis Siegelbaum and Andrei Sokolov. New Haven, Conn.: Yale University Press, 2004. ISBN 0-300-10127-9. Glossary. Notes. Indexes. Pp. xix, 343. Paper. $24.00. This abridged edition of the larger volume published in 2000 contains 99 documents, mostly from Russian archives, which illuminate life in Stalinist Russia; from the Annals of Communism Series.

Tales of a Cold War Submariner. By Dan Summit. College Station: Texas A&M University Press, 2004. ISBN 1-58544-360-3. Illustrations. Appendix. Index. Pp. 266. $60.00. Memoirs of a submarine officer from conventional boats in the immediate post–World War II years to command of a nuclear Polaris boat.

Tannenberg: Erich Ludendorff and the Defense of the Eastern German Border in 1914. By Perry Pierik. Soesterberg, The Netherlands: Aspekt, 2003. ISBN 90-5911-106-0. Map. Photographs. Bibliography. Pp. 102. Paper. $19.95. This brief monograph on the critical World War I battle in 1914 shows how Ludendorff turned the German defensive maneuver against Russia into a successful counter-offensive.

Tarawa 1943: The Turning of the Tide. By Derrick Wright. Westport, Conn.: Praeger, 2004. ISBN 0-275-98271-8. Maps. Photographs. Illustrations. Appendixes. Index. Pp. 96. $35.00. Reissue by the Praeger Illustrated Military History Series of the original Osprey edition of 2000.

Target: America. Hitler's Plan to Attack the United States. By James P. Duffy. Westport, Conn.: Praeger, 2004. ISBN 0-275-96684-4. Photographs. Figures. Notes. Bibliography. Index. Pp. xiv, 178. $39.95. The author documents the German plans and weapons development efforts aimed at providing the capability of directly attacking the United States during World War II.

Thach Weave: The Life of Jimmie Thach. By Steve Ewing. Annapolis, Md.: Naval Institute Press, 2004. ISBN 1-59114-248-2. Maps. Photographs. Appendix. Notes. Bibliography. Index. Pp. x, 338. $34.95. Biography of a famous naval aviator whose career spanned World War II and the Cold War and who developed the weaving tactic of aerial combat named after him.

This Man's Army: A Soldier's Story from the Front Lines of the War on Terrorism. By Andrew Exum. New York: Gotham Books, 2004. ISBN 1-592-40063-9. Pp. 238. $25.00. This is an eyewitness account of the on-going war in Afghanistan from an officer in the 10th Mountain Division.

Tobruk 1941: Rommel's Opening Move. By Jon Latimer. Westport, Conn.: Praeger, 2004. ISBN 0-275-98287-4. Maps. Photographs. Illustrations. Bibliography. Index. Pp. 96. $35.00. Reissue by the Praeger Illustrated Military History Series of the original Osprey edition of 2001.

Verdun 1916: 'They Shall Not Pass'. By William Martin. Westport, Conn.: Praeger, 2004. ISBN 0-275-98294-7. Maps. Photographs. Illustrations. Notes. Bibliography. Index. Pp. 96. $35.00. Reissue by the

Praeger Illustrated Military History Series of the original Osprey edition of 2001.

Victory on the Potomac: The Goldwater-Nichols Act Unifies the Pentagon. By James R. Locher, III. College Station: Texas A&M University Press, 2004. ISBN 1-58544-398-0. Illustrations. Notes. Index. Pp. 524. Paper. $20.00. Reissue of the 2002 study of the passage of the legislation which created the contemporary joint services organization of the Department of Defense under which the United States' current military efforts are being conducted; from the Texas A&M University Military History Series.

Viet Cong at Wounded Knee: The Trial of a Blackfeet Activist. By Woody Kipp. Lincoln: University of Nebraska Press, 2004. ISBN 0-8032-2760-4. Photographs. Notes. Index. Pp. 157. $24.95. Autobiography of a Native American and Vietnam veteran who became an activist in the American Indian Movement.

War Stories: Remembering World War II. By Elizabeth Mullener. New York: Berkley Publishing, 2004. ISBN 0-425-19641-0. Photographs. Bibliography. Index. Pp.

xxiii, 332. Paper. $14.00. First published in 2002, this is a collection of 53 eyewitness accounts of key events of World War II, from the invasion of Poland to the Nuremburg trials, as collected by a reporter for the *New Orleans Times-Picayune* beginning in 1989.

The War with Japan: The Period of Balance, May 1942–October 1943. By H. P. Willmott. Wilmington, Del.: SR Books, 2002. ISBN 0-8420-5033-7. Maps. Table. Notes. Bibliography. Index. Pp. xvii, 180. $60.00. The author covers the early naval battles of the Coral Sea and Midway and the land forces operations in New Guinea and the Solomon Islands in the Pacific in World War II.

We Felt the Flames: Hitler's Blitzkrieg, America's Story. By Charles Kupfer. Newville, Pa.: Sergeant Kirkland's Press, 2003. ISBN 1-887901-34-5. Illustrations. Notes. Bibliography. Pp. 225. Paper. $18.95. How American media coverage of events in Europe in 1940 effected a major shift in public opinion in the United States away from isolationism.

Recent Journal Articles

☆

Wendy A. Swik, *U.S. Military Academy Library*

T HE bibliography is compiled by the systematic search of approximately four hundred periodicals, a check of several general journal bibliographies, and the welcomed contribution of interested subscribers. Many times older citations will be included simply because the compiler had not come across them earlier or, more frequently, because the periodicals are behind publication schedule. Those wishing to be assured of having their articles listed in this section are urged to notify the compiler. References should include the following: author(s), full title (including subtitle), name of periodical, volume number, issue date, and pagination. Address all contributions to Wendy Swik, Military Affairs Librarian, U.S.M.A. Library, West Point, NY 10996–1799.

General Military Affairs

Athwal, Amardeep. "The United States and the Sino-Soviet Split: The Key Role of Nuclear Superiority." *Journal of Slavic Military Studies* 17 (April-June 2004)· 271–97.

Forsyth, Michael. "Finesse: A Short Theory of War." *Military Review* 84 (July-August 2004): 17–19.

Goldman, Emily O. "Introduction: Information Resources and Military Performance." *Journal of Strategic Studies* 27 (June 2004): 195–219.

Herrera, Geoffrey L. "Inventing the Railroad and Rifle Revolution: Information, Military Innovation and the Rise of Ger-

many." *Journal of Strategic Studies* 27 (June 2004): 243–71.

Reed, George E. "Toxic Leadership." *Military Review* 84 (July-August 2004): 67–71.

Showalter, Dennis E. "Information Capabilities and Military Revolutions: The Nineteenth-Century Experience." *Journal of Strategic Studies* 27 (June 2004): 220–42.

Stentiford, Barry M. "Two Volumes on the Richardson Light Guard of Wakefield, Massachusetts." *Military Collector & Historian* 56 (2004): 90–93.

Ancient and Medieval Warfare

Brysac, Shareen Blair. "The Scythian Scourge." *MHQ: Quarterly Journal of*

Military History 16 (Winter 2004): 6–13.

1500–1815 Military Affairs

Barker, Thomas M. "The Friedrich von Germann Watercolors." *Journal of the Johannes Schwalm Historical Association* 7 (2004): 29–38.

Blumberg, Arnold. "British Army's Galloping Gunners." *MHQ: Quarterly Journal of Military History* 16 (Winter 2004): 62–65.

Chartrand, René. "Troops of Portuguese Brazil from the 1780s to 1808." *Military Collector & Historian* 55 (Winter 2003–2004): 198–211.

Daly, Gavin. "Napoleon's Lost Legions: French Prisoners of War in Britain, 1803–1814." *History* 89 (July 2004): 361–80.

Franklin, Carl E. "Draught Harness, Royal Horse Artillery, circa 1814." *Journal of the Society for Army Historical Research* 82 (Autumn 2004): 242–52.

Hill, Steven W. "Hessian Flags in the American War for Independence, 1776–1783." *Military Collector & Historian* 55 (Winter 2003–2004): 226–32, i–vii.

Kappes, Jeramias. Tr. Henry J. Retzer. "March Route from Hessen to America." *Journal of the Johannes Schwalm Historical Association* 7 (2004): 7–14.

Kerry, P. J. "'He fought at Waterloo': Thomas Josiah Wedgwood." *Journal of the Society for Army Historical Research* 82 (Autumn 2004): 190–203.

Londahl-Smidt, Donald M. "Das combinierte Bataillon—The Combined Battalion of Hessen-Cassel, 1776–1778. Part 1: December 1776–July 1777." *Journal of the Johannes Schwalm Historical Association* 7 (2004): 21–28.

Manders, Eric I. "More on the Conococheague Rangers of 1763." *Military Collector & Historian* 55 (Winter 2003–2004): 223.

Meiners, Jorn. Tr. Henry J. Retzer. "Portraits of Hessian Jäger Officers in the Museum of Marburg University." *Journal of the Johannes Schwalm Histori-cal Association* 7 (2004): 15–19.

Neely, Sylvia. "Lafayette's Mémoires and the Changing Legacy of Two Revolutions." *European History Quarterly* 34 (July 2004): 371–402.

Rees, John U. "'We . . . got ourselves cleverly settled for the night . . .': Soldiers' Shelter on Campaign during the War for Independence, Part V." *Military Collector & Historian* 55 (Winter 2003–2004): 213–23.

————. "'We . . . got ourselves cleverly settled for the night . . .': Soldiers' Shelter on Campaign during the War for Independence, Part VI." *Military Collector & Historian* 56 (2004): 98–106.

Retzer, Henry J. "Frederick Augustus Dezeng—Hessen-Cassel Captain and Upstate New York Enterpriser." *Journal of the Johannes Schwalm Historical Association* 7 (2004): 57–60.

Selig, Robert A. "Hessians Fighting for American Independence? German Deserters Recruited for Lauzun's Legion in America, 1780–1782." *Journal of the Johannes Schwalm Historical Association* 7 (2004): 39–51.

Showalter, Dennis E. "Gustavus' Greatest Victory." *MHQ: Quarterly Journal of Military History* 16 (Winter 2004): 82–93.

Storkel, Arno. "The Ansbach-Bayreuth Flags Lost at Yorktown." *Journal of the Johannes Schwalm Historical Association* 7 (2004): 1–6.

Weaver, Philip D. "Update on 4th New York Uniforms in 1775." *Military Collector & Historian* 55 (Winter 2003–2004): 247–48.

Zlatich, Marko. "Newspaper Extracts Describing Military and Naval Dress of the American Revolutionary War, 1775–1783, Part III, Pennsylvania Continental and State Line Infantry." *Military Collector & Historian* 56 (2004): 116–20.

1816–1869 Military Affairs

Bigham, John Mills. "Fort Warren Confederate Signature Albums, 1861–1862: Boston Harbor, Massachusetts." *Military Collector & Historian* 56 (2004): 126–29.

Bowery, Charles R. "Encounter at the Triangular Field: the 124th New York and the 1st Texas at Gettysburg, July 2, 1863." *Gettysburg Magazine* 30 (July 2004): 49–62.

Callihan, David L. "Passing the Test: George G. Meade's Initiation as Army Commander." *Gettysburg Magazine* 30 (July 2004): 30–48.

Coco, Gregory A. "Where Defeated Valor Lies: A Rose Farm Mystery Solved." *Gettysburg Magazine* 30 (July 2004): 114–28.

"Confederate Faces from Georgia: From the Collection of David W. Vaughan." *Military Images* 26 (September/October 2004): 7–31.

Cooksey, Paul Clark. "Forcing the Issue: Brig. Gen. Henry Hunt at Gettysburg on July 3, 1863." *Gettysburg Magazine* 30 (July 2004): 77–88.

Custer, Andie. "John Hammond's 'mistake': How a Misplaced Wooden Stake Altered the History of Farnsworth's Charge at Gettysburg." *Gettysburg Magazine* 30 (July 2004): 98–113.

Ellis, John D. "'Left to the streets and the workhouse': The Life, Visual Representation and Death of John Baptist, 3rd Scots Fusilier Guards." *Journal of the Society for Army Historical Research* 82 (Autumn 2004): 204–9.

Field, Ron. "The Vigilant Rifles: A Profile of Confederate Fire Company Volunteers in the Civil War." *Military Collector & Historian* 55 (Winter 2003–2004): 249–51.

Gaede, Frederick C. "An Early Percussion Cap Packing Bag." *Military Collector & Historian* 56 (2004): 112–14.

Gero, Anthony. "Additional Observations on Mourning Dress in the Militia: 1800–1841." *Military Collector & Historian* 56 (2004): 96–97.

Goss, Thomas. "Gettysburg 'decisive battle'." *Military Review* 84 (July-August 2004): 11–16.

Gutknecht, David R. "What Mean These Stones? Another Monumental Controversy." *Gettysburg Magazine* 30 (July 2004): 89–97.

Hill, Steven W. "British Swords in America, and a Hybrid." *Military Collector & Historian* 56 (2004): 110–11.

Hutchinson, Matthew W. "Bringing Home a Fallen Son: The Story of Lt. Willis G. Babcock, 64th New York Volunteer Infantry." *Gettysburg Magazine* 30 (July 2004): 63–73.

McLaughlin, W. F. "A Mexican War Letter." *Military Collector & Historian* 56 (2004): 93–95.

Mosser, Jeffrey S. "Garrison flags at Fort McAllister." *Military Collector & Historian* 56 (2004): 121–23.

Ryan, Thomas J. "A Battle of Wits: Intelligence Operations during the Gettysburg Campaign." *Gettysburg Magazine* 30 (July 2004): 7–29.

Shaffer, John E. "Grant, His Canal, and Clausewitz." *Military Collector & Historian* 56 (2004): 80–82.

Stahl, Joe. "Pvt. David D. P. Alexander, Company G, 11th Pennsylvania Reserve Infantry." *Gettysburg Magazine* 30 (July 2004): 74–76.

Symonds, Craig L. "Johnston's Toughest Fight." *MHQ: Quarterly Journal of Military History* 16 (Winter 2004): 56–61.

Vaughan, David Wynn. "A Brief History of the Georgia Military Institute and a Study of Its Uniform, 1851–1864." *Military Images* 26 (September-October 2004): 32–36.

Veit, Chuck. "The First Battle of Shiloh." *Naval History* 18 (October 2004): 42–45.

1870–1920 Military Affairs

Bundt, Thomas S. "Gas, Mud, and Blood at Ypres: The Painful Lessons of Chemical Warfare." *Military Review* 84 (July-August 2004): 81–82.

Cook, Kevin L. "The Army Buys an Airplane." *MHQ: Quarterly Journal of Military History* 16 (Winter 2004): 66–75.

Cunningham, Roger D. "Black Troops in the Philippines, 1901." *Military Collector & Historian* 55 (Winter 2003–2004): 224–25.

Emerson, William K. "The World War I American Red Cross Uniform of Miss Annie L. Wheeler." *Military Collector & Historian* 55 (Winter 2003–2004): 243–47.

Echevarria, Antulio, II. "Fortune also Favors the Deliberate." *MHQ: Quarterly Journal of Military History* 16 (Winter 2004): 34–45 [Battle of Mars-la-Tour].

Hamby, Joel E. "Striking the Balance: Strategy and Force in the Russo-Japanese War." *Armed Forces & Society* 30 (Spring 2004): 325–56.

Harris, Stephen L. "Harlem's Hell Fighters." *MHQ: Quarterly Journal of Military History* 16 (Winter 2004): 46–55 [369th Infantry Regiment].

Horn, W. Donald. "Custer Mystery." *Research Review* 18 (Summer 2004): 2–11, 31.

Marshall, Alex. "Russian Military Intelligence, 1905–1917: The Untold Story behind Tsarist Russia in the First World War." *War in History* 11 (November 2004): 393–423.

Noyes, C. Lee. "A Dispatch from the Battlefield: Major James S. Brisbin's Observations on the Little Big Horn." *Research Review* 18 (Summer 2004): 18–31.

Wasti, Syed Tanvir. "The 1912–13 Balkan Wars and the Siege of Edirne." *Middle Eastern Studies* 40 (July 2004): 59–78.

Wilson, Graham. "Listed for the Connaught Rangers." *Sabretache: The Journal and Proceedings of the Military Historical Society of Australia* 45 (June 2004): 31–39.

1921–1949 Military Affairs

Bernstein, Marc D. "A 'black and dismal record.'" *MHQ: Quarterly Journal of Military History* 16 (Winter 2004): 76–81 [Burma].

Citino, Robert. "Beyond Fire and Movement: Command, Control, and Information in the German Blitzkrieg." *Journal of Strategic Studies* 27 (June 2004): 324–44.

Connelly, Mark, and Walter Miller. "The BEF and the Issue of Surrender on the Western Front in 1940." *War in History* 11 (November 2004): 424–41.

Corum, James S. "Unchartered Waters: Information in the First Modern Joint Campaign—Norway 1940." *Journal of Strategic Studies* 27 (June 2004): 345–69.

Davidson, I. A. "The Evacuation of the Heraklion Garrison from Crete, 28–29 May 1941." *Journal of the Society for Army Historical Research* 82 (Autumn 2004): 210–26.

D'Este, Carlo. "MacArthur's Whipping Boy." *MHQ: Quarterly Journal of Military History* 16 (Winter 2004): 24–33.

Emerson, William K. "The U.S. Army's General Staff Badge and the Officer's Reserve Corps Badge." *Military Collector & Historian* 56 (2004): 83–89.

James, Karl. "'Uncle Stan' and the Staff Corps." *Sabretache: The Journal and Proceedings of the Military Historical Society of Australia* 45 (June 2004): 5–9.

Landis, Erik C. "Waiting for Makhno: Legitimacy and Context in a Russian Peasant War." *Past and Present*, May 2004, 199–236.

Richmond, Keith. "Nakano Agents and the Japanese Forces in New Guinea, 1942–1945." *Sabretache: The Journal and*

Proceedings of the Military Historical Society of Australia 45 (September 2004): 29–39.

Rosenzweig, Paul A. "Rabaul 1942: The Sacrifice of John Eshott Carr (1922–1942)." Sabretache: The Journal and Proceedings of the Military Historical Society of Australia 45 (June 2004): 11–18.

Seydi, Suleyman. "The Activities of Special Operations Executive in Turkey." Middle Eastern Studies 40 (July 2004): 153–70.

Military Affairs after 1950

Blackford, Mansel G. "Environmental Justice, Native Rights, Tourism, and Opposition to Military Control: The Case of Kaho'olawe." Journal of American History 91 (September 2004): 544–71.

Bluth, Christopher. "The Warsaw Pact and Military Security in Central Europe during the Cold War." Journal of Slavic Military Studies 17 (April-June 2004): 299–331.

Croissant, Aurel. "Riding the Tiger: Civilian Control and the Military in Democratizing Korea." Armed Forces & Society 30 (Spring 2004): 357–81.

Rubin, G. R. "Military Law and Politics: The Labour Government and the Parkes Affair, 1967." Journal of the Society for Army Historical Research 82 (Autumn 2004): 227–41.

Saxer, Carl J. "Generals and Presidents: Establishing Civilian and Democratic Control in South Korea." Armed Forces & Society 30 (Spring 2004): 383–408.

Yechezkel, Dar, and Shaul Kimhi. "Youth in the Military: Gendered Experiences in the Conscript Service in the Israeli Army." Armed Forces & Society 30 (Spring 2004): 433–59.

Air Force

Alexander, Kristin. "Cleaning the Augean Stables. The Morotai Mutiny?" Sabretache: The Journal and Proceedings of the Military Historical Society of Australia 45 (September 2004)· 5–28.

Brugioni, Dino. "The Effects of Aerial and Satellite Imagery on the 1973 Yom Kippur War." Air Power History 51 (Fall 2004): 1–13.

Eisel, Braxton. "Signal Aircraft Warning Battalions in the Southwest Pacific in World War II." Air Power History 51 (Fall 2004): 14–23.

Hamady, Theodore M. "Fighting Machines for the Air Service, AEF." Air Power History 51 (Fall 2004): 24–37.

Scheib, James A. "Flight to Korea, June 25, 1950." Air Power History 51 (Fall 2004): 38–43.

Zimmerman, David. "Information and the Air Defence Revolution, 1917–40." Journal of Strategic Studies 27 (June 2004): 370–94.

Naval Affairs

Bowden-Dan, Jane. "Diet, Dirt, and Discipline: Medical Developments in Nelson's Navy—Dr. John Snipe's Contribution." Mariner's Mirror 90 (August 2004): 260–72.

Lambert, Nicholas A. "Transformation and Technology in the Fisher Era: The Impact of the Communications Revolution." Journal of Strategic Studies 27 (June 2004): 272–97.

Langley, Harold D. "Squadron Flags of the United States." Military Collector & Historian 55 (Winter 2003–2004): 234–42.

Langley, Harold D. "Warren Opie's Sailor Uniform at Winterthur." *Winterthur Portfolio* 38 (Summer-Autumn 2003): 132–41.

Martin, Tyrone. "The Intrepid Infernal." *Naval History* 18 (October 2004): 46–49.

Smith, Janet Gwendolyn. "U.S. Marine Uniforms of 1798–1806 and the Sandwich at Puerto Plata, May 1800: Research of a Recently Discovered Painting." *Military Collector & Historian* 56 (2004): 107–9.

Taylor, John M. "Sailing the Seas of Manifest Destiny." *MHQ: Quarterly Journal of Military History* 16 (Winter 2004): 14–20.

Till, Geoffrey. "Maritime Airpower in the Interwar Period: The Information Dimension." *Journal of Strategic Studies* 27 (June 2004): 298–323.

Traynor, Leonard. "Great Britain Views United States Naval Officers and Marines." *Military Collector & Historian* 56 (2004): 124–25.

Willis, S. B. A. "Fleet Performance and Capability in the Eighteenth-Century Royal Navy." *War in History* 11 (November 2004): 373–92.

Letters to the Editor

We are always pleased to have letters to the editor because this shows that people are reading our Journal seriously. However, due to space limitations, we ask that you keep your letters under 500 words.

To the Editor:

There are, it seems, relatively few selfless friendships in the academic world. Gunther Rothenberg was a major exception to this rule. I consider him to have been one of the finest individuals I have ever known. I first learned of his existence when he beat me out for a job in New Mexico (for which he was better qualified than I). Years later when I published my study on the second Turkish siege of Vienna he wrote a review for the *American Historical Review*. He praised the book but made one mistaken criticism. When I discussed this with him, he said he would take it back in a letter to the *AHR* which he actually did. From that point onward we remained very close to each other and this notwithstanding the fact that we worked in the same field of Habsburg military history! We helped each other out with recommendations for grants, had a lot of uproarious, alcoholic fun at meetings and corresponded at great length, first by snail mail and later electronically. We talked of guns, politics, and strictly personal issues.

He regretted moving to Australia both because of his Purdue students and the powerful leftist atmosphere in that country. Gunther was anything but politically correct. I recall that he was especially indignant about the confiscation of muzzleloaders Down Under. He came from a culturally assimilated Berlin Jewish family and in the best sense of the word was a very Prussian character. His father was a war hero. Despite the grievous harm done to him and his family by the Nazis, he remained objective about things German. I cannot say how much I miss him.

Thomas M. Barker

Emeritus, University at Albany
Albany, New York

To the Editor:

Reading a review of one's own work (in my case, Kleinschmidt's review of *Firearms* in the January 2004 issue of the *JMH*) can be a surreal experience.

My argument goes like this: (1) prior to the spread of flintlocks in the 1700s, firearms were impractical to use on horseback; (2) prior to the invention of the railroad in the 1800s, large masses of slow-moving infantry could only support themselves by foraging in densely populated agricultural lands; therefore (3) prior to 1700, firearms were primarily used by infantry in densely populated agricultural lands. While early firearms were wildly inaccurate, they could still hit large targets like infantry formations or city walls.

However, along the edges of the steppe or desert, against fast-moving nomads who lived in tents and fought on horseback, early firearms were largely ineffective. Consequently, only areas insulated from the steppe or desert would rely on firearms. Such areas included Western Europe and Japan—and also south China when firearms were first invented, though only until China was unified in 1276.

This is the argument that Kleinschmidt caricatures as "the weather." My supposed argument from the "availability and proper use of saltpeter" is simply a figment of Kleinschmidt's imagination. The fact is, saltpeter is not even mentioned once in my introduction or conclusion, and except to document the by-now-uncontroversial point that gunpowder and firearms were invented in China, it is hardly discussed at all.

Regarding cultural preferences, Kleinschmidt's favored explanation, the only credible argument concerns the Mamluks, which I address at some length. The cultural argument for Japan that Kleinschmidt finds so convincing was dreamed up by an American professor of English literature during the Cold War as an allegory for nuclear disarmament. Even the Japanese translator of that book recognized it as a fable (albeit one that appeals to Japanese readers), and Japanese military historians just find it puzzling or irritating. I follow the experts here.

Kleinschmidt airily refers to a "plethora" of East Asian sources that supposedly would undermine my argument, but since his résumé and publications show no signs that he can read primary sources in any East Asian language, I have to wonder why he thinks he knows what they would say. Curiously, while Kleinschmidt chooses to introduce me as having been "trained as a lawyer," he neglects to add that I hold a Ph.D. in East Asian history from Harvard. I can't imagine why he would bring up my being a lawyer at all in this context, except to mislead readers about my credentials—perhaps he can explain.

Whatever its shortcomings, *Firearms* is the first book to address the origins, spread, and use of firearms in medieval and early modern times on a global scale while giving due weight to evidence from all the areas involved: drawing on numerous sources in Chinese, Japanese, and Korean, and selected sources in Arabic, Persian, and Turkish, in addition to European scholarship. I think it deserves a fair hearing, which it does not get from this review.

Kenneth Chase

Hong Kong

Professor Kleinschmidt declined to respond.

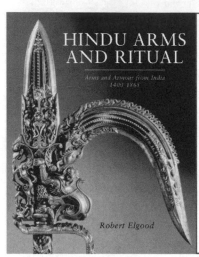

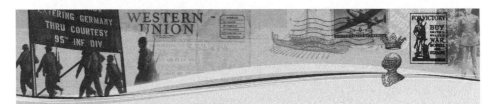

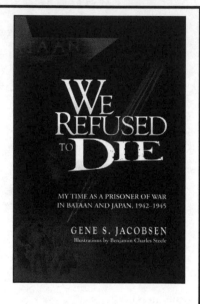

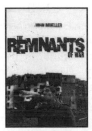

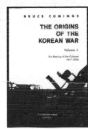

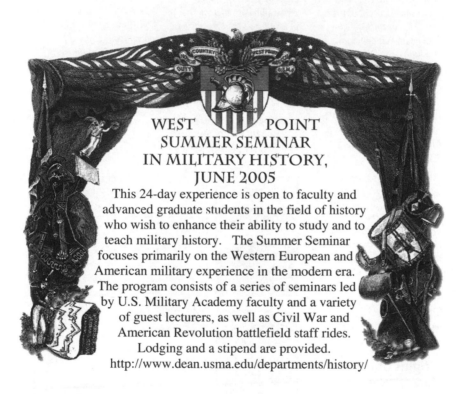

WEST   POINT
SUMMER SEMINAR
IN MILITARY HISTORY,
JUNE 2005

This 24-day experience is open to faculty and
advanced graduate students in the field of history
who wish to enhance their ability to study and to
teach military history.   The Summer Seminar
focuses primarily on the Western European and
American military experience in the modern era.
The program consists of a series of seminars led
by U.S. Military Academy faculty and a variety
of guest lecturers, as well as Civil War and
American Revolution battlefield staff rides.
Lodging and a stipend are provided.
http://www.dean.usma.edu/departments/history/